THE SCIENCE OF THE SWASTIKA

THE SCIENCE OF
THE SWASTIKA

Bernard Mees

Central European University Press
Budapest New York

Published in 2008 by
CENTRAL EUROPEAN UNIVERSITY PRESS

An imprint of the
Central European University Share Company
Nádor utca 11, H-1051 Budapest, Hungary
Tel: +36-1-327-3138 or 327-3000
Fax: +36-1-327-3183
E-mail: ceupress@ceu.hu
Website: www.ceupress.hu

400 West 59th Street, New York NY 10019, USA
Tel: +1-212-547-6932
Fax: +1-646-557-2416
E-mail: mgreenwald@sorosny.org

ISBN 978-963-9776-18-0 cloth

LIBRARY OF CONGRESS CATALOGING-IN-PUBLICATION DATA

Mees, Bernard (Bernard Thomas)
  The science of the swastika / Bernard Mees.
      p. cm.
  Includes bibliographical references and index.
  ISBN 978-9639776180 (cloth : alk. paper)
1. Swastikas. 2. Symbolism (Psychology) 3. National socialism. 4. Nationalism—
Germany—History—20th century. I. Title.

  DD256.5.M3975 2008
  929.9—dc22

                      2008025537

Printed in Hungary by
Akaprint Nyomda

Table of Contents

Preface

Hidden away in the stacks of many Western libraries are a range of works printed in German blackletter: on Vikings, dead languages, skull shapes and runes. There was a time when such writings were considered essential additions to any proper liberal arts collection. They represent the remnant of a tradition that is largely now lost, its last memory quickly receding. Indeed last year the University of Melbourne abolished the teaching of Viking Studies, bringing to a close a teaching tradition of some 50 fruitful years—the university's former associations with eugenics, Sanskrit and Gothic are even longer forgotten. This book is an investigation into that old world of philological and historical study, of old literatures, old symbols, pots and bones. Once these things were especially popular in universities other than just in Central Europe, and they thus represent a key, albeit murky chapter in the history of Western ideas.

In writing this book I used knowledge that I gained from my University of Melbourne doctoral dissertation on *Sinnbildforschung*, submitted in 2001. I owe considerable gratitude for the help and guidance of my doctoral supervisor Steven R. Welch and his associate Charles Zika. Other teachers and colleagues at the University who had considerable influence on the current work include Tim Mehigan, Ronald T. Ridley, Mindy MacLeod, Neile A. Kirk and John S. Martin—and I should also acknowledge Bernard Muir, W. Ann Trindade and the late Ian Robertson for their valuable support, encouragement and advice over the course of the last ten years or so. The manuscript was also improved by the input of three referees who were gracious enough to pass useful comment on it: Malachi H. Hacohen, Suzanne L. Marchand and Uwe Puschner. Research for the work was undertaken in Germany, England, the United States and Australia, and I must also acknowledge here the financial support of the Diebold Foundation as well as those who found the time to help me with many and varied matters along the way, particularly Reinhold Bollmus, Jutta and Klaus Burghard, Thomas L. Markey, Gerd Simon and Maria Wilkinson.

I have recently begun teaching a course in another part of intellectual history—at RMIT University, a place that seems very far away from the world of ancient sun symbols and spears investigated in this work. Yet the deeper theoretical questions and understandings I developed while writing this study seem to me still of particular relevance to a proper understanding of the key intellectual currents of the previous century. The broader Western intellectual tradition is notoriously difficult to navigate where the Holocaust and the years of Nazi rule in Central Europe are concerned. But this is what makes the area so sharp, so fraught and often so crucial too, and the largely forgotten blackletter culture that informed so much of the intellectual debate of the time such an important part of the twentieth-century history of ideas.

April 2008   *Bernard Mees*

"Issues concerning the Teutons"

in intellectual history the cranks
and fools are important too
Martin Green

It is a cool Viennese evening. The trees of the Ringstraße are all green buds and white flowers, and the setting sun now daubs them in pinks and lilacs too. A young doctoral student makes his way to the University—he has been advised to leave behind the Heuriger this evening and take instead the opportunity to experience a literary event, one not to be missed. It is spring 1959 and the young Australian has been invited to a celebration of the latest work of the Viennese master of his field.

The student converses in the hall a while with a North German colleague. The Viennese welcome someone from the New World, but Prussians remain a plague. A hush eventually settles among the collection of students, instructors and professors: the Old Germanic master has arrived.

The event is managed like an opera; it begins with a sudden hush and an expectant silence. The work being launched is on Arminius, the hero who saved ancient Germany from enslavement by the Romans. The old master argues to an enraptured audience that the character Siegfried, the hero of the *Song of the Nibelungs*, is a symbolic refiguring, 1,000 years later, of the ancient savior of Germany. It is part of the master's thesis that German "cultural morphologies"—the symbolic expressions discernable in national literature—are essentially timeless.[1]

The atmosphere in the auditorium is electric. It is so charged, the young man feels he can almost touch it. But suddenly he realizes that this is not a literary occasion; it is a religious event. Billy Graham is not here. Instead, as thunderous applause breaks out, the young man realizes he is in a place of the ancestors. He has joined the antiquarian worshippers at the Semnonian grove.

To a new scene. Now it is autumn, 1982, and a group of professors have retired to a watering hole in a small resort town in West

Germany. They are here participating at a conference entitled "Issues concerning the Teutons from a contemporary perspective" that every-one agrees has been a great success.[2] The Transatlantic guests seem unaware that the conference has occasioned a homecoming for its con-venor, though; many of his continental contemporaries are well aware that he has long been a party to a Teutonic problem of a less antiquar-ian nature. And after a few drinks the aging professor allows his reserve to diminish.

The convenor lets his mind run back to some 40 years before. He was something very special then. Politicians had regularly visited his archeological digs—in fact the national police minister seemed to take a special shine to his work. One of his present-day colleagues—a testy chap from Frankfurt—had asked that a paper be read at the con-ference, one that sought to tarnish the memory of this gilded past.[3] Our professor instead preferred to reminisce about his halcyon years in the convivial company of both his local and foreign colleagues. As one of the American participants at the conference subsequently noted in his journal, the old professor still seemed proud of his time as an academic in the SS, his personal relationship with Heinrich Himmler, and even recounted later that night that he had been a witness to the Holocaust.[4]

The professors who feature in these two accounts are no longer with us, but in their lifetimes they shared much in common. They were both born into communities which are no longer part of Germany; they were both brought up in households with politically active fathers; both also became university professors who specialized in the study of Ger-man antiquity; and during the years of the dictatorship they had both become members of the Nazi Party and also of the SS.

Both professors were also dismissed from their posts in 1945, but both equally were subsequently able to reclaim academic positions of the highest standing; the first in Munich, then Vienna in the late 50s, the second at Göttingen, the university of the brothers Grimm. Both have been the subject of attacks and apologies in recent times, and both evidently not only chose to remain silent, but also to lie after the war about the extent of their dealings with the Nazis. They were both political conservatives and resented the humiliation Germany suf-fered in 1945. Both had also evidently revelled in their roles as Nazi academic show ponies. It is hard to see why either should have been allowed a publicly funded teaching post again, let alone command the respect and even adulation of a new generation of academic fellows. There seems to be something peculiar about the discipline in which they made their names: it has an ambiguous, if not uncomfortable, relationship with the Nazi past. The years of the National Socialist dictatorship were boom years for these professors and their fellows. This book seeks to explain why.

This book is not just about Nazi professors though, but also about the discipline in which these two men were important figures. It was a discipline that bore extraordinary connections with Nazism—indeed many aspects of National Socialism were clearly influenced by German antiquarians. The most emblematic sign of Nazism, the swastika, is a symbol from the primordial German past; and it was clearly an antiquarian understanding that formed the basis upon which the Nazi adoption of the swastika was built. In 1931 a German antiquarian suggested that the swastika might serve as a guide to an investigation of Old Germanic culture.[5] It also seems a logical place to begin an investigation of Old Germanic studies and its role in the emergence of Nazism, Nazi culture and the intellectual history of the Third Reich.

Many of the ideological works produced by right-wing thinkers in Germany in the 1920s and up until 1945 are infused with ideas that were first produced within German antiquarian studies. The glorious past of ancient Germany—represented most strikingly in the defeat of three invading Roman legions by the ancient Germanic chieftain Arminius in A.D. 9—had long been employed as a symbol of the one-time greatness of the German people. German patriots usually had to experience this past through the writings of antiquarians or popularizers indebted to antiquarian research. Yet not surprisingly, over the decades preceding the Nazi accession to power, Old Germanic studies (*ältere Germanistik*), or as it was usually styled in German at the time, Germanic antiquarian studies (*germanische Altertumskunde*), had also become politically radicalized as nationalistic students gravitated toward the new patriotic disciplines of Old Germanic philology, legal history, linguistics, anthropology, folklore and archeology. Ideals usually regarded today as generic to fascist belief systems underpinned theories that were hailed as new conceptual paradigms within Germanic antiquarian discourse at the time. Notions of cultural renewal, racial purity and the fulfillment of destiny in martial struggle are clearly present in the works of German and Austrian antiquarian scholars of the 1920s. Yet most of the new ideals of Germanic antiquarianism were not derived directly from contemporary political agendas promoted by the radical right. In fact sometimes the direction of influence was clearly from academic antiquarian to political discourse. There are many specimens of "brown" literature from the 1920s–40s replete with new words and new concepts borrowed directly from studies of Germanic antiquity—and the pronouncements of leading Nazis from Hitler to Himmler, R. Walther Darré and Alfred Rosenberg sometimes even make deliberate references to the practices of Germanic antiquity as revealed through the works of contemporary scholars. This is most evident in some of the otherwise symbolically impenetrable practices that went on within the SS, many of which were suggested by the findings of contemporary academics. Himmler was clearly an enthusiastic consumer of antiquarian literature, mirroring the love for antiquity already shown earlier by Rosenberg and the Führer himself. Old Germanic studies made an essential contribution to the mythoepic core of Nazism and what, reflecting the model of the racial utopia of ancient Germanic times, Hitler emphatically hoped to make "*a Germanic State of the German Nation.*"[6]

Germanic antiquity became in Hitler's Germany what ancient Rome was to that of Mussolini's *Fascisti* (*fascismo* or Fascism proper)— an image of former national greatness that was called upon to legitimize the aims of the new regime.[7] So it is no surprise to find that the production of utopian visions of the old Germanic past was seen as supportive of Nazism. Modern scholarship does not recognize, however, that much of the vision of antiquity promoted in National Socialist circles was identical to that held in some sections of the academic community before 1933; not merely in terms of what had happened in Germany many hundreds, even thousands of years before, but in what lessons the study of the old Germanic past could teach a contemporary German society that in the 1920s was widely perceived as racked with uncertainty, disharmony and weakness. Instead, today these "brown" thinkers are usually dismissed as grubstreet cranks—hopeless polemicists who understood the past mostly as a treasure chest filled with precedents which could be used to force their points home. Yet prominent professional antiquarians were calling for a national reawakening many years before the Nazis came to power, employing the im-

age of an ancient heroic German golden age, a time when a society of
warrior peasants rooted to the soil had flourished, one imbued with
special cultural or racial qualities which had to be rediscovered and
reclaimed, and one that had once dominated Europe culturally and politically, and had set a historical precedent for a fight for living space in
the Slavic East. National Socialist ideology is often dismissed as a grab
bag of frequently conflicting ideals; nevertheless, many of these ideals
achieved their feeling of correctness, interconnectedness and consistency in the tradition of the works of the popularizers and even scholars of
Germanic antiquity. This tradition was one in which political ideas of
an extreme right-wing bent had already taken firm root before it was
turned to for support by ideologues of a more overtly activist persuasion. In fact it was especially in a field of study which had grown up
about interpretations of the swastika where the influence of reactionary
thought was most patently reflected in scholarship. Within Old Germanic studies as a whole, it was in a new field developed from a tradition of swastika studies where the rediscovery of the past was most
overtly considered a political enterprise—a service to the nation—and
an enterprise that in 1945 with the downfall of the National Socialist
regime would also founder.

In the latter half of the nineteenth century, advancements in new
sciences such as archeology and linguistics first proffered the hope that
symbolic expressions associated with cultures generally thought to be
pre-literate might for the first time be understood. It was in reflection
of this hope that a new field of study consequently developed in Germany in the 1920s that was termed *Sinnbildforschung* or *Sinnbildkunde*.
Quite obscure today, the focus of this study was symbols or rather
ideographs of German history and prehistory. The rise of ideographic studies, however, was contemporary with the rise of Nazism—and
strangely enough in 1945 ideographic studies also collapsed just as
this new political belief did, as if their destinies had somehow become
linked. Ideographic studies became so entwined with National Socialism that it shared a similar fate after the German defeat, and today,
much like neo-Nazism, is usually only to be found sporadically and
then only at the margins of European experience.

Sinnbildforschung encompassed the study of ancient German symbols and written characters: from pictographs of the late Stone Age
to the first alphabetic characters employed in ancient Germany, the

Germanic runes. All sorts of symbols came under scrutiny: from those found among prehistoric rock carvings, on pottery and other manufactures such as spearheads and jewellery, to traditional medieval designs such as the hallmarks of medieval artisans and the traditional familial symbols employed in housing designs in rural Germany. To these were added the Germanic runes, an alphabetic script whose use had died out in Germany in the early Middle Ages, and also several apparently related characters commonly found in connection with runic inscriptions. The principal aim of ideographic studies was to make these symbols readable, after determining their ideographic values, and thus reveal a new set of sources which would lead to a better understanding of early German history and prehistory. As such, *Sinnbildforschung* aimed to further the project that medievalists had set out upon in the nineteenth century: by rediscovering the content of early ideographic messages, the readable history of the German people could hopefully be traced further back in time, perhaps lengthening the pedigree of what could fairly be reconstructed as culturally German as far back even as the Stone Age.

With the Nazi accession to power in 1933, *Sinnbildforschung* was soon supported directly by the state through university appointments and the manipulation of streams of research funds. Moreover, in 1935 an organization was founded within Hitler's bodyguard, the SS, to further its study. This organization, the SS-Ahnenerbe or Ancestral Inheritance foundation, was officially styled the Learned Society for Intellectual Prehistory (Studiengesellschaft für Geistesurgeschichte). Most infamous as the organ through which medical experiments were arranged to be performed on the inmates of concentration camps, the Ahnenerbe was founded as a historical or rather prehistorical research institution before it expanded its horizons to medical torture. At first glance it seems strange indeed that the police apparatus of the Nazi state would become involved in archeological digs, historical research and museum exhibitions. Yet the National Socialists recognized a need actively to support investigations of the ancient Germanic past, bringing resources to bear never before (or since) available for the study of early Germanic history and prehistory. Amid this new project for the uncovering of Germanic antiquity, *Sinnbildforschung* remained a development held in high esteem by the new regime, concerned principally as it was with investigating the origin and meaning of symbols such as the swastika and other expressions of early Germany which had become part of the symbolic repertoire of the Nazi Party.

The institutional focus brought to bear on the study of Germanic antiquity led to the enrollment of German prehistorians, linguists, philologists, legal historians, folklorists and anthropologists within bodies such as the Ahnenerbe. These scholars can generally be classed as Germanists—they focused on the study of German culture, especially from a historical perspective; hence the two late professors, the Viennese philologist and the East Prussian-born archeologist recalled at the outset here, both saw themselves as contributors to the same broad field. Of course Germanists who focused on expressions of antiquity which had been adopted by the National Socialists to symbolize aspects of their political platform might be expected to have come under special attention in Nazi Germany and certainly this in part explains why so many antiquarian Germanists became so politicized at the time. Yet the intellectual origins of *Sinnbildforschung* predate the formation of the Nazi Party or its adoption of the swastika. Indeed many of its proponents had been associated with the Party long before the Nazi accession to power. But it was not merely openly National Socialist academics who were attracted to the new science of *Sinnbildforschung*.

Sinnbildforschung reflected a radical new attitude that had emerged in Old Germanic studies in Hitler's day. Most attempts by Germanist antiquarians to come to terms with the direction their field took during the years of National Socialism, however, have been anecdotal and bereft of sustained or measured criticism. The past is often still too close and too painful for its legacy to be acknowledged properly within their field. Even when it is, though, the Nazi pasts of such individuals typically highlight the occasional qualms these scholars had, much as several of the Nuremberg defendants did. The development and acceptance of a fascistic form of Old Germanic studies during those years have proven especially difficult to explain by those who were once its practitioners or have an emotional attachment to those who once were. Moreover, *Sinnbildforschung* itself is represented, if at all, merely as a product of dilettantes or enthusiastic scholarly over-interpretation.

Suzanne Marchand in her assessment of the career of the Austrian art historian Josef Strzygowski writes of a radical Grub Street that existed in the 1910s and 20s, one which obviously fed the superlative ideal of Germanness and the Aryan shared by Hitler and many of his

reactionary contemporaries.[8] Many of these grubstreet figures were
seminal contributors to swastika studies. Like the grubstreet writers of
the French Revolution, these authors were often the less talented, less
remarkable counterparts of the ideologues, who in the French instance
were the great liberal authors—the Voltaires, the Montesquieus—of
enlightenment France. But in contrast, most of these Aryanist grubstreet figures like Strzygowski were academic writers holding publicly
funded positions—German and Austrian university men proved more
of a muse to the ideologists of Nazism than the image of the ivory-
tower scholar might at first suggest. The relationship to the Nazis of
Germanists like those considered in this book was inspirational, useful
and direct in a way which the figures of Robert Darnton's study of the
revolutionary French literary underground could only have dreamt.[9]
Sinnbildforschung, as the most overtly radicalized development in Germanic antiquarian studies of its day, proved the most useful, the most
functional channel in which academic theories could contribute to
Nazism. As swastika studies grew to become the new science of *Sinnbildforschung*, the old Aryanist Grub Street gave way to a new, more
sophisticated and established academic tradition in which mainstream
understandings of the old Germanic past were generated that were
widely recognized as politically useful contributions to the National
Socialist present day.

NOTES

1 O. Höfler, "Siegfried, Arminius und die Symbolik," in W. Rasch (ed.), *Festschrift für Franz Rolf Schröder* (Heidelberg: Winter, 1959), 11–121 [= monograph, Heidelberg: Winter, 1961]. The student was John Stanley Martin, to
whom we are grateful for the recollection.
2 H. Beck (ed.), *Germanenprobleme in heutiger Sicht* (Berlin: De Gruyter,
1986).
3 K. von See, *Barbar, Germane, Arier* (Heidelberg: Winter, 1994), 363.
4 T.L. Markey, "A Tale of Two Helmets," *Journal of Indo-European Studies*
29 (2001): 140.
5 E. Richter, "Das Hakenkreuz als Führer zu altgermanischer Kultur," *Mannus* 23 (1931): 1–23.
6 A. Hitler, *Mein Kampf*, 44th ed. (Munich: Eher, 1933), 362 [= trans. R.
Mannheim, Boston: Houghton Mifflin, 1943, 299].

7 R. Visser, "Fascist doctrine and the cult of *romanità*," *Journal of Contemporary History* 27 (1992): 5–22; B. Mees, "Hitler and *Germanentum*," *Journal of Contemporary History* 39 (2004): 255–70.

8 S.L. Marchand, "The Rhetoric of Artifacts and the Decline of Classical Humanism," *History and Theory*, suppl. 33 (1994): 106ff.

9 R. Darnton, *The Literary Underground of the Old Regime* (Cambridge, Mass.: Harvard University Press, 1982).

CHAPTER 1.

The Tradition of *Völkisch* Germanism

Ohne Juda, Ohne Rom,
Wird erbaut Germanias Dom
Schönerer

Blue night with mild waves!
In the open country, the cry of the delighted rings,
Where still Holle's bushes bloom.
Fire shines through the valleys,
Like Balder's monuments,
And from the wheel sparks glow.
Let the sun-rune spark,
Swastika radiant in the dark,
Be welcome, exalted Phol!
A thousand standing-stones counsel,
Druidic wisdom, Edda, Vedas,
From you, eternal "symbol"!

These are the words of *Solstice (Sonnenwende)*, an anonymous poem first published in the German journal *Heimdall* in 1899.[1] It glorifies the swastika, an ancient symbol known in an Old Norse source as the *sólarhvel* ("sun-wheel"). The poem, drawing on a farrago of references to German, Norse, Celtic and Indian traditions, is typical of many contributions which appeared in journals from Wilhelmine times with titles that evoked antiquarian themes—Heimdall is the god who guards the way to heaven in Old Norse myth. All of the groups which published these journals had one trait in common apart from an interest in antiquity: they were all also devotees of a new movement of the political far right that had been christened by an adjective that is not properly translatable into English.

Over the course of its long development, German nationalism developed an idiosyncratic offshoot described as *völkisch* by its proponents. This political tradition is central to an understanding of the politics that gave birth to National Socialism. It is usually not recognized that the *völkisch* tradition is also essential to the development of German antiquarian discourse too, and not merely of the overtly politicized sort represented by journals such as *Heimdall*.

Even before the accession to power of the National Socialists, Old Germanic studies had developed a range of blatantly political aspects. With the development of an extreme form of nationalism bound up in a reliance on ideals often thought best represented in the Germany of the distant past, it is perhaps not surprising to find that some expressions of German antiquarianism had become infused with extreme nationalist ideas. A *völkisch* aspect to, and indeed discourse within, Old Germanic studies developed during the course of the what historians now commonly call the long nineteenth century, the period between the revolutionary late 1700s and the end of the First World War.[2] *Sinnbildforschung*, the form of German antiquarian discourse most radically influenced by *völkisch* concerns, was born after this antiquarian tradition had mostly reached a mature form. Yet this *völkisch* form of Germanic studies could only have emerged after several other premises had been built into German antiquarian scholarship. A revolution had begun in Old Germanic studies in the years before the Nazi assumption of power, one that transformed most of the disciplines within the German antiquarian tradition. Most of the different strands of Old Germanic studies had some influence on the development of *Sinnbildforschung* and the new thinking in the antiquarian discourse of the 1910s and 20s clearly contributed to the form it took at the time of its emergence. The work from 1928 that gave birth to a continuous tradition of ideographic studies, however, is almost impenetrable outside the context of the politically charged world of Germanic antiquarianism of the late 1920s. Hence an investigation is required of the *völkisch* tradition of Germanic studies before a proper analysis of *Sinnbildforschung* can be attempted.

The term *Sinnbildforschung*, though (which alternated occasionally with the style *Sinnbildkunde*), was coined only as late as the mid-1930s to describe the research most closely identified with Herman Wirth, a controversial academic of Dutch extraction who had been active in his field for several years before it gained a widely accepted designation.[3] Although an expression like swastika studies often seems a more appropriate way to describe the field from which Wirth's work most obviously emerged, the expression *Sinnbildforschung* was modelled, rather, on *Runenforschung* or *Runenkunde* (runic studies or runology), a branch of Old Germanic studies that held much in common with *Sinnbildforschung* and in fact one upon which ideographic studies was fundamentally reliant. The German term *Sinnbild* is in origin a seventeenth-century calque on French *emblème*, but had been re-analyzed by some German thinkers in the nineteenth century as a term closer in form and meaning to the Graecisms symbol or ideograph.[4] Expressions such as *Zeichenforschung* or more commonly *Symbolforschung* (both literally "symbol studies") are normally used in its stead for those Germanophones who study ancient ideographs today. Wirth's contribution to the study of ancient ideography is similarly usually ignored in modern German *Symbolforschung*. He claimed at the time, however, that he was pursuing his ideographic studies in a scholarly tradition that reached back into the nineteenth century; and though he pursued and expressed his research in an idiosyncratic manner, there certainly was an earlier tradition of the study of ancient and prehistoric ideographs such as the swastika that he could and did call upon. But ideographic study was not consolidated in the form in which it was to be expressed during its peak in the years of the National Socialist dictatorship until Wirth's particular take on pre-modern ideography appeared in the late 1920s.

The National Socialists used the term Weltanschauung to describe the set of political beliefs shared by the complete Nazi, an expression that was conterminous at the time with what in English is usually described as ideology.[5] What the Nazis called their Weltanschauung was referred to in their literature as the *völkisch* ideal or *völkisch* thought (*der völkische Gedanke*), and it has its origins in a tradition of German and Austrian experience that dates back to well before the days of Hitler. The origins of *völkisch* thought, the place and time of its first cultural and political expression, and its status within Nazi thinking were all to prove important concerns in the growth and acceptance of *völkisch* Germanism and the *Sinnbildforschung* that developed out of it. It seems necessary, therefore, to come to a historical understanding of the *völkisch* ideal before considering the textual and conceptual genealogy of ideographic studies.

After the war, Baldur von Schirach, the former Hitler Youth leader, claimed that the Nazi Weltanschauung meant different things to different Nazi leaders, and there has long been a tradition of treating what Hitler termed a Weltanschauung as only a hodgepodge of beliefs which never attained the status of an ideology in the sense of liberalism or Marxism, for example.[6] In many ways the National Socialists also had an ambiguous relationship with the *völkisch* tradition: more obviously infused with the militarism of the "front generation," of the veterans groups that emerged at the end of the Great War, Hitler often sought to distance his party from older expressions of the radical right.[7] The adoption of the label *völkisch* by the Nazis was even contested by some longer-established radical groups. Indeed the National Socialists only ever attempted the feat of setting out their party's program once, in the 25 articles of the Party produced by Hitler and Gottfried Feder in 1920; and after 1933, the Nazis even chose not to implement a number of their 1920 articles.[8] Hitler was famously opportunistic; he was more interested in expediency than dogma—he did not like be tied down by programmatic statements.

Mein Kampf, after all, is a rambling work, more like a collection of sound bites than an ideological statement—refrains taken from Hitler's speeches that were intended to sound profound and to agitate, rather than to argue a coherent political platform.[9] Statements like "All who are not of good race in this world are chaff"[10] seemed more important than his deliberations on foreign policy or Party organization (which even changed over time). Hitler's genius was his understanding of political demagogy, a gift reflected in his insights on how to win power from a base in popular support. He was a practical politician and had little interest in, or understanding of, the nuances or complexities of ideology.

It is instead in the writings of the *völkisch* literati that we find more deliberate attempts to explain the *völkisch* ideal under National Socialism. The Führer's ideological role seems more to have been that of Party arbiter, rather than that of an ideologue in the usual sense. There were members of the Party such as Alfred Rosenberg, the editor of the Party's paper the *Völkischer Beobachter,* who in effect had been deputized as ideologues—Hitler even called Rosenberg his dogmatist. Nonetheless there were others, too, who wrote in a similar mode and who of course were not personally so close to the Führer. Although many of these *völkisch* ideologues or literati were inclined to cite passages from *Mein Kampf* or one of Hitler's speeches in order to show their unswerving allegiance to the Führer, it is perhaps more correct to talk of *völkisch* ideals as the ideologists of Nazism tried to enunciate their political beliefs in a mode of "working towards the Führer"—the charismatic figure of their own imaginings, to use Ian Kershaw's Weberian model—rather than the man himself.[11] Yet even under a totalitarian, *völkisch* regime, political understandings remained substantially bound by tradition, often based in the public perceptions of the ideals of the Führer rather than those he personally maintained. There is a popular perception that Nazi ideology was all embracing or monolithic—yet Hitler evidently had no desire to describe his party's ideology programmatically. While he had ideologues "working towards the Führer," there was no need to produce a program of National Socialist political belief. As Martin Broszat has argued, the indolence of the dictator and his notion of survival after struggle ensured that the whole administrative structure of the National Socialist state was a chaotic, lumbering behemoth.[12] There is no reason to expect National Socialist ideology to be more than a morass of half-formed notions, often still evolving and only loosely coordinated by the aim of working towards a Führer whom few of the *völkisch* literati personally knew. But the effect of the political thought accepted by supporters of Nazism could not be so incoherent and so fragmented as its weak coordination might at first suggest; else the call of National Socialism would never have been strong enough to entice a generation of German intellectuals of the right, profound thinkers of the calibre of the philosopher Martin Heidegger or the political scientist Carl Schmitt among them. Instead, the ideologues, political hacks and spruikers of National Socialism worked more or less together toward an ideal, one that was incarnated in a *völkisch* messiah who may personally and privately have been a morass of contradictions, but in the public view was the focus of an ideal shaped by notions moulded in a received tradition of *völkisch* thinkers as much as by the public pronouncements of Hitler himself.

The *völkisch* ideal was only ever loosely articulated in terms of a platform or program and was flexible enough to tolerate some divergence in interpretation. However, some of the features essential to *völkisch* thought that developed over time—extreme nationalism, fanatical activism and renewalistic spirit—are typical of fascist thought in general.[13] Nazism, viewed in comparison to similar movements of the radical right, seems to be merely the most extreme historical form of fascism. Yet other, culture-specific aspects of *völkisch* thought not stressed so strongly by other fascist traditions—anti-modernism, anti-Semitism and Social Darwinism—also make it typically German in its expression. Culture, as Roger Griffin has argued, seems to have a primacy in fascisms and Nazism certainly has its German particularities.[14] Hitler's last command was for the German people always to protect their racial integrity—a dictate that is hard to interpret in the light only of a generic theory of fascism given racialism seemed of little importance to many other fascist movements.[15] But Nazi Germany was much more than merely a racial state.[16] It is factors in its historical development, its growth and change, as well as the extreme manner in which it was expressed when it emerged in the form of the Nazi Party that makes the *völkisch* ideal often seem so difficult to classify or even, admittedly, just to pin down as a political expression.

The origins of the notion of the *Volk* can be traced back to the late eighteenth century, to the writings of Johann Gottfried von Herder.[17] A Lutheran preacher, Herder launched a series of attacks on the Francophilia prevalent among the German literati of his day. He was the first influential figure to speak of an essential Germanness that he wished to see cultivated rather than suppressed as he claimed those who looked outside Germany for their culture would and did. Herder spoke of a national spirit or soul of the *Volk*, a spirit of Germanness that united the German-speaking peoples of Central Europe—what would later be called the German *Volksgeist*.[18] In his day, however, there was no German state—the German *Volk* was not reconciled with the idea of nation in the days of Herder as, say, the French *peuple* was with the political bounds of Bourbon France.

Herder lived at the time of the birth of a new patriotic German literature. Although there was no German nation, there was a German *Kulturnation*—an elite, at first substantially Francophile (and often even Francophone) literary culture that served as some sort of binding agent for the manifold Central European, culturally German states.[19] The glue that held the *Kulturnation* together, however, was shattered and then formed anew with the shock of the victories of Napoleon's armies—German Francophilia was soon transformed into Francophobia. Johann Gottfried von Fichte's *Addresses to the German Nation (Reden an die deutsche Nation)* that rang out during what to that time were the years of the lowest ebb of German military fortune called on the banishment of all Francophilia throughout German-speaking Europe and the institution of German as the supreme language of Central European culture.[20]

The *Kulturnation* of Fichte's day produced the most vibrant period German literature has seen, the years of the German classical period (*Deutsche Klassik*) and the German Romanticism that followed the *Sturm und Drang* of Herder's generation.[21] It was the time, too, of the rediscovery of earlier German literature and even the period of the appearance of the first collection of German folk tales, those of the brothers Grimm. It also saw the rise in popularity of a new conceptualization of the German nation as the German *Volk* was elevated to a supreme ideal of Germanness and became a central feature of the growing German notions of *Bildung* (cultivation) and *Kultur* (cultural heritage). All manner of thinkers during this time of unprecedented German cultural activity—from the brothers Schlegel, the Humboldts and Grimms, to Goethe and Schiller, in the fine arts, in the universities—all incorporated some aspect of the notion of the *Volk* in their works. Idealized and popularized, Herder's *Volksgeist* was developed at the time into a pillar of Germanness, of German culture, of German nationalism.[22] We might note that the very term Germanness (*Deutschtum*) first appeared in the German language in those heady days, if only at first mostly ironical in use.[23] The surge in the awareness of Germanness manifested itself in the Frankfurt Diet of 1848 that demanded the establishment of a liberal all-German state to reflect the cultural reality expressed by the *Kulturnation*.[24] Liberal German nationalism failed to win German unification that day and the cause when taken up again was expressed in authoritarian and militaristic terms. Yet clearly, the failed greater Germany of 1848 was founded in notions of Herder's *Volksgeist*, the notion of the cultural and familial unity of the German *Volk*, and the *Volksgeist* did not vanish after the liberal failure of 1848.

When German unification did come, it was only achieved imperfectly—it excluded the German-speaking lands under Hapsburg sovereignty.[25] Prussian–Austrian rivalry over who would lead the new Germany was decided on the battlefield at Königgrätz in 1866 and led to the latter's exclusion from the new Reich. The unified Germany of the Prussian "iron" chancellor Otto von Bismarck that followed in 1871, however, seemed an incomplete achievement for many critics while it excluded German Austria. In fact even within the new German Reich it was felt by some radical thinkers that this Germany was merely a political and military construction—that the real struggle to Germanize the country properly had only just begun. After the founding of the Prusso-German Reich in 1871 (this time at the military expense of France), thought conceptualized around the *Volk* in Germany became focused on other questions: externally in relation to the rights and wellbeing of Germans still dwelling outside the bounds of the German Empire; and within, the struggle to raise the *Volksgeist* to a preeminent position. Nevertheless, it was in Austria that the most radical form of early *völkisch* agitation appeared and gave the associated political movement its name. Some Austrian Germans continued to clamor for the creation of the Greater Germany (*Groß-deutschland*, or less commonly *All-Deutschland*) seemingly forgone after the war of 1866. It is also from this eastern tradition that radical impulses in the development of *völkisch* thought would continue to emanate for the next half a century, most prominently of course in the figure of Hitler himself.

Early activist *völkisch* politics was epitomized in the leading Austrian Pan-Germanist (*Alldeutsch*) figure of Georg von Schönerer.[26] A delegate to the Austrian parliament, the popular fervor whipped up by Schönerer's group (the *Schönerianer*, or later the *Alldeutsche*) in the 1880s and 90s over local German linguistic and cultural issues received great prominence in the Bismarckian Reich, and was conterminous if not concomitant with the rise of a similar Pan-German League (Alldeutscher Verband) in the German Empire.[27] Schönerer and his followers firmed support for a politics focused on the inalienable superiority of Germanness and the German language, and embraced a vituperous radicalism never before seen in Central Europe as their preferred mode of political expression. Munich-based *Heimdall* was one of the first pan-German politico-cultural journals spawned by this emergent *völkisch* movement.

It was also in Austria that the Romance term *Nation* first most clearly developed a different series of connotations to its indigenous counterpart *Volk* in German. Although related to the English term folk, *Volk* has come to inhabit a semantic sphere not translatable properly into English.[28] German speakers in Imperial Austria saw themselves as no less German than those in Prussia, but were instead one of many nations within the Hapsburg state. The term *Volk* at the time took on a more Romantic and ethnic, rather than a liberal and civic tone. All sorts of radical *völkisch* or "popular" patriotic parties like Schönerer's Pan-Germans emerged in the late nineteenth century. Liberalism seemed to have failed Germany—in the 1880s a new form of politics appeared that rejected liberal mercantilism and arrogated to itself the patriotic role that German liberals had once claimed as their own.

Most of those sympathetic to *völkisch* politics classed themselves German National (*Deutschnational*) rather than pan-Germanist per se. Nonetheless, for those who prided themselves on being most German, patriotism was usually seen to be best expressed in terms of the *Volk*. Whatever their background, by the late nineteenth century most of those who felt themselves to be strongly German came to express their patriotism in a manner that appeared to reflect a *völkisch* ideal. They may not have always been happy with the antics of Schönerer's Pan-Germans or even the curmudgeonly posturing of journals like *Heimdall*. But many German Nationals came to associate liberalism with its industrialist supporters, not the most essential expressions of Germanness—rootedness (*Bodenständigkeit*), reliability and empathy for the countryside. Perhaps the clearest link of *völkisch* thought with the Romantic movement, the exaltation of the German landscape and the doughty peasantry became essential to *völkisch* writers—a vision of Germanness that seemed incompatible with deruralization, modern industry and the rise of the big cities.

This dissatisfaction with the realities of industrialization (and the politicization of the masses that seemed inexorable with urbanization) was soon reflected in a philosophical tradition. Literary cultural pessimists emerged who bemoaned the impoverished state of the *Volk* as things stood in the new society. The writings of profoundly anti-liberal, anti-modern and anti-Socialist thinkers now joined the developing tradition of *völkisch* thought. The use of the term *völkisch* to refer to this movement is not noted before the 1880s.[29] Yet by this date the *völkisch* ideal had already taken on its most obvious characteristics, chief and most pointed among which was anti-Semitism.

Immoderate attacks on Jews were one of the features that marked out Schönerer most in the early stages of his political career. A growing tide of criticism of liberalism and its press bastion had led to a new form of anti-Semitism that associated Jewry with all the economic and social ills of the time. This anti-Semitism developed a picture of European Jews as a corrupting people or rather an anti-*Volk*, not a religious community, stressing the physical features shared by many European Jews as a sign that they were a race of parasitic aliens.[30] The Jewish question to the new breed of anti-Semite was biological as well as moral and religious; assimilation through conversion, once the panacea of devotional anti-Semites, could only now be a partial remedy. The Jewish question became one of blood for the more radical anti-Semites. For many *völkisch* thinkers, anti-Semitism proved to be the negative side of their idealizing of the *Volk*—the *Volk* was everything not Jewish within German society, while concomitantly everything Jewish was irredeemably wrong.

The *völkisch* critique of the political and social order, rather than exclusionist and negative, was essentially utopian, however, a feature perhaps especially striking in light of how the *völkisch* politics of men like Schönerer was usually practiced.[31] The *Volk* was increasingly to be seen to have existed in its ideal form in a lost, innocent, pre-industrial past.[32] Some nationalists such as Felix Dahn expressed their patriotism in their increasingly popular fictionalized accounts of ancient and early medieval times.[33] An even more antique gaze and, moreover, a clearly more political and gnostic vision, however, was to be found in the writings of Paul de Lagarde. His essays, collected together as his *German Writings (Deutsche Schriften)* in 1878, engendered an especial political importance to Germanic antiquity.[34] Lagarde was later to be proclaimed one of the foundational Nazi ideologues and it was in his writings that an overtly gnostic aspect to *völkisch* thought first developed.

Lagarde had a much more developed notion of the historicity of the *Volk* than his predecessors. He recognized an original *Volksgeist* immanent among the tales of the old Germanic past, one which, moreover, included a Germanic spiritualism similar to that seen by some Protestant theologians to have emerged in Luther's rejection of Rome. Lagarde thought an equal rejection of the oriental "pollution" he saw typified in Pauline dogma would return the German Protestant to a state closer to the *Volksgeist* of old Germanic times. Writing in the heyday of the new anti-Semitism, Lagarde recognized this oriental pollution most clearly in the excessive ritualism of Judaism. Only a rejection of Catholicism, the Jew and an understanding of old Germanic faith could return the modern German to spiritual harmony. For Lagarde, a spiritual Teutonism must awaken, a positive, German Christianity stripped of the layers of empty, suffocating ritual.[35]

This gnostic feature of *völkisch* thought led to the adoption of the *Los von Rom* (Break with Rome) movement by Pan-Germans like Schönerer in Austria.[36] The *Los von Rom* movement saw rejecting the Catholic Church and embracing the faith of Luther as a sign of one's uncompromised fidelity to the Protestant Prusso-German Empire. But the spirituality of German Christianity could be taken further—by the time of the adoption of the *Los von Rom* by his Pan-Germans, Schönerer had already made contact with the circle of the Austrian mystic Guido List who had made a more fundamental break with Rome. At the time of the dawning of modern German occultism, both List's and Schönerer's *Los von Rom* included their acceptance of Wotanism, a neo-paganism based in the writings not of theorists such as Lagarde, but instead in List's own interpretation of Germanic antiquity.[37] Neither was interested in Lutheranism for any truly confessional motive in the Christian sense: they were Lutheran when they were pro-Prussian, Wotanist when more fundamentally pan-German. Their true religion was the greater German *Volk*.

Much as was the contemporary rise of Druidism in Wales, however, Wotanism was clearly a development of the Romantic movement, and it is in this sense that *völkisch* often seems closest to "folkish." List, after all, had first become well known through his naturalist essays that in 1891 were collected as *German Mythological Landscapes (Deutsch-Mythologische Landschaftsbilder)*.[38] These landscapes also included ruins, medieval and ancient, and List, the leading *völkisch* mystic of the day (and an enthusiastic mountaineer), would later recount he had first celebrated his Wotanism as early as 1875 in a Roman-age ruin outside Vienna.[39] Yet where Romantic artists and antiquarians cherished a past lost in time's mists, some *völkisch* thinkers came to demand its recreation in varying measures of actuality. Authors such as Bernhard von Cotta stressed the influence of landscape in the creation of the *Volksgeist*—the criterion of blood came to be amplified by soil.[40] As the influence of the German cult of nature grew, one first realized in the philhellenism of the *Sturm und Drang*, a naturalist reform movement had arisen in German-speaking Europe.

The notion of reform appeared in several expressions of German and Austrian society at the end of the nineteenth century, and was often not seen only in terms of the new politics that idolized the *Volk*. Among the young it was manifested in the Youth Movement, a loose back-to-nature organization that would go on to inspire the British Scouting movement.[41] There was also the Life Reform Movement, whose followers participated in athletic events and reformed their diets.[42] Like Schönerer before him, Hitler was a vegetarian[43]—many aspects of Nazism grew out of the ideals of these movements of social critique and so did much of its imagery. Participation in the Youth Movement gave its members a feeling of *esprit de corps*, for instance, later glorified as a *bündisch* (corporate or fraternal) ideal, as well as closeness to the natural world.[44] A fascination with symbols from the ancient Germanic past, perhaps most notably the swastika, was also prevalent in such groups—and the books of radical reformists such as List soon became influential in Youth Movement and Life Reform circles. In fact, like List, many of the leading early *völkisch* figures had similarly been devotees of the German reformatory and back-to-nature craze.

The anti-modern *völkisch* emphasis on naturalism was also to have its effect in the development of German art and design. After all, an emphasis on the medieval German past had become an official motif of Bismarckian art, especially in the philhellene historicist tradition of the German art establishment. Where a specifically *völkisch* approach differed was a rejection of the mere preservationist social agenda of the conservatives and a focus on recapturing a specifically Germanic antiquity. In a manner influenced by the naturalism of the *Jugendstil* (*art nouveau*), but perhaps showing a deeper connection with the Pre-Raphaelites, from the 1890s Hugo Höppener, a Youth Movement artist who called himself Fidus (i.e. "trusty"), developed a folksy, woodcut-emulating style that seemed to capture the spirit of the Vikings, the woodcuts of the Reformation and the cultural otherworldliness of the runes.[45] More *völkisch* artists soon appeared, their book art appearing most commonly in journals like *Heimdall*, and led to the development of a dense German archaizing aesthetic or kitsch. Some members of the developing German graphic design industry adopted a *völkisch* Teutonic style which favored the use of a woodcut sensibility and heavy *Fraktur* (German Gothic or Blackletter) type, one that by the time of the First World War was considered respectably German enough to appear in government posters. Adolf Reinecke, the editor of *Heimdall*, was a particular critic of the growing dominance of international Roman (plain or Antiqua) type and by the 1920s *Fraktur* had come to be championed even in mainstream German typography journals as a somehow organic expression of Germanness.[46] This penchant for a woodcut feeling in type was extended by some *völkisch* designers to the use of rune-like type or even runes themselves. A catalogue of runic jewellery tailored for the *völkisch* market had also appeared by 1917.[47] Instead of ancient Greece and Rome, a mythologized antiquarian Germany of warriors and runes supplied the vision of antiquity which served as a model for the project of *völkisch* reform.

The preeminent form of exposure to the new political thinking in respectable German society at the time, however, was in the operas of Richard Wagner.[48] Wagner had had great success when he put a medieval German tale to music in his *Tannhäuser* of 1844 and again with *Lohengrin* four years later. Instead of merely dabbling in motifs from the German literary past as had Mozart in his *Magic Flute*, however, Wagner soon came to appreciate more fully the Germanness in medieval German literature. He reached a height with his four-part *Ring of the Nibelungs* (1853–74) and *Parsifal* (1882) where the medieval German tales, the anonymous *Song of the Nibelungs* and Wolfram von Eschenbach's much-embellished retelling of the legend of Sir Percival, are reworked into sweeping allegorical commentaries on the fate of Germany and her Christian racial mission.[49]

Wagner also incorporated a new form of political understanding in his operas as well as his writings that was similarly to become an essential pillar of the *völkisch* ideal. In a culturally pessimistic work typical of the period, in the 1850s a French nobleman, Arthur, Count de Gobineau, had ascribed the malaise of his times to racial miscegenation.[50] Taking in a long tradition of French anthropological theorizing, Gobineau blamed the ills of his day on bad blood; he extended class prejudice (a family of bad blood) to racial prejudice (a race of the same). Mostly ignored in France, his writings nevertheless eventually gained him many converts in Germany: cultural pessimists, anti-Semites and national xenophobes could all see their agendas explained in terms of the new racial thinking that began with Gobineau. Moreover, as Darwin's theory of evolution became more accepted in the course of the 1870s, especially in the form promoted by the German naturalist Ernst Haeckel, biology, race and blood seemed to become an especially important concern to those who pined for national renewal not to mention those who had turned anti-Semitic prejudice into a form of patriotism.[51] The new racial science and its attendant Social Darwinism were to grow in standing, discussed and promulgated in a growing body of Social Darwinist publications which in the spirit of *völkisch* renewal came to call for a racial as well as cultural hygiene. In the 1890s the French thinker Georges Vacher de Lapouge firmly linked the Aryan with the new race-based politics.[52] But the most developed form of political racialism came in the new century with the studies of Hans F.K. Günther (nicknamed *Rassen*-Günther) who gave the new thinking a new designation: the racialist *völkisch* ideal would become the Nordic ideal (*nordische Gedanke*).[53] To the new thinkers it was the racial purity of the Germans stressed by the first-century Roman historian Tacitus that seemed to explain the most laudable features of the *Volk*. In fact by the turn of the new century, for many *völkisch* theorists the racialist thinking that began with Gobineau seemed to have become the scientific glue that held the rest of their thought together—which is, no doubt, why Hitler's ideas seem most coherent when he opines on the question of race.[54]

Much as with anti-Semitism, however, racialist thinking was not essential to the concept of the *Volk*. It seemed that an extremely nationalistic focus on antiquity could hold *völkisch* thought together without its attendant sciences of prejudice. While pan-Germanists were generally anti-Semitic and accepted racialist thought, there were still many notable examples of those who classed themselves German National who did not subscribe to the full-blown form of the new *völkisch* ideal—and it is evident that many German Nationals thought their rune-fancying and race-obsessed radical rightwing brethren ridiculous. There were even aborted attempts in late Wilhelmine times to develop a left-wing form of *völkisch* politics similar to that which arose in Sweden (which has its own *völkisch* or rather *folklig* tradition), e.g. the Bavarian anarchist Gustav Landauer's *völkisch* socialism.[55] In general, though, *völkisch* politics readily became both anti-Semitic and racialist. Racialism seemed to feed off anti-Semitism, and hatred of Jews—the anti-*Volk*—increasingly appeared to be a necessary part of German patriotism. In fact, acceptance of *völkisch* or fascist thought often led to anti-Semitism and racism even outside Germany: both Oswald Mosley's British Union of Fascists and even Mussolini's *Fascisti* became increasingly anti-Semitic over time.

There was one more ingredient to be added to the development of *völkisch* thought, however, that also seemed to be essential. From the

1880s *völkisch* discourse, like most radical movements of the day, also became infused with the ideas of Wagner's former disciple Friedrich Nietzsche.[56] Under the influence of Nietzsche, *völkisch* thought developed aspects which led to a further radicalizing of the nationalist vision.

Völkisch thought took on several of Nietzsche's main themes. First, it became Dionysian—it became increasingly impatient of received tradition and glorified knowledge derived from inspiration and intuition—much as Nietzsche had prescribed in his earlier works.[57] Nietzsche's investigations of social and political inequality also influenced much of the language of the racialist, Social Darwinist theorizing of later writers. Most palpably, Nietzsche's ideals of a *Herrenvolk* (master race) and a *Herrenethik* (masterly moral) came to resonate widely in *völkisch* thought.[58] *Völkisch* thinking after Nietzsche also came to bathe in the aura of his *Übermensch*, the creative genius and enlightened superman.[59] Indeed not only did they share Nietzsche's focus on inequality, his concept of will to power was soon bowdlerized by some of his *völkisch* interpreters to the point where it became a call only for single-minded, fanatical action.[60] After Nietzsche, *völkisch* writers adopted much of his language and thematics, even if they did not share his humanism and insight. Nevertheless, it was the promise that the *Volksgeist* would from time-to-time be epitomized in a certain reforming *Übermensch* that became the most seductive element of *völkisch* thought after Nietzsche. The German-National "conservative revolutionary" Arthur Moeller van den Bruck summed up this messianic vision most influentially in 1923 in his prophetic *The Third Reich (Das Dritte Reich)*.[61] Even Carl Jung seemed to accept the notion of a *völkisch* superman—Hitler, the personification of the German *Volksgeist*.[62] The *Volk* after Nietzsche increasingly seemed to be framed in terms more of the sword of Arminius than of the pen of Herder. But the *völkisch* reception of Nietzsche had decked out the radical German ideal in a resplendent new linguistic, zealous and visionary garb nonetheless.

One of Schönerer's pan-German mottos was "Germania's cathedral will be built without Judah, without Rome." This temple of the *Volk*, described by the Roman description for ancient Germany, had changed since his day to encompass more of the antiquarian Romanticism clear in the pan-German poem *Solstice*, but also in other ways too. The *völkisch* critique of the political and social order had led to the rise of a movement whose principal pillar was a demand for social renewal, one which idealized pre-industrial Germany, but increasingly saw that the true German golden age had been in pre-Christian times.[63] This ancient Germany had long been seen as a time of racial purity. It consequently allowed the aim of renewal, legitimized in an ideal past, to dovetail with the new Social Darwinism and the reformatory notion of racial purity first extolled in the late nineteenth century. The calls for social renewal and racial hygiene met at the barriers of the new anti-Semitism, and after being infused with an uncompromising Nietzsche-anism, the *völkisch* critique also became increasingly radical. German society had to be transformed, rid of its undesirable elements and remade according to the splendid ideal of ancient Germany. Its negative side seems now to many critics to define the new politics, but Schö-nerer and his latter-day followers were most interested in building, not destroying, although many maintained that along the way some radical racial and cultural surgery might be necessary to achieve their ultimate goal.

Notes

1 Anon., "Sonnenwende," *Heimdall* 14 Apr. 1899, 95.
2 E.g. D. Blackbourn, *The Fontana History of Germany 1780–1918* (London: Fontana, 1997).
3 H.-L. Janssen, "Grundsätzliches zur vor- und frühgeschichtlichen Sinn-bilderforschung," *Altpreußen* 1 (1935): 183–85; S. Lehmann, "Der Kampf um die Sinnbildforschung," *Nationalsozialistische Monatshefte* 7 (1936): 832–35.
4 J. & W. Grimm, *Wörterbuch der deutschen Sprache* XVI, (Berlin: Hirzel, 1905), 1153–54; *Meyers Lexikon* XI, 7th ed. (Leipzig: Bibliographisches Institut, 1929), 1192–93.
5 Both expressions are early-twentieth–century political bowdlerisms; see J.A. Simpson et al. (eds.), *The Oxford English Dictionary*, 22 vols., 2nd ed. (Oxford: Clarendon, 1989), VII, 622; XX, 149; C. Schmitz-Berning, *Vokabu-lar des Nationalsozialismus*, 2nd ed. (Berlin: De Gruyter, 1998), 686ff.; and cf. R. Cecil, *The Myth of the Master Race* (London: Batsford, 1972), 61ff.; E. Jäckel, *Hitler's Weltanschauung*, trans H. Arnold (Middleton: Wesleyan University Press, 1972), 13–26; and R. Zitelmann, *Hitler*, trans. H. Bo-gler (London: London House, 1999), 52ff., 130ff.; B. Zehnpfennig, *Hitlers Mein Kampf*, 2nd ed. (Munich: Fink, 2002), 284ff.
6 B. von Schirach, *Ich glaubte an Hitler* (Hamburg: Mosaik, 1967), 87; Cecil, 65; F. Stern, *The Politics of Cultural Despair* (Berkeley: University of California Press, 1961), xi, xiv; M. Broszat, *German National Socialism 1919–*

1945, trans. K. Rosenbaum & I.P. Boehm (Santa Barbara: Clio, 1966), 31ff.; W.D. Smith, *The Ideological Origins of Nazi Imperialism* (New York: Oxford University Press, 1986), 13ff. and 232ff.

7 R.G.L. Waite, *Vanguard of Nazism* (Cambridge, Mass.: Harvard University Press, 1952); R. Bessel, "The 'Front' Generation and the Politics of Weimar Germany," in M. Roseman (ed.), *Generations in Conflict* (Cambridge: Cambridge University Press, 1995), 121–36; S. Breuer, *Grundpositionen der deutschen Rechten* (Tübingen: Niemeyer, 1999); idem, *Nationalismus und Faschismus* (Darmstadt: Wissenschaftliche Buchgesellschaft, 2005), 145ff.

8 G. Feder, *Das Programm der N.S.D.A.P. und seine weltanschaulichen Grundgedanken* (Munich: Eher, 1927).

9 D.C. Watt, "Introduction," in Hitler, *Mein Kampf*, trans. Mannheim, xi–xii; W. Maser, *Hitler's Mein Kampf*, trans. R.H. Barry (London: Faber & Faber, 1970), 36ff.

10 Hitler, *Mein Kampf*, 324; trans. Mannheim, 269.

11 M. Broszat, "Soziale Motivation und Führer-Bindung des Nationalsozialismus," *Vierteljahrshefte für Zeitgeschichte* 18 (1970): 392–409; I. Kershaw, *The "Hitler Myth"* (Oxford: Clarendon, 1987); idem, "'Working Towards the Führer'," *Contemporary European History* 2/2 (1993): 103–18; idem, "Hitler and the Uniqueness of Nazism," *Journal of Contemporary History* 39 (2004): 239–54.

12 F. Neumann, *Behemoth* (London: Gollancz, 1942); M. Broszat, *The Hitler State*, trans. J.W. Hiden (London: Longmann, 1981); H. Mommsen, *From Weimar to Auschwitz*, trans. P. O'Connor (Cambridge: Polity, 1991), 163ff.

13 R. Griffin, *The Nature of Fascism* (London: Pinter, 1991), 26.

14 R. Griffin, "The Primacy of Culture," *Journal of Contemporary History* 37 (2002): 21–43.

15 Hitler's last testament, International Military Tribunal document no. 3569 apud H. Trevor Roper, *The Last Days of Hitler*, 2nd ed. (London: Pan, 1962), 212; cf. Griffin, *Nature*, 110.

16 M. Burleigh and W. Wippermann, *The Racial State* (Cambridge: Cambridge University Press, 1991).

17 R.R. Ergang, *Herder and the Foundations of German Nationalism* (New York: Columbia University Press, 1933); T. Nipperdey, *Germany From Napoleon to Bismarck 1800–1866*, trans. D. Nolan (Dublin: Gill & Macmillan, 1996), 262ff.

18 Ergang, 44–45; 85, n. 6; 102 & 110.

19 J.J. Sheehan, *German History 1770–1866* (Oxford: Clarendon, 1989), 144ff.; Blackbourn, 47ff.; J. Echternkamp, *Der Aufstieg des deutschen Nationalismus* (Frankfurt a.M.: Campus, 1998), 44ff.

20 J.G. von Fichte, *Reden an die deutsche Nation* (Berlin: Realschuhbuchhandlung, 1807–8); Blackbourn, 88ff.

21 W. Scherer, *Geschichte der Deutschen Literatur*, 13th ed. (Berlin: Weidmann, 1915), 470ff.; H.G. Rötzer, *Geschichte der deutschen Literatur* (Bamberg: Buchner, 1997), 86ff.

22 Sheehan, 165ff.; Echternkamp, 99ff.

23 Grimms *Wörterbuch* II (1866), 1053.

24 Sheehan, 656ff.; W.J. Mommsen, *1848*, 2nd ed. (Frankfurt a.M.: Fischer, 1998), 104ff.

25 L. Gall, *Bismarck*, trans. J.A. Underwood, 2 vols. (London: Allen & Unwin, 1986), I, 227ff.; O. Pflanze, *Bismarck and the Development of Germany I*, 2nd ed. (Princeton: Princeton University Press, 1990); W.J. Mommsen, *Das Ringen um den nationalen Staat* (Berlin: Propyläen, 1993), 72ff.; Nipperdey, 627ff.

26 A.G. Whiteside, *The Socialism of Fools* (Berkeley: University of California Press, 1975); cf. J.W. Boyer, *Political Radicalism in Late Imperial Vienna* (Chicago: Chicago University Press, 1981), 88ff.

27 U. Lohalm, *Völkischer Radikalismus* (Hamburg: Leibniz, 1970), 27ff.; G. Eley, *Reshaping the German Right* (New Haven: Yale University Press, 1980), 48ff.; R. Chickering, *We Men Who Feel Most German* (Boston: Allen & Unwin, 1984).

28 R. Koselleck et al., "Volk, Nation, Nationalismus, Masse," in O. Brunner et al. (eds.), *Geschichtliche Grundbegriffe* VII (Stuttgart: Klett–Cotta, 1992), 141–431.

29 G. Hartung, "Völkische Ideologie," *Weimarer Beiträge* 33 (1987): 1174–85; idem, "Völkische Ideologie," in U. Puschner et al. (eds.), *Handbuch zur "Völkischen Bewegung" 1871–1918* (Munich: Saur, 1996), 22f.; Schmitz-Berning, 645f.

30 R. & J. Patai, *The Myth of the Jewish Race* (Detroit: Wayne State University Press, 1989), 21ff.; A. Kiefer, *Das Problem eine "jüdischen Rasse"* (Frankfurt a.M.: Lang, 1991).

31 J. Hermand, *Old Dreams of a New Reich*, trans. P. Levesque (Bloomington: Indiana University Press, 1992), 26ff.; U. Puschner, "Anti-Semitism and German Voelkish Ideology," in H. Cancik and U. Puschner (eds.), *Anti-Semitism, Paganism, Voelkish Religion* (Munich: Saur, 2004), 55–63.

32 W.H. Riehl, *Die Naturgeschichte des Volkes als Grundlage einer deutschen Sozialpolitik*, 4 vols. (Stuttgart: Cotta, 1851–69); G.L. Mosse, *The Crisis of German Ideology* (New York: Grosset & Dunlap, 1964), 19–20; S. Schama, *Landscape and Memory* (New York: Knopf, 1995), 112–19; W.D. Smith, *Politics and the Sciences of Culture in Germany 1840–1920* (New York: Oxford University Press), 1991, 40–44; J. von Altenbockum, *Wilhelm Heinrich Riehl 1823–1897* (Cologne: Böhlau, 1994).

33 See esp. F. Dahn, *Ein Kampf um Rom*, 4 vols. (Leipzig: Breitkopf & Härtel, 1876–87) and M. Titzmann, "Die Konzeption der 'Germanen' in der deutschen Literatur des 19. Jahrhunderts," in J. Link and W. Wülfling (eds.), *Nationale Mythen und Symbole in der zweiten Hälfte des 19. Jahrhunderts* (Stuttgart: Klett–Cotta, 1991), 120–45; R. Kipper, *Der Germanenmythos im Deutschen Kaiserreich* (Göttingen: Vandenhoeck & Rupprecht, 2002), 118ff.

34 P.A. de Lagarde, *Deutsche Schriften* (Göttingen: Dieterich, 1878); Stern, 3–94; R.W. Lougee, *Paul de Lagarde 1827–1891* (Cambridge, Mass.: Harvard

University Press, 1962); I.U. Paul, "Paul Anton de Lagarde," in U. Puschner et al. (eds.), *Handbuch zur "Völkischen Bewegung" 1871–1918* (Munich: Saur, 1996), 45–93.

35 Stern, 35ff.; Lougee, 131ff.

36 Whiteside, 243ff.

37 N. Goodrick-Clarke, *The Occult Roots of Nazism* (Wellingborough: Aquarian, 1985), 8ff.; C. Treitel, *A Science for the Soul* (Baltimore: Johns Hopkins University Press, 2004).

38 G. List, *Deutsch-Mythologische Landschaftsbilder* (Berlin: Lüstenöder, 1891).

39 Goodrick-Clarke, 34–35.

40 B. von Cotta, *Deutschlands Boden* (Leipzig: Brockhaus, 1853).

41 W. Laquer, *Young Germany* (London: Routledge & Kegan Paul, 1962); Mosse, *Crisis*, 171ff.; P.D. Stachura, *The German Youth Movement 1900–1945* (New York: St Martin's Press, 1981).

42 W.R. Krabbe, *Gesellschaftsveränderung durch Lebensreform* (Göttingen: Vandenhoeck & Ruprecht, 1974); D. Kerbs and J. Reulecke (eds.), *Handbuch der deutschen Reformbewegungen 1880–1933* (Wuppertal: Hammer, 1998); K. Buchholz et al. (eds.), *Die Lebensreform*, 2 vols. (Darmstadt: Häusser, 2001); cf. also M. Green, *Mountain of Truth* (Hanover: University of New England Press, 1986); K. Repp, *Reformers, Critics and the Paths of German Modernity* (Cambridge, Mass.: Harvard University Press, 2000).

43 Mees, "Hitler and *Germanentum*," 267.

44 F. Raabe, *Die bündische Jugend* (Stuttgart: Brentano, [1961]); H. Siefert, *Der bündische Aufbruch* (Bad Godesberg: Voggenreiter, [1963]); H.W. Koch, *The Hitler Youth* (New York: Stein & Day, 1976); Stachura, 45ff., 113ff.

45 J. Frecot et al., *Fidus 1868–1948* (Munich: Rogner & Bernhard, 1972); cf. R. Hamann and J. Hermand, *Naturalismus* (Berlin: Akademie, 1959), 12ff.; J. Döring, "Beispiele englischer Buchkunst," in J. Lammers and G. Unverfehrt (eds.), *Vom Jugendstil zum Bauhaus* (Münster: Westfälisches Landesmuseum für Kunst & Kulturgeschichte, 1981), 18–33.

46 A. Reinecke, *Die deutsche Buchstabenschrift* (Leipzig–Borsdorf: Hasert, 1910); S. Hartmann, *Fraktur oder Antiqua* (Frankfurt a.M.: Lang, 1998); J. Aynsley, *Graphic Design in Germany* (London: Thames & Hudson, 2000), 17–19, 182–88; G. Newton, "Deutsche Schrift," *German Life and Letters* 56 (2003): 183–211.

47 Haus Ecklöh, *Runenschmuck. Werbeschrift* [S.l., n.d.]; Goodrick-Clarke, 129.

48 R.W. Gutman, *Richard Wagner* (Harmondsworth: Penguin, 1971); M. Gregor-Dellin, *Richard Wagner*, trans. J.M. Brownjohn (London: Collins, 1983); M. Tanner, *Wagner* (London: HarperCollins, 1996).

49 C. von Westerhagen, *Richard Wagner* (Zürich: Atlantis, 1956), 116ff.; T.W. Adorno, *In Search of Wagner*, trans. R. Livingstone (London: NLB, 1981), 18ff.; P.L. Rose, *Wagner, Race and Revolution* (London: Faber, 1992); M.A. Weiner, *Wagner and the Anti-Semitic Imagination* (Lincoln:

University of Nebraska Press, 1995); J.M. Fisher, *Richard Wagners "Das Judentum in der Musik"* (Frankfurt a. M.: Insel, 2000).

50 A. Compte de Gobineau, *Essai sur l'inégalité des races humaines*, 4 vols. (Paris: Firmin Didot, 1853–54); M.D. Biddiss, *Father of Racist Ideology* (London: Weidenfeld & Nicholson, 1976).

51 E. Haeckel, *Natürliche Schöpfungsgeschichte* (Berlin: Reimer, 1868); idem, *Anthropogenie* (Leipzig: Engelmann, 1874); H.-G. Zmarzlik, "Der Sozialdarwinismus in Deutschland als geschichtliches Problem," *Vierteljahreshefte für Zeitgeschichte* 11 (1963): 246–73; D. Gasman, *The Scientific Origins of National Socialism* (London: MacDonald, 1971); A. Kelly, *The Descent of Darwin* (Chapel Hill: University of North Carolina Press, 1981); J. Sandmann, *Der Bruck mit der humanitären Tradition* (Stuttgart: Fischer, 1990).

52 G. Vacher de Lapouge, *Les Selections sociales* (Paris: Fontemoing, 1896); idem, *L'Aryen* (Paris: Fontemoing, 1899).

53 H.F.K. Günther, *Rassenkunde des deutschen Volkes* (Munich: Lehmann, 1922); H.-J. Lutzhöft, *Der Nordische Gedanke in Deutschland 1920–1940* (Stuttgart: Klett, 1971); L. Poliakov, *The Aryan Myth*, trans. E. Howard (London: Heinemann, 1974); G.G. Field, "Nordic Racism," *Journal of the History of Ideas* 38 (1977): 523–40.

54 Puschner, "Anti-Semitism," 62f.

55 E. Lunn, *Prophet of Community* (Berkeley: University of California Press, 1973); L. Trägårdh, "Varieties of Volkisch Ideologies," in B. Stråth (ed.), *Language and the Construction of Class Identities* (Gothenburg: Department of History, Gothenburg University, 1990), 25–54.

56 W. Kaufmann, *Nietzsche*, 4th ed. (Princeton: Princeton University Press, 1975); D. Fischer-Dieskau, *Wagner and Nietzsche*, trans. J. Neugroschel (New York: Seabury, 1976); P. Bergmann, *Nietzsche, "The Last Antipolitical German"* (Bloomington: Indiana University Press, 1987); S.E. Aschheim, *The Nietzsche Legacy in Germany 1890–1990* (Berkeley: University of California Press, 1992).

57 F. Nietzsche, *Die Geburt der Tragödie* (Leipzig: Fritsch, 1871).

58 R. Hamann and J. Hermand, *Gründerzeit* (Berlin: Akademie, 1965), 172ff.; B.H.F. Taureck, *Nietzsche und der Faschismus* (Hamburg: Junius, 1989).

59 F. Nietzsche, *Also sprach Zarathustra*, 4 vols. (Chemnitz: Schmeitzer and Leipzig: Naumann, 1883–91).

60 F. Nietzsche, *Der Wille zur Macht*, ed. E. Förster-Nietzsche (Leipzig: Naumann, 1901).

61 A. Moeller van den Bruck, *Das dritte Reich* (Berlin: Ring, 1923); Stern, 183–266; H.-J. Schwierskott, *Arthur Moeller van den Bruck und der revolutionäre Nationalismus in der Weimarer Republik* (Göttingen: Musterschmidt, 1962); Aschheim, 193–94; and cf. A. Mohler, *Die konservative Revolution in Deutschland 1918–1932*, 2nd ed. (Darmstadt: Wissenschaftliche Buchgesellschaft, 1972); S. Breuer, *Anatomie der konservativen Revolution* (Darmstadt: Wissenschaftliche Buchgesellschaft, 1993); idem, *Ordnungen der Ungleich-*

heit (Darmstadt: Wissenschaftliche Buchgesellschaft, 2001); M. Travers, *Critics of Modernity* (New York: Lang, 2001).

62 C.J. Jung, *Nietzsche's* Zarathustra, ed. J.L. Jarrett, 2 vols. (Princeton: Princeton University Press, 1989), II, 826–27; Aschheim, 258ff.; R. Noll, *The Jung Cult* (Princeton: Princeton University Press, 1994); idem, *The Aryan Christ* (New York: Random House, 1997), 223ff.

63 Cf. H. Glaser, *The Cultural Roots of National Socialism*, trans. E.A. Menze (London: Croom Helm, 1978), 147ff.

CHAPTER 2.

History and Intuition

Lies Tacitus, da findest du ihren Charakter
... da ward in Norden neuer Mensch gebohren

Herder

The development of *völkisch* politics was also contemporary with a substantial change in the focus of German academic culture. In the mid-nineteenth century, German universities were particularly focused on philhellenism and the classics—something superlative in the Greek spirit seemed to accord particularly well with German hopes and identity at the time. Thus Latin and especially ancient Greek studies were disciplines held in the highest regard, and the study of ancient Greek philosophy and culture was considered the most favored avenue to education and understanding.[1] By the time of the Nazi assumption of power, however, university classicism was on the wane, largely at the expense of the study of modern languages and literatures as well as the physical sciences, but also of a growing and confident, if not mature field of Germanic antiquarian studies. The popularity of the old Germanic past had come to threaten to surpass that of Greece and Rome in terms of university courses, enrollments, publications and eventually state funding too. A growing public fascination with German antiquity was reflected in a new development in the universities that threatened to eclipse its elder classicist antiquarian sibling.

The old Germanic past could only be accessed, however, through a complex, fragmentary and often indirect record, one which was much less readily accessible than that of Greco-Roman antiquity. The medieval Germanic equivalent to Homer was not even written in German, and what could be rescued from early native literature often seemed a poor cousin to the better-known Latin, French or Scandinavian works. Much patient empirical groundwork was required to assemble the evidence required to reach an understanding of old Germanic culture and the ancient German soul. The difficult nature of the record of Germanic antiquity also made it an area where historical imagination seemed particularly necessary, and its rescuing and understanding a project that lent itself particularly well to becoming subservient to other, less purely antiquarian concerns.

Nonetheless it is clear that the Germanism of those early cultural warriors, Wagner, Lagarde and other thinkers and writers who would come to be seminal sources for later generations of *völkisch* enthusiasts, was derived from notions of the past which ultimately stemmed from a tradition of German antiquarian study. As much as for any academic working at the same time, the views of antiquity formed by these men were the reflection of a scholarly tradition of a lengthy pedigree. But it was a tradition of discontinuity and rupture, although it clearly went back as far as 1473, the year of the first German printing of the *Germania*, the ethnographical study of ancient Germany by Tacitus.[2]

Tacitus' *Germania* is a moral study that favorably contrasts ancient Germanic simplicity with Roman degeneracy. It rapidly became a golden book after its German rediscovery, however, and was soon complemented by the publication of a number of other relevant classical works.[3] An age of humanist Germanomania ensued in which ancient German figures were hailed in poems, dramatic works and songs.[4] Yet by the early 1700s, interest in this German antiquity had given way to classicism and the dominance of French verse and fashion.[5]

The Renaissance had seen the rebirth of all sorts of classical learning. The first German humanists, though, also had to contend with the Italian notion that all things out of the north were barbaric. The ancient Goths had sacked Rome twice in late antiquity and the label Gothic had long been applied by Italian writers to anything that had followed them out of the north—even the great tradition of medieval northern European architecture was derogated as "Gothic" by Italian humanists. Yet with the decline of Italy, German minds no longer felt the need to extol ancient Germany, but instead had become more interested in Greco-Roman antiquity than the Tacitean German past.

Nonetheless at a time of pronounced Francophilia, this focus on classical learning eventually led to the emergence of a similar interest in German literature. The first steps toward a tradition of the study of the *belles lettres* of the German nation appeared at the same time as French style and even language first began to be adopted in German high society.[6] Although this Germanistic study did not achieve the status of a discrete discipline in universities until the next century, it clearly laid the groundwork for the first surveys of German literary history and critique of the late 1700s.[7] Moreover, in the shadow of classical philology, the study of German literature came to be styled *Germanistik* (as opposed to *Romanistik*) seen at the time as a suitably grandiose, Latinate title, even though the literature was more properly *deutsch*.[8] Such coins reflected a linguistic confusion that is still especially evident in English today.

The term *German* is first recorded in the sixteenth century where it is obviously a loan from Latin.[9] It and the adjective *germanisch* (Germanic), however, have otherwise achieved a quite separate meaning in modern German. *Germanisch* is more properly 'Old German'—it describes the Germany of ancient times. Yet the Germans of Tacitus are also ancestors not only of the modern Austrians, Swiss and Germans, but also the modern Scandinavians, Dutch and Anglo-Saxons. Hence English (historically and linguistically) is properly equally as Germanic as German is. Yet the former homonymy in German where the Latinate term was felt to be a prestige form of the native one is clearly the reason why the German National Museum at Nuremberg is styled the Germanisches Museum and *Germanistik* refers to what at school level is merely termed *Deutsch*.

Almost the reverse development has taken place in English where the term German stands for *deutsch* and Germany for *Deutschland*. In contrast, the distinction between the ancient Germans and ancient Germany that in German today is reserved to the terms *Germanen* and *Germanien* has no unambiguous counterpart in English. For a time the ancient Germans were called Teutons, repeating the error of medieval scribes who associated *Deutsch* with an early wandering northern tribe called the Teutones. Nonetheless, under the influence of German linguistics the language associated with the inhabitants of ancient Germany has come to be called Germanic (formerly Teutonic). Thus despite the similarity of this term to the adjective Germanic (meaning 'German'), it has become customary to refer to the ancient Germans as Germanic peoples in English. Teutonic is also often used in English today for an attribution 'German,' much as Gallic (i.e. Gaulish) is used for 'French.' But German should be recognized as separate from the antiquarian and linguistic identity which is Germanic (*germanisch*), even though in common usage these terms might easily be regarded almost as synonymous.

Samuel Johnson refers to English in his *Dictionary*, however, as both Teutonic and a Gothonic tongue; by his day Germanic antiquarianism had been reborn in the light of the full flowering of European Gothicism.[10] The picture of the Goths in Gothicism was not the negative stereotype of the Italian humanists, though, but presented the Goths of ancient times, instead, in an idealized manner.[11] In Spain this Gothicism was a Visigothicism that looked back to the early Middle Ages of Visigothic Christian rule before the conquest of the Moors in the early eighth century.[12] In France the Goths were romanticized by authors such as Montesquieu as the liberators of Western Europe from the tyranny of Imperial Rome.[13] In Sweden, however, the connection was stronger: there the Goths were claimed to be the greatest of the early Scandinavians to mark their place in history.[14]

A connection of the Goths with Scandinavia is recounted by the sixth-century Ostrogothic historian Jordanes.[15] The Goths had also been a popular subject among German humanists;[16] but it was the representation of the Goths as ancient Scandinavians in the works of the Swedish humanists Johannes and Olaus Magnus that had the most lasting influence in the North.[17] Antiquarianism soon became a pan-Scandinavian concern and when the Danish antiquarian Peder Resen discovered a number of manuscripts preserving medieval Icelandic literature, a new chapter in Scandinavian antiquarian interest began.[18] With Resen's publication of the *Prose Edda*, a tradition of Old Norse studies was born.

The publication of the *Prose Edda* had an immediate impact on antiquarian studies outside Scandinavia. The highpoint of Scandinavian Gothicism was reached soon thereafter with the four-volume *Atlantica (Atland eller Manheim)* of Olof Rudbeck the elder, a celebrated study in which the author sought to link Scandinavia, Jordanes' *vagina nationum* (womb of nations), with the mythical Atlantis of Plato.[19] Yet it is clear that far more important for the reception of the fruits of Gothicism outside Scandinavia was the appearance of the works of the Genevan Paul Henri Mallet.[20] This one-time pupil of Montesquieu introduced the new Nordic component of Gothicism to a popular, Europe-wide audience and inaugurated the interest in Scandinavian antiquity to Germany.

The translation of the *Prose Edda* in Mallet's *Northern Antiquities (Introduction à l'Histoire de Dannemarc)* was clearly the source of inspiration that in 1771 led the German poet Friedrich Gottlieb Klopstock to reject classicism and embrace Gothicism in its stead; upon acquaintance with Mallet, Klopstock's subject matter became Norse, or as he rediscovered the Germany of Caesar and Tacitus, ancient Germanic personages.[21] Klopstock's metrical innovations inaugurated a new German poetry, no longer straightjacketed by classicist forms; coupled with his adoption of Gothicism and calling also on contemporary "bardic" Celticism, Klopstock's new German poetry led straight to the Romantic naturalism exemplified in the *Sturm und Drang* and the ardent Germanism of its herald, Herder.

The foremost example of the new treasuring of ancient Germany at the time is the 1808 *Battle of Hermann (Hermannsschlacht)* of Heinrich von Kleist. Penned in response to the seeming inability of Austria and Prussia to launch a concerted resistance against Napoleon, instead of a contemporary or classical figure, Kleist focused on Arminius, who as head of a combined army of ancient Germany had routed three Roman legions invading from Gaul.[22] Kleist's play re-established the essential Germanness of Arminius—his *Battle of Hermann* refocused attention on ancient Germany. German antiquarianism was reinvigorated in light of the nationalist response to Napoleon.

Most of the figures associated with the German classical period, although essentially often philhellenes, nevertheless wrote about the ancient Germans. Herder's remark that "a new man had been born in the North" was to be the touchstone of nineteenth-century German nationalism.[23] The German antiquarian tradition was reborn during the time of Herder, and for many of its figures, shadowing his call, the rediscovery of Germanic antiquity became a patriotic duty. A German who read the antiquarian works which followed Herder did not always find a considered picture of the old Germanic past. As often as not, national chauvinism dictated the picture of Germanic antiquity even in the works of the most respectable antiquarians writing before the days of Schönerer.

Old Germanic philology, the part of *Germanistik* that deals with early German (and increasingly Norse, Gothic and Old English) literature, was seen as a lesser cousin to the study of the great Latin and Greek writers in the early nineteenth century. But the emerging discipline brought a new nationalistic aspect to philological work. Linguistics was also born in Germany at the same time as a rapid growth in Germanic philology and history. Yet despite the illusion of scientification that the discipline often suggests, nineteenth-century German linguistics also harbored a deep chauvinism that also affected the development of Germanic antiquarianism.

In 1808, the Berlin Orientalist Friedrich Schlegel had pointed out the statement made by Sir William Jones, the President of the Royal Asiatic Society of Bengal, in which the Welshman had expressed the opinion that

Sanskrit, the ancient language of the writings of the Indian Brahmans, must surely be genetically related to a number of European languages, citing in this connection Greek, Latin, Celtic and Gothic.[24] Schlegel's student Franz Bopp sought to investigate Jones's claim and went to Paris to study Sanskrit, a language that had only recently become noted in Europe with the first translations of the Hindu epics.[25] Bopp returned to Berlin to publish his proof in 1816, his *Conjugation System*, the foundation work of modern linguistics.[26] Similar investigations of northern European languages had been inaugurated with the publication in 1665 of the Gothic translation of the Bible attributed to the fourth-century Visigothic bishop Wulfila. A tradition of scholars from Franciscus Junius, George Hickes and even to Samuel Johnson stated that Gothic was the oldest of the Teutonic (or 'Gothonic') languages.[27] The wider positioning of Teutonic within Europe, however, was not well understood until the appearance of the seminal study of the Göttingen philologist Jacob Grimm who with his four-volume *Deutsche Grammatik* of 1819–37 produced the twin to Bopp's *Conjugation System*, the foundation work of historical linguistics.[28]

At the same time as Bopp and Grimm were involved in their empirical studies, however, Wilhelm von Humboldt, the Rector of the University of Berlin, was building upon the tradition of Herder, Klopstock and the *Sturm und Drang*, and researching language as an expression of culture.[29] Observing that language is a creation of people, Humboldt thought to see in language the essential representation of culture and nation. In a cross-linguistic or what would now be termed a typological approach, he noted an apparent link between the level of the complexity of the verbal and nominal systems of a language and the level of civilization or culture enjoyed by its speakers. He explained this in terms of a *Sprachgeist*: primitive languages were spoken by primitive minds, whereas complex languages such as German were the product of and represented complex cultures.[30] This of course represented a Eurocentricism and was essentially false. But based in part on Herder's idea of a *Volksgeist*, it also represented the evolution of an ideal of the study of language as an expression of German patriotism.

In his grammar Jacob Grimm set out in a formal manner the phonological relationships between each of the related Germanic languages. Grimm was the first to formulate regular sound laws and indeed one of these laws still bears his name today. Unfortunately, he also indulged in a deliberate display of patriotism in the title of his *Deutsche Grammatik* as clearly it was not a German grammar that he had produced, but a Germanic (*germanisch*) one. Grimm rejected the terms Gothonic, Teutonic or Germanic which had been proposed by other investigators of the correct relationship between these languages. *Deutsch*, he claimed, was the only indigenous term that had once designated all of these languages.[31] But *deutsch* was 'German' and was not accepted by other linguists, not even in Germany. Yet when Jacob and his brother Wilhelm came to publish less linguistically based works, they retained the term *deutsch*, although few could be seen as German in the usual nineteenth-century sense.[32]

The formalist tradition of linguistics represented by Grimm's concept of a sound law and the culture-bound tradition represented by Humboldt, the father of the German research-oriented university tradition, were to continue on side-by-side throughout the nineteenth century. On the other hand as the nineteenth century progressed, the literary philologists, now increasingly separated from the pure linguists, continued the project launched by the Gothicists. Editions of medieval German works such as what would become the national epic, the anonymous *Song of the Nibelungs*, and the compositions of medieval court poets such as Walther von der Vogelweide and Wolfram von Eschenbach were prepared by contemporaries of the Grimms—a new wave of experts in old Germanic literatures appeared, the most famous of whom was probably Karl Lachmann, the inaugurator of philology's text-critical method.[33] Along with increasingly sophisticated editions of the old Germanic classics, throughout the century lesser-known Greco-Roman and northern works continued to appear under both German and Scandinavian imprimaturs. Indeed a monographic series had even been launched in 1826 whose aim was to provide accessible editions of all manuscripts of historical interest to Germans and Germany. This *Monumenta Germaniae historica* comprised the best editions of classics such as the works of Jordanes, but also the writings of medieval epistlers and legists, and the annals kept by medieval clerics.[34] The appearance of the *Monumenta* signalled the beginning of an enormous increase in the production of historical and philological study. In fact soon the first academic journals dedicated to German antiquity appeared, the most prominent being Moritz Haupt's *Zeitschrift für deutsches Alterthum* (*Journal of German Antiquity*, *ZfdA*) of 1841ff., which unlike many others of contemporary provenance such as Franz Pfeiffer's *Germania* (1856–92) continues to this day.[35] The launch of Haupt's *ZfdA* marks the beginning of a new period in German scholarship—previously the journals of institutions such as those of the Göttingen Academy of Sciences and literary magazines had been the main organs for the promulgation of philological scholarship. Soon after the appearance of the *ZfdA*, however, came Adalbert Kuhn's *Zeitschrift für vergleichende Sprachforschung (Journal of Comparative Language Research, KZ)* of 1852ff.,[36] followed by Heinrich von Sybel's *Historische Zeitschrift* of 1859ff., which is now the premier German history journal.[37] The middle of the nineteenth century was the age of the new German academic periodical. Yet by the time of the establishment of the German Empire in 1871, the *ZfdA* had become but one in a sea of competing publications. After German unification, it seemed to become the patriotic duty of every historical society and foundation to produce its own journal, and amateur historians and philologists clamored to contribute to the more prestigious titles.[38] Many were rebuffed. But it is clear that the patriotic surge among the broader public of the time came to influence some writings of academic origin. The enormous growth in the amount and range of editions and critical scholarship had now made old Germanic studies a field that demanded considerable erudition of those who wished to engage with the mainstream of antiquarian philological discourse. Nonetheless Leopold von Ranke's famous dictum that historians should attempt to reconstruct the past "as it actually was" was soon compromised by the growing numbers of enthusiasts who flocked to the study of historical disciplines—philology, linguistics, anthropology, antiquarianism and history proper itself—many of whom did not display the patience, let alone learning, that the empirical tradition of the Grimms, Lachmann and Haupt demanded.

It was during the period of this explosion in academic Germanic studies and its growing popular reception that Wagner adopted his spiritual Teutonism.[39] Wagner's position in the evolution of the new notion of the *Volk* is much more pronounced than any other figure of the German arts, even more than the national conservative literati who emerged at the time such as Julius Langbehn, Gustav Freytag and Felix Dahn. It was with Wagner that Germanic medievalism was first linked strongly to racialism and the destiny of the German nation. This spirituality is termed Teutonic in English today and reflected a form of neoconservatism that had particular resonance in the *völkisch* movement.

One of the features of Wagner's approach to the past was his incorporation of non-German elements into his work. It did not at all concern him that most of the major motifs in his *Ring* were borrowed not from the old German epic it is ostensibly based upon, but rather a medieval Norse retelling. He even added the Nordic Ragnarok to the tale in the form of the *Götterdämmerung* (*Twilight of the Gods*) of the last cycle, although such a motif is unknown from German sources and is not at all linked with the Norse tale of the downfall of the house of the Nibelungs.[40] Wagner adopted ideas which Klopstock and the Grimms had brought to philological study—that medieval Scandinavian literature could be claimed as German. Yet he managed to bring Germanic antiquity to an audience that scholars had not been able to access and did so in a manner which included elements of the broader Germanic identity that had developed in academic circles, but in this case also rather more clearly under the influence of *völkisch* thought.

Wagner's thought was deeply political and not merely nationalistic. He had distilled much of his politics from a range of contemporary philosophers, in fact from doyens of the *völkisch* ideal: from the German Christianity of Lagarde, the racialism of Gobineau and the cultural ennui of Arthur Schopenhauer.[41] The concerns of these three writers had become the intellectual pillars of the respectable neoconservatism of the time that disdained democracy and came to see parliament as squabbling and un-German. Classing themselves as German National rather than *völkisch* per se, these neoconservatives were also members of a respectable elite, not the crass populists typical of early Pan-Germanism. Nevertheless, in his political writings and even in his later operatic works Wagner extolled the vision of his own version of the *völkisch* ideal, marrying others' notions with his own understanding of medieval German and Norse literature. It is difficult to gauge precisely how influential the racial aspect Wagner brought to his Teutonism was outside the group of sycophants that gathered around him and after his death his widow Cosima in Bayreuth.[42] Nevertheless, Wagnerian symbolism and themes became widespread in the *völkisch* press at the time. For many of its proponents, the new conservatism seemed too genteel to become involved in the antics of Schönerer and his anti-Semitic fellows in the German Empire. Yet Wagnerian Teutonism invoked a spirit that reflected an extreme, all-or-nothing ideal, reflecting Wagner's notion of "total art."[43] Wagnerian clubs soon became hotbeds for *völkisch* political enthusiasm and Schönerer for one periodically used Wagnerian *soirées* as launching places for political demonstrations. The *Bayreuther Blätter* (*Bayreuth Pages*, 1878–1938), a journal set up by patrons of the Wagnerian festival at Bayreuth, did much to expand upon the themes of *The Ring* and *Parsifal*, and Wagnerian concerns often came to be reflected in the more overtly political journals of the time.[44] The boundary between the new conservatism of the cultured, opera-going elites and the *völkisch* radicalism of the crasser, populist anti-Semitic agitators (and their excitable counterparts among the student fraternities) was all-too easily crossed—indeed some proponents of the new, reactionary right did not recognize any such boundary at all. Radical student fraternities, so important to the rise of the Austrian Pan-Germans, often took Wagnerian names, as did leading *völkisch* journals such as *Heimdall* (1896–1932) and *Hammer* (1902–1940).[45] This identification with Wagnerian expressions of the Germanic past was eventually reflected in the *völkisch* political clubs of the 1910s and 20s such as the Germanic Orders (Germanenorden) and Munich's Thule Society. After Wagner and his spiritual Teutonism, Germanic antiquity was cemented in the minds of champions of the *völkisch* ideal as the preeminent path to the rediscovery of the untrammelled, untainted Germany. Many respectable neoconservatives like those of the Bayreuth circle disliked the radicalism of the Pan-Germans and the other anti-Semitic, *völkisch* agitators—the coarseness of men like Schönerer offended elite sensibilities.[46] Nevertheless figures such as Wagner ensured conservative thought would maintain a notion of Germanism in common with their more radical brethren, and the respectable and the common came to enjoy a synergy as the new century dawned. In contrast to their Austrian fellows, both expressions of the new right were represented among the Pan-Germans within the German Empire. Yet many German-National neoconservatives maintained their distance from the more activist radical right well into the 1920s. For some it was not until the Nazi accession to power that neoconservative reserve and distance from the broader *völkisch* movement was surrendered altogether.

The most articulate exponent of the Teutonism and neoconservatism that began with Lagarde and Wagner, and a leading historian of a new type that emerged in the later nineteenth century, was an Englishman who had become a devoted Germanophile and Wagnerite (and eventually Wagner's son-in-law), but had moved away from a focus solely on ideas stemming from Bayreuth. Houston Chamberlain, a biologist by training, had achieved some status as a dilettante by 1896 when he was asked to write a reflective study to be published in the last year of the 1800s.[47]

Published as the *Foundations of the Nineteenth Century (Grundlagen des neunzehnten Jahrhunderts)*, this account immediately became a bestseller upon its appearance in 1899.[48] Writing in Vienna, which had been his home for most of the decade, Chamberlain had aimed to capture the essence of the nineteenth century, and for him the emergent racialism was the most fundamental feature of that essence. Chamberlain's work was read and accepted by a large conservative audience—although Schönerer and his fellows in Vienna made no approaches to him, the German Emperor Wilhelm II proclaimed the *Foundations* his favorite book and was given to reading out passages from it to acquaintances.[49] Chamberlain had managed to popularize much of the racialist thought of Wagner that went back to Gobineau, but more importantly first encapsulated a neoconservative view of world history, one which, as a Germanophile, stressed the centrality of the cultural mission of the German *Volk*.

The standing of Chamberlain among the German right was to become great enough for Hitler to attend his funeral in 1927. The erstwhile Briton had become for Hitler the successor to Wagner as bearer of the "spiritual sword" of the new German right, forged in the fire of Wagnerism.[50] Chamberlain had become one of the principal early upper-class proponents of the Nazi Party; the divide between neoconservative reserve and *völkisch* radicalism was not the only thing that had begun to blur.

In Austria, the threat to Germanness was palpable with the rise of national consciousness among the Slavs and other nations of the Hapsburg patrimony—Schönerer had consequently won electoral support from all manner of German nationalists. In the German Empire, in contrast, *völkisch* politics had never been successfully promoted as a broad parliamentary movement. The early anti-Semitic parties formed after the stock market collapse in 1873 proved failures in the Reichstag—they had all but disappeared in terms of parliamentary representation by the early 1900s.[51] Thereafter, anti-Semites and other radical right-wing groups instead came to favor a different approach to activism. Many leading *völkisch* thinkers at the time formed clubs and established journals in which to debate if not promulgate their views. The leading anti-Semite Theodor Fritsch, for example, had set up the publishing house Hammer in 1887 to publish his *Anti-Semitic Catechism (Antisemitische Katechismus)*; from 1907 it would subsequently appear as the infamous *Handbook of the Jewish Question (Handbuch der Judenfrage)*.[52] Moreover, whereas his earlier *Antisemitische Korrespondenz* (1885–1903) eventually failed, from 1902 Fritsch's publishing house produced an eponymous journal that survived for some forty years.[53] A similar periodical was begun by the Social Darwinist Ludwig Woltmann that year, suitably entitled the *Politisch-Anthropologische Revue*.[54] Both *Hammer* and the *Revue* soon became favored by all manner of *völkisch* thinkers. *Heimdall* was also founded in this period by the pan-German agitator Adolf Reinecke as the bulletin of a radical splinter from the General German Language Association (Allgemeiner Deutscher Sprachverein). The Association had been formed in 1885 to protect the German mother tongue from foreign influence; yet its policies had proved not radical enough for patriots like Reinecke. In 1898 Reinecke's splinter would become the Pan-German Language and Writing Association (Alldeutscher Sprach und Schriftverein), a promoter of "pan-Germanism and pure Germanness."[55] Newspapers with clearly *völkisch* sympathies also soon appeared as did all manner of mystical and life reform journals which stressed antiquarian and racialist themes. Another leading and more established figure was Eugen Diederichs, sometime editor of the respected literary journal *Die Tat* (1909–39), who published many radical works from his publishing house in Jena.[56] Diederichs, however, was closer to the right-wing Austrian and German cultural societies which reflected a longer tradition than those of their *völkisch* counterparts, one stretching back to the 1870s and groups such as the German language societies. The later years of the century had similarly seen the emergence of nationalistic lobby groups like the Navy League and the Pan-German League in the German Empire.[57] But new, more radical groups had emerged with the new century. Fritsch, for example, was also a leading figure in the founding of the Imperial Hammer League (Reichshammerbund) in 1912, an umbrella organization for *völkisch* groups who were associated with his journal *Hammer*.[58] Moreover, the same year the secretive Germanic Orders emerged from these *Hammer* groups: modelled upon the lodges of Freemasonry, many of their rituals were founded in those of the teachings of the Austrian mystic List and his Wotanism.[59] One of these groups, which came to operate under the aegis Thule Society, began the journal *Runen (Runes)* in 1918—the leader of the Thule Society, Rudolf von Sebottendorff, even bought the Eher publishing house (whose lead title would become the *Völkischer Beobachter*) before selling it to the Nazis in 1922.[60] In 1924 a similar journal for 'Nordic Life and Ideology' entitled *Die Sonne (The Sun)* was begun by a political group in Weimar dedicated to the ideas of List whose publishing mark was the asterisk-like Scandinavian **h**-rune (✴). And not only did the Nazi Party develop out of this *völkisch* milieu, National Socialist understandings of history were largely influenced by the new historical discourses that developed in these publications of the *völkisch* Grub Street.[61]

For most of the early adherents to *völkisch* belief the picture of Germanic antiquity represented in schoolbooks and historical novels that ultimately went back to academic titles was clearly sufficient. Yet from the late 1880s, as part of the explosion in historical societies and the general wave of production of enthusiastic accounts of Germanic antiquity, some *völkisch* thinkers began to produce some such works of their own. At first outside the academic and popular mainstream, their contributions soon began to appear in journals that were not principally *völkisch*. At a similar time, however, *völkisch* thought had already entered academia: although it was often hidden under the guise of neoconservatism, the dilettantes of the *völkisch* Grub Street had found academic counterparts, many of whom were university Germanists. Several academic Germanists began careers of reinterpreting Germanic antiquity from what was increasingly to be a clearly *völkisch* perspective at the time. Both the dilettantes and their counterparts within academia became fundamental figures in a *völkisch* antiquarian project that developed in earnest, especially from the second decade of the new century.

Chamberlain, however, relied on more mainstream sources—with the addition, of course, of the principal neoconservative authorities. His work was decried by professionals as loose with historical facts, misrepresentative of the authors he cited, opinionated and indeed quite woolly intellectually—the Englishman had often seemed more interested in turn of phrase than in intellectual consistency.[62] Nevertheless, his approach to Germanic antiquity became important to the *völkisch* Germanists of the following years, much as would his penchant for grandiloquence. The most powerful image of the *Foundations* was his portrayal of the ancient Germans in his sixth chapter 'The Entry of the Teutons into World History' as the racial prophets who cleansed the multiethnic travesty of late imperial Rome, destroying the Empire and replacing it with the medieval nation-states. Whereas Edward Gibbon had seen the decline of Rome in terms of the moral debasement bemoaned of by Roman authors as early as Tacitus, Chamberlain explained this decline in terms of miscegenation.[63]

As Gobineau and Wagner had before him, Chamberlain thought that miscegenation was the prime factor in the ruination of civilizations, but that, nevertheless, only two races had remained unadulterated throughout world history: Germans and Jews. The Germans were the racial elite of Europe, the Jews a force for corruption. Yet physical anthropology had developed far enough by Chamberlain's time that skull shapes and other physical features could be shown to be quite transient features. In order to explain away the scientific evidence that ran counter to his essentially racist view of history, Chamberlain made a logical leap of a type that was to become common in later *völkisch* histories. Unlike some later authors, however, Chamberlain did bother to explain how science could be ignored when it did not accord with his basic views:[64]

> The hieroglyphs of nature's language are in fact not so logically mathematical, so mechanically explicable as many an investigator likes to fancy ... very small children, especially girls, frequently have a marked instinct for race. It frequently happens that children ... begin to cry as soon as a genuine Jew or Jewess comes near to them! The learned can frequently not tell a Jew from a non-Jew; the child that scarcely knows how to speak notices the difference. Is not that worth something? To me it seems worth as much as a whole anthropological congress ... There is still something in the world besides compass and yardmeasure. Where the expert fails with his artificial constructions, one single unbiased glance can illuminate the truth like a sunbeam.

Yet in his glorification of intuition, Chamberlain was not alone. By the time he set about writing his *Foundations* in 1896, the empiricist tradition epitomized by Ranke had already come to be considered passé by German theorists of history. In 1883 Wilhelm Dilthey had brought positivist history under the fire of Kantian thought, rejecting the notion that history was concerned only with the acts of politicians, diplomats and the will of God.[65] The new German historical school that followed aimed to investigate historical consciousness in terms of experience and intuitive understanding, and moved subtly away from an empirical epistemology.[66] The neo-Idealist school that developed in the 1880s and 90s, however, was soon bowdlerized by popularizers. Historical understanding became an intuition for the past and popular historians could defend their intuitive histories in terms of a cheapened version of contemporary historical theory. Populists like Chamberlain glorified their dilettantism as a holistic remedy to the accelerating fragmentation of knowledge. Objectivity was now a sham, interpretation was all and understanding was guided through historical intuition, a gut feeling about what was essentially right about the past.[67] Thus it is no surprise to find Chamberlain expressing that his *Foundations* derived from an understanding of what is "experienced":[68]

> Though many factual statements may be old mistakes, though many judgements may arise from prejudice ... nothing is totally false ... a single thought can be without content, the error of an isolated individual, but a deep conviction is rooted in something outside and above the individual ... it must contain at its core a living truth.

Chamberlain had turned a philosophy of history into a justification for the dominance of ideology. He had transcended mere bias, dismissed the aim of impartiality and helped inaugurate a new form of history—*völkisch* history—one in which an undisguised prejudice was upheld as a leading virtue. His approach was quickly adopted by his fellow grub-street dilettantes and eventually even by some of the less reticent academic investigators of the past.

Bias of course became a patriotic duty of German academics after the Nazi accession to power, but it had already been a feature of earlier years, especially in German antiquarianism which itself had a political dimension of lengthy pedigree. The entire German antiquarian project, whether philological, linguistic or more properly historical, was riddled with political agendas even before it was joined by authors of an actively *völkisch* persuasion. It was at first anti-Italian, then it was anti-French. After 1871 in some expressions it turned on German society itself. For writers like Chamberlain the antiquarian tradition became racialist, pan-Germanist, anti-Semitic and anti-modern. Moreover, Chamberlain, with his cheapened form of neo-Idealism, had opened up the path to an ever more subjective manner in which to rescue the German past—a third way, between the rigors of empirically based academic discourse and the intuitive obscurantism of Romantic origin. This third way was not held by its historians to be less valid than that of the academy, however. Indeed many expressed feelings of superiority in their work, as if they held a key to historical understanding that was not available to professional scholars. Apparently this new history was more essential than that produced in the academies as it was closer to an understanding of the *Volksgeist* first hailed by Herder, one that, seemingly, only those who felt most German truly experienced, only those who carried a particular concern for the *Volk* deep in their hearts. By the end of the nineteenth century the *völkisch* movement had now added its own form of history to its art, poetry and political theory. It was a history distinct from that written by professionals and one that often railed against the offerings of the academic establishment. The ideological foundations of *völkisch* belief had been firmly established. But the new century was to add new interpretations of other traditional disciplines to this *völkisch* history, which in turn would lead to new developments in the evolving manner in which the *völkisch* ideal was expressed.

NOTES

1 S.L. Marchand, *Down from Olympus* (Princeton: Princeton University Press, 1992).
2 Tacitus, *Germania* ([Nuremberg: Creusner, 1473]); L. Krapf, *Germanenmythus und Reichsideologie* (Tübingen: Niemeyer, 1979); M.F. Tenney, "Tacitus through the Centuries to the Age of Printing," *University of Colorado Studies* 22 (1935): 341–63; D.R. Kelley, 'Tacitus Noster,' in T.J. Luce and A.J. Woodman (eds.), *Tacitus and the Tacitean Tradition* (Princeton: Princeton University Press, 1993), 152–67.
3 Caesar, *De bello gallico* ([Esslingen: Fyner,] 1473); Jordanes, *De rebus Gothorum*, ed. C. Peutinger (Augsburg: Miller, 1515); Tacitus, *Historia Augusta*, ed. A. Alciato (Basel: Froben, 1519); K. von See, *Deutsche-Germanen Ideologie* (Frankfurt a.M.: Athenäum, 1970), pp.14ff.; J. Ridé, *L'Image du Germain dans le pensée et la littérature Allemande*, 3 vols. (Paris: Champion, 1977).
4 C. Celtes, *Protucij* (Nuremberg: [s.n.,] 1502); idem, *Cornelii Taciti ... de situs Germanie ... Poeta fragme(n)ta queda(m)* (Vienna: Singren, 1515); F. Irenicus, *Germaniae exegesos* (Hagenau: Koberg, 1518); U. von Hutten, *Arminius* (Hagenau: Sec[er], 1529); Beatus Rhenanus, *Rerum Germanicarum* (Basel: Froben, 1533).
5 H. Tiedemann, *Tacitus und das Nationalbewußtsein der deutschen Humanisten* (Berlin: Ebering, 1913); R. Kuehnemund, *Arminius* (Chapel Hill: University of North Carolina Press, 1953); U. Muhlack, "Die Germania im deutschen Nationalbewußtsein vor dem 19. Jahrhundert," in H. Jankuhn and D. Timpe (eds.), *Beiträge zur Verständnis der Germania des Tacitus*, 2 vols. (Göttingen: Vandenhoeck & Ruprecht, 1989), I, 128–54; and cf. Schama, 77ff.
6 J. Hermand, *Geschichte der Germanistik* (Reinbek bei Hamburg: Rowohlt, 1994), 17ff.
7 C.D. Ebeling, "Kurze Geschichte der deutschen Dichtkunst," *Hannoverische Magazin* 5 (1767): 81–92, 97–128 & 6 (1768): 81–94, 97–118,

353–84, 401–58, 529–52; J.J. Rambach, *Versuch einer pragmatischen Literairhistorie* (Halle a.S.: Gebauer, 1770).

8 J. J. Müller, "Germanistik—eine Form bürgerlicher Opposition," in idem (ed.), *Germanistik und deutsche Nation 1806–1848* (Stuttgart: Metzler, 2000), 6.

9 Grimms *Wörterbuch* V (1897), 3716–17.

10 S. Johnson, *A Dictionary of the English Language*, 2 vols. (London: Knapton et al., 1775).

11 Von See, *Deutsche-Germanen Ideologie*, 27f.

12 J. Nordström, "Goter och spanjoner," *Lychnos* (1944–45): 257–80 & (1971–72): 171–80.

13 C.L. de Secondat, Bon de la Brède et de Montesquieu, *Lettres Persanes*, 2 vols. (Amsterdam: Brunel, 1721), no. 136; idem, *De l'Esprit de Loix*, 2 vols. (Geneva: Barrilot & Sons, 1748), XI, 8.

14 J. Svennung, *Zur Geschichte des Goticismus* (Stockholm: Almqvist & Wiksell, 1967); F. Hillebrecht, *Skandinavien* (Berlin: Humboldt-Universität zu Berlin, 1987).

15 Jordanes, *Getica* 25, 4.

16 Cassiodorus, *Antiqua regum Italiae Gothicae gentis rescripta*, ed. J. Cochlaeus ([Leipzig: Schmidt] 1529), J. Cochlaeus, *Vita Theoderici* (Ingolstadt: Weissenhorn, 1544).

17 J. Magnus, *Historia ... de omnibus Gothorum Svemque regibus* (Rome: De Viotti, 1554); idem, *Historia metripolitanae ecclesias Upsaliensis* (Rome: De Ferrari, 1557); O. Magnus, *Historia de gentibus septentrionalibus* (Rome: De Viotti, 1555); K. Johannesson, *The Renaissance of the Goths in Sixteenth-Century Sweden*, trans. J. Larson (Berkeley: University of California Press, 1982).

18 P.J. Resenius, *Edda Islandorum* (Copenhagen: Gödianus, 1665).

19 O. Rudbeck, *Atland eller Manheim*, 4 vols. (Uppsala: Curio, 1679–1702).

20 P.H. Mallet, *Introduction à l'Histoire de Dannemarc II* (Copenhagen: Phillibert, 1756); idem, *Histoire de Dannemarc* (Copenhagen: Phillibert, 1758).

21 F.G. Klopstock, *Oden und Elegien* (Hamburg: Bode, 1771); idem, *Die deutsche Gelehrtenrepublic I* (Hamburg: Bode, 1774), 229 [= *Klopstocks sämmtliche Werke*, 10 vols. (Leipzig: Göschen, 1848), VIII, 169]; von See, *Deutsche-Germanen Ideologie*, 34ff.; K. Düwel and H. Zimmermann, "Germanenbild und Patriotismus in der Literatur des 18. Jahrhunderts," in H. Beck (ed.), *Germanenprobleme in heutiger Sicht* (Berlin: De Gruyter, 1986), 358–95; U. Hafner, *"Norden" und "Nation" um 1800* (Trieste: Parnaso, 1996).

22 W. Kittler, *Die Geburt des Partisanen aus dem Geist der Poesie* (Freiburg i.Br.: Rombach, 1987).

23 J.G. von Herder, *Auch eine Philosophie der Geschichte zur Bildung der Menschheit* ([Riga: s.n.,] 1774), 65–66 [= *Werke*, ed. B. Suphan, 33 vols. (Berlin: Weidmann, 1877–1913), V, 514–15]; H. Kohn, *The Mind of Germany*, 2nd ed. (London: MacMillan, 1962), 54ff.

24 W. Jones, "The Third Anniversary Discourse," in J. Shore, Baron (Lord) Teignmouth (ed.), *The Works of Sir William Jones*, 13 vols. (London: Stockdale, 1807), III, 34; F. von Schlegel, *Ueber die Sprache und Weisheit der Indier* (Heidelberg: Mohr & Zimmer, 1808); T.R. Trautmann, *Aryans and British India* (Berkeley: University of California Press, 1997); A. Morpurgo Davies, *History of Linguistics. Volume IV* (London: Longman, 1998), 59ff., S. Arvidsson, *Aryan Idols*, trans. S. Wichmann (Chicago: University of Chicago Press, 2006).

25 D.M. Figueira, *Aryans, Jews, Brahmins,* (New York: SUNY, 2002), 12ff.

26 F. Bopp, *Über das Conjugationssystem der Sanskritsprache in Vergleichung mit jenem der griechischen, lateinischen, persischen und germanischen Sprache* (Frankfurt a.M.: Andreä, 1816); H. Pedersen, *Linguistic Science in the Nineteenth Century*, trans. J.W. Spargo (Cambridge, Mass.: Harvard University Press, 1931), 254ff.; Morpurgo Davies, 124ff.

27 F. Junius (ed.), *Gothicum glossarium* (Dordrecht: Junius, 1665); G. Hickes, *Linguarum Vett. Septentrionalium* (Oxford: Sheldon Theatre, 1705); L. ten Kate, *Gemeenschap tussen de Gottische Spraeke en de Nederduitsche Sprake*, 2 vols. (Amsterdam: Rienwertsz, 1710).

28 J. Grimm, *Deutsche Grammatik*, 4 vols. (Göttingen: Dieterich, 1819–37).

29 K.W. von Humboldt, *Über die Verschiedenheit des menschlichen Sprachbaues und ihren Einfluß auf die geistige Entwicklung des Menschengeschlechts* (Berlin: Dümmler, 1836) [= *On Language*, trans. P. Heath (Cambridge: Cambridge University Press, 1988)]; H. Scurla, *Wilhelm von Humboldt* (Düsseldorf: Claasen, 1976), 589ff.

30 H. Ivo, *Muttersprache—Identität—Nation* (Opladen: Westdeutscher Verlag, 1994), 92ff.; Morpurgo Davies, 98ff.

31 H.F. Nielsen, "Jacob Grimm and the 'German' Dialects," in E.H. Antonsen (ed.), *The Grimm Brothers and the Germanic Past* (Amsterdam: Benjamins, 1990), 25–26.

32 W. Grimm, *Ueber deutsche Runen* (Göttingen: Dieterich, 1821); J. Grimm, *Deutsche Rechts-Alterthümer* (Göttingen: Dieterich, 1828); idem, *Deutsche Mythologie*, 2 vols. (Göttingen: Dieterich, 1835) [= *Teutonic Mythology*, trans. J.S. Stallybrass, 4 vols. (London: Bell & Sons, 1888–1900)].

33 *Der Nibelunge Not*, ed. C. Lachmann (Berlin: Reimer, 1826); Walther von der Vogelweide, *Die Gedichte*, ed. K. Lachmann (Berlin: Reimer, 1827); Wolfram von Eschenbach, *Parcival*, ed. C. Lachmann (Berlin: Reimer, 1833), M. Hertz, *Karl Lachmann* (Berlin: Hertz, 1851); H. Sparnay, *Karl Lachmann als Germanist* (Bern: Francke, 1948); S. Timpanaro, *La genesi del metodo del Lachmann*, 2nd ed. (Padua: Liviana, 1985).

34 G.H. Pertz et al. (eds.), *Monumenta Germaniae historica* (Hanover: Hahn, and Berlin: Weidmann, 1826ff.); W.T.M. Gamble, *The Monumenta Germaniae historica* (Washington: The Catholic University of America, 1927).

35 *Zeitschrift für deutsches Altert(h)um (und deutsche Lit(t)eratur)* 1ff. (Leipzig/Berlin: Weidmann, Wiesbaden/Stuttgart: Steiner, 1841ff.); *Germania* 1–37 (Stuttgart: Metzler, then Vienna: Gerold, 1856–92).

36 *Zeitschrift für vergleichende Sprachforschung (auf dem Gebiete der indoger-manischen Sprachen)* 1-100 (Berlin: Dümmler, Gütersloh: Bertelsmann, Göt-tingen: Vandenhoeck & Ruprecht, 1856–1987); continued now as *Historische Sprachforschung* 101ff. (Göttingen: Vandenhoeck & Ruprecht, 1988ff.).

37 *Historische Zeitschrift* 1ff. (Munich: Oldenbourg, 1859ff.).

38 Cf. Marchand, *Down from Olympus*, 162ff.; E. Leroy, *Konstruktionen des Germanen in bildungsbürgerlichen Zeitschriften des deutschen Kaiserreiches* (Frankfurt a.M.: Lang, 2004).

39 Rose, *Wagner*, 89ff., 135ff.

40 W.O. Lord, *The Teutonic Mythology of Richard Wagner's* The Ring of the Nibelung, 3 vols., (Lewiston: Mellen, 1989–1991).

41 A. Schopenhauer, *Parerga und Paralipomena* (Stuttgart: Cotta, 1850); D.C. Large, "Wagner's Bayreuth Disciples," in D.C. Large and W. Weber (eds.), *Wagnerism in European Culture and Politics* (Ithaca: Cornell Univer-sity Press, 1984), 77ff.; L.J. Rather, *Reading Wagner* (Baton Rouge: Louisi-ana State University Press, 1990), 7ff.

42 W. Schüler, *Der Bayreuther Kreis* (Münster: Aschendorff, 1971); Large, "Wagner's Bayreuth Disciples"; R. Stackelberg, *Idealism Debased* (Kent, Ohio: Kent State University Press, 1981), 10ff.; H. Châtellier, "Wagnerism in der Kaiserzeit," in U. Puschner et al. (eds.), *Handbuch zur "Völkischen Bewegung" 1871–1918* (Munich: Saur, 1996), 575–612; A. Hein, *"Es ist viel 'Hitler' in Wagner"* (Tübingen: Niemeyer, 1996).

43 M. Tanner, "The Total Work of Art," in P. Burbidge and R. Sutton (eds.), *The Wagner Companion* (London: Faber & Faber, 1979), 140–220.

44 *Bayreuther Blätter* 1–61 (Chemnitz: Schmeitzer, 1878–1938).

45 *Heimdall* 1–37 (Berlin: Hafert, then Zeitz: Sis, Stade i. H.: Zwei Welten, Einsiedel: Winkler, Leonberg: Die Schwertsmiede, 1896–1932); *Hammer* 1–39 (Leipzig: Hammer, 1902–1940).

46 J.N. Retallack, *Notables of the Right* (Boston: Unwin Hyman, 1988), 91ff.

47 H.S. Chamberlain, *Lebenswege meines Denkens*, 2nd ed. (Munich: Bruck-mann, 1922); G.G. Field, *The Evangelist of Race* (New York: Columbia University Press, 1981), 169ff.

48 H.S. Chamberlain, *Die Grundlagen des neunzehnten Jahrhunderts*, 2 vols. (Munich: Bruckmann, 1899), 14th ed. 1922 [= idem, *Foundations of the Nineteenth Century*, trans. J. Lees, 2 vols. (London: Lane, 1910)].

49 Whiteside, 324; Field, *Evangelist*, 232, 250–55.

50 A. Hitler/S. Wagner 5.5.1924 apud M. Karbaum, *Studien zur Geschichte der bayreuther Festspiele* (Regensberg: Bosse, 1976), 65–66.

51 R. Levy, *The Downfall of the Anti-Semitic Parties in Imperial Germany* (New Haven: Yale University Press, 1975).

52 T. Fritsch, *Antisemitische Katechismus* (Leipzig: Hammer, 1887); idem, *Handbuch der Judenfrage*, 25th ed. (Leipzig: Hammer, 1925), 49th ed. (Berlin: Hammer, 1944).

53 *Antisemitische Correspondenz* 1–18 (Leipzig: Hammer, 1885–1903); *Ham-mer*, cit. supra n. 45; R.H. Phelps, "Theodor Fritsch und der Antisemitis-

mus," *Deutsche Rundschau* 87 (1961): 442–49; M. Bönisch, "Die 'Hammer' Bewegung," in U. Puschner et al. (eds.), *Handbuch zur "Völkischen Bewegung"*, 341–65.

54 *Politisch-Anthropologische Revue* 1–13 (Eisenach: Thüringische Verlags-Anstalt, then Berlin-Steglitz: Politisch-Anthropologischer Verlag, 1902–14); continued as: *Politisch-Anthropologische Monatsschrift* 13–21 (Hamburg: Politisch-Anthropologischer Verlag, 1914–23); P.E. Becker, *Wege ins Dritte Reich*, 2 vols. (Stuttgart: Thieme, 1988–90), II, 328ff.

55 U. Puschner, *Die völkische Bewegung im wilhelminischen Kaiserreich* (Darmstadt: Wissenschaftliche Buchgesellschaft, 2001), 31ff.; idem, "'One People, One Reich, One God,'" *Bulletin of the German Historical Institute London* 24 (2002); 10; cf. also idem, "Germanenideologie und völkische Weltanschuung," in H. Beck et al. (eds.), *Zur Geschichte der Gleichung "germanisch-deutsch"* (Berlin: De Gruyter, 2003), 103–29.

56 *Die Tat* 1–20 (Jena: Diederichs, 1909–39); W.G. Oschilewski, *Eugen Diederichs und sein Werk* (Jena: Diederichs, 1936); G.D. Stark *Entrepeneurs of Ideology* (Chapel Hill: University of North Carolina Press, 1981), 58ff.; E. Viehöfer, "Der Verleger als Organisator," *Archiv für Geschichte des Buchwesens* 30 (1988): 1–147 [= monograph, Frankfurt a.M.: Buchhändler, 1988]; J.H. Ulbricht and M.G. Werner (eds.), *Romantik, Revolution und Reform* (Göttingen: Wallstein, 1999).

57 Eley, 41ff.; Chickering, 24ff.

58 Lohalm, 56ff.; Goodrick-Clarke, 123ff.

59 Goodrick-Clarke, 127ff.

60 R.H. Phelps, "'Before Hitler Came'," *Journal of Modern History* 25 (1963): 245–61; Goodrick-Clarke, 135ff.; H. Gilbhard, *Die Thule-Gesellschaft* (Munich: Kesseling, 1994); D. Rose, *Die Thule-Gesellschaft* (Tübingen: Grabert, 1994).

61 *Die Sonne* 1–16/4–6 (Weimar: Duncker, then Leipzig: Armanen-Verlag, 1924–39); cf. Mees, "Hitler and *Germanentum*," 268.

62 Field, *Evangelist*, 225ff.

63 Ibid., 214ff.

64 Chamberlain, *Grundlagen* I, 546 [= *Foundations* I, 537].

65 W. Dilthey, *Einleitung in die Geisteswissenschaften* I (Leipzig 1883), 87ff.

66 G.G. Iggers, *The German Conception of History*, 2nd ed. (Middleton, Conn.: Wesleyan University Press, 1983), 124ff.

67 Field, *Evangelist*, 174–78.

68 Chamberlain, *Grundlagen*, x; trans. Field, *Evangelist*, 177.

CHAPTER 3.

The Origins of Ideographic Studies

Was euch nicht angehört,
Müsset ihr meiden;
Was euch das Inn're stört,
Dürft ihr nicht leiden!
Goethe

Ostensibly, ideographic studies developed out of runology and investigations of the history of the alphabet, matters which traditionally had been concerns of linguistic-philological inquiry. In the second half of the nineteenth century, however, early writing systems had also come under scrutiny from literary philologists, art historians, archeologists, anthropologists and those scholars who in the German tradition are classed folklorists. All these disciplines were also notable for their struggles with empiricism: most were founded as antiquarian fields that relied on common, Christian sense for their argument; some were, in consequence, slower than others to develop an elaborate evidential rather than generally philosophical basis. Others already carried with them a significant amount of Romantic or speculative baggage long before they were subjected to the new intuitive idealism of Chamberlain's generation or had otherwise been seen more publicly to be of national concern. All in their Germanophone expressions eventually became riddled with clearly *völkisch* agendas too, but it is not always a simple matter to disentangle these later political concerns from issues of a more longstanding nature in these disciplines.

RUNIC STUDIES

Runology is the scientific study of runic inscriptions. It has its foundations in the seventeenth century in the form of two publications by the Danish polymath Ole Worm,[1] although the plates of rune-stones prepared by the Swedish antiquarian Johan Bure perhaps make him the first runic scholar.[2] The development of runic studies in Scandinavia was clearly linked to the growth of Gothicism, and the Magnus brothers, the Swedish founders of this tradition, even called the runes Gothic. Yet with the growth in linguistic-philological studies towards the end of the eighteenth century, runic studies was brought within the sphere of Germanic philology, an increasingly predominantly German field of study. In fact among the first properly philological studies of the runes were those of Wilhelm Grimm.[3] Runology soon came to be seen as a preserve of linguists.

The runic script or futhark is the ancient alphabet of the Germanic tribes: the old Norse, Anglo-Saxons, Frisians, Dutch, Franks, Germans, Lombards, Burgundians and Goths. Inscriptions in runic characters are known from throughout most of Europe, in fact almost wherever Germanic peoples wandered: from Ireland to Italy and Greece to Russia. The great majority are found in Scandinavia, where runic was a living alphabet down to modern times. Yet until the middle of the nineteenth century, no runic inscriptions had yet been found that were recognized as such on the Continent. Nevertheless in 1856 a runic inscription was noted on a brooch excavated from Charnay in Burgundy and soon more continental runic finds were uncovered; the first in German territory was found near Dahmsdorf, south of Berlin, during railway works in 1865 and similar discoveries were unearthed in the next years in Franconia, Thuringia, Bavaria and Swabia.[4] Most of the continental finds had been discovered through archeology, although as the language of the runic inscriptions was not immediately transparent, philology remained the main interpretative discipline. Runology is still practiced today principally as a branch of historical linguistics.

Yet studies of runic finds in Germany were soon linked with other concerns. The first of all such discoveries, on the Dahmsdorf spearhead, also featured non-runic signs: a circle, a crescent and a magical symbol of Bosporan origin (a tamga) appear on the obverse, and a triskelion and a swastika appear on the reverse. The discovery of these non-alphabetic signs in connection with runes was one of the developments which came to link runology with non-linguistic disciplines in Germany in the later nineteenth century.

It is clear from the works of nineteenth-century scholars, however, that little about these inscriptions, especially the earliest ones, was properly understood until the advent of the publications of the Danish linguist Ludvig Wimmer. Over a period of years, Wimmer came to put on firm ground the correct reading of previously obscure runes such as **z** (Ƴ) and in many cases provided the first reasonably accurate readings of the great majority of the oldest inscriptions. Yet *Sinnbildforschung* has its origins in a time before runology had actually developed a firm linguistic basis.

It is also clear, though, that German runic studies was an enterprise heavily dependent on works from Scandinavia. The contributions of the early, nineteenth-century proponents of German runology pale into insignificance before those of the leading Scandinavian authorities such as Wimmer. Runology in Germany was a branch of Nordic studies in the nineteenth and early twentieth centuries, and Scandinavian authors were generally regarded as the masters of the field. Runic studies was not a discourse that developed out of the nineteenth-century linguistic tradition, but was rather a development of Scandinavian antiquarianism that developed a strong linguistic focus.

THE IDEOGRAPHIC THESIS

The intellectual origins of the central premise of the *Sinnbildforschung* that emerged in 1928 can be traced back to the late eighteenth century. One of the first questions asked by early Scandinavian antiquarians was where the runes had come from. At first scholars such as Worm linked the runes with Hebrew, agreeing with the prevailing interpretation of the biblical story of the Tower of Babel that all languages and scripts derived from that of the ancient Israelites.[5] In 1770, however, the enlightened Swedish antiquarian Johan Ihre linked the question of the origin of the runes to the runic alphabet most commonly used in Hälsingland, Sweden, now often known as staveless runes.[6] These runes are so unlike any of the Mediterranean scripts that Ihre sought an indigenous origin for them, reasoning with the great, often Deluvial antiquity assumed for the earliest inscriptions at the time that other variants of the runic script only became more like the Mediterranean alphabets through later development or contact. The Hälsing runes seemed to show little or no connection with any known southern tradition.

This observation was repeated by another Swede, Johan Liljegren, in a work from 1832 that appeared in a German edition sixteen years later, an edition that was destined to become more important to later German understandings of the runes than the immediate impact of its scholarship might at first seem to warrant.[7] This German edition of Liljegren's *Runic Learning (Run-Lära)* was reviewed by the Kiel philologist Rochus von Liliencron and the review together with some more observations from his fellow Kiel professor, the renowned antiquarian Karl Müllenhoff, appeared as a book in 1852 entitled *On Runic Learning (Zur Runenlehre)*.[8] In this work Liljegren's suggestion that the runes might be an autochthonous creation of the North was developed into a thesis, later called the hieroglyphic or *Urschrift* (proto-script) thesis, one that would continue to win German converts long after Scandinavian scholars had ruled out the possibility of an indigenous origin. The weight of Müllenhoff's word was especially important as he soon became the most outstanding figure in Germanic antiquarian studies of the late nineteenth century. Indeed Wilhelm Grimm also seemed to offer support for this interpretation: he had dismissed attempts to prove a Greek or Latin origin for the Germanic script as fruitless, compared the runes to Egyptian hieroglyphs and suggested that all European scripts had developed from a common source.[9] Consequently, many German scholars continued to voice the opinion that the runes were an indigenous creation until as late as the 1890s when Wimmer's seminal *The Runic Script's Origin and Development in the North (Runeskriftens Oprindelse og Udvikling i Norden)*, especially in its revised German edition *The Runic Script (Die Runenschrift)* of 1887, seemed to have finally laid the autochthonous theory of the origin of the runes to rest.[10]

Von Liliencron and Müllenhoff had developed a complex theory, based on Liljegren's observations, that was developed further by the Germanists Friedrich Losch and Richard M. Meyer some decades later.[11] The theory focused on the use of runes as ideographs and a passage from Tacitus' *Germania*.[12] It is evident from medieval sources that unlike the case in Greek or Latin, the names of the runic letters are meaningful, and thus can be and were used logographically—i.e. a rune could be used to represent its name without spelling it out alphabetically. Thus, much as the hieroglyphs of the Near Eastern cultures eventually came to represent only their initial sound, a similar process was imagined in the evolution of the runes. The runes must then have developed out of the assortment of pre- (or in the thesis proto-) runic ideographs known from rock carvings and prehistorical manufactures, among them the swastika and less infamous symbols such as the triskelion (ᘏ) and the fulmen (ᚺ).

The end of the autochthonous theory in Scandinavian scholarship came with the pioneering work of Wimmer. Wimmer had given sense to the bewildering array of runic variants and linked them chronologically, showing that the Hälsing runes were a late development of a tradition that went back to a script now known as the elder futhark or Common Germanic runes. Over time the runes had become less and less like the oldest forms and consequently increasingly unlike the prototype upon which they were based—Latin according to Wimmer. It was now quite clear that the original shape of the Hälsing rune ᛏ was ᚠ, and as the phonological value of this rune was *f* in both cases, this runic **f** could hardly be disassociated from Mediterranean letters such as Latin F. Wimmer's *Runic Script* demolished the case for an autochthonous origin of the runes and the hieroglyph-like explanation that had developed alongside it. Or at least it should have.

SWASTIKA MYSTICISM

Of all of the pre-runic symbols, the swastika has always been the most popular among scholars. It is found in Bronze Age contexts not just in northern Europe, but also as far south as North Africa, and east as far as India, China and Japan. In fact the term swastika itself is of Indian derivation, although in German it is instead called the *Hakenkreuz*, the 'hooked cross,' a calque on the description *croix gammé* (gamma cross or gammadion) favored by some nineteenth-century French Orientalists.

The origin of swastika studies must be traced to the excitement generated by the archeological finds of Heinrich Schliemann at Troy. Schliemann's discovery of scores of swastikas employed in decorations among these earliest of Greek remains soon inaugurated a tradition of swastika scholarship.[13] Major studies were presented by Ludvig Müller, Michael von Zmigrodski, Eugène, Count Goblet d'Alviella, Thomas Wilson, Oscar Montelius and Joseph Déchelette, none of whom, of course, were Germans.[14] Müller theorized that the swastika must have been a religious expression of the ancient Indo-European peoples, i.e.

the symbol of a sun god; Von Zmigrodski claimed it was a particular symbol, a coat-of-arms of the Aryan race. Despite Goblet d'Alviella's revelation that the swastika was known in many cultures other than Indian or European (including, as Wilson noted, those of many American Indian tribes), the notion that the swastika was a symbol of the prehistoric Aryans consequently entered academic prehistorical discourse, and thence anthropology, art history and German folklore as well.[15]

Sir William Jones's connection of ancient Indic to early European languages had become associated with the notion of an Indo-European people and a homeland—at first an Indian one, as most of the early nineteenth-century experts claimed. While the Indo-Europeans remained geographically more firmly Indian than European, though, the swastika could not be seen as particularly German. It was, after all, known to Orientalists as a lucky charm still in use among the modern Hindus.[16] Nevertheless, in a climate of European fascination with all things Indian, the Russian mystic Madame Blavatsky had adopted the swastika as the crest of the emblem for her Theosophical Society; in Britain under the name fylfot the symbol had become popular as a lucky charm, even appearing at one time in a Scout badge.[17] Archeologists began to make it clear, however, that a significant number of ancient swastikas seemed to be of European origin. But while the Indo-European identity remained oriental it could be of little use to those who mythologized the German *Volk*.

Yet archeology also showed that the swastika continued to be used in Northern Europe well into the historical period. Most of the other cultures had forgotten it by the time of the dawning of their respective Iron Ages. It remained in use in the North down to medieval times where it is recorded in Old Norse as a 'sun-wheel'; and although it became confused with the Thor's hammer in Scandinavian folklore, it seems to symbolize the sun rolling across the heavens.

In 1883, however, an Austrian schoolmaster, the gymnasium professor Carl Penka, published a monograph that made the claim that the Indo-Europeans were indigenous to Europe and had expanded into the Orient by conquest.[18] This notion of indigeneity soon began to receive support from German academics and by the turn of the century had achieved some level of academic respectability. The early proponents of an Indo-European origin in Germany clearly fed off anthropological speculation; yet they were also obviously arguing a national question.

Very soon the connection between German, Germanic and Indo-European (the latter identity still to this day usually termed *indogermanisch*, i.e. Indo-Germanic, in German) was also to become a mainstay of *völkisch* thought too.

With the siting of the Aryan homeland in the German North, the Aryan identity received new importance.[19] Chamberlain, after all, had bound classical antiquity and ancient Germany together as chapters in an Aryan antiquity. He had used the term Aryan only in its anthropological sense (which is more clearly described as Nordic or Caucasian), but as the realization of the implications of Indo-European linguistics entered anthropological and archeological discourse in the later decades of the nineteenth century, the anthropological identity Aryan had become fused with the linguistic one. Aryan only properly designates the Indo-European peoples of India and Iran (and indeed the latter place-name derives from 'Aryan').[20] Yet when Schliemann discovered symbols identical to Hindu swastikas among his much-publicized discoveries at Troy, swastikas became the symbols of an occidental Aryan identity. The Greeks of Homer, no longer the mythical figures they had once seemed, now represented the oldest of occidental Indo-European cultures, one even as old as ancient India and Persia. As an occidental hallmark of Aryan culture, Schliemann's swastika soon also came to penetrate *völkisch* literature: the connection between Aryan (Indo-Germanic) and Teuton (Germanic) had achieved a physical, concrete and easily recognizable symbol. Goblet d'Alviella's study was also employed to show that although the swastika was widely known throughout the world's cultures, the earliest examples of the symbol were attested only in Central Europe. D'Alviella's diagrammatic depiction of the distribution of swastikas in Europe and Asia became a mainstay of both academic and *völkisch* interpretations of the origin and nature of the swastika. The swastika became the symbol *par excellence* of the Aryan, or in anthropological terms, the White Race.

By the 1920s swastika studies had developed a number of theories about the swastika and what were thought to be related prehistorical symbols: the circle, the circle-cross and the cross itself (which according to Montelius had been adopted by the church from prehistoric practice).[21] The connection of the sun with these symbols also led to the notion of primitive Aryan sun worship, a cult which in description was clearly monotheistic. An influence of the swastika came to be seen

in the development of the Mediterranean alphabets and primitive notions of cosmology; swastika studies had produced an academic swastika mania.[22] Perhaps the most extreme example was Erwin Richter's
1931 article "The swastika as guide (Führer) to Old Germanic culture."
Although at first glance this title might be mistakenly thought to head
an article calling upon German academics to follow Hitler, the paper
in fact aims to be a serious empirical study, discovering the swastika or
its arms in the designs of Old Germanic brooches, decorations such as
spirals and meanders, military salutes and even Scottish dancing.

The connection between *völkisch* thought and the swastika, however, took another vital step forward in 1907. After reading the German
translation of Blavatsky's *Secret Doctrine*, the Viennese mystic Guido
List found that his visions began to take on a more recognizable, Theosophical form.[23] He had already been fascinated by the swastika, but
now also by what he believed were the uniquely Germanic reflexes of
the Aryan symbol: the runes. Blinded for most of 1902 by an operation
to remove cataracts, the next year the first of his purely occult studies
appeared in the obscurantist journal *Gnosis*.[24] Soon his mystical teaching would crystallize into a more-or-less coherent doctrine. In 1907 as
Guido von List he published his account of the mystical powers of the
Germanic-Aryan runes and single-handedly founded runic mysticism.[25]

VÖLKISCH ALPHABET HISTORY

List's *Secret of the Runes (Das Geheimnis der Runen)*, became the foundation work for a brand of runic mysticism he called Armanism;[26] and
as Armanism developed, List's version of Theosophy, Germanicized
and indeed Aryanized, became Ariosophy. After List, the runes were
bound up with the racialism of the *völkisch* movement (which had already adopted the swastika of course). Not surprisingly, a distinctly
völkisch brand of runic learning also developed over the next few decades, one based in the writings of List.[27]

Apart from its influence in the development of the autochthonous
thesis in German scholarship, the German edition of Liljegren's *Runic
Learning* also became the guide for this new development in the German understanding of the runes. In preparing his *Secret of the Runes*
and its sequels, List did not use the work of Wimmer, but relied in-

stead on the works of popularizers who were indebted to Grimm, Liljegren and von Liliencron and Müllenhoff. Reflecting the state of runic scholarship before Wimmer, List chose the younger Scandinavian runic alphabet as the basis for his Armanen runes. Furthermore, List, inspired by the eighteen runic songs described in the gnomic Old Norse lay *The Sayings of the High One (Hávamál)*,[28] thought that the sixteen-letter younger runes were incomplete, so he took the liberty of adding two more staves to his younger model: his e-rune (ᛂ), named Eh, and his g-rune (ᚷ) which he named Gibur. This last rune he claimed to be a substitute for the swastika, "intentionally incomplete."[29] List's Armanen runes thus represent only a pseudo-alphabet and the inclusion of his pseudo-runes is a telltale sign of the influence of List in the works of later runic enthusiasts.

Many of the elements that would later appear in *Sinnbildforschung* are also present in List's work. List supported the notion that the runes "in distant days of yore, had the function of a syllabic script" and were "word-symbols of the prehistoric age."[30] He also saw runic symbols continued on in an ideographic form in many aspects of German representation: from designs in Gothic architecture, German heraldry, the symbols of the German legal tradition and even the traditional shapes of German breads and cakes. His ideas, however, are always couched in the terminology of his mystical systems: most commonly his "trifidic-triune triad"—the runes bore an immediate (prosaic) form, an exoteric form (an outward religious meaning) and an esoteric message (a secret mystical truth), and the esoteric meaning itself often bore a triple message based in the eternal trifidic-triune triadic semantic spheres of arising, being and passing-away. List's interpretations relied on a multiplicity of meaning produced by naive etymological and semantic fancies, guided by his occult insight. The secret of the runes for List was that through knowledge of their (multiple) meanings based in the shapes of his eighteen-character runic alphabet, all sorts of prosaic and often everyday German symbols and forms could be read for their deeper exoteric and esoteric meanings.

The enthusiasm for Germanic (and Aryan) antiquity generated by the *völkisch* movement in the 1890s saw the swastika and the runes become the clearest, most essential symbols of the new German and Austrian radical far right. List's books on runes were bought widely by members of the *völkisch* politico-cultural groups which had developed out of the fraternities and language and cultural societies of the previous decades; Listian rune-lore rapidly spread throughout *völkisch* circles.[31] As symbols of Germanic antiquity, though, the runes had already been adopted by *völkisch* groups before 1907 as had the swastika. *Heimdall*, for example, had its pan-Germanist motto written in a strange form of younger Nordic runes, and the swastika appeared in all sorts of *völkisch* contexts, from poems, to mastheads, to the paintings of Fidus. Yet in the wake of List's *Secret of the Runes*, even people not prone to the most overt obscurantism of his circle soon began to take on elements of his runic learning. Hence just as the ideographic thesis was losing credibility in academic circles, a new discourse arose that could only support an overweeningly chauvinistic interpretation of the origin and nature of the runes.

Nonetheless in the same decade as Richard M. Meyer, a Jewish professor at Berlin, made the last contribution to the old ideographic thesis, a new form of it had already emerged. A self-declared *völkisch* thinker and anti-Semite, the physician and amateur antiquarian Ludwig Wilser began to support the *Urschrift* thesis, unaware at first of the previous contributions of von Liliencron, Müllenhoff and Losch.[32] Although he seemed a lone voice in the early years, Wilser was to spend the rest of his life promoting this theory, publishing scores of reviews, essays and even books promoting his view that the runes were a creation of primordial Germanic antiquity. His views were ridiculed by most of his academic counterparts. By the 1920s, however, he was to seem a pioneer to a new generation of runic enthusiasts.

Wilser began his career as a popularizer of Germanic antiquity in 1885.[33] At the time he was a member of the Karlsruhe Antiquarian Society (Karlsruher Altertumsverein) and his extreme, Germanomaniacal portraits of antiquity did not receive much comment among the academic community. By the 1890s, however, he had made himself something of an expert in things runic and had begun contributing reviews of runological works to respected anthropological periodicals such as the German Anthropological Society's review journal, the *Zentralblatt für Anthropologie*. He also became involved with the *völkisch* press, most notably Woltmann's *Politisch-Anthropologische Revue*, and though he attained a large following for many of his views, his publishing career never truly moved out of the twilight *völkisch* world that developed between right-wing extremist politics and regular academic discourse at the time.

As a member of respected organizations such as the German Society for Anthropology, Ethnology and Prehistory (Deutsche Gesellschaft für Anthropologie, Ethnologie und Urgeschichte), Wilser was known personally to many German and Austrian academics.[34] In fact his studies on racial anthropology which emerged in the early 1900s were often well received. But his principal concern was the runes and their origin. Indeed he is by far the most prolific of all producers of papers on the subject, although few of his essays are any more than repetitions of views he first put together most completely in 1895.[35]

Wilser called for a nationalistic interpretation of the question of the origin of the runes. Citing a range of authors who had been equally as patriotic in their interpretations, Wilser called for a renaissance in antiquarian studies, clearly with the fantastic Gothicism of Rudbeck's time in mind.[36] This attitude to scholarship in which patriotism could override the need for empirical objectivity riddled his work for the rest of his lifetime. Like Chamberlain, Wilser was a neo-Idealist and a post-empiricist, a *völkisch* antiquarian grubstreet post-empiricist. Yet in spite of the glaring flaws in his scholarship, his obviously patriotic approach sometimes led to the promotion of his ideas by more respectable scholars.

After stating his basic principles in 1895, the rest of Wilser's musings on the subject of runic origins are essentially reactions to the works of other authors. He clearly saw himself as an expert, in a sense like Chamberlain with his cavalier approach to evidentiality, and was confident his understanding was superior to that of the professors. Wilser ignored the careful arguments of his academic critics, railed against their judgement and supported his often-fabulous claims with lists of authors he admired like Count Gobineau, even if their opinions were quite irrelevant.[37] A penchant for name-dropping and a stubborn refusal to accept criticism did not win him academic acceptance, however. Few bothered to enter into exchanges with him—instead, he increasingly became an object of academic scorn.

Wilser, however, seemed to think that the views of professional runologists required correcting. For instance his short 1905 monograph *On Runology (Zur Runenkunde)* is mostly an attack on the Swedish scholar Otto von Friesen's seminal *On the Origin of the Runes (Om runeskriftens härkomst)* which inaugurated the thesis of a Bosporan

Greek origin of the runic script (one that would subsequently feature in encyclopedias such as the *Brittanica*).[38] Wilser's book provoked several caustic reviews, bringing the further development of the hieroglyphic thesis to the attention of serious runologists.[39] But Wilser remained undaunted.

A quite different attitude was held by some other academics to the work of dilettantes like Wilser though. A revealing case was that of the 1911 publication of the Brünn (Brno) schoolmaster Karl Schirmeisen's long paper on the origin of the runes by Gustaf Kossinna, the editor of the archeological journal *Mannus*.[40] Knowing little about runology, Kossinna had sent Schirmeisen's manuscript to the Swedish archeologist Bernhard Salin for comment, as Salin had written on runes in his seminal study *Old Germanic Zoomorphism (Die altgermanische Thierornamentik)*.[41] Salin duly replied to Kossinna that:[42]

> Schirmeisen's study is absolutely worthless; [he is] one of the wildest of dilettantes. It is in this area of scholarship, where the ground is still imperfectly prepared, that the worst weeds develop. Men like Schirmeisen and Wilsner [sic] believe that one can throw any old facts together ...

After some delay, in 1911 Kossinna published Schirmeisen's contribution regardless as a long article in *Mannus*. He did write an editorial introduction, however, referring to some of the points raised by Salin and the long genesis of the article.[43] Kossinna evidently liked the direction of Schirmeisen's research and, moreover, came to publish even more of this type of speculation in his journal. Schirmeisen's paper was clearly the most fantastic of all the variations on the *Urschrift* thesis to have appeared to that date, but the next year saw a similar article appear in *Mannus* by Reinhold, Baron von Lichtenberg, along with, of course, Wilser's seemingly obligatory reply.[44]

Academic authors specializing in fields such as archeology, fine arts, anthropology and folkloric studies continued to produce variations on the hieroglyphic thesis, often under the influence of swastika studies, but often also in ignorance of recent developments in alphabet history itself. Building on a preliminary work from 1913, Hermann Schneider, a professor of philosophy at Leipzig (and who is not to be confused with his Germanist contemporary at Tübingen), produced a long study of this type in 1924, where the runes are portrayed as a development of Cretan hieroglyphs, but still, nonetheless, the root of all Aryan alphabets.[45] In the same year the Königsberg-based Orientalist Ferdinand Bork had even tried to link the runic alphabet with the representation of the zodiac, basing his argument in an earlier tradition of alphabet-historical speculation and swastika mania.[46] All manner of speculation about ideographs, swastikas and runes moved in and out of academic discourse at the time. Nevertheless this discourse did not become continuous until the *Urschrift* thesis and the question of the nature of Germanic and Aryan ideographs was brought squarely back into the mainstream of academic and dilettantish discourse in a spectacular manner in 1928.

Before 1928, however, swastika studies and the question of the origin of the runes had developed into a discourse only at the margin of alphabet history and runic studies proper. It was supported most of all by professional archeologists and anthropologists, scholars from disciplines where the structuralist principles common in linguistic scholarship were not so commonly to be found. The interest in these signs and symbols of Germanic and Aryan antiquity was also informed by political matters, both overtly obscurantist as in the case of the followers of List, but also by those of a more mundanely *völkisch* mien. Few of the speculative studies published at the time were developed in an atmosphere discrete from the dictates of the political agenda so blatantly represented in the works of the *völkisch* antiquarian fringe. Yet German antiquarianism already harbored a tradition of some pedigree of overvaluing the accomplishments of their ancestors without the need for the intrusion of the radicalism of *völkisch* grubstreet thinkers such as Wilser. Some senior scholars also lent their names to this new development in German antiquarianism, and when *Sinnbildforschung* proper emerged after 1928, many reviewers linked the inauguration of the tradition of investigation into the ideographs of Germanic and Aryan prehistory with established academics like Kossinna and Montelius. Despite the intrusions of the Lists and the Wilsers, the nascent *Sinnbildforschung* of the latter part of the nineteenth century and the early decades of the twentieth was clearly substantially an academic discourse, though already one quite separate from the philological mainstream of Old Germanic studies in general.

NOTES

1 O. Wormianus, [*Runer*] (Copenhagen: Martzen, 1636); idem, *Danicorum monumentum* (Copenhagen: Moltke, 1643).

2 J. Bureus, [*Runakänslanäs lärä-span unde runr*] (Uppsala: [s.n.,] 1599); idem, *Runa ABC-boken* (Stockholm: Gutterwitz, 1611); idem, *Monumenta lapidum aliquot Runicorum* (Uppsala: Curio, 1664); E. Svärdström, *Johannes Bureus' arbeten om svenska runinskrifter* (Stockholm: Wahlström & Widstrand, 1936).

3 Grimm, *Ueber deutsche Runen*; idem, "Zur Literatur der Runen," *Jahrbücher der Literatur* 43 (1828): 1–42 [= *Kleinere Schriften*, ed. Gustav Hinrichs, 4 vols, Berlin and Gütersloh, 1881–87, III, 85–131].

4 Grimm, *Ueber deutsche Runen*, 82; W. Bell, "On the Discoveries of Runic Characters on Spears, etc.," *Journal of the British Archaeological Association* 23 (1867): 385–87.

5 Wormianus, [*Runer*], cap. XI.

6 J. Ihre, *Dissertatio de runarum patria et origine* (Uppsala: Stenberg, 1770).

7 J.G. Liljegren, *Run-Lära* (Stockholm: Norstedt & Söner, 1832) [= *Die nordischen Runen*, ed. and trans. C. Oberleitner (Vienna: Haas, 1848)].

8 R. von Liliencron, review of J.G. Liljegren, *Die nordischen Runen* and A. Kirchhoff, *Das gothische Runenalphabet*, *Allgemeine Monatsschrift für Wissenschaft und Literatur* 1852, 169–93; K. Müllenhoff, "Ueber altdeutsche Loosung und Weissagung," *Allgemeine Monatsschrift für Wissenschaft und Literatur* 1852, 310–48; R. von Liliencron and K. Müllenhoff, *Zur Runenlehre* (Halle a.S.: Schwetschke & Son, 1852).

9 Grimm, *Ueber deutsche Runen*, 4–5, 11, 25–26; cf. similarly K. Faulmann, *Ilustrirte Geschichte der Schrift* (Vienna: Hartleben, 1880).

10 W. Weingärtner, *Die Ausprache des Gothischen zur Zeit des Ulfilas* (Leipzig: Weigel, 1858), 20; F. Dietrich, *Ueber die Ausprache des Gothischen während der Zeit seines Bestehens* (Marburg: Elwert, 1862), 6; L.F.A. Wimmer, "Runeskriftens Oprindelse og Udvikling i Norden," *Aarbøger for nordisk Oldkyndighed og Historie* 1874, 1–270 [= monograph, Copenhagen: Prior, 1874], 2nd ed. = *Die Runenschrift*, trans. F. Holthausen (Berlin: Weidmann, 1887).

11 F. Losch, "Zur Runenlehre," (Pfeiffer's) *Germania* 34 (1889): 397–405; R.M. Meyer, "Runenstudien," *PBB* 21 (1896): 162–84.

12 Tacitus, *Germania* 10.

13 H. Schliemann, *Trojanische Altertümer* (Leipzig: Brockhaus, 1874), 49, 51 [= *Troy and Its Remains*, ed. P. Smith (London: Murray, 1875), 101–6 et seq.].

14 L. Müller, "Det saakaldte Hagekor's Anvendelse og Betydning i Oldtiden," *Det Kongelige Danske Videnskabernes Selskabs Skrifter*, 5:e Række, Hist. og Phil. Afd., Bd. 5, no. 1, 1877 (1877–92), 1–114; R.P. Greg, "On the Meaning and Origin of the Fylfot and Swastika," *Archaeologia* (48): 1884, 293–326; C. Sterne, *Tuisko-Land* (Glogau: Flemming, 1891), 344ff.; M. von Zmigrodski, "Zur Geschichte der Suastika," *Archiv für Anthropologie*

19 (1891): 173–84; E. Compte Goblet d'Alviella, *La Migration des symbols* (Paris: Leroux, 1891); T. Wilson, "The Swastika," *Report of the U.S. National Museum* 1894, 757–1011; O. Montelius, "Das Rad als religiöses Sinnbild in vorchristlicher und christlicher Zeit," *Prometheus* 16 (1905): 241–48, 259–66, 277–84; J. Déchelette, "Le culte du soleil aux temps préhistoriques," *Revue archéologique* 4ième serie, 13 (1909): 305–57.

15 J. Lechler, *Vom Hakenkreuz* (Leipzig: Kabitzsch, 1921); K. Weißmann, *Schwarze Fahne, Runenzeichen* (Düsseldorf: Droste, 1991), 58–73; M. Quinn, *The Swastika* (London: Routledge, 1994), 22ff.

16 E. Burnouf, *Le Lotus de la bonne loi, traduit du sanscrit* (Paris: Imprimérie Nationale, 1837), 625; idem, *Dictionaire classique sanscrit-francais* (Paris: Maisonneuve, 1866), 746; idem, *La Science des religions*, 2nd ed. (Paris: Maisonneuve, 1872), 256.

17 Weißmann, 73 & tab. xix, d.

18 C. Penka, *Origines Ariacae* (Vienna: Prochaska, 1883); idem, *Die Herkunft der Arier* (Vienna: Prochaska, 1886).

19 R. Römer, *Sprachwissenschaft und Rassenideologie in Deutschland*, 2nd ed. (Munich: Fink, 1989), 62ff.

20 H. Siegert, "Zur Geschichte der Begriffe 'Arier' und 'arisch'," *Wörter und Sachen* 22 (1941–42): 73–99.

21 O. Montelius, "Das Sonnenrad und das christliche Kreuz," *Mannus* 1 (1909): 53–69 & 169–86; idem, "Das lateinische Kreuz," *Mannus* 7 (1915): 281–314.

22 K. von den Steinen, "Prähistorische Zeichen und Ornamente," *Festschrift für Adolf Bastian* (Berlin: Reimer, 1896), 249–88; W. Schultz, "Das Hakenkreuz als Grundzeichen des westsemitischen Alphabets," *Memnon* 3 (1909): 175–200; H. Steinmetz, "Versuch einer astronomischen Deutung des Hakenkreuzes," *Archiv für Anthropologie* NF 15 (1917): 206–13.

23 H.P. Blavatsky, *The Secret Doctrine*, 2 vols. (London: Theosophical Publishing, 1888) [= idem, *Die Geheimlehre*, trans. R. Froebe (Leipzig: Vollrath, 1900)].

24 G. List, "Die esoterische Bedeutung religiöser Symbole," *Gnosis* 1 (1903): 323–27; Goodrick-Clarke, 41ff.

25 G. von List, *Das Geheimnis der Runen* (Gross-Lichterfelde: Zillmann, [1907]), rev. ed. (Leipzig: Steinacker, 1908) [= *The Secret of the Runes*, trans. S.E. Flowers (Rochester, Vermont: Destiny, 1988)].

26 According to List, the Armanen were an ancient pagan order of Germanic priests who had fled the Christian missionaries for Iceland, and whose wisdom had been preserved by the Knights Templar, the Rosicrucians and other apparently occultic groups. It derives from the Herminones of Tacitus, *Germania* 2.

27 G. von List, *Die Armanenschaft der Ario-Germanen*, 2 vols. (Leipzig: Steinacker, 1908–11); idem, *Die Rita der Ario-Germanen* (Leipzig: Steinacker, 1908); idem, *Die Bilderschrift der Ario-Germanen* (Leipzig: Steinacker, 1910); idem, *Die Religion der Ario-Germanen in ihrer Esoterik und Exoterik* (Zürich: Bürdecke, 1910); idem, *Der Übergang von Wuotanstum zum Christentum* (Zürich: Bürdecke, 1911); Goodrick-Clarke, 44ff.

28 *Hávamál* 139–65.

29 List, *Geheimnis*, 21 [= *Secret*, 64].

30 List, *Geheimnis*, 2 [= *Secret*, 42–44].

31 Goodrick-Clarke, 43, 123ff.

32 L. Wilser, "Über die Stellung der germanischen Runen" (1888), *Der Karlsruher Altertumsverein* 1 (1892): 27ff.

33 L. Wilser, *Ueber einen Fall von Ausgedehnter Thrombose der Sinus und Venen des Gehirns in Folge von Insolation* (Freiberg: Loggen & Son, 1875); idem, *Die Herkunft der Deutschen* (Karlsruhe: Braun, 1885); idem, "Die Herkunft der Germanen," *Correspondenz-Blatt* 16 (1885): 122–24.

34 H.A.L. Degener, *Wer ist's*, 3rd ed. (Leipzig: Degener, 1908): 1510–11.

35 L. Wilser, "Alter und Ursprung der Runenschrift," *Korrespondenzblatt der Gesamtvereins der deutschen Geschichts- und Alterthumsvereine* 43 (1895): 137–43.

36 Ibid., 140–41.

37 L. Wilser, "Zur Geschichte der Buchstabenschrift," *Beilage zur Allgemeinen Zeitung* 5 May 1899, no. 103, 3.

38 O. von Friesen, "Om Runeskriftens härkomst," *Språkvetenskapliga sällskaps i Uppsala förhandlingar* 2 (1904–6): 1–55 [= monograph, Uppsala: Akademika, 1904]; idem, "Runes," in W. Yust (ed.), *Encyclopædia Britannica*, 24 vols, 14th ed. (London: Encyclopædia Britannica, 1929), XVII, 659–64; L. Wilser, *Zur Runenkunde* (Leipzig: Akademischer Verlag für Kunst und Wissenschaft, 1905).

39 S. Feist, notice of Wilser, *Zur Runenkunde, Jahresbericht* 27 (1905): I, 67; idem, "Runen und Zauberwesen im germanischen Altertum," *Arkiv för nordisk filologi* 35 (1919): 250.

40 K. Schirmeisen, "Buchstabenschrift, Lautwandel, Göttersage und Zeitrechnung," *Mannus* 3 (1911): 97–120 & 225–78.

41 B. Salin, *Die altgermanische Thierornamentik*, trans. J. Mestorf (Stockholm: Wahlström & Widstrand, 1904), 146–48.

42 Salin/Kossinna, 15.1.1905 [1909?], in H. Gräfin Schwerin von Krosigk, *Gustaf Kossinna* (Neumünster: Wachholtz, 1982), 177–78.

43 G. Kossinna, "Vorbemerkung," *Mannus* 3 (1911): 97–98.

44 L. Wilser, "Ursprung und Entwicklung der Buchstabenschrift," *Mannus* 4 (1912): 123–29; R. Freiherr von Lichtenberg, "Das Alter der arischen Buchstabenschrift, ihre Entwicklung und ihre ferneren Einflüße," *Mannus* 4 (1912): 295–305. Von Lichtenberg's article was in fact a response to Wilser's criticism of his earlier hieroglyphic contribution, "Beiträgen zur Schriftgeschichte," published in the *Heimdall* splinter/successor, the *Mitteilungen des Allgemeinen Deutschen Schriftvereins* NF 3/4 (1911) [n.v.].

45 H. Schneider, *Der kretische Ursprung des "phönikischen" Alphabets* (Leipzig: Hinrichs, 1913); idem, "Ursprung und Sinn unseres Alphabets," *Gesammelte Aufsätze* (Leipzig: Kroner, 1924), 3–113.

46 F. Bork, "Zur Entstehungsgeschichte des Futharc," *Mannus* 16 (1924): 127–37.

CHAPTER 4.

Germanic Resurgence

Das höchste Gut des Mannes ist sein Volk,
Das höchste Gut des Volkes ist sein Recht.
Des Volkes Seele lebt in seiner Sprache
Dem Volk, dem Recht, und unsrer Sprache treu,
Fand uns der Tag, wird Tag jeder uns finden.
Felix Dahn

The most acclaimed summation of Germanic antiquity in the late nineteenth century was Karl Müllenhoff's magisterial *Study of German Antiquity (Deutsche Altertumskunde).*[1] The rune-fancying Müllenhoff was held in similar esteem to the Grimms in his lifetime, and students of the Old Germanic past flocked to him and his lectures at the University of Berlin (where he had been called in 1858). Müllenhoff inculcated in many of his students a mixture of philological rigor and nationalism that is not so evident in earlier works. The third Grimm saw all philological study as an avenue to better understanding the roots of the German nation and made his guiding political principles quite explicit in his publications.

Müllenhoff's *magnum opus*, however, is essentially classicist. His main sources, unlike the Grimms, were classical commentators on the early Germanic tribes, though he was clearly the first to bring together the many hundreds of classical references to early Germanic civilization and history in a masterly way.[2] Müllenhoff also taught early Germanic languages, but he was essentially teaching a German outgrowth of classical philology. The classics-dominated form of Germanic antiquarian studies of his time would give way to a vastly different approach to the old Germanic past in the new century. In fact it was one that can already be seen in the posthumously published fifth volume of his masterwork from 1900 which contains notes on the Old Norse poem the *Seeress's Prophecy (Völuspá)*, perhaps the richest mythological piece from the *Poetic Edda* and the inspiration for Wagner's *Twilight of the Gods.*

Yet the nationalist Germanophilia of Müllenhoff's day had become partnered by something altogether different in the new century. The rise of Schönerer and the Pan-Germans of Austria and Germany, and the antiquarian-enthusing *völkisch* movement had lent a new radicalism to antiquarian Germanistic discourse. Many university scholars were supporters of pan-Germanism and the new politics which grew up in Schönerer's wake. They may not have become contributors to journals like *Heimdall* and *Hammer*, but found other outlets in which to express their patriotism instead.

The development and acceptance of *Sinnbildforschung* within German academic discourse was a natural progression in part for individuals relying on the theoretical premises of several German and Austrian schools of thought in archeology, philology and linguistics that developed between the time of Müllenhoff's death in 1884 and the late 1920s. Some changed the disciplines in which they developed fundamentally; all represented new directions in the understanding of Germanic antiquity. These developments also hold one other thing in common: clearly *völkisch* sensibilities informed them. For some scholars, however, it was not even a subtle, but rather an explicit acceptance of *völkisch* thinking in academic discourse.

The clearest early example of *völkisch* thought at play within one of these schools was in the methodology stressed by Berlin's Kossinna or settlement school of archeology. Gustaf Kossinna and his pupils not only served to validate some marginal notions raised by *völkisch* amateurs, they promoted ideas that became an essential plank for the theoretical framework accepted within ideographic studies. The influence of the East Prussian-born Kossinna was so strong that German archeology was severely compromised by political concerns over the course of the Weimar Republic and the Nazi dictatorship. Kossinna's most firmly held thesis, his rejection of foreign influence in the prehistorical roots of Germanic culture, however, was founded in a quite developed discourse. His work also had both a powerful influence on the development of *Sinnbildforschung* and played a seminal role in the growth of the Aryanist Grub Street.

At the same time a contemporary of Kossinna at the University of Berlin, the Swiss philologist Andreas Heusler, also set out upon a comparable though less overtly *völkisch* mission. A German-National conservative, Heusler focused on early Germanic literature and in his studies attempted to distill the heroic Germanicness of the past, one he and his followers maintained was a tragic loss in spirit compared to that which prevailed in contemporary German society. His concept of Germanicness became a new paradigm in Germanic antiquarian studies: in fact it heralded the emergence of a new Germanic studies, one that would fundamentally transform academic approaches to the Old Germanic past. Much as with the concepts developed by Kossinna, Heusler's notion of Germanicness became dominant in the new discourses emerging within Germanic antiquarianism at the time.

A comparable conservative influence can be seen at work in the new school of historical religious studies inaugurated in 1913 by the University of Marburg Germanist Karl Helm that tied in to the idea of German Christianity promoted by Lagarde. Helm's new historicist understanding would lead to the development of a new way of studying cult and mythology. The most remarkable offshoot of this new approach, however, was centred about the Viennese Germanist Rudolf Much and his students. The Much school produced the most radical branch of *völkisch* Germanism at the time and by the 1930s began to influence the manner in which other schools of thought developed. In fact the most mature form of the theories of the Much school almost developed as a rival to ideographic studies. Nonetheless *Sinnbildforschung* might not have become so influential without Helm staking out this new direction in the study of pre-Christian religion.

At a similar time as the Kossinna school was developing in Berlin, another group of thinkers were developing a school of historical semantic scholarship in Austria that would also serve to ready Germanophonic academic discourse for the arrival of ideographic studies. Linked to the Much school, this development of linguistics, the *Wörter und Sachen* ("words and things") movement was heavily influenced by *völkisch* thought, its main proponents often being outspoken Nazis. In its most developed and radical form, the *Wörter und Sachen* movement became associated with the emergent neo-Humboldtian school whose proponents sought to investigate language in terms of a chauvinistic mystique that idolized the German mother tongue. Unlike the neo-Humboldtians proper, however, the *Wörter und Sachen* movement eventually became allied with ideographic studies in a concrete sense when in the late 1930s *Wörter und Sachen* studies were coordinated along with *Sinnbildforschung* under the umbrella of the SS. Yet the first Germanistic antiquarian field to succumb to the lure of *völkisch* thought was German archeology.

ARCHEOLOGY AND LANGUAGE

The contribution of nationalistic discourse to nineteenth-century philology was a touchstone for later German authors. In archeology, however, the entire discipline as it was practiced in Germany had become so influenced by nationalistic concerns that *völkisch* influence in early-twentieth-century German archeology was not only patent in publications of the time but often ubiquitous. Nevertheless, archeology was hardly a developed discipline in Germany until the close of the nineteenth century. Most German and Austrian archeology had not yet risen far above the level of Near Eastern tomb-robbing at the time and the study of antiquities from Central Europe had yet to be put on any firm empirical basis. Instead, the development of a scientific archeology was mainly a Scandinavian phenomenon.

The growth of the discipline of prehistory in Germany is principally to be ascribed to the achievement of Gustaf Kossinna. Kossinna was a philologist by training, however, and soon came to apply notions current in linguistic theory at the time in his work.[3] This included the notion developed by Humboldt that language was the most highly developed expression of an ethnic culture (or as Felix Dahn put it, "the soul of the people lives in its language"). When Kossinna applied a similar reasoning to archeological material, he managed to transform the study of Germanic antiquities into a fundamentally nationalistic enterprise, one firmly focused on the recovery of Germanness from the soil. Although archeology was a quite immature science in Wilhelmine Germany and, as with runology, had mostly been adopted from Scandinavian works, it soon became entwined in a broader self-consciously German antiquarian endeavor that with Kossinna would ultimately lead to the development of a *völkisch* form of archeology.

The antiquarian excitement surrounding indigenous archeological discoveries at the time of the Grimms was not at first shared in the broader community. Most German antiquarian works of the time were little more than collections of ceramic oddities, "thunder stones" (microliths) and bronze manufactures of rather poor workmanship—obviously the work of uncultured heathens.[4] They were, consequently, little valued. Such was not the case in Scandinavia, however.

The state antiquarians in Scandinavia, first appointed with the full blooming of Gothicism in the seventeenth century, had been given a mission to preserve and study the ancient monuments of the North. The earliest antiquarians such as Bure began with runic monuments; Denmark's Worm similarly formed a collection of antiquities (and natural oddities), which upon his death was opened as the first public museum.[5] The study of physical antiquities was soon to become termed archeology (as *archeo* literally means 'archaic'), although it was not yet at that time principally a matter of digging up the past. That was a development of the Enlightenment with the excavation of sites such as the burial mounds of Uppsala (to discover if they really were the homes of elves) and the megalith graves previously associated with giants. Still, no systematic archeology existed until the early 1800s when the Danish archeologist Christian Jurgensen Thomsen arranged according to type of material the collection of the Royal Committee for the Preservation and Collection of National Antiquities of Denmark (founded in 1806). Thomson's three materials-cum-age periodization (Stone Age, Bronze Age, Iron Age) was the first step in the establishment of prehistoric chronology.[6]

The first displays of the Danish Commission for Antiquities (Oldsags kommissionen) were so successful that a permanent place for their display was soon created, the result being the founding of the Danish National Museum (Nationalmuseet) in Copenhagen in 1819. Yet it is quite clear that archeology in Denmark was no mere bourgeois form of entertainment: it was a public, patrimonial and national archeology.[7] This growing concern was recognized as one of national importance and in 1855 the first European chair in archeology was created at the University of Copenhagen. The empirical Scandinavian endeavor of the mapping out of Germanic prehistory then began in earnest.

Although German archeologists had received the permission of the Turkish Sultan to pillage sites in the Near East, in the mid-nineteenth century Central European archeology of an indigenous nature was still in its infancy. The findings of the scientific expedition sent by Napoleon to Egypt in 1798, published as *Description de l'Egypte* (1809–22),[8] had inaugurated an industry of antiquarian pillage, however—an industry represented perhaps most controversially by the marbles taken down from the Acropolis by Lord Elgin in 1802. This interest in oriental and classical antiquities, however, eventually led to the appearance of museums of locally discovered archeological finds too—after all, most of Europe held a tradition of Roman patrimony in common. An interest in Germano-Roman remains was kindled by the establishment of local museums in Austria, the southern German states and in the Rhineland. Yet influential early German establishments such as the Romano-Germanic Central Museum in Mainz (Römisch–Germanisches Zentralmuseum Mainz), founded in 1852, were interested only in the archeology of the local Roman provinces, those which coincided with the modern geographical bounds of Germany. The rest of Germany, called Free Germany (Germania libera) by the Romans, was of little interest to archeology as practiced by the nineteenth-century German establishment.

Kossinna, the Arminius of the archeology of free Germany, had published several articles on ancient Germanic history before taking up prehistory in earnest. To that time his field had seemed mainly the interest only of dilettante enthusiasts. In fact one of these amateurs, Ludwig Wilser, had become quite successful in Kossinna's day, by applying an overweeningly chauvinistic approach to all things Germanic, from runes to weapons and European origins. More established figures such as Rudolf Virchow, the leading name in German archeology at the time, had publicly chided Wilser for allowing patriotism to dictate all his findings.[9] But rather than rebuff Wilser's contribution, Kossinna soon came to complement it. He applied the same unabashedly chauvinistic approach as did Wilser, but Kossinna was better able to enunciate his nationalism in a manner he deemed suitable of serious study.

Where indigenous archeology came into play in broader nineteenth-century German discourse was on the question of the origins of Europe. Before the time of Kossinna the origin of European culture had usually been discussed exclusively in anthropological terms, i.e. as a matter of explaining the superlative achievements of the White Race. The question of European origins, however, also led to developments in linguistic and archeological theory which would later be used, as Léon Poliakov has dubbed them, as a "tyranny" in anthropological thought.[10]

Sir William Jones's observation that the languages spoken by a number of geographically widespread Eurasian communities were related led to the construction of a linguistic identity, the Indo-European or Aryan identity. Initially it was dominated by Sanskrit, the "exquisitely refined" language of ancient India according to Jones,[11] much as that of Germanic had formerly been by Gothic. Indeed at the same time, in a climate of growing fascination with all things Indian, a form of (Indo-)Aryanism had arisen in Europe.[12]

Friedrich Schlegel's 1808 study *On the Language and Wisdom of the Indians (Über die Sprache und Weisheit der Indier)* firmly accredited to India the origin of European language and indeed civilization.[13] In the 1830s Schlegel's supporter August Friedrich Pott went further, however, when he inaugurated "linguistic paleontology," i.e. the notion that the etymological prehistory of words could be studied as the bones of a prehistoric language (Indo-European) and that these bones in turn reflected the culture that had spawned this language.[14] By the end of the 1850s, the Frenchman Adolphe Pictet had further developed this notion in a two-volume *Essai de paléontologie linguistique* where he described the Indo-European or primitive Aryan culture, one that with its common words for 'horse,' 'cart' and 'copper' or 'bronze' could now be matched with the findings of archeology.[15]

The first notable German-speaking author to attempt to do so was the Viennese antiquarian Matthäus Much, a sometime member of the Austrian Diet and an associate of Schönerer.[16] An autodidact holding a doctorate in law, Much has been described as the "Nestor of Austrian prehistory"; independently wealthy, he directed several important excavations in Cisleithian Austria.[17] He also prepared a handful of studies of Bronze Age discoveries from Central and Eastern Europe, studying them in terms of the Indo-European/Aryan identity promoted by contemporary linguists.[18] Matthäus Much's contribution to *völkisch* antiquarianism is perhaps overshadowed by that of his son Rudolf, but the elder Much's studies were valued much more highly in his day than were those of authors like Wilser and Penka. Nor had anthropological sceptics such as Robert Latham or Theodor Poesche made much of an impression among prehistorians when they had claimed the Aryans were indigenous to Europe.[19] Nevertheless as Much could plainly see, archeology did not reveal any influx of Indo-European speakers into Central Europe at the time estimated by linguists such as Pictet: the archeological record as the late Stone Age moved into the Bronze Age seemed to show continuity, not rupture. Thus Much concluded that the Aryans were indigenous to Central Europe. For those who agreed, archeology and linguistics could now bolster the Aryan myth, and as racialist explanation entered *völkisch* discourse with the followers of Gobineau, archeology and linguistics became avenues for racialist discourse and thus *völkisch* concerns of a fundamental nature.

It was at this point, when the racial imperative had first come to be applied to the Aryan question, that Kossinna appeared on the scene. As the Danish archeologist Jakob Worsaae had observed, though, the collections of the German archeological museums were disorganized and it would take someone with immense fortitude and patience to put together a principled examination of all their holdings.[20] In 1895 Kossinna took up this challenge and began a new chapter in German archeology with the appearance of his study "On the prehistoric spread of the Germanic peoples in Germany."[21] Due to his diligence, energy and care, he soon surpassed Much as the leading Germanophonic voice in the study of Germanic and Aryan prehistory.

Kossinna, however, saw his archeology in terms of the *Volk*; his method relied on the notion of culture embodied in language that he had learned from the linguistic pronouncements of Humboldt. He thought that sharp distinctions in the archeological record could be equated with the limits of settlement areas of different ethnic groups. In short he extended Humboldtian thought to archeology—his "settlement method" stressed the Germanness of prehistorical artifacts; they were concrete expressions of the roots of German civilization.

Much has been written on settlement archeology and the "Kossinnism" or "Kossinna syndrome" that Kossinna inaugurated and which continued to permeate German archeology after his death in 1931.[22] Kossinna had become a giant. His students evangelized his thought throughout the profession in the 1930s and 40s, and the *völkisch* implications of his and their work on a purely indigenous archeology were eventually recognized through the financial and institutional support of the National Socialist government.

Kossinna also thought that with his archeological method he could demonstrate the prehistoric movements of peoples in Central Europe and he soon began to make a number of pronouncements on the prehistory of Germany that agreed with theories that had already been proposed by the *völkisch* Grub Street. Wilser, for instance, thought he had demonstrated a continuous tradition of Germanness in race and archeological finds reaching back to the Stone Age. Increasingly for Wilser the continuity of Germanness was guaranteed not only by the appearance of symbols of the *Volk*, such as swastikas, among finds from the German Stone Age, but also by his racial theories—by the early 1900s he had published dozens of studies on racial typology and diffusion.[23] Wilser claimed to have originally decided upon a Central European homeland for the Indo-Europeans already by 1881, two years before the publication of Penka's *Origines Ariacae*.[24] Yet in 1904 Kossinna himself dismissed Wilser's arguments as "groundless" and bemoaned that:[25]

> it was a peculiarly unlucky star for this idea of a northern European origin of the Indo-Europeans ... that it was first founded so superficially and was developed in the wilderness of blind-alley dilettantism ... which was the case with Wilser then and still is now.

Wilser, however, would soon seem like a visionary.

In a famous article from 1902, Kossinna set out to prove essentially the same thesis as Wilser had promulgated in 1899 and as had been adumbrated by Penka in 1883 and Matthäus Much in 1886.[26] Using his settlement method, Kossinna located the various archeological complexes required to show immigrations of the Indo-Europeans from Germany into the south and east. With Kossinna, an essentially anthropological theory which stated that the Germans were the paragons of the White Race was granted a new archeological foundation.

But Kossinna's contribution did not end with his conversion to Aryanism, and he was not at first successful in convincing many of his peers of the wisdom of his method. Even before he proclaimed his new approach to archeological description, he had already fallen afoul of a number of senior academics for his chauvinistic approach to proto- and prehistory. After falling out with Virchow, he launched a splinter to the German Society for Anthropology, Ethnography and Prehistory. His publications also became more personalized at the time: he increasingly came to see archeology as a battleground and himself as the champion of indigenous prehistory.

Kossinna was also concerned about the future of Germany and became active in national politics at the time. His review of Wilser's *The Germanic Peoples (Die Germanen)* had even appeared in one of the new political-anthropological journals of the day and he soon became associated with other *völkisch* publications such as the Armanen press's *Die Sonne* as well as conservative groups such as the Gobineau Society. His own journal, *Mannus*, increasingly also became an organ for the promotion of *völkisch* antiquarianism. His attitude to politics and prehistory, though, is exemplified in his famous 1912 monograph *German Prehistory: A Pre-eminently National Science (Die deutsche Vorgeschichte: Eine hervorragend nationale Wissenschaft)*, a popular archeology with each chapter headed by a quotation from a figure from the German nationalist tradition.[27] The preface to the second (1914) edition even begins with a quotation from Lagarde and another is discussed within it: "Germanness does not lie in the blood, rather in character."[28] Yet Kossinna quotes this most gnostic of the early *völkisch* sources here only to correct him: "Today we know otherwise and confess aloud: blood makes character first."[29] By this date Kossinna's settlement method had also come to entail an acceptance of the new racialist thinking too.

In the introduction to his *German Prehistory* Kossinna also spelled out a rejection of a paradigm that at the time dominated European archeology, an idea summarized by the Latin phrase *ex Oriente lux*, "light comes from the East." Kossinna rejected the notion that technological and cultural innovation diffused to the North from the South and ultimately from the East. According to Kossina the notion of *ex Oriente lux* was a "baseless fantasy."[30] Against most of the opinion of Scandinavian, French and English archeologists, some of whom he counted as friends, Kossinna rejected the notion that much of the culture of the North was dependent on that of the classical South.

In a sense this bombast was a rejection of extremist diffusionist claims that the root of all civilization could be found in the Near East and usually principally in Egypt. After all, by the 1890s several leading prehistorians had come to rail against the overuse of the *ex Oriente lux* in archeological argument. The French archeologist, Salomon Reinach, had inaugurated the attack on "*le mirage oriental*" in 1893 and Much had written a monograph under a similar title in 1907.[31] Under Kossinna's influence, however, the expression *ex Oriente lux* came to be used derisively in German archeological discourse—it indicated the contempt of the author for an outmoded perception of Germanic culture. Rejection of the *ex Oriente* was a radical new development in Germanic antiquarian thought, one that by the 1930s would also make its presence felt in philology.[32]

Kossinna's proof of the fallacy of such a position was, of course, his evidence first published in 1902 that the Indo-Europeans were indigenous to Germany and therefore that the Mediterranean civilizations, as Indo-European, in fact physically stemmed from the North. If culture was only to be measured by blood, the South instead was dependent on the North. Centuries of prejudice from authors in a line from Greek or Roman antiquity and through the Italian renaissance could now be swept away. This rejection, however, also paved the way for its reverse, a veritable *ex Septentrione lux*. The seventeenth-century Gothicist Rudbeck in his fantastic *Atlantica* had already spoken of a *lux in tenebris Cimmeriis* ("light in the Cimmerian darkness"); by the 1910s all manner of *völkisch* enthusiasts were hailing this new nationalist approach.[33] They held quite different statuses in the academic community, but Wilser and Kossinna had clearly come to enjoy a synergy by the end of Wilhelmine times. Wilser accepted and championed the *ex Septentrione lux* of Kossinna in his works and Kossinna, obviously respecting Wilser's patriotic drive, came to support Wilser's right to have his speculation promulgated in academic channels. Despite his earlier criticism of Wilser's "wilderness of blind-alley dilletantism," Kossinna duly came to support Wilser's ideographic theory for the origin of the runes and, as we have seen, allowed Wilser and other dilettantes a platform to promote this ideographic theory in his increasingly radical prehistorical journal *Mannus*.

Kossinna had not just rescued indigenous German archeology from Scandinavian dominance, he had nationalized it so thoroughly that it became a discourse for *völkisch* agitation. Consequently, he was duly recognized after his death in 1931 as a champion of the *völkisch* movement.[34] Members of the Kossinna school were also to have a pronounced influence on archeology in Nazi Germany. Kossinna's greatest achievement was to develop the archeology of non-Roman Germany, but in his day his more broadly recognized achievement was his solidifying of the picture of the Germans as the original Aryans and his development of this Aryanism to a level such that the ancient Germans could be seen as the prehistoric culture-bringing people *par excellence*. Moreover, in fulfillment of this vision he had also encouraged radical amateur reflections on prehistory, allowing even the most ludicrous theories space in his journal *Mannus*. The legacy of the Arminius of German archeology was as much that of German racism or even Richter's Aryan swastika dance as it was the development of a proper national tradition of indigenous archeology.

FROM GERMANNESS TO GERMANICNESS

A further influence in the establishment of the new Germanic antiquarian studies that arose in the Wilhelmine and Weimar years was more clearly philological. Kossinna himself did much to instill in younger generations of academics how important an understanding of the ancient past was in achieving a proper cognizance of the Germany of the present-day. Yet a greater role in the development of this new attitude to Germanic antiquity was surely played by the man who has proven to be the most important Germanophonic figure in Old Germanic studies of the twentieth century, the Swiss-born Berlin lecturer in German language and ultimately professor of Nordic studies from 1894–1919, Andreas Heusler.

Heusler's contribution to our understanding of the literary aspect of Germanic antiquity is immense. He has even been compared in this respect to the Grimm brothers.[35] Most of his major monographs were reissued unaltered after the war and have never been properly superceded. His *Old Germanic Poetry (Die altgermanische Dichtung)* of 1923 and *History of German Verse (Deutsche Versgeschichte)* of 1925–29, written after he had returned home to Switzerland, remain fundamental works in the study of Old Germanic literatures.[36] In fact he is credited by the leading German philologist Heinrich Beck as the first scholar properly to define Old Germanic studies as a self-contained discipline: linguists, archeologists or historians could never fully understand the culture of Germanic antiquity—only a student dedicated to Old Germanic literatures could.[37] Moreover, Old Germanic studies itself was dedicated to the study of a defined cultural entity. In 1908 in his induction address to the Prussian Academy of Sciences Heusler defined Old Germanic culture as:[38]

[the] civilization of the Germanic peoples, that comes before the conversion, the literate age, the towns and feudalism; that which slowly retreats before the Christian-Roman culture and through battle and exchange with this superior power produces an idiosyncratic spirit that continues into the later feudal period.

Heusler called this spirit "Germanicness" (*Germanentum*), and although a similar notion of a unitary Old Germanic culture had long been shared by *völkisch* enthusiasts and was accepted in varying degrees by many nineteenth-century philologists and historians, the main object of Heusler's scholarship came to be the Germanicness of Norse heroic mythological literature, not some ancient German study. This appropriation of Old Norse literature in the form of a Germanic inheritance was in fact a Germanizing of the Nordic sagas. Wagner had done much the same in the previous century but to rather less effect in the scholarly community. Heusler was more persuasive. He wove a web of argument that tied Nordic literature into a history of German culture in a novel manner, one that was subtle and ultimately for many academics, one that was very convincing.

Heusler saw that Old Norse verse could be construed as representative of a form that had mostly been lost in Germany during the early Middle Ages—most of the early German works that had been rescued by Lachmann and others were expressions of the French tradition of courtly love or tales of Arthurian knights. Instead, early German verse of a more clearly indigenous nature is more similar metrically and thematically to that of the Scandinavian Eddas; hence Norse heroic verse could be seen as representative of a poorly or even largely unattested early German heroic tradition. Both his renowned study of the *Song of the Nibelungs* and his metrical histories from the 1920s focused squarely on this shared Germanicness.[39] Yet Heusler could move even beyond meter and genre in his appropriation of the medieval Icelandic tradition.

Not only are there Norse versions of the German *Song of the Nibelungs*, Heusler thought to trace in these works what he held were common Germanic motifs. In his later scholarship he even became influenced by Nietzsche and discovered in his Norse sources what he claimed were pan-Germanic themes such as the struggle between the law of the jungle and that of society.[40] When it came to issues of Germanic sensibility he readily admitted: "we rely on the people of the

Icelandic sagas for help"[41]—Germanicness could not be reconstructed from the surviving literature of medieval Germany, but only through an appreciation of Nordic sources. Yet in Heusler's opinion "the thought that [the Scandinavian] Eddas have a common Germanic background no longer excites Nordic hearts and minds."[42] For him, evidently, a true awareness of Germanicness lived on only in the German-speaking lands. Heusler came to see that the very essence of the social and cultural condition of ancient and early medieval Germany could be re-discovered in Old Norse literature: in effect he called for the recognition of what the medievalists of the Annales school might have called a *mentalité* of Germanicness. Very little of pre-Christian German thought had survived in medieval German literature. Yet with Heusler, heroic tales of Vikings had come to be held to exhibit the same *Volksgeist* as that which was presumed to have existed in early Germany. The study of Norse literature became a surrogate for the study of a mostly lost German tradition.

A sign of the new attitude to Old Norse literature at the time was the project begun by the Nordicist Felix Niedner to have all the best of the Old Norse tales translated into German. This project took the form of the monograph series *Thule* published by Eugen Diederichs.[43] Diederichs was a leading publisher of *völkisch* works and had adopted the promotion of old Nordic culture as part of his New Romanticism, a revival of the ethos of the first German Romantic period—Romantic and nationalist.[44] His publishing house soon came to be the most important of all the conservative publishers in terms of *völkisch* antiquarianism. By 1933, sales of the translations in the *Thule* series had reached 98,000 volumes. Now all sorts of amateur and professional antiquarians had access to a treasure trove of literature that they believed was seminal to an understanding of ancient Germany and Germanicness.[45]

In 1926 Heusler contributed an essay to a work that aimed to tap this popular audience. Edited by Herman Nollau, it had the grand, although *völkisch*-sounding title *Germanic Resurgence (Germanische Wiedererstehung)*, and its subtitle "A Work on the Germanic Foundations of Our Civilization" presages much of the attitude taken to the sources it interprets.[46] Like Heusler, most of the contributors to *Germanic Resurgence* were political conservatives, early academic supporters of the Nazi Party who were alarmed at what had become of German society after the loss of the Great War. A cultural pessimist, Heusler marked out the way for many of his contemporaries and successors to become more surely enthralled by an interpretation of history in terms of the *Volk* and inaugurated a discourse in which those with more overt political leanings could feel justified in advancing their patriotic views of the soul of the Germanic past.

But German National as he was, Heusler was no Kossinna and often privately expressed his dislike of his Berlin colleague. He also was aware of, and bemoaned the encroachments on his field by the *völkisch* right, especially the more fantastic studies of grubstreet interpreters of Nordic antiquity such as Willy Pastor.[47] The excitement that ushered in Heusler's "Nietzschean winter" of 1932/33 would soon fade as the realities of a Nazi dictatorship became clearer to him, his relationships with Diederichs and other acquaintances from Berlin becoming increasingly strained. Yet he did little to make his disenchantment clear as his name increasingly became attached to all manner of forms of radical antiquarianism as the 1930s marched on.

Much of Heusler's vision of Germanicness is to be found set out in a collection of essays first published under his name in 1934 but some of which ranged back as far as 1921. The timing for the publication of this collection could not have been better. Heusler had already been recognized by this stage as one of the greatest of all contributors to the understanding of the Germanic past. In 1936 Hans Taeger gave an address to the National Socialist Teachers' Federation (Nationalsozialistischer Lehrerbund) in which he acknowledged:[48]

Heusler has given us an appreciation of the artistic quality of the Eddas, of characteristically Germanic art and Germanic humanity, and in sympathy with Nietzsche's moral challenge has forged a bridge from the past to the present.

In 1925 Heusler had summarized Germanic mores up into a number of characteristics of Germanicness and Taeger went on and repeated them. But by the mid-1930s Heusler's studies were clearly beginning to affect more than just academic perceptions of the past.

The influence of Heusler on the image of the old Germanic past and its importance in the present-day can most clearly be seen by the spread of the word *Germanentum* itself.[49] As Heusler had reflected, German historians had long seen that Germanicness and Romanness had come into contact at the end of antiquity and by their interaction had produced medieval culture.[50] One of the main questions, especially for German historians, had traditionally been to what extent medieval culture was Germanic and what part was Roman. Yet rather than define Germanicness in an oppositional manner, Heusler was influenced by Leo Berg's use of the word in attempting to explain why the Norwegian playwright Henrik Ibsen's realism appealed so much to Germans: Berg considered that Ibsen's works drew on a shared Germanic experience.[51] With its adoption by Heusler, however, the term suddenly exploded in use and it soon became ubiquitous in Old Germanic studies.

By 1944, Heusler's concept of Germanicness had even become part of the Weltanschauung promoted in Nazi literature. The Nazi political scientist Friedrich Alfred Beck in his meandering *Rise of the Germanic World-Age (Der Aufgang des germanischen Weltalters)* wrote that year:[52]

> German Germanicness is a metaphysical form of character, derived from a Nordic racial essence, which reveals itself in a creative power based on a heroic attitude located in the personality as the unique representation of the *völkisch* organic existence, in order, while transcending that state of being which is conditioned by space–time and causality, but still within that state of being, to achieve an infinite, eternal and free life as a perfect organic unity between the nation's conception of its essence and the form taken by the reality of the people within the order of the Reich.

This passage is deeply influenced by the Heuslerian view of antiquity. Not only in Taeger's view had Heusler "forged a bridge from past to present." As the influential University of Tübingen Germanist Hermann Schneider, himself the author of a work on Germanic heroic literature (and a good friend of Heusler's), reflected in 1939:[53]

> The year 1933 witnessed the victory of an attitude towards the history of the culture of Germany which gave the Germanic element of all that is German a significance previously unthought of. "The best of what is German," it was declared, "is Germanic and must be found in purer form in early Germanic times."

Heusler's Germanicness was reworked by later scholars to incorporate the racial identity that became wedded to Germanicness as part of the Nordic ideal. The entry of racial discourse to Old Germanic studies, though, is bemoaned by Heusler in his letters and was never part of his own formulation.[54] For many, Germanicness readily became a description of race as well as *Geist*. In fact by the 1940s, Germanicness seemed even to have eclipsed Aryanness in some Nazi publications (compare the combination of "Nordic racial essence" and "German Germanicness" by the Nazi theorist Beck). There was not a marked radicalization of the concept of Germanicness only in 1933; it had been developing over the course of the 1920s. And when a younger generation of philologists were to work towards a further politicization of their field, by the 1930s much as young archeologists could point to Kossinna, so philologists could and did cite the approach of their hero Heusler, even as the expression of their research increasingly seemed to become no more than *völkisch* propaganda. But there were other fields to which the *völkisch* approach to antiquity could now be applied, perhaps most obviously and most radically in understandings of the religion of the pagan ancestors.

RELIGION AND CULT

In a review article published in the *Zeitschrift für Deutschkunde* in 1938, the German philologist Jost Trier noted that a significant change of emphasis had occurred in the interpretation of Germanic mythology in the past generation.[55] The occasion of the review was the appearance of a monograph on Germanic mythology by the Dutch Nordicist Jan de Vries.[56] De Vries had been hailed in 1930 by Gustav Neckel, Heusler's successor in Berlin, for a Dutch-language work he had written as an example of what could be achieved when the notion of Germanicness was applied properly to antiquarian study.[57] De Vries's new work did not represent merely an advancement on Heusler's Germanicness to Trier, however, but instead was a culmination in another development in the study of the old Germanic past whose genesis Trier traces to the first installment of Karl Helm's *History of Old Germanic Religion (Altgermanische Religionsgeschichte)* from 1913.[58] De Vries's book was published as part of an encyclopedic monograph series and had replaced an earlier work on the subject of Germanic mythology contributed by the German scholar Eugen Mogk.[59] Trier noted that while Mogk's work discussed the general form of the myths (genre, manner) and some of the aspects of Germanic belief that they reveal (magic, sacrifice etc.), they did little to locate Germanic mythology within the development of Germanness: they lacked any sense of the now. De Vries's evidently more suitable work situated Germanic myth within its Indo-European context and related modern Germanness to its Germanic pedigree. In effect, he historicized it.

Helm was the first German scholar to seek to explain Germanic mythology in terms of the development of German religiosity: thus *History of Religion* not *Mythology*. Jacob Grimm and his contemporaries had spoken of history of religion, but had not been properly historicist or developmental in their approach. Helm, though, was merely applying an approach that had begun to be used in studies of classical religion and was far from prolific. Vilhelm Grønbech, a Danish literary philosopher, had similarly had a transforming effect on mythological scholarship with his emphasis on what Old Norse literature could reveal about the personal spirituality of the medieval Norse in his *Culture of the Teutons (Vor Folkeæt i Oldtiden)* of 1909–12.[60] Nevertheless, it was clearly Helm who inaugurated a revolution in the way Old Germanic religiosity was assessed at the time. Helm was one of the many antiquarians who added their names to 1933's *Vow of Allegiance of the Professors of German Universities and High-Schools to Adolf Hitler*,[61] but was more famous in his day for developing a new way in which Germanic literature could be interpreted in terms of the *Volk*. Moreover, his new approach was to have an especially pronounced effect most of all in the field of *Volkskunde*.

Volkskunde is literally the study of the German *Volk*, and although originally modelled on British folklore studies, *Volkskunde* is not adequately translated by the English expression 'folklore.' In a sense *Volkskunde* is closer to ethnology (*Völkerkunde*) or anthropology, but with its singular focus upon *Volkstümer* (national traditions), i.e. the traditional cultural expressions of the German *Volk*, it is a field of study that cannot be easily compared with folklore or ethnology as they are practiced in another national tradition.

When the Grimms were collecting their famous fairy tales, they did so in the hope of preserving some vestiges of the ancient stories that they had focused upon in their more textual philological works. German *Volkskunde* has always had a penchant, though, of not only studying fairy and folk tales, but just about any aspect of the entire Germanic antiquarian tradition that might conceivably be open to cultural analysis. By the 1920s, *Volkskunde* was thus merely what it literally means, study of the *Volk*, using just about any expression conceivable.

Sinnbildforschung can thus be described as *Volkskunde*, more readily, perhaps, than it can be classed as philological, archeological or historical. The developments in *Volkskunde* at the time, then, would seem even more important than those in literary philology and archeology, and perhaps even separate from them. Yet contemporary *Volkskunde* was dominated by notions current in archeology and philology. And as Hannjost Lixfeld points out, by 1920 *Volkskunde* had already produced its equivalent to Nollau's *Germanic Resurgence* in the form of *German Custom (Deutsche Sitte)*, a popular work by the respected German folklorist Otto Lauffer (another signatory to the 1933 *Vow of Allegiance*).[62]

Perhaps the most infamous school of *Volkskunde* of the early twentieth century, however, is the Viennese school named for Rudolf Much. The son of the archeologist Matthäus, the younger Much was brought up in Vienna in an atmosphere of *völkisch* agitation and was no less political than his father. A philologist by training, Much is recorded preaching the religion of the Greater German nation at academic conferences, in his published works and in his classes. From his desk at the University of Vienna hundreds of pages of studies of ancient Germany flowed, all characterized by one mission: to demonstrate the glory of the Germanic ancestors.

Hermann Schneider's 1939 review surveys the burgeoning Old Germanic studies of the first five years of the dictatorship. He notes the growth in publications on new areas such as runology as well as literary studies. But the author he singles out most for comment is Much and the controversial publications of his students which had appeared in recent times:[63]

> It is here that excess of zeal and of penetration admittedly find their most fertile field; the tendency to discern Germanic elements in the present often leads to the envisaging of the present as a function of the Germanic

past and thus to arbitrary standards of judgement. Excellent examples of a bold advance into new land are provided above all by R[udolf] Much's school ...

Although he taught Old Norse, in his research Much was faithful to the classicistic tradition of Müllenhoff, maintaining his principal focus on the Germanic past of Roman times. More overtly politicized than Müllenhoff, however, Much had become associated with pan-Germanism from an early stage in his career, although it was only relatively late in his life that he began to declare his political affiliations brazenly. In 1925 he plagiarized Chamberlain's chapter title "The Entry of the Teutons into World History" to head a tendentious study which attempted to prove the existence of Germanic tribes in the Alps as early as the fifth century B.C., some four centuries earlier than had been accepted before.[64] The influence of his politics was not limited only to the direction and manner of his research, however. Not only had he made a confessional *Los von Rom*, in 1929 he went as far as to pen a fourth verse for the *Deutschlandlied (Deutschland über Alles)*, the national anthem of Germany, and presented it to a meeting in Vienna of the German Women Teachers' Association (Deutsche Lehrerinnen Verein):[65]

> In the lap of the mother country
> return there Austria,
> Only in the league of brother tribes
> freedom calls us, happiness blooms!
> From the banks of the Danube it also sounds
> like an oath to the firmament:
> Germany, Germany above all else ...

Much's approach to Old Germanic culture was less obviously structured than most of his linguistic contemporaries and tended all too readily to descend into speculative, nationalist fantasy. Already in 1896, the leading German linguist Herman Hirt had felt the need to chastise Much for relying on arrant etymologies "built upon prejudices of the worst sort."[66] Intellectually, however, Much recognized Kossinna as a like spirit, for example supporting Kossinna in a long-standing exchange with the French Celticist Henri d'Arbois de Jubainville.[67] Going somewhat further than his father had, he even supported Kossinna's new paradigm of *ex Septentrione lux*, in 1928 even attacking Theodor Mommsen, the celebrated nineteenth-century historian of Rome, for his depiction of the ancient Germans as uncouth barbarians.[68] A radical pan-Germanist and antiquarian fantasist, Much died in 1936, only two short years before Hitler made his dream of *Anschluß* a reality.

Nevertheless, the main influence of Much after his death was in Austrian *Volkskunde*, two schools of which had developed during his time at the University of Vienna. One group, the "mythologist" school studied Old Germanic mythology and its effects on folk traditions; the other, the Much school, saw mythology instead as a reflection of social belief.[69] Neither school was strictly dealing with folklore per se. Instead, in Vienna the study of Old Germanic mythology had come to be seen as the best avenue to the exploration of folk dance, folk music and other such traditions. These Germanists interpreted German folk culture as a means to rescuing the core of ancient Germanic culture while demonstrating the continued Old Germanic legacy in the folk beliefs of the present-day. In fact as the new form of *Volkskunde* became accepted more generally, a new attitude arose in German and Austrian folkloric study: Christianity was increasingly to be denigrated as a foreign imposition that had usurped native traditions or remade them in a bastardized form. This new, often anti-Christian *Volkskunde* also enjoyed a clear political aspect and in many ways was the logical conclusion of a *völkisch* history of religion.

Much's student Lily Weiser inaugurated a new form of historical investigation with her 1927 study of *Old Germanic Juvenile Devotions and Men's Leagues (Altgermanische Jünglingsweihen und Männerbünde)*, one that would prove to have particular resonance after 1933.[70] Her sources were the usual stuff of Old Germanic studies: Tacitus and the Eddas. It seems fairly clear, however, that ideas stemming from the Youth Movement at the time tacitly influenced her thought, especially in her notion of juvenile devotions within the context of a *Bund*. The *Bund* had become one of the planks of the *völkisch* conception of German community and by the early 1920s the *völkisch* construction of the *Bund* had even developed its own genre of *bündisch* thought.[71] The importance of the notion of the *Bund* to the later National Socialist regime can be seen semantically in the number of German professional, social and cultural associations and federations that were replaced by Party organizations termed *Bünde*. The same construction also seems to have influenced Much's students to develop a *bündisch* form of Germanic philology that revolved around the continuity of the *Männerbund* as a social expression throughout German and Germanic history.[72]

Ostensibly the idea of ancient Germanic fraternities stems from classical descriptions of some early Germanic tribes, perhaps most notably that of the Harii in Tacitus' *Germania*. The Harii are described by the Roman as exponents of a rather exotic, almost shamanistic warrior cult:[73]

> They black their shields and dye their bodies, and choose pitch-dark nights for their battles. The shadowy, awe-inspiring appearance of such a ghoulish army inspires mortal panic; for no enemy can endure a sight so strange and hellish. Defeat in battle always starts with the eyes.

In 1902 Heinrich Schurtz, a German ethnologist, had focused on *Männerbünde* and secret societies in a seminal work on the development of modern society. Citing descriptions of groups like the Harii, Much's pupils thought they had discovered the description of an important early social group in old Germanic times.[74] The Harii seem to have been an ancient warrior retinue that had broken away from the usual kinship-based group and it might be reasonable to assume that a group of Germanic bachelors might also develop their own notion of cult and honor. But the political resonances were so patent that by the 1930s Weiser's description of the Old Germanic *Männerbund* had become one of the models for the SS. Helm's notion of development in Germanic and German religiosity had been transformed by Much's students. Their investigations of putatively ancient and medieval *Männerbünde* created an Old Germanic pedigree for the modern *Bünde*—it served to validate contemporary *völkisch* theories of masculinity as well as validating the existence of Nazi paramilitary groups by demonstrating their rootedness in ancient traditions.

Other members of the Much school who focused on more traditional folkloric concerns such as Richard Wolfram and Robert Stumpfl had come to see the influence of these secret pagan cultic societies in folk dances and festivals.[75] Yet Himmler is known to have been especially fascinated by the *Männerbund* theories of Otto Höfler, a particularly ambitious scholar who by the 1930s had become the most influential and adventurous of Much's students.[76] Höfler had completed his professional thesis in Vienna in 1931 and had had it published in 1934 as *Secret Cultic Leagues of the Germanic Peoples (Kultische Geheimbünde der Germanen)*, the same year he took up a position at the University of Kiel (with Himmler's help).[77] It was published by Moritz Diesterweg's, Frankfurt, who by this time had become involved with the Armanen press, a leading publisher of *völkisch* works.[78] Stressing the demonic aspect of these leagues such as Tacitus appears to describe so vividly for the Harii, Höfler concluded that "this demonic aspect has been a force throughout [German] history."[79] The impressionistic manner in which Much's students approached their leagues has continued among some less than reputable philology even until today.[80] At the time, however, the notion that the legacy of barbarian military societies could still be felt (and treasured) in the present-day was immediately seized upon by *völkisch* groups. Höfler's thesis was considered by many a breakthrough work at the time and became one of the favorite books of the Reichsführer-SS.

Reviews of Höfler's *Secret Cultic Leagues* by members of the academic community were mixed. Some senior Germanists were wary or even dismissive of an interpretation that linked a bevy of cultural expressions from different eras and places, and attempted to link them genetically.[81] The German folklorist, Friedrich von der Leyen, noting Höfler's interpretation of the Old Norse Einherjar (the troop of the souls of slain warriors) as a mythologized celestial cultic league, even ironically suggested:

> If the *Einherjar* derive from a secret cultic league, then the Valkyries are similarly in reality a secret cultic league of Germanic girls and the precursors to the BDM.

The Much school had wedded Heusler's Norse-based Germanicness to *bündisch* thought and now Germanic social and political expressions could be added to the list of elements of present-day culture that could be construed to be essentially and originally Germanic. In the late 1930s Höfler became even more adventurous, expanding on his themes in respected journals, eliciting further accolades and at the same time criticisms from more senior researchers in his field.[82] His new method even inspired a Swedish scholar with fascist leanings, Stig Wikander, to attempt to do for Indo-Iranian sources what Höfler had done for the Germanic in his 1938 study *The Aryan Men's League (Der arische Männerbund)*.[83] Höfler's clearly *völkisch* continuity theories were inspired by Helm's historicist approach to Germanic religion and both the new and old concepts of Germanicness viewed through the tinted lenses of *völkisch* politics. His theories seemed to capture the radical political spirit of Nazi Germany and helped make him one of the most influential Germanists in the Third Reich.[84]

Höfler continued to extol the need for *Volkskunde* to be useful throughout the years of the dictatorship. In 1942 in a paper given to the SS in light of German "political contact" with Scandinavia after the invasions of 1940, he attacked "'harmless *Volkskunde*,' that which opines on the 'nature' of the Nordic phases of the moon, happiness or whatever."[85] For him *Volkskunde* needed to concern itself with bigger, more relevant questions such as "what is it that always makes the Nordic race the bearer of political power?"; or in 1944, what "the origins of the Germanic propensity for state-building" were.[86] This legacy of the ancient Germanic tribes also fascinated contemporary German archeologists—from those like Wilhelm Unverzagt who deliberated on how an early Germanic ethnic stratum had taught the Slavs how to build their first fortified dwellings,[87] to the new obsession that prehistorians like Höfler's SS colleague at Kiel, Herbert Jankuhn developed on social formation and hierarchy among the early Germanic tribes at the time.[88] Höfler's postwar deliberations on "cultural morphology," a notion derived from Oswald Spengler's neoconservative classic *The Decline of the West (Der Untergang des Abendlandes)*, continued this project in an unapologetic, although less abjectly Nazified form down to the time of his celebrated Arminius oration in 1959.[89]

The methodological problem with the Much school, however, was recognized by critics such as Schneider:[90]

> Existing interest in the study of the Germanic past reaches its highest point where it touches upon the spiritual life of the early Germans, their conceptions of a higher being, in a word, upon their religion in the widest sense. Naturally it is in this sphere that the danger of distortion, of

overestimation of more recent documents, and of interpolation in place of interpretation is greatest.

In light of Schneider's earlier hailing of the "victory" of 1933, this warning seems quite schizophrenic and underlines an important feature of the new paradigms. On the one hand less overtly political Germanists such as Hermann Schneider hailed the new era in Germanic studies ushered in by the Nazi accession to power.[91] Yet at the same time they were critical of the approach of those who were patently interpreting Germanic antiquity in terms which ultimately reflected a *völkisch* tradition, those who sought to rescue the *Geist* of old Germany in order better to seek a renewal of this *Geist* in their own day. Like other commentators Schneider could recognize that some of his contemporaries had begun to be affected by the Germanomaniacal mood of the times, and many disdained the basely *völkisch*. But Schneider was so heavily steeped in theory that had arisen among Germanophiliacally minded scholars in previous decades, he could not articulate clearly what it was that the new academically trained Germanomaniacs were doing wrong. Worse still, Germanists like Schneider often could not see *völkisch* themes present in their own publications.

Helm's developmental approach to the study of Old Germanic belief had become an important new paradigm in the Old Germanic studies of the Weimar period. In Vienna it was reflected in its most radical form in the continuity theories of the Much school. The Much school, however, was infested with *völkisch* thought to such a degree that the continuities promoted by its members were not only obviously specious, but blatantly *völkisch* continuities to boot, ones which dovetailed all too neatly with contemporary political concerns. The Much school was recognized as the most extreme expression of academic Germanomania at the time by critics such as Schneider. But a *völkisch* influence in the study of Germanic religion and cult had already become ubiquitous in Old Germanic studies by the time. Heusler's manufactured concept of Germanicness was applied to the belief systems of ancient Germany, a process in which as it became more radicalized, by the 1930s had reached the logical extreme: it claimed that the *Geist* of ancient Germany was the most essential representation of Germanness. Academic thought had come to legitimize *völkisch* theory; it was as if Lagarde had joined Herder and the Grimms as a seminal theorist in the understanding of the old Germanic past.

WÖRTER UND SACHEN

The last major intellectual development to have an important effect in Germanist circles in the 1920s and 30s was probably the most complex. This time it came from the heart of the discipline that had provided the humanities with structuralist thought; in fact it emerged just as structuralism was first making substantial inroads upon traditional language studies.

Linguistic structuralism was a development of the Neogrammarian school of the 1870s, a group of (mostly) German linguists who were particularly antipathetic to the thought of Humboldt and his emphasis on the cultural element in language.[92] The Neogrammarians instead stressed the mechanistic nature of language and language change, an idea which reached full bloom under the influence of Ferdinand de Saussure's posthumously published *Course in General Linguistics (Cours de lingustique générale)* from 1916.[93] At first the Neogrammarians (*Junggrammatiker*) were only successful in convincing a collection of (mostly) young scholars who were centered about Jena and Leipzig, and the figure of Saussure's teacher Eduard Sievers. Nevertheless, the Humboldtian tradition of language lived on after the Neogrammarian revolution, albeit in a somewhat changed form.

The Neogrammarians rigidly refrained from speculating on aspects of language that their mechanistic method could not establish. Before their day, however, language had been seen, prevailingly, as organic—a living, growing and sometimes dying entity. The Neogrammarians dismissed this organicist principle; yet the approach to language of Humboldt had survived. In the 1850s Heymann (Haim) Steinthal inaugurated a psychological approach to language that was continued by Wilhelm Wundt in the first part of his influential *Collective Psychology (Völkerpsychologie)* at the close of the century.[94] Where Neogrammarian thought reduced language to its structural essences, Wundt and others continued to view language in terms of culture, mass psychology and nation.

The burgeoning new linguistics inspired by Saussure's *Course* in the 1920s and 30s was not accepted by many scholars in Germany. Nonetheless, the *Wörter und Sachen* or historical semantics approach represented an area where Saussure's ideas would eventually have quite an obvious influence, even though in origin it has more patent connections with the work of the psychological linguists such as Steinthal as well as the tradition of linguistic paleontology founded by Pott and Pictet.

Inaugurated in the first decade of the 1900s by Hugo Schuchardt and Rudolf Meringer, the culture-focused *Wörter und Sachen* approach saw words as the building blocks of language (representing the culture they describe). *Wörter und Sachen* linguistics is often claimed to be a resurrection of the etymological studies of Jacob Grimm, but it reached new heights in the 1930s and 40s and led to the production of several linguistic classics. Jost Trier was a leading member of this school and was particularly well known for his structuralist *Wörter und Sachen* studies.

Schuchardt and Meringer both taught in Austria and developed the *Wörter und Sachen* method in a climate of rejection of the rigidity of their Neogrammarian forebears. Witnessing recent work on dialectology (predominantly of German, French and Italian dialects) they sought to return to linguistic scholarship the cultural aspect that the dry formulae of the grammars of the Neogrammarians lacked. The new area of study focused around terms that described culture (*Kulturwörter*), for example the terminology of kinship or color, and in an approach that is almost anthropological, investigated what these terms could reveal about the collective psychology or semiotic particularities that they described.

Meringer founded a journal to promote the new field of research. Called *Wörter und Sachen* (a coin of Meringer's)[95] it aimed to promote the investigation of Indo-European culture and society through linguistic means. But *Wörter und Sachen* also had a clear political edge; not only was Rudolf Much a foundation member of the editorial board of *Wörter und Sachen*, as Hermann Güntert would write in 1927: "language history is a type of intellectual history as changes in language can only occur upon a change in the intellectual understanding of the linguistic community."[96] Moreover, after succeding Meringer as editorial director of *Wörter und Sachen* (now the "Journal for Indo-European Linguistics, Ethnology and Cultural History") Güntert explained more expansively in 1938:[97]

> ... a language brings together, indeed facilitates in a certain sense, all hu-
> man cultural achievement ... as language facilitates, so in a reverse man-
> ner the culture of a language community always works back on the lan-
> guage and forms it ... What a decline it is from the intellectual sum-hold-
> ing of the conception of language of a Herder, Humboldt or Grimm to
> the insipidity of Paul's *Principles* ... "Phonological laws" operate some-
> where in an empty space, a knitted jumble of thousands and ever more
> thousands of "analogical forms" spanning over the great line of evolu-
> tion of linguistic development. General "driving forces" stand firm in the
> comparison of all that is comparable without reflection upon specific eth-
> nic and temporal-cultural conditions and historical rootedness. A type of
> general language mathematics remains with the illusion and tacit premise
> of a generally valid, universal concept of language ...

Güntert understood that the new general linguistics had its origin in
the works of Neogrammarians like Hermann Paul rather than Saussure. (He singles out Paul's *Principles of Historical Linguistics [Prinzip-
ien der Sprachgeschichte]* here, one of the most important theoretical
tracts of the Neogrammarians.[98]) Güntert evidently also saw a need for
a revival of the original spirit of German linguistic enquiry. He did not
bemoan the practical consequences of the Neogrammarian revolution;
as Antoine Meillet had observed in 1905: "these scholars are only separated by nuances; all agree on fundamental principles, all argue in the
same way."[99] Güntert merely attacked the notion that the abstract laws
of Neogrammarian theory reflected an underlying reality and hence actually explained linguistic phenomena. He had already speculated that
the most distinctive sound laws of the Germanic languages represented
the "result of a particularly energetic colonization activity"[100] and the
Wörter und Sachen movement clearly grew out of the recognition that
Neogrammarian principles could not explain behavior directly attested
in the here-and-now studies of dialectologists.[101] Güntert was rearticu-
lating the argument of Schuchardt and Meringer that the Neogrammarians had gone too far in their abstraction and had neglected semantic and dialectal concerns. His criticism reflected the general mood of
Germanic studies at the time:[102]

> Specifically, Indo-European linguistics investigates the character, fate and
> history of our Aryan inheritance; it labors above all on the developmental

history of the Germanic and German language as a reflection of the growing together and development of the Germanic peoples and of German
ethnicity ... From there the individual studies, original researches and ex-
positions of scholars should ... join themselves together in the sense of the
great national-political tasks of the present day under the common motto:
service to our people.

Although he became an outspoken Nazi, Güntert remained suspicious
of the claims of Kossinna and others of an Aryan homeland in Central
Europe.[103] He also singled out Schirmeisen's paper from Kossinna's
journal *Mannus* as "absurd" and was sceptical of the *Urschrift* theory
of the origin of the runes.[104] A Party member, he was a supporter of
some aspects of radical antiquarianism. Yet his modus operandi was
clear and consistent: he was a sober, empirical searcher for truth in the
service of the *Volk*.

The implications of the *Wörter und Sachen* approach to *völkisch*
Germanists were obvious: it was a German approach to linguistics that
rejected the cosmopolitan general linguistics hailed at the time elsewhere in Europe, and being culture-bound it served to further the work
of both German and Old Germanic studies. *Wörter und Sachen* studies
seemed to return linguistic enquiry to the nationalistic discourse it had
been in the time of the Grimms. It was also a theoretically progressive
discipline, however, and made a lasting contribution to both historical
linguistics as well as linguistic semantics.

This mixture of chauvinism and innovation is especially clear in
the work of the leading *Wörter und Sachen* semantician Trier. Trier's
work revolved around describing *Kulturwörter* within *sprachliche Felder*
(semantic fields).[105] His work on semantic fields was a major breakthrough at the time and launched a new *Wörter und Sachen* wrapped up
in its own structuralist semantic jargon. His studies from the National
Socialist period, however, nearly all focus on practices from antiquity
that he thought to reconstruct from the development of vocabulary. His
investigations of the semantics of the Germanic *Thing* or tribal meeting place were published at a time when Himmler's SS were setting up
Thing-places throughout Germany in the hope the SS could revive the
custom described in the Norse sagas of tribal assemblies in hallowed
Things.[106] Similarly, his 1943 attempt to prove that the German term
Reich was not a loan word from Celtic (as the vocalism clearly shows)

was patently specious and reveals again the chauvinistic nature of his semantic work.[107] Clearly, although many of the theoretical postulates of Trier remain valid for any type of historical semantic study, his focus was decidedly *völkisch*: for Trier his studies of historical semantics were not merely of linguistic or historical interest, they served to demonstrate the continuity of Germanness from antiquity into modern times by means of rescuing heretofore obscure patterns in language that represented a superlative inherited patrimony. His project was just like that of the Much school, but followed a more proper (and theoretically progressive) linguistic method. In fact Trier's investigations of the semantic fields of German community and rulership from the early 1940s were clearly influenced by Höfler and his focus on Germanic political thought and expression. Although not as outspoken, like Güntert, Trier had also answered the *völkisch* call and became a Party member (although not until 1937, after the restrictions on new members that had been imposed in the middle of 1933 were briefly relaxed).[108] But it is in the work of Trier that *Wörter und Sachen* most clearly reveals itself as deeply *völkisch* in its focus: the *raison d'être* of *Wörter und Sachen* studies was to recover the culture, if not the *Volksgeist*, of the ancient Germanic past as it was expressed linguistically. Trier was not alone in his mixture of progress and regression, however: a similar figure to Trier was the even more famous *Wörter und Sachen* linguist Leo Weisgerber who is also hailed today as a leading figure in German structuralism.

A Celticist by training, Weisgerber joined Güntert as an editor at Meringer's *Wörter und Sachen* in 1933 and his contributions dominated the journal in the early 1930s.[109] His *oeuvre* was different to that of Trier and most clearly represents a sophisticated form of what Christopher Hutton has rather unfortunately described as "mother-tongue fascism."[110] Weisgerber achieved fame in the 1950s as the leading neo-Humboldtian in West Germany, a development that makes him appear rather unrepentant in light of the development of "mother tongue" ideology in general. In the 1920s he had become caught up in the mother-tongue (*Muttersprache*) movement within German linguistics, a movement expressed in its most chauvinistic form in a work by Georg Schmidt-Rohr published by Diederichs in 1932 as *Language as the Educator of Peoples (Die Sprache als Bildnerin der Völker*, retitled *Mutter Sprache* in its 1933 edition).[111] A form of mother-tongue ideology can be traced back to the German language societies of the sixteenth century, through Herder, Humboldt and then to the General German Language Association.[112] The Association had become involved in pan-Germanism from the 1880s (and in fact had renamed its journal *Muttersprache* in the 1920s).[113] Mother-tongue ideology had thus readily been caught up by *völkisch* thought—the German language was their weapon as Schmidt-Rohr had put it in 1917.[114] Under Schmidt-Rohr and his contemporaries a whole genre of apparently progressive linguistic theory developed (progressive in that it was inspired in part by the new linguistic paradigm associated with the appearance of Saussure's *Course*), but that in fact represented an overwhelmingly chauvinistic approach to language that championed German and Germanness above all else. Weisgerber, the *Wörter und Sachen* theorist, was one of the leading exponents of this mother-tongue scholarship, focussing on the peculiarities of the development of German terms, for instance, for the senses, color and taste.[115] He claimed he was especially focused on the "intellectual interstice" (*geistliche Zwischenwelt*) between the outward expression of the German language and the speaker's perception. But his approach to language can be summed up by its logical extreme: as Weisgerber opined in 1933, a true bilingual is a sort of cultural cripple—as one cannot be fully at home in two cultures, a bilingual cannot master the cultural core of either language.[116] It is no surprise to see Weisgerber penning books on *völkisch* concerns under the dictatorship such as the origin and meaning of the term *deutsch* and treating language as cultural consciousness.[117] Like Güntert, the mother-tongue linguists rejected a cosmopolitan approach and focused instead on the "wholeness" of language—on the cultural aspects of language, not merely the soulless abstractions beloved by linguistic generalists. But this wholeness was only ever applied to German as foreign languages were not the concern of mother-tongue theorists.[118] It is scarcely surprising then to discover that Weisgerber was employed as a propagandist by the SS during the war.[119] Like the *Wörter und Sachen* movement in general, Weisgerber represents both the continuity of Humboldtian thought in German linguistics and how *völkisch* sentiment could penetrate even to the core of the discipline that gave the humanities the new structuralism.

A series of new ideas had entered the discourse of Old Germanic studies in Wilhelmine and Weimar times. The Kossinna school, echoing the call of *völkisch* enthusiasts such as Penka and Wilser, rejected the consensus view of the world of archeology that civilization in terms of technology and most aspects of material life had diffused from the East into the North and turned this argument on its head. With their reassignment of the Aryan homeland to North-Central Europe, European civilization was now a culture-bringing, indigenous Aryan one, and all sorts of items, practices and indeed ideas once thought to have been Egyptian, Semitic or Greco-Roman in origin might now well be thought to have originated instead in the North. Many philologists and linguists, too, directed their energies towards properly patriotically centered assessments of language and literature, developing new jargon and concepts with which to cloak the main concern of their research: the study of language and culture as a key to an understanding of the time-transcending semiotics, psychology and consciousness of the German *Volk*. Heusler's Germanicness and Nollau's *Germanic Resurgence* are the clearest signs that a *völkisch* project in Germanic philology was already well underway before 1933. In Vienna, even the fundamental principles of linguistic and literary study were surrendered in favor of a nebulous *Volkskunde* where only the concept of the *Volk* mattered: the laws of linguistics and empirical logic could comfortably be violated when the concern was driven by a *völkisch* sentiment. Language, race and religion were the three key themes stressed by the *völkisch* movement according to Uwe Puschner[120]—and each of these concerns was reflected by the new paradigms in old Germanic studies: in archeology, literary philology, *Volkskunde* and linguistics. Even among the structuralist linguists whose concern for evidentiality and method seemed to be stronger, the general cultural focus of their research, their neo-Humboldtian approach, was dominated by *völkisch* concerns. It was much more than poor or misguided scholarship. Historical intuition had come to be accepted in Old Germanic studies cloaked in the mantle of academic respectability and girded by a tradition of nationalist sophistry. Germanic archeology and philologically based studies had developed radical nationalist schools of interpretation in both Germany and in Austria by the late 1920s, ones which were all too ready to serve the *völkisch* resurgence which was to overwhelm German and Austrian democracy in the 1930s and reject the liberal tradition of the Grimms in which the respective Germanistic antiquarian disciplines had been founded.

Notes

1 K. Müllenhoff, *Deutsche Altertumskunde*, 5 vols. (Berlin: Weidmann, 1870–1900).

2 Cf. J.K. Zeuss, *Die Deutschen und die Nachbarstämme* (Munich: Lentner, 1837).

3 G. Kossinna, *Die ältesten hochfränkischen Sprachdenkmäler* (Strasbourg: Trübner, 1881); R. Stampfuss, *Gustaf Kossinna* (Leipzig: Kabitzsch, 1935); H. Grünert, *Gustaf Kossinna* (Rahden i.W.: Leidorf, 2002); I. Wiwjorra, *Der Germanenmythos* (Darmstadt: Wissenschaftliche Buchgesellschaft, 2006).

4 B.F. Hummel, *Bibliothek der deutschen Alterthümer*, 2 vols. (Nuremberg: Grattenauer, 1781–91); J.G.G. Büsching, *Abriß der deutschen Alterthums-Kunde* (Weimar: [s.n.,] 1824); G.F. Klemm, *Handbuch der germanischen Alterthumskunde* (Dresden: Walther, 1836); S.C. Wagener, *Handbuch der vorzüglichtes, in Deutschland entdeckten Alterthümer aus heidnischer Zeit* (Weimar: Voigt, 1842); L. Lindenschmidt, *Die Alterthümer unserer heidnischen Vorzeit*, 5 vols. (Mainz: Von Zabern, 1858–1911).

5 O. Worm, *Museum Wormianum* (Leiden: Elsevier, 1655).

6 O. Klindt-Jensen, *A History of Scandinavian Archaeology*, trans. G.R. Poole (London: Thames & Hudson, 1975); G.E. Daniel, *A Short History of Archaeology* (London: Thames & Hudson, 1981), 55ff.; B. Gräslund, *The Birth of Prehistoric Chronology*, trans. N. Tomkinson and J. Taffinder (Cambridge: Cambridge University Press, 1987).

7 M.L.S. Sørensen, "The Fall of a Nation, the Birth of a Subject," in M. Díaz-Andreu and T. Champion (eds.), *Nationalism and Archaeology in Europe* (London: UCL Press, 1996), 24–47.

8 E.-F. Jomard et al., *Description de l'Egypte*, 20 vols. (Paris: Imprimérie impériale/royale, 1809–22).

9 R. Virchow, comment on Wilser, "Die Herkunft der Germanen," *Correspondenz-Blatt* 16 (1885): 124–25; J.H. Ottaway, "Rudolf Virchow," *Antiquity* 47, (1973): 101–8; C. Andree, *Rudolf Virchow als Prähistoriker* (Cologne: Böhlau, 1976); idem, *Rudolf Virchow* (Munich: Langen Müller, 2002); C. Goschler, *Rudolf Virchow* (Cologne: Böhlau, 2002); cf. A. Zimmermann, *Anthropology and Antihumanism in Imperial Germany* (Chicago: University of Chicago Press, 2001), 112ff.

10 Poliakov, 255.

11 Jones, "The Third Anniversary Discourse," in his *Works*, 34.

12 A.L. Willson, *A Mythical Image* (Durham, N.C.: Duke University Press, 1964).

13 Schlegel, *Ueber die Sprache*; Morpurgo Davies, 59ff.

14 A.F. Pott, *Etymologische Forschungen auf dem Gebiete der indo-germanischen Sprachen*, 4 vols. (Lemgo: Meyer, 1833–36).

15 A. Pictet, *Les Origines indo-européennes ou les Aryas primitifs*, 2 vols. (Paris: Cherbuliez, 1859–63).

16 Whiteside, 94.

17 O.H. Urban, "Much. 1) Matthäus," *Neue deutsche Biographie* XVIII (Berlin: Dunker & Humblot, 1997), 249.

18 M. Much, *Die älteste Besiedlung der Länder des Österreichischen Kaiserstaates durch die Menschen und deren Cultur-Entwicklung* (Vienna: self-pub., 1884); idem, *Die Kupferzeit in Europa und ihr Verhältnis zur Kultur der Indogermanen* (Vienna: K. u. K. Hof- u. Staatsdrückerei, 1886); idem, *Die Heimat der Indogermanen im Lichte der urgeschichtlichen Forschung* (Jena: Costenoble, 1902).

19 R.G. Latham, *The Germania of Tacitus* (London: Taylor, Walton & Marberly, 1851), epilogomena; T. Poesche, *Die Arier* (Jena: Costenoble, 1878).

20 J.J.A. Worsaae, "Den nationale Oldkyndighed i Tyskland," *Annaler for nordisk Oldkyndighed og Historie* 1846, 116–40 [= idem, *Die nationale Alterthumskunde in Deutschland* (Copenhagen: Eibe, 1846)].

21 G. Kossinna, "Über die vorgeschichtliche Ausbreitung der Germanen in Deutschland," *Correspondenz-Blatt* 26 (1895): 109–12; idem, "Die vorgeschichtliche Ausbreitung der Germanen in Deutschland," *Zeitschrift des Vereins für Volkskunde* 6 (1896): 1–14; H. Jankuhn, "Das Germanenproblem in der älteren archäologischen Forschung," in H. Beck (ed.), *Germanenprobleme in heutiger Sicht* (Berlin: De Gruyter, 1986), 298–309.

22 L.S. Klejn, "Kossinna im Abstand von vierzig Jahren," *Jahresschrift für mitteldeutsche Vorgeschichte* 58 (1974): 7–55; G. Smolla, "Das Kossinna-Syndrom," *Fundberichte aus Hessen* 19/20 (1979–80): 1–9; idem, "Gustaf Kossinna nach 50 Jahren," *Acta praehistorica et archaeologica* 16/17 (1984–85): 9–14; idem, review of Schwerin von Krosigk, *Gustaf Kossinna*, *Germania (RGK)* 64 (1986): 682–86; K. Sklenář, *Archaeology in Central Europe*, trans. I. Lewitová (Leicester: Leicester University Press, 1983), 147ff.; U. Veit, "Ethnic Concepts in German Prehistory," in S. Shennan (ed.), *Archaeological Approaches to Cultural Identity* (London: Unwin Hyman, 1989), 35–56.

23 E.g. L. Wilser, *Die Rassengliederung des Menschengeschlechts* (Leipzig: Thüringische Verlag-Anstalt, 1906); idem, *Rassentheorien* (Stuttgart, Strecker & Schröder, 1908); idem, *Rassen und Völker* (Leipzig: Thomas, 1912).

24 L. Wilser, *Herkunft und Urgeschichte der Arier* (Heidelberg: Hornung, 1899), 54.

25 G. Kossinna, review of Wilser, *Die Germanen*, *Archiv für Rassen- und Gesellschaftsbiologie* 1 (1904): 780.

26 G. Kossinna, "Die indogermanische Frage archäologisch beantwortet," *Zeitschrift für Ethnologie* 34 (1902): 161–222.

27 G. Kossinna, *Die deutsche Vorgeschichte* (Würzburg: Kabitsch, 1912).

28 Lagarde, 24.

29 G. Kossinna, *Die deutsche Vorgeschichte*, 7th ed. (Leipzig: Kabitsch, 1936), 4.

30 Ibid., 10–11.

31 S. Reinach, *L'Origin des Aryens* (Paris: Leroux, 1892); idem, "Le mirage oriental," *L'Anthropologie* 4 (1893): 539–78 & 699–732; M. Much, *Die*

Trugspiegelung orientalischer Kultur in den vorgeschichtlichen Zeitaltern Nord-und Mitteleuropas (Jena: Costenoble, 1907); I. Wiwjorra, "'Ex oriente lux' – 'Ex septentrione lux'," in A. Leube (ed.), *Prähistorie und Nationalsozialismus* (Heidelberg: Synchron, 2002), 73–106; idem, *Germanenmythos*, 77ff.

32 Heusler/Ranisch 7.7.35, no. 179 in K. Düwel and H. Beck (eds.), *Andreas Heusler an Wilhelm Ranisch* (Basel: Helbing & Lichtenhahn, 1989), 583.

33 Puschner, *Völkische Bewegung*, 82–88, B. Mees, "*Germanische Sturmflut*," *Studia Neophilologica*, 78 (2006): 184-98. The expression is an allusion to the "Cimmerian darkness" of the eleventh chapter of Homer's *Odyssey*.

34 H. Reinerth, "†Gustav Kossinna," *Nationalsozialistische Monatshefte* 3 (1932): 259–61; idem, "Gustaf Kossinna als Vorkämpfer und Begründer der völkischen Vorgeschichtsforschung," *Germanen-Erbe* 3 (1938): 354–62.

35 S. Sonderegger, "Vorwort," in A. Heusler, *Kleine Schriften* II, ed. S. Sondregger (Berlin: De Gruyter, 1969), v; H. Beck, "Andreas Heusler (1865–1940)," in H. Damico (ed.), *Medieval Scholarship* II (New York: Garland, 1998), 283.

36 A. Heusler, *Die altgermanische Dichtung* (Berlin: Athenäum, 1923); idem, *Deutsche Versgeschichte* (Berlin: De Gruyter, 1925–29).

37 H. Beck, "Andreas Heuslers Begriff des 'Altgermanischen'," in idem (ed.), *Germanenprobleme in heutiger Sicht* (Berlin: De Gruyter, 1986), 396–412.

38 A. Heusler, "Antrittsrede in der Preußischen Akademie der Wissenschaften," *Sitzungsberichte der Preußischen Akademie der Wissenschaften, Phil.-Hist. Klasse* 1908, 712 [= *Kleine Schriften*, ed. H. Reuschel and S. Sonderegger, 2 vols. (Berlin: De Gruyter, 1942–69), II, 14].

39 A. Heusler, *Nibelungensage und Nibelungenlied* (Dortmund: Ruhfus, 1921).

40 A. Heusler, "Die Herrenethik in der isländischen Sage," *Germanentum* (Heidelberg: Winter, 1934), 63–78; K. von See, "Andreas Heusler in seinen Briefen," *ZfdA* 119, 1990, 387–88 [= *Barbar, Germane, Arier*, 271–72].

41 A. Heusler, "Von germanischer und deutscher Art," *Zeitschrift für Deutschkunde* 39 (1925): 753 [= *Germanentum* (Heidelberg: Winter, 1934), 87 = *Kleine Schriften* ed. H. Reuschel and S. Sonderegger, 2 vols. (Berlin: De Gruyter, 1942–69), II, 605].

42 Ibid., 746 [= *Germanentum*, 79 = *Kleine Schriften* II, 598].

43 F. Niedner (ed.), *Thule*, 24 vols. (Jena: Diederichs, 1911–30).

44 Stark, 93–94, 191ff.; G. Hübinger, *Versammlungsort moderner Geister* (Munich: Diederichs, 1996); I. Heidler, *Der Verleger Eugen Diederichs und seine Welt 1896–1930* (Wiesbaden: Harrassowitz, 1998); M.G. Werner, *Moderne in der Provinz* (Göttingen: Wallstein, 2003).

45 Stark, 94; cf. J. Zernack, *Geschichten aus Thule* (Berlin: FU Berlin, 1994).

46 A. Heusler, "Altgermanische Sittenlehre und Lebensweisheit," in H. Nollau (ed.), *Germanische Wiedererstehung* (Heidelberg: Winter, 1926), 156–204 [= *Germanentum* (Heidelberg: Winter, 1934), 7–62].

47 I. Wiwjorra, "Willy Pastor," in M. Meyer (ed.), "*… trans Albium fluvium*" (Rahden i.W.: Leidorf, 2001), 11–24.

48 Heusler, *Germanetum*; H. Taeger, "Germanentum und wir," *Zeitschrift für Deutschkunde* 50 (1936): 409.

49 Mees, "Hitler and *Germanentum*."

50 J. Venedy, *Römerthum, Christenthum und Germanenthum* (Frankfurt a.M.: Meidinger, 1840); H. Gollwitzer, "Zum politischen Germanismus des 19. Jahrhunderts," in J. Fleckenstein et al. (eds.), *Festschrift für Hermann Heimpel*, 3 vols. (Göttingen: Vandenhoeck & Ruprecht, 1971–72), I, 282–356.

51 L. Berg, *Henrik Ibsen und das Germanenthum in der modernen Literatur* (Berlin: Eckstein, 1887).

52 F.A. Beck, *Der Aufgang des germanischen Weltalters* (Bochum: Feldmüller, 1944), 44–45; trans. W.J. McCann, "'Volk und Germanentum,'" in P. Gathercole and D. Lowenthal (eds.), *The Politics of the Past* (London: Unwin Hyman, 1990), 74; L. Poliakov and J. Wulf (eds.), *Das Dritte Reich und seine Denker* (Berlin: Arani, 1959).

53 H. Schneider, *Germanische Heldensage*, 2 vols. (Berlin: De Gruyter, 1928–34); idem, "Die germanische Altertumskunde zwischen 1933 und 1938," *Forschungen und Fortschritte* 15 (1939): 1 [= "The Study of Germanic Antiquity in the Years 1933–1938," *Research and Progress* 5 (1939): 135].

54 Heusler/Ranisch 2.2.1930, no. 156 in Düwel and Beck (eds.), 522.

55 J. Trier, "Germanische Religionsgeschichte," *Zeitschrift für Deutschkunde* 52 (1938): 382–86; cf. W.H. Vogt, "Altgermanishe Religiosität," *Forschungen und Fortschritte* 15 (1939): 246–48.

56 J. de Vries, *Altgermanische Religionsgeschichte*, 2 vols. (Berlin: De Gruyter, 1935–37).

57 G. Neckel, review of J. de Vries, *De germaansche oudheid*, *DLZ* 51 (1931): 1168–71.

58 K. Helm, *Altgermanische Religionsgeschichte*, 2 vols. (Heidelberg: Winter, 1913–53).

59 E. Mogk, "Mythologie," in H. Paul (ed.), *Grundriß der germanischen Philologie*, 2 vols. (Strasbourg: Trübner, 1891–93), I, 982–1138 [= 2nd ed., 1900, III, 230–406].

60 V. Grønbech, *Vor Folkeæt i Oldtiden*, 4 vols. (Copenhagen: Pios, 1909–12) [= *The Culture of the Teutons*, trans. W. Worster, 2 vols. (Oxford: Clarendon, 1932)].

61 A. Göpfert et al., *Bekenntnis der Professoren an den deutschen Universitäten und Hochschulen zu Adolf Hitler und dem nationalsozialistischen Staat* (Dresden: Limpert, 1933), 129ff. The *Vow* of November 1933 (which represented academics from the universities of Göttingen, Hamburg, Leipzig, Marburg and several *Hochschulen*) includes antiquarian Germanists and Indo-Europeanists such as Felix Genzmer, Karl Helm, Eduard Hermann, Alfred Hübner, Hans Kuhn, Otto Lauffer, Walther Mitzka, Robert Petsch, Emil Sieg, Adolf Spamer, Ludwig Wolff and Ferdinand Wrede.

62 O. Lauffer, *Deutsche Sitte* (Leipzig: Quelle & Meyer, 1920); idem, "Die Entwicklungsstufen der germanischen Kultur," in H. Nollau (ed.), *Germanische Wiedererstehung* (Heidelberg: Winter, 1926), 17-155; H. Lixfeld, *Folklore and Fascism*, trans. James R. Dow (Bloomington: Indiana University Press, 1994), 13–15.

63 Schneider, "Die germanische Altertumskunde," 2 [= trans. p. 137].

64 R. Much, *Der Eintritt der Germanen in die Weltgeschichte* (Vienna: Österr. Bundesverlag für Unterricht, Wissenschaft und Kunst, 1925); H. Schmeja, *Der Mythos der Alpengermanen* (Vienna: Gerold, 1968).

65 J. von Uthmann, "Ein garstig Leid?," *Frankfürter Allgemeine Zeitung: Bilder und Zeiten* Nr. 10, 12 Jan. 1980, 2; H. Reichert, "Much, Rudolf," in J. Hoops, *Reallexikon der germanischen Altertumskunde* XX, 2nd ed. (Berlin: De Gruyter, 2002), 274.

66 H. Hirt, "Nochmals die Deutung der germanischen Völkernamen," *PBB* 21 (1896): 127; and cf. R. Much, *Deutsche Stammsitze*, Halle a.S.: Niemeyer, 1892 [= idem, "Die Südmark der Germanen," "Die Germanen am Niederrhein," "Goten und Ingvaeonen," and "Berichtigung und Nachträge," *PBB* 17 (1893): 1–224]; idem, "Die Deutung der germanischen Völkernamen," *PBB* 20 (1895): 1–19; H. Hirt, "Die Deutung der germanischen Völkernamen," *PBB* 18 (1894) 511–19.

67 H. d'Arbois de Jubainville, "Unité primitive des Italo-celtes," *Comptes rendus des séances de l'Académie des inscriptions et belles-lettres* 13, 1885, 316–25 [= *Celtes et Germains* (Paris: Imprimérie Nationale, 1886)]; idem, "Les témoignages linguistique de la civilisation commune aux Celtes et aux Germains pendant le Ve et le IVe siècle avant J.-C.," *Revue archéologique* 17 (1891): 187–213; idem, "Recherches sur la plus ancienne histoire des Teutons," *Revue celtique* 12 (1891): 1–19; G. Kossinna, "Die Sueben im Zusammenhang den ältesten deutschen Völkerbewegungen," *Westdeutsche Zeitschrift für Geschichte und Kunst* 9 (1890): 199–216; idem, "Die Grenzen der Kelten und Germanen in der La Tène Zeit," *Correspondenzblatt* 38 (1907): 57–62; Much, *Deutsche Stammsitze*, 9 [= idem, "Die Südmark," 9]; idem, review of O. Bremer, *Ethnographie der germanischen Stämme*, *DLZ* 23 (1902): 486; idem, "Kelten," in J. Hoops, *Reallexikon der germanischen Altertumskunde* III (Strasbourg: Trübner, 1915–16), 25–27; idem, "Die angebliche Keltenherrschaft in Germanien," *Volk und Rasse* 1 (1926): 100–5; B. Mees, "Linguistics and Nationalism," *Melbourne Historical Journal* 25, 1997, 46ff.

68 R. Much, "Die Germanen bei Theodor Mommsen," *Volk und Rasse* 3 (1928): 101–4.

69 O. Bockhorn, "Der Kampf um die 'Ostmark'," in G. Heß et al. (eds.), *Willfährige Wissenschaft* (Vienna: Verlag für Gesellschaftskritik, 1989), 17 [= J.R. Dow and H. Lixfeld (eds.), *The Nazification of an Academic Discipline* (Bloomington: Indiana University Press, 1994), 135].

70 L. Weiser, *Altgermanische Jünglingsweihen und Männerbünde* (Bühl i. Baden: Konkordia, 1927); cf. C. Neim, "Lily Weiser-Aall (1898–1987)," *Zeitschrift für Volkskunde* 94 (1998): 25–52.

71 Stachura, 45ff.; N. Sombart, "Männerbund und Politische Kultur in Deutschland," in J.H. Knoll and J.H. Schoeps (ed.), *Typisch deutsch, die Jugendbewegung* (Opladen: Leske & Budrich, 1988), 155–76.

72 K. von See, "Politische Männerbunde-Ideologie von der wilhelmischen Zeit bis zum Nationalsozialismus," in G. Völger and K. von Welck (eds.),

Männerbünde, Männerband, 2 vols. (Cologne: City of Cologne, 1990), I, 93–102 [= a revised version in *Barbar, Germane, Arier*, 319–42]; S. von Schnurbein, "Geheime kultische Männerbünde bei den Germanen," in Völger and von Welck (eds.), II, 97–102; O. Bockhorn, "Von Ritualen, Mythen und Lebenskreisen," in W. Jacobeit et al. (eds.), *Völkische Wissenschaft* (Vienna: Böhlau, 1994), 477–88.

73 Tacitus, *Germania* 43; trans. H. Mattingly, 2nd ed. (Harmondsworth: Penguin, 1970), 137.

74 H. Schurtz, *Altersklassen und Männerbünde* (Berlin: Reimer, 1902); J. Reulecke, "Das Jahr 1902 und die Ursprünge der Männerbund-Ideologie," in G. Völger and K. von Welck (eds.), *Männerbünde, Männerband*, 2 vols. (Cologne: City of Cologne, 1990), I, 3–10.

75 R. Wolfram, "Sword Dances and Secret Societies," *Journal of the English Folk Dance and Song Society* 1/1 (1932): 34–41; idem, *Schwerttanz und Männerbund* (Kassel: Baerenreiter, 1936); R. Stumpfl, "Der Ursprung des Fastnachtspiels und die kultischen Männerbünder der Germanen," *Zeitschrift für Deutschkunde* 48 (1934): 286–97; idem, *Kultspiele der Germanen als Usrprung des mittelalterlichen Dramas* (Berlin: Junker & Dünnhaupt, 1936–37).

76 E. Gilch et al., *Volkskunde an der Münchener Universität 1933–1945* (Munich: Münchener Vereinigung für Volkskunde, 1986), 54ff., 82–83.

77 O. Höfler, *Kultische Geheimbünde der Germanen I* (Frankfurt a.M.: Diesterweg, 1934); H. Birkhan, "Vorwort," in O. Höfler, *Kleine Schriften*, ed. H. Birkhan (Hamburg: Buske, 1982), XI.

78 Diesterweg's and the Armanen-Verlag published joint catalogues in the early 1930s: cf. "Kulturpolitik und Erziehung: Neues Schriftum aus dem Armanen-Verlag und dem Verlag Moritz Diesterweg, Frankfurt-M. u. Leipzig," in M.R. Gerstenhauer, *Der völkische Gedanke in Vergangenheit und Zukunft* (Leipzig: Armanen, 1933), after p. 165.

79 Höfler, *Kultische Geheimbünde*, 341.

80 A.H. Price, *The Germanic Warrior Clubs*, 2nd ed. (Tübingen: Niemeyer, 1996).

81 F. von der Leyen, review of Höfler, *Kultische Geheimbunde, AfdA* 54 (1935): 156. Cf., also, H. Hempel, notice of Höfler, *Kultische Geheimbunde, Jahresbericht* 56, NF 14 (1934): 161; F. Ranke, "Das Wilde Heer und die Kultbünde der Germanen," *Niederdeutsche Zeitschrift für Volkskunde und Blätter für niedersächsische Heimatpflege* 18 (1940): 1–33.

82 O. Höfler, "Der germanische Totenkult und Sagen vom Wilden Heer," *Oberdeutsche Zeitschrift für Volkskunde* 10 (1936): 33–49; idem, "Über germanische Verwandlungskulte," *ZdfA* 73 (1936): 109–15; idem "Antwort," *Oberdeutsche Zeitschrift für Volkskunde* 11 (1937): 97–102; F. von der Leyen, "Erwiderung auf Otto Höfler," *Oberdeutsche Zeitschrift für Volkskunde* 11 (1937): 94–97.

83 S. Wikander, *Der arische Männerbund* (Lund: Gleerup, 1938); B.D. Lincoln, *Theorizing Myth* (Chicago: University of Chicago Press, 1999), 126.

84 J. Hirschbiegel, "Die 'germanische Kontinuitätstheorie' Otto Höflers," *Zeitschrift der Gesellschaft für Schleswig-Holsteinische Geschichte* 117 (1992): 181–98.

85 O. Höfler, "Die Entwicklung der geistigen Lage in Skandinavien," lecture given 23 Nov. 1942 to an RSHA conference; BA PA Höfler 240–74.

86 Höfler, "Entwicklung"; idem, "Der Ursprünge der germanischen Staatsbildnerkraft," late 1944, BA R 15/329, 23–66.

87 W. Unverzagt, "Zur Vorgeschichte des ostgermanischen Raumes," in A. Brackmann (ed.), *Deutschland und Polen* (Munich: Oldenbourg, 1933), 6ff. [= *Germany and Poland in their Historical Relations*, trans. S.M. Bouton (Munich: Oldenbourg: 1934), 6ff.]; idem, "Zusammenfassung," in A. Brackmann and W. Unverzagt (eds.), *Zantoch* (Leipzig: Hirtzel, 1936), 131ff.; S. Brather, "Wilhelm Unverzagt und das Bild der Slawen," in H. Steuer (ed.), *Eine hervorragend nationale Wissenschaft* (Berlin: De Gruyter, 2001), 484–87; cf. M. Burleigh, *Germany turns Eastward* (Cambridge: Cambridge University Press, 1988), 58.

88 H. Jankuhn, "Gemeinschaftsformen und Herrschaftsbildung in frühgermanischer Zeit," *Kieler Blätter* (1938): 270–381; idem, "Politische Gemeinschaftsformen in germanischer Zeit," *Offa* 6/7 (1941/42): 1–39; H. Steuer, "Herbert Jankuhn und seine Darstellungen zur Germanen- und Wikingerzeit," in idem (ed.), *Eine hervorragend nationale Wissenschaft* (Berlin: De Gruyter, 2001), 441–45; cf. O. Höfler, "Die politische Leistung der Völkerwanderungszeit," *Kieler Blätter* (1938): 282–97 [= *Kleine Schriften*, ed. H. Birkhan (Hamburg: Buske, 1982), 1–16] and the September 1937 SS conference in Buchenhagen, Kiel on the "History of Germanic Social Forms" (program, BA AE 21/345).

89 O. Spengler, *Der Untergang des Abendlandes* (Munich: Beck, 1923).

90 Schneider, "Die germanische Altertumskunde," 2 [= trans. pp. 139–40].

91 On Schneider, see K. von See and J. Zernack, *Germanistik und Politik in der Zeit des Nationalsozialismus* (Heidelberg: Winter, 2004), 13ff.

92 Morpurgo Davies, 226ff.

93 F. de Saussure, *Cours de linguistique générale*, ed. C. Bally and A. Sechechaye (Lausanne: Payot, 1916).

94 H. Steinthal, *Grammatik, Logik und Psychologie* (Berlin: Dümmler, 1855); idem, *Einleitung in die Psychologie und Sprachwissenschaft* (Berlin: Dümmler, 1871); W.M. Wundt, *Völkerpsychologie. I. Die Sprache*, 2 vols. (Leipzig: Engelmann, 1900); idem, *Sprachgeschichte und Sprachpsychologie* (Leipzig: Engelmann, 1901); Morpurgo Davies, 201ff.

95 R. Meringer, "Wörter und Sachen," *Indogermanische Forschungen* 16 (1904): 101–96; H. Schuchardt, "Sachen und Wörter," *Zeitschrift für romanische Philologie* 29 (1905): 620–22; *Wörter und Sachen* 1–34 (Heidleberg: Winter, 1909–44); D. Heller, *Wörter und Sachen* (Tübingen: Narr, 1998), 13ff.

96 H. Güntert, "Über die Ursache der germanischen Lautverschiebung," *Wörter und Sachen* 10 (1927): 1–2.

97 H. Güntert, "Neue Zeit—neues Ziel," *Wörter und Sachen* 19, NF 1 (1938), 1–11.

98 H. Paul, *Prinzipien der Sprachgeschichte* (Halle a.S.: Niemeyer, 1880).

99 A. Meillet, "Avertissement," in K. Brugmann, *Abrégé de grammaire comparée des langues indo-européennes*, trans. J. Bloch et al. (Paris: Klincksieck, 1905), iv.

100 H. Güntert, "Zum heutigen Stand der Sprachforschung," *Wörter und Sachen* 12 (1929): 390.

101 R.H. Robins, *A Short History of Linguistics*, 3rd ed. (London: Longmann, 1990), 207–8.

102 Güntert, "Neue Zeit," 11.

103 H. Güntert, *Der Urpsrung der Germanen* (Heidelberg: Winter, 1934), 37–38 (with Hitlerite preface). Cf. also idem, *Deutscher Geist* (Bühl i. Baden: Concordia, 1932).

104 H. Güntert, "Über die Ursache," 1; idem, *Ursprung*, 102, 181–82; idem, "Runen, Runenbrauche und Runeninschriften der Germanen," *Oberdeutsche Zeitschrift für Volkskunde* 8 (1934): 51–102.

105 J. Trier, "Sprächliche Felder," *Zeitschrift für deutsche Bildung* 8 (1932): 417–27; idem, "Das sprächliche Feld," *Neue Jahrbücher für Wissenschaft und Jugendbildung* 10 (1934): 428–49; C.M. Hutton, *Linguistics and the Third Reich* (London: Routledge, 1999), 86–105.

106 J. Trier, "First," *NAWG, Phil.-Hist. Klasse* 1940, no. 4, 55–137; idem, "Über das Sprechen in ringförmiger Versammlung," *GGA* 203 (1941): 423–64; idem, "Zaun und Mannring," *PBB* 66 (1942): 232–64; S. Behrenbeck, *Der Kult um die toten Helden* (Vierow bei Greifswald: SH-Verlag, 1996), 242–58.

107 J. Trier, "Zur Vorgeschichte des Wortes Reich," *NAWG, Phil.-Hist. Klasse* 1943, no. 14, 535–82; cf. B. Mees, "Celtic Influence in the Vocabulary of Hierarchy in the Common Germanic Period," *Zeitschrift der Savigny-Stiftung für Rechtsgeschichte, Germanischtische Abteilung* 115 (1998): 376.

108 M. Kater, *The Nazi Party* (Cambridge, Mass.: Harvard University Press, 1983), 73.

109 See esp. L. Weisgerber, "Die Stellung der Sprache im Aufbau der Gesamtkultur," *Wörter und Sachen* 15 (1933): 134–224 & 16 (1934): 97–236.

110 Hutton, 106ff.; cf. Ivo, 152–80.

111 G. Schmidt-Rohr, *Die Sprache als Bildnerin der Völker* (Jena: Diederichs, 1932); idem, *Mutter Sprache* (Jena: Diederichs, 1933); G. Simon, "Wissenschaft und Wende 1933," *Das Argument* 158 (1986): 527–42.

112 C. Ahlzweig, "Die deutsche Nation und ihre Muttersprache," in K. Ehlich (ed.), *Sprache im Faschismus* (Frankfurt a.M.: Suhrkamp, 1989), 35–57.

113 *Zeitschrift des (Allgemeinen) Deutschen Sprachvereins* 1–39 (Brunswick/Berlin: Der Sprachverein, 1886–1924), thereafter *Muttersprache* 40–53 (Berlin: Der Sprachverein, 1925–43); P. von Polenz, "Sprachpurismus und Nationalsozialismus," in E. Lämmert et al., *Germanistik*, 2nd ed.

(Frankfurt a.M.: Suhrkamp, 1967), 116ff.; G. Simon, "Sprachpflege im 'Dritten Reich'," K. Ehlich (ed.), *Sprache im Faschismus* (Frankfurt a.M.: Suhrkamp, 1999), 58–86; Hutton, 285ff.

114 G. Schmidt, *Unsere Muttersprache als Waffe und Werkzeug des deutschen Gedankens* (Jena: Diederichs, 1917).

115 L. Weisgerber, "Das Problem der inneren Sprachform und seine Bedeutung für die deutsche Sprache," *GRM* 14 (1926): 241–56 [= *Zur Grundlegung der ganzheitlichen Sprachauffassung*, ed. H. Gipper (Düsseldorf: Schwann, 1964), 36–66]; idem, "Der Geruchsinn in unserem Sprachen," *Indogermanische Forschungen* 46 (1928): 121–50 [= *Zur Grundlegung*, 99–121].

116 L. Weisgerber, "Zweisprachigkeit," *Schaffen und Schauen* 9 (1933): 5–10 [= *Zur Grundlegung*, 423–30]; Hutton, 122.

117 L. Weisgerber, *Theudisk* (Marburg: Elwert, 1940); idem, *Deutsch als Volksname* (Stuttgart: Kohlhammer, 1953); Hutton, 106–43.

118 C. Knobloch, "Sprachwissenschaft," in F.-R. Hausmann (ed.), *Deutsche Geisteswissenschaften im Nationalsozialismus* (Munich: Oldenbourg, 2002), 305–27.

119 J. Lerchenmüller, "Arbeiten am Bau Europa?," *Ein Germanist und seine Wissenschaft = Erlanger Universitätsreden* 53 (1996), 3. Folge, 62ff.; idem, *"Keltischer Sprengstoff"* (Tübingen: Niemeyer, 1997), 400ff.; Hutton, 134ff.

120 Puschner, *Völkische Bewegung*, 14ff.

CHAPTER 5.

National Socialism and Antiquity

Der Jude kann mit Mythus und Symbol
nichts beginnen
Alfred Rosenberg

Despite the many and varied expressions of *völkisch* thought in the years leading up to 1933, it is usual—given the absolute authority of Hitler and his chief cronies after the Nazi assumption of power—to concentrate on what each held to be *völkisch* and how each responded to the developments of the period.[1] The actual thoughts of Hitler and other senior Nazis on the antiquarian activities of *völkisch* enthusiasts and other antiquarians who came under the influence of *völkisch* thought might not seem so important when one places their researches and claims in the context of "working towards the Führer." Yet Hitler, and especially a number of his lieutenants, had a special fascination for the ancient past and expressed that fascination not just verbally but with financial and institutional aid as well. The merits of the new study of ancient ideographs were also considered by senior Nazi Party members and a fascination with runes and the like penetrated the upper echelons of the Party.

The two major supporters of antiquarian discourse from within the Party were Rosenberg and Himmler. Hitler himself did not bother much with the enthusiasts and scholars of Germanic antiquity—he was more interested in ancient Greek and Roman culture.[2] Rosenberg and Himmler, both of whom considered themselves to be ideologues, however, clearly had other ideas. Both saw Germanic antiquity as important to a true understanding of the *Volk*. Moreover, Germanic antiquity was clearly an area of German culture that was free from Jewish or Christian taint—both Himmler and Rosenberg were not merely anti-Semitic, but also anti-Christian.[3] These two senior Nazis saw that Germanic antiquity was a fundamental reference point for their views on what Rosenberg called the Nazi mystique or mythos that they both thought would replace the Judeo-Christian Weltanschauung. Both

Rosenberg and Himmler judged that a Weltanschauung rooted in the Judeo-Christian tradition was ultimately irreconcilable with the ideal that informed the *völkisch* revolution. As a result, both became involved in organizing the study and promotion of knowledge of Germanic antiquity in the belief that Old Germanic studies would provide the foundation of an emerging Nazi mystique. Both men were actively involved in the support and control of the institutions in which Germanic antiquity was studied. Not all Germanists were affected directly by this Old Germanic duopoly, but ultimately the most influential scholars were those who joined one of the new Nazi research institutions. In fact the Germanists aligned to Rosenberg and Himmler often came to fall into opposing camps, a development which even led to the emergence of conflict over *Sinnbildforschung*.

Hitler, however, was often critical of those who were fascinated by Germanic antiquity. For example his disdain for the Germanomaniacal leanings of groups like the Germanic Orders is indicated in *Mein Kampf* when he dismisses as "wandering scholars" and "*völkisch* Methuselah[s]" those ineffectual old "cowards" who "rave about old Germanic heroism, about dim prehistory, stone axes, spear and shield."[4] Antiquarian trappings like the old Germanic month names and *Fraktur* lettering were removed from the *Völkischer Beobachter* after it was acquired by the Nazis in the early 1920s.[5] The German dictator also had little respect for archeologists who like Kossinna overvalued the modest cultural achievements of the Germanic ancestors; despite his public statements that were fetishized by the archeological community, in 1942 Hitler opined privately: "at a time when our forebears were producing the stone troughs and clay vessels about which our archaologists have made such a to-do, the Greeks were building the Acropolis,"[6] and furthermore: "the Germani ... had reached no higher cultural level than the Maori of today."[7] Hitler had no time for patent Germanomania; the runes looked Greek to him.[8] Nevertheless, his call in *Mein Kampf* for "a Germanic State of the German Nation" is a double reference, both to the medieval Holy Roman Empire of the German Nation, but also the sublime Germanic racial identity first stressed by Tacitus.[9] Hitler even claims several times in *Mein Kampf* that his dictatorial position within the Party was modelled on the precepts of "Germanic democracy"—i.e. the election (for life) of early medieval kings.[10] Notwithstanding his disdain for the Germanomania of *völkisch* antiquity enthusiasts, Hitler evidently understood that the image of the old Germanic past bequeathed by sources such as Tacitus could be of use to National Socialism.

Yet as Reinhard Bollmus points out, Hitler's notion of the relationship of scientific knowledge to ideology was the reverse of that of Rosenberg—Rosenberg saw ideology as the determinant of scientific understanding, whereas Hitler thought that ideology was built up from a scientific base.[11] On the other hand, Himmler, a man whose character was full of paradoxes, evidently never even thought this relationship through. Himmler liked utility, but at the same time harbored a credulousness that seems irreconcilable with considered scholarship. Hitler, Rosenberg and Himmler seem to represent three methodological extremes: Hitler claimed to be a sober man of facts, Rosenberg, like Chamberlain, was an idealist, and Himmler, like List, often proved to be an outright fantasist. Hitler was not interested in the myth-making possibilities of Germanic antiquity, while to Rosenberg and Himmler it was the ideological potential of Old Germanic studies that was the fundamental concern. Hitler derided antiquarian Germanomania, Rosenberg and Himmler encouraged it.

Part of Hitler's disdain for the adventurous researchers of Germanic antiquity is explained by his dislike of Wotanists. In *Mein Kampf* he especially criticizes those "so-called religious reformers" who wanted to return German religiosity to "an old Germanic basis."[12] Schönerer and other leading *völkisch* figures had embraced Wotanism in the past, and so had a number of members of the Party: Hitler's criticism of "*völkisch* Methuselah[s]" appears to represent in part merely a desire to distance the "young movement" from the prewar *völkisch* tradition of List, Schönerer, the Germanic Orders and the Thule Society. Still, some of the more obviously mystical enthusiasts not well connected enough to gain Party protection were persecuted after 1933. Friedrich Bernhard Marby, for example, the main promoter of the *völkisch* rune-yoga or rune-gymnastics that has found converts in the New Age, was interned in concentration camps from 1936–45 as punishment for bringing the Germanic ancestors into disrepute.[13] Similarly, the leading Austrian Ariosophist Jörg Lanz von Liebenfels's Ordo Novi Templi (Order of the New Templars) was one of many occult groups investigated by the Gestapo in the late 1930s.[14] Some Ariosophists had

managed to inveigle their way into the confidence of Himmler, however, and sometimes the work of the researchers of the Ahnenerbe is
confused with the creations of these men. Obscurantism, though, was
generally curtailed within the Party by Hitler. He specifically stated in
1938 that National Socialism was not a cult, presumably in reaction
to the erection of *Thing*-places throughout the country, a development
that had been encouraged by Himmler.[15] The Führer did allow Himmler license to accumulate rune-occultists and seers in his entourage
within the SS and encourage a National Socialist form of *völkisch* paganism. Yet the less credulous among the Party's elite usually took a
more sedate approach to ancient history than did the Reichsführer-SS,
albeit not always as sedate as was Hitler's.

Hitler had little direct role in the development of Old Germanic
studies during the Third Reich. Instead the responsibility for study
of Germanic antiquity under the dictatorship was split between the
Party's other two chief ideologues. Of course by 1933 Rosenberg, the
older and more earnest of the two, had already established a reputation
as a leading *völkisch* thinker in his own right. By the 1940s, Himmler,
on the other hand, had become the second most powerful figure in the
Reich next to Hitler himself. The coincidence of interest between the
two men did not lead to a concerted effort to encourage the field of
Germanic studies, however. It led instead to rivalry; in the end perhaps
a more creative and certainly more radical dynamic than cooperation
usually proved to be within the administratively chaotic and combative
world that was the National Socialist Reich.

Much of the Germanic philology of the 1930s was not specifically coordinated into the camp of one particular ideologue or the other. Not
all academic Germanists were enrolled into organizations established
by Rosenberg or Himmler for the promotion and coordination of the
study of Germanic antiquity. Many Germanists responded to the new
valuing of Old Germanic studies in ways that reflected the new political situation without any deliberate political attempt to encourage or
coerce them.

Instead, in the course of the 1930s there was a cumulative intrusion of ideas that first appeared in academic circles into broader political discourse. This intrusion often took the form of *völkisch* publicists
borrowing claims made by academic Germanists and applying them

in considerations of more immediate political concerns. These authors often worked for Himmler or Rosenberg, but others were employed in organs of the Party independent of the two. The publicists proved to be an audience for the writings of university Germanists and developed their findings in ways more overtly useful to the regime. These writers served to reinforce the importance of Old Germanic studies to the *völkisch* Weltanschauung and encouraged even more Germanists to show their support for the *völkisch* revolution by deliberately casting their research in a politicized guise.

There were many ways in which *völkisch* writers were influenced by ideas from Old Germanic studies in the 1930s. Some were blatant and remain quite transparent today. For example, apart from its importance to understanding the Nazi Weltanschauung, after 1933 *völkisch* writers soon found that the picture of the ancient Germans could serve practical purposes; the glorious Germanic past could be employed as justification for the imperialist aims of the present. Hitler's desire to dominate continental Europe was explained in Nazi periodicals in the late 1930s as merely a fulfillment of Germanic destiny, repeating the prehistoric Aryan and then later Germanic migrations throughout the Continent during late antiquity.[16] The image used in the quest for *Lebensraum* in the East was similarly extended from its origin in medieval colonization and the development of Prussia to embrace the Gothic expansions into Eastern Europe in classical and late antiquity.[17] These claims soon found their way into educational literature prepared by members of the Party, for example in 1937's *Nazi Primer (Handbuch für die Schulungsarbeit in der HJ)*, the official history handbook for the Hitler Youth.[18] The maps used in these publications are often obviously taken directly from the works of antiquarians such as Kossinna. Yet even living Germanists could lend their support to the *völkisch* cause. Moreover, the opportunity to actually apply the findings of antiquarian scholarship would later emerge with the conquests of the Wehrmacht.

The Germanizing of the East after September 1939 required German names for all the conquered cities and districts, and it is clear that the renaming of some Eastern European towns with Gothic names was a reflection of philological interest. In fact this is most clearly reflected in an article surveying Gothic names in the East from the *Proceedings of the Göttingen Academy of Sciences* in 1941, the same year the ancient Gothic empire in Eastern Europe was being explained in the SS's monthly magazine as the historical precedent for the current search for *Lebensraum*.[19] Its author, the Indo-Europeanist Eduard Hermann, begins his survey with the sentiment:

> In the course of this war the small fishing village of *Gdingen* which lies on the western port has again fallen into German hands, and its tongue-twisting name had to be replaced with the more comprehensible *Gotenhafen* [i.e. *Goths-haven*]...

The Polish toponym Gdynia (Gdingen in German) seems to be formed from the Slavic root *gd-* (earlier *gud-*) "Goth." Hermann goes on to seek out other names of putatively Gothic pedigree too, such as Danzig (Gdańsk) and Graudenz (Grudziądz), yet to some extent he misses the point. The labelling of foreign towns with names that referred to archaic polities such as the ancient empire of the Goths had been a part of *völkisch* discourse since the late nineteenth century. Long-forgotten names from medieval times (e.g. Bisanz for Besançon) or even ones newly created from philological theory (such as Gotenhafen for Gdingen) had been apportioned to places that were slated one day to join the Greater German Reich of pan-Germanist fantasy (and Hitlerian reality). This *völkisch* predilection for place-name theorizing led to the promotion of similar discussions on the place-names of Eastern Europe and the cannibalizing of the *Zeitschrift für Ortsnamenforschung (Journal for Toponymic Studies)* by the SS's learned society in 1937.[20] In fact so highly regarded were place-names at the time that a toponymic study by the Leipzig Slavicist Reinhold Trautmann was seized on the presses by the Gestapo in 1939—Trautmann's intention had been to refute the notion that place-names with Slavic origins like Berlin and Leipzig had anything to do with Polish, but Goebbels's intervention resulted in Trautmann's dry linguistic study being the only book of its type actually to be banned under the Nazis.[21] His Berlin contemporary Max Vasmer, although one of the few German scholars to protest the brutal suppression of the Jagiellonian University of Cracow in 1939, nevertheless spent much of the early 1940s seeking out evidence for Germanic place-names in the Balkans.[22] After reading a work which surveyed the Frankish place-names of Northern France, Hitler is even recorded proclaiming in 1942 that "the place-names and so on indicate this is ancient German land that was stolen from us and which we are fully within our rights to reclaim";[23] and it is in this light that similar works from the 1930s by linguists such as Theodor Frings and Ernst Gamillscheg must be seen.[24] As much an amateur project as it was academic, this expansion in place-name theorizing is clearly a reflection of a desire to cement the German identity of places of disputable ethnicity through rendering their names transparently German or Germanic.

A more clearly academic, although equally political expression of philological sophistry was employed to attempt to convince Bretons under German domination that the Germans were the natural allies of Celts, not the (putatively) bastardized and Romanized Gallic oppressors whose Celtic identity was (apparently) a sham. The willingness of German Celticists to be coopted by the Party (most infamously among them Weisgerber) is clearly part of a broader pattern of readiness among German philologists to submit to the realities of the new Reich; and at the same time indicates how useful their new masters thought the philological disciplines could be. Although the notion seems quite ridiculous on first acquaintance, the philological and archeological discovery in the late nineteenth century that much of Germany was originally inhabited by Celtic speakers was somehow thought to render Germany a natural ally of Brittany and Ireland. There had always been a close scholarly connection between Germanophonic Celticists and Irish scholars—many of the earliest records of Irish had turned up in continental monastic collections founded by medieval Irish missionaries. Yet it was the grand delusion of ancient German–Celtic ethnic ties that rang truer with the Nazi authorities and in 1940 philologists were dispatched to Brittany to propagandize the notion that the Germans were the natural allies of a Breton separatist nationalism.[25]

It comes as little surprise, then, to see Germanic studies employed as part of German imperial propaganda in occupied Holland, Belgium, Denmark and Norway during the war. The haphazard responses of academic Germanists, however, were gradually organized into a more deliberate political enterprise. The enrollment of Germanists into Party organizations became the goal of Himmler, Rosenberg and their functionaries. However disjointed it was initially, though, the first wooing of Germanists to the Party and the use of the findings of antiquarian Germanists in Nazi propaganda began even before the Nazis came to power. It was especially prevalent within the so-called brown arm of the Party, the regular Political Organization or PO.

Brown Germanism

Rosenberg's standing as an ideologue was not maintained just through his writings. His commentary on the fraudulent *Protocols of the Elders of Zion* and especially his *Mythos of the Twentieth Century (Mythus des XX. Jahrhunderts)* may have been based on falsehood, Chamberlain and the world of the *demi-lettré*, but they were also outstanding contributions to the growth of what to this day is termed brown literature.[26] It was also not merely a function of his leading position within the early Party propaganda machine as editor of the *Völkischer Beobachter*. Hitler acknowledged him as the Party dogmatist, mainly because he had studied the works of *völkisch* literati such as Lagarde and Chamberlain as well as for his detailed knowledge, first-hand experience and wild theories about Bolshevism. A Baltic German who had studied in Moscow and witnessed the Russian Revolution at first hand, Rosenberg was a well-educated man, an architect, and one with a developed sense of German *Kultur*. In 1928, reaction to the apparent decline of German culture (thought exemplified by the expressionism of the Weimar years) had led to the founding of the Combat League for German Culture (Kampfbund für deutsche Kultur), an organization that quickly drew together a number of similarly minded conservative critics. Rosenberg soon came to move in the world of German-National academia, cultivating papers from leading conservative thinkers for his journalistic interests (which had been expanded by the foundation of the *Nationalsozialistische Monatshefte* in 1930) and mustering support within the upper echelons of the universities for the Nazis.[27] Although it focused primarily on what was seen as degeneracy in the visual and performing arts, academics from other fields were drawn to Rosenberg's organization. In fact, Rosenberg and the Kampfbund soon developed an interest in reforming the universities too. In 1930 this connection between the PO and academia led the Dean of the Philosophy (i.e. Liberal Arts) Faculty of the University of Berlin to call for the intellectual life of the university to be visualized in not only National Socialist, but in *bündisch* terms. That year the Kampfbund's Alfred Baeumler, a leading *völkisch* interpreter of Nietzsche, praised the *bündisch* ideology exemplified by the SA and called for the *Männerbund* model theorized by Rudolf Much's student Weiser to be applied to academia.[28] Upon the

Nazi accession, Rosenberg argued that the Party should take a leading role in reforming German education and regularize *völkisch* ideology into a more dogmatic form. Hitler agreed and in January 1934 gave him a commission to set up an institution to that end. The Führer's Commission for the Supervision of the Entire Intellectual and Ideological Schooling and Education of the NSDAP (Beauftragung des Führers für die Überwachung die gesamte geistige und weltanschauliche Schulung und Erziehung der NSDAP) soon came to be known simply as the Amt Rosenberg, the Rosenberg Office.

The core of the Amt Rosenberg was those academics who had previously belonged to the Kampfbund. Although perhaps most famous for its pronouncements on the paintings of the German Expressionists and the new musical styles and theatrical forms developing at the time, the Kampfbund held that its mission was to reform the whole of German cultural and intellectual life. In the second half of 1932, for example, a study group for prehistory was founded within the Kampfbund. With the creation of the Amt Rosenberg in 1934 it became the Reich Federation for German Prehistory (Reichsbund für deutsche Vorgeschichte). Both were headed by Hans Reinerth, a leading exponent of settlement archeology of Transylvanian (Siebenbürger Saxon) origin. An adjunct lecturer (Privatdozent) at the University of Tübingen when he first joined Rosenberg's association, late in 1933 with help from the Party he was appointed to Kossinna's old chair in prehistory in Berlin. In the figure of Reinerth, Kossinna's approach to prehistory soon became the official archeology of Nazi Germany.[29]

Reinerth is probably best known for his *magnum opus*, the three-volume *Prehistory of the German Tribes (Vorgeschichte der deutschen Stämme)* from 1940.[30] In parts a collaborative effort, this book marks the most successful popularization of German prehistory since the days of Kossinna and Wilser. In short, it is a triumph of *völkisch* prehistory. But its success stands in marked contrast to the fate of Reinerth and the Amt Rosenberg's Reich Federation for German Prehistory.

Despite serving as Hitler's regent while the future dictator served out his term in Landsberg prison, Rosenberg had never been an effective power-player in the Party. He always seemed to be on the losing side of contests with the other senior Nazis. For example, in 1933 the Propaganda Ministry under the control of Goebbels clashed with Rosenberg over who should control the arts, and Robert Ley who led the Kraft durch Freude (Strength through Joy or KdF), although for some time an ally, by late 1934 was also working to undermine Rosenberg's position.[31] Nevertheless, neither of these two rivals of Rosenberg was interested in controlling the direction of Old Germanic studies.

The area of Germanic antiquarian endeavor that attracted most interest from the Amt Rosenberg was archeology. Rosenberg had first developed a fascination for archeology in his youth,[32] but there were also clear ideological reasons to seek to coordinate archeological research. In the figure of Kossinna and his school, Germanic prehistory had already assumed a *völkisch* mantle. It is perhaps not surprising, then, that German archeology developed an intimate relationship with the new regime almost immediately after the National Socialist triumph in January 1933.

In May 1933 at a public lecture at the University of Tübingen, Reinerth set out an agenda for the reform of German archeology.[33] With Kossinna's school and its focus on indigenous prehistory, a divide had been created between East German archeology and the traditional West and South German schools whose main concern was the archeology of Roman Germany and the classical world. The Archeological Institute of the German Reich (Archäologisches Institut des Deutschen Reiches) was led by Theodor Wiegand, held by Reinerth to be a supporter of those whom Kossinna had dismissively dubbed the "Romelings," and in the form of the Roman Germany Commission (Römisch–Germanische Kommission, RGK) of the Institute, the West and South German archeologists had an umbrella organization that Reinerth saw as an institutional barrier to continuing on Kossinna's struggle against the archeology of *ex Oriente lux*. Reinerth denounced the RGK in his Tübingen speech and was later rebuked by his own university for the intemperate and personalizing manner of his attack. Reinerth wanted a new archeology in Nazi Germany, one that admitted the centralism of race and ethnic identity, that eschewed the internationalism represented by the RGK, and focused instead on matters such as Aryan origins, *völkisch* continuity and the Germanic proprietorship over Eastern Europe.[34]

It was perhaps predictable, then, that when the Reich Institute for German Prehistory was first established in 1934, West and South German archeologists refused to be drawn into it. Wiegand had managed to get Hitler to stop it being instituted as an official organ of the Party and many of his contemporaries ignored Reinerth's attempts to build up a coordinating Party umbrella for all German prehistorical organizations: curatorial, academic and even at the level of the popular antiquarian societies. The *Gleichschaltung* that had been applied to most of the other professional and labor organizations was only partially successful in German archeological circles. Reinerth did succeed in enrolling the Kossinna-founded Society for German Prehistory (Gesellschaft für deutsche Vorgeschichte) and the East German members of the Federation of German Historical and Antiquarian Societies (Gesamtverein der deutschen Geschichts- und Altertumsvereine) split from the parent umbrella organization in order to join his Reich Federation. The Amt Rosenberg also sponsored several large conferences (or rather rallies) on German prehistory or what Rosenberg called the "Old Testament of the German people."[35] Yet despite his active campaigning against the RGK and its half-Jewish leader Gerhard Bersu, the personal animosity many prehistorians felt for Reinerth served to institutionalize the split that Kossinna had inaugurated in German archeological circles in the form of the settlement school-dominated Reich Institute for German Prehistory.[36]

In terms of Germanic studies of a philological nature, however, the prize recruit of the Amt Rosenberg was Bernhard Kummer, a young Nordicist at Leipzig and later Berlin and Jena. Heusler had become less and less enthused by National Socialism after 1933. For a younger generation of scholars, however, the new regime afforded new possibilities. With *Rassen*-Günther and his stress on the Nordic, antiquity had taken on a larger significance in racialist thinking, and for some *völkisch* thought had become Nordic thought. Many of the Nordicists of the time had quickly become enamoured of the racialist imperative, and the blurring between the Nordic type and Old Norse studies was to lead to the development of a new radicalism in Norse philological circles.

Nevertheless, Kummer began his studies as a more traditional, philologically focused scholar. He was a student of Eugen Mogk and had graduated with a dissertation on "Midgards Decline" ("Midgards Untergang"). Midgard is the Old Norse description for the world of men and reviewers of his work were aware of the obvious connection between Kummer's vision and that painted by Oswald Spengler in his 1923 neoconservative classic *The Decline of the West*.[37] Kummer's dis-

sertation went through several published editions and in the spirit of
Grønbech's *Culture of the Teutons* is a recreation of what a superlative
expression of the Old Germanic *Geist* old Nordic society was (and what
a tragedy it was that it had been destroyed by the Christian missionaries too). It is so steeped in fantasy and overvaluation of the positive
aspects of Nordic religion and culture, however, that it is of little use
today as a serious work. A similarly culturally pessimistic approach is
to be found in the works of Heusler, but the Swiss master had no time
for the young upstart, deriding Kummer in his letters as the "Beküm-
merer" (the worrier).[38] He seemed to know how to play the political
game, however, and there were fears in the academic community that
Kummer's prestige in Party circles would lead to his gaining a senior
chair. Kummer had joined the Nazi Party and SA in 1928, and although he let his membership lapse upon winning a government stipend the next year, had already been noted by that time as a supporter
of the right kind of scholarship in Rosenberg's Kampfbund. By 1936
he had even won a position at the University of Jena where he gave lectures on the new version of Nordic studies he was developing.[39] Yet he
fell afoul of the SS in 1937 when he publicly ridiculed the editor of the
SS's main antiquarian journal and his critique of Kummer's interpretation of Nordic paganism.[40] Kummer's mistake, apparently, had been
to ignore the contention of Otto Höfler that the Old Norse themes and
expressions of violence and destruction which Kummer had attributed
to the decline of pagan Nordic society, were in fact to be celebrated as
essential (and eternal) features of the Germanic *Volksgeist*. Kummer's
criticism of his SS counterparts subsequently saw him forced to resign
as editor of his own journal, *Nordische Stimmen (Nordic Voices)*, to offer
a public and grovelling retraction, and his influence declined dramati-
cally thereafter.[41]

Kummer had been a regular contributor to *völkisch* antiquarian
journals since at least the late 1920s and was editor for much of the
30s not just of *Nordische Stimmen*, but also of its monograph series,
*Reden und Aufsätze zur nordischen Gedanke (Speeches and Essays on the
Nordic Ideal)*.[42] He sought to explain the Viking past terms of *völkisch*
ideology and influenced the popular image of Viking culture through
publications financed by the Amt Rosenberg as well as other *völkisch*
sources. His influence can clearly be seen in *Germanic Storm Tide (Ger-*

manische Sturmflut), a collection of Viking tales from 1943 written as an introduction to Nordic antiquity for school children.[43] It also seems to have provoked other young Nordicists such as Hans Kuhn who similarly began to promote themselves at the time by producing essays for a *völkisch* audience.[44] With Kummer, for a time the Amt Rosenberg was the Party organization with the most influence over the teaching and research of Old Norse studies in the Third Reich.

Apart from the Amt Rosenberg, the Party developed other historical institutes within the PO over the years. Walter Frank, a modern historian who had been aligned to Hitlerite circles since the early 20s, was rewarded with his own Reich Institute for the History of the New Germany (Reichsinstitut für die Geschichte des neuen Deutschlands) in 1935. But in the mid-1930s the Amt Rosenberg, headed as it was by the Party's leading ideologue, was clearly the most influential and important. Frank's Institute was mainly patronized by Rudolf Hess, the leader of the PO and the Führer's nominated successor. Höfler became involved with Frank's Institute at the time and took part in a number of historical conferences patronized by Frank, including at least one of the infamous Researches into the Jewish Question (*Forschungen zur Judenfrage*) conferences.[45] He also gained backing from the Reich Institute for a translation of Grønbech's now seminal *Culture of the Teutons*.[46] Yet Frank's organization was more closely wedded to the history profession proper, not to the broader historical studies of archeology, philology and *Volkskunde*.

Unlike with Frank's organization, in archeology the Amt Rosenberg once again shared an area of abiding interest with another arm of the Party. This time, however, the main duty of this partner was not a cultural–political one, but a grimmer responsibility altogether. In archeology, Rosenberg's interests intersected with those of Himmler, the state police chief and leader of Hitler's bodyguard. As the regime came more and more to rely upon arbitrary force and with the emasculation of the SA after the Night of the Long Knives in 1934, the SS began to assume ever more power within the National Socialist state. In a mirror to the power shift within Nazi Germany at large, the SS's own historical-cultural division soon threatened to eclipse both Frank's Reich Institute and the Amt Rosenberg as the principal center for historical studies in the Third Reich.

BLACK GERMANISM

Himmler held history to be a central concern and one that could serve great national purposes. Reflecting on the restoration of the tomb of the medieval German Emperor Henry I at Quedlingberg cathedral he announced in 1936:[47]

> A people lives happily in the present and the future so long as it recognizes its past and the greatness of its ancestors. For centuries we Germans have forgotten not only our thousands of years old, ancient past, but also the great ancestors and leader figures of the last ten centuries.

In a survey of the role of the SS from 1937, Himmler explained his interest in archeology in terms of propaganda:[48]

> The Race and Resettlement Office [RuSHA] is, for all practical purposes, the scientific agency in charge of matters relating to excavations, and prehistoric things—with which we are very much involved. We are also actively participating in excavations, such as those in East Prussia ... The enemy on the other side of the border is forever contending that this land in the east is Slavic and therefore rightly belongs to them. Consequently they are engaged in excavations on the other side of the German border, in the East, but are only digging in the Slavic strata. But when they come across a Germanic layer they simply fill in the cavity and state: there is only Slavic material here ... Our task, scientifically and ideologically viewed, must be to investigate these things, not to falsify ... These things interest us because they are of greatest importance in the ideological and political battle ... We want to make it clear to our men, and to the German people, that we do not have a past of only roughly 1,000 years, that we were not a barbaric people that had no culture of its own, but had to acquire it from others. We want to make our people proud again of our history. We want to make it clear that Germany is more eternal than Rome, which is only 2,000 years old!

In a sense these words are a victory speech for a struggle between the Amt Rosenberg and Himmler that had begun in 1934. Himmler's description of Rome as only 2,000 years old and his rejection of the notion that the ancient Germans were barbarians clearly show the influence of *völkisch* archeology on the thinking of the Reichsführer-SS. His comments about Slavic strata are also mirrored in polemics by some Nazi archeologists and seem to have their ultimate origin in the vociferous reaction of Kossinna and his pupils to the works of the Polish archeologist (and former student of Kossinna's) Józef Kostrzewski.[49] Yet apart from sharing a crass Slavophobia, it is not clear that Himmler actually understood the approach of the Kossinna school as such, as a rejection of *ex Oriente lux* and an overvaluing of the cultural achievements of the ancient Germans are also to be found in the works of *völkisch* popularizers.

Himmler's introduction to Germanic antiquity was in the works of popularizers and novelists such as Felix Dahn.[50] He also favored the approach of the *völkisch* antiquarian fringe and not always one that valued the trappings of scholarship as much as had even Wilser. Unlike in the Amt Rosenberg, the focus of the researchers in the SS usually merely mirrored Himmler's own personal interests. The Reichsführer-SS even hired an obscurantist to work in the RuSHA to help the SS with historical matters. Such a step might seem to be at odds with the eventual enrollment of serious academics within the SS. But the SS approach to antiquity was always rather Janus-like, much as was its leader. Rosenberg saw his mission to capture academics in terms of education policy and an ideological competence built up from study. Himmler's approach, however, was instinctive and dilettantish, and in terms of antiquarian study, one derived directly from the *völkisch* tradition, at least as much Listian as it was academic in origin. The institutionalization of the antiquarian activities of the SS within the Ahnenerbe, then, was well suited in terms of symbolism when Herman Wirth, the academic-obscurantist founder of *Sinnbildforschung*, was made its first president in July 1935.

Yet already in 1933 a number of academic archeologists had been attracted into the SS. Archeologists such as Alexander Langsdorff, Julius Andrée and Herbert Jankuhn established *ad hoc* connections with the SS that usually involved the help of Himmler's men in fieldwork. The results of archeological fieldwork have always seemed to attract more interest among the general public than its more philological counterpart and the National Socialists certainly put effort into ensuring that the results of Nazi archeology were readily accessible in the form of regular SS archeological exhibitions.[51]

Langsdorff seems to have been the seminal figure in the institu-
tionalizing of the SS involvement in archeology. A war hero, "Sandro"
Langsdorff was a longstanding Nazi—he had been present at the failed
Nazi beer-hall putsch in 1923 and had joined the SS in 1933. Oddly
enough, though, his fame as an archeologist was due to his work with
his Jewish doctoral supervisor, Paul Jacobsthal, at the University of
Marburg. After joining the Berlin Prehistorical Museum (Museum für
Vor- und Frühgeschichte), Langsdorff won Himmler's support for a
dig outside Cologne in 1935 and soon found himself acting as a Nazi
foreign-affairs specialist as well as an SS propagandist.[52] The involvement of the SS in fieldwork would inevitably lead to friction between
the initially *ad hoc* SS responses to requests from men like Langsdorff
and Jankuhn, however, and the plans of Reinerth and his Reich Federation. The official establishment of the Reich Federation for German Prehistory had finally been agreed to by Hitler in mid-1936. But,
somewhat perversely, after Wiegand's death at the end of 1936 (and
the dismissal and flight to England of the RGK's Bersu), the savior of
West German archeology turned out to be the SS. Himmler's archeologists were unable to apply the same sort of pressure as had been
used on Kummer. So they at first worked instead to undermine the
legitimacy of Reinerth's organization through influence with the Education Ministry (Reichs erziehungsministerium) and the German Research Council (Deutsche Forschungs gemeinschaft, DFG). It was
not until 1938 that SS archeological fieldwork was brought under the
control of one body, but Reinerth's standing was rapidly undermined
nonetheless. In the mid-1930s Baeumler, now the head of the universities section of the Amt Rosenberg, had mooted the creation a Hohe
Schule, a Nazi School of Advanced Studies or Party university. Yet
by the 1940s when plans for the Hohe Schule were made official by a
decree of Hitler, it was Jankuhn, since 1939 in charge of SS fieldwork,
who was slated by Rosenberg's people to fill the post of professor of
Nazi archeology.[53]

West German archeology became an SS protectorate. Langsdorff
and others produced regular fieldwork reports for the SS's antiquarian journals.[54] In fact Himmler had come to the tomb of Henry I at
Quedlingberg after an SS-sponsored excavation had led to its restoration. There were SS-sponsored archeological sites all over the country
and although the Amt Rosenberg might have had some control over

curatorial and theoretical studies, the SS was literally at the cutting edge. Jankuhn, later to become one of the foremost archeologists of the FRG, received considerable financial backing from the SS for his excavations and then publication of the findings from the Viking Age settlement at Haithabu (Hedeby), in Schleswig-Holstein and occupied Denmark in 1938–40. SS-Sturmbannführer Jankuhn even led a special group (SS-Sonderkommando) in occupied Russia from 1941–44 whose remit was to safeguard any Germanic antiquities that might fall into their hands. During the war, Jankuhn acted as Himmler's archeological Girl Friday, travelling all over the Nazi empire, chasing up curatorial details for his master and supervising digs in Northern France as well as occupied Scandinavia and the Ukraine.[55] Langsdorff also became involved in imperial German archeology and antiquities looting, his last publication being a 1945 guide to the protected ancient monuments in the part of Italy that was (more-or-less) still under German control.[56] Despite Rosenberg's status as Party expert on eastern matters and his eventual installment as minister responsible for the occupied eastern territories, the Amt Rosenberg only participated in a limited manner in the pillaging of archeological collections in the occupied East. Instead it was SS archeologists such as Langsdorff, Jankuhn and (in Poland) Peter Paulsen[57] who led the cultural looting that represents the nadir of professional German archeology.

None of the numerous archeological digs of the Ahnenerbe investigated Romano-German sites and Himmler made quite clear that the purpose of SS archeology was unabashedly nationalistic. As Jankuhn had reported to his Ahnenerbe masters from the Ukraine in May, 1941:[58]

> … we have already discovered important graves from the region about Kiev which shed new light on the question of the southeastern relations of the Vikings … But given the circumstances it seems to me that the possibility of making more important archeological contributions to the study of the Gothic realm from Southern Russia is at hand. Besides, the region is also of the greatest importance for the Indo-Europeanizing of the South East during the Stone Age.

SS archeology was Germanic (and even Indo-Germanic) through and through, and in the tradition of Kossinna, had no time for other prehistories.

The general support of archeology in the Third Reich is represented most obviously by the eight new chairs in German archeology and two research institutes for prehistory (in Bonn and Cologne),
along with a number of new prehistorical museums that were established after 1933.[59] To symbolize the victory of the approach of the
Kossinna school, the museum for Romano-German antiquities in
Mainz was even rechristened as a center for the pre- and protohistory
of Germany (Zentral Museum für Deutsche Vor- und Frühgeschichte). The RGK had become increasingly Germanophile since the 1920s.
Yet the struggle between the Reinerth-led eastern archeology and the
SS-aligned professors raised in the better-established western tradition
maintained the fundamental split between the settlement school and
the "Romelings." There were denunciations of their elders by ambitious young western archeologists.[60] But as the SS remained focused
on the assembling of antiquities rather than their analysis, the National
Socialist coordination of German archeology remained fragmented. It
was certainly not controlled in terms of ideology. Jankuhn could even
criticize Kossinna in his publications, but still argue like a Kossinnist in
cause and effect.[61] In this atmosphere, in 1940 the former Kossinnist,
Ernst Wahle, launched an attack on the settlement school in an address
to the Heidelberg Academy of Sciences.[62] Wahle's attack would lead to
the intellectual dissolution of Kossinna's settlement theory well before
the German military disaster at Stalingrad marked the beginning of the
end for Hitler's Germany.

Somewhat in the manner of Rosenberg's *Nationalsozialistische
Monatshefte* and the journals run by Reinerth and Kummer, the SS
developed a range of publication interests, from the journalistic *Das
Schwarze Korps* (*The Black Corps*) to the more serious *SS-Leithefte* (*SS
Lead-issues*).[63] From the mid-30s, the SS also began to take control of
other journals, much as it later would incorporate research groups not
otherwise closely aligned to another organ of the Party. SS scholarship
was a mixture of irrationality, propagandizing and cannibalizing—in this
sense very much in line with the character of the Reichsführer-SS—and
thus proved to be a much more dynamic instrument for the Nazification of antiquarian discourse than any other expression of the Party.

Moreover, as Himmler understood it, Nazi antiquarian study was
also hampered by the inaccessibility of many of the sources. In a plan

for "The Reconstruction and Tapping of the Germanic Inheritance" from 1937 (and a mooted 50-volume edition of the sources essential to the study of Germanic antiquity), Himmler's office set out clear instructions that the first requirement was the "collection and editing of all as yet unheard of scattered sources," whether philological or archeological.[64] Höfler's name was mooted in connection with the plan although it was the historian Karl A. Eckhardt who received money to set up a German Law Institute (Deutschrechtliche Institut) at the University of Bonn in the hope of fulfilling at least part of this task. Yet the project was never realized or even planned out properly in SS circles. A plan to produce an encyclopedia of Germanic antiquity along the lines of the classical studies encyclopedia of August Friedrich Pauly similarly never developed beyond the planning stage.[65] A Nazi equivalent of the *Monumenta Germaniae historica* had even been founded in the form of a Reich Institute for Older German Historical Studies (Reichsinstitut für ältere deutsche Geschichtskunde). It was instituted instead by the Education Ministry, however, and remained outside the control of the SS. Even still, the Nazi *Monumenta* never progressed much further than the planning phase.[66]

Although Himmler aimed ultimately to capture all antiquarian scholarship within the SS, Rosenberg had Hitler's backing when it came to Nazi education policy. The SS-Ahnenerbe was established amid a series of battles among the various National Socialist institutions that had responsibility for areas which touched upon antiquarian studies. While Rosenberg's Kampfbund represented the first such body, its institutional successor in terms of Nazi schooling policy was often at the losing end of the institutional power struggles that typified government in the Third Reich. Academics who ended up on the wrong side of one of these battles could be marginalized within academia, especially if they had not yet been able to find themselves a tenured position. Others recognized this state of affairs, however, as one that they could exploit. A connection with the right Nazi institution could win one all sorts of aid that perhaps would otherwise be unavailable. Nevertheless, the pressure to conform to the ideological premises of leading Party officials was limited. The example of German archeology shows that it was not always mandatory for a scholar to toe any particular ideological line. Senior Party officials did not always share the need for scholarship to conform to ideological niceties if they were not directly interested in the theoretical developments of the discipline so concerned. Although the totalitarian environment required certain cosmetic changes, some form of ideological resistance was certainly possible as Wahle so clearly showed in his public attack on Kossinna's methodological excesses at Heidelberg in 1940. An approach such as that of the Kossinna school may have been favored by Party ideologues, but it did not require the experts' abject intellectual submission. There were still places to resist and indeed to hide.

NOTES

1 F.-L. Kroll, *Utopie als Ideologie* (Paderborn: Schöningh, 1998).

2 Kroll, 72ff.; Mees, "Hitler and *Germanentum*," 264ff.

3 J. Ackermann, *Heinrich Himmler als Ideologe* (Göttingen: Musterschmidt, 1970), 32ff.; Cecil, 82ff.

4 Hitler, *Mein Kampf*, 395–96 [= trans. Mannheim, 326–27]; cf. Puschner, *Völkische Bewegung*, 10; Mees, "Hitler and *Germanentum*," 265–66.

5 Newton, p. 195, n. 45.

6 Hitler, 7.7.1942, in H. Picker, *Hitlers Tischgespräche im Führer Hauptquartier*, 3rd ed. (Stuttgart: Seewald, 1976), 426 [= trans. in W. Maser, *Hitler*, trans. P. & B. Ross (London: Allen Lane, 1973), 138–39].

7 Hitler, 4.2.1942, in Picker, 101 [= trans. in Maser, 139].

8 Hartmann, 195.

9 Mees, "Hitler and *Germanentum*," 265.

10 Hitler, *Mein Kampf*, 95, 99, 100, and a further in Mannheim's translation (from the 1st ed.), p. 312, which was purged from later editions; see Mees, "Hitler and *Germanentum*," 265.

11 R. Bollmus, "Alfred Rosenberg," in R. Smelser and R. Zitelmann (eds.), *The Nazi Elite*, trans. M. Fischer (London: MacMillan, 1993), 187; cf. Zitelmann, 331ff.

12 Hitler, *Mein Kampf*, 399 [= trans. Mannheim, 328].

13 F.B. Marby, *Runenschrift, Runenwort, Runengymnastik* (Stuttgart: Marby-Verlag, 1931); idem, *Marby-Runen-Gymnastik* (Stuttgart: Marby-Verlag, 1932); idem, *Runen raunen richtig Rat!* (Stuttgart: Marby-Verlag, 1934); idem, *Rassische Gymnastik als Aufrassungsweg* (Stuttgart: Marby-Verlag, 1935); Goodrick-Clarke, 160–61; B. Wedemeyer-Kolwe, "Runengymnastik," in S. von Schnurbein and J.H. Ulbricht (eds.), *Völkische Religion und Krisen der Moderne* (Würzburg: Königshausern & Neumann, 2001), 367–85; idem, *"Der neue Mensch"* (Würzburg: Königshausern & Neumann, 2004), 174–88.

14 W. Daim, *Der Mann, der Hitler die Ideen gab*, 3rd ed. (Vienna: Ueberreuter, 1994), 181–82 and 188–90; E. Hieronimus, *Lanz von Liebenfels* (Toppenstedt: Uwe Berg-Verlag, 1991), 18.

15 R. Glunk, "Erfolg und Mißerfolg der nationalsozialistischen Sprachlenkung," *Zeitschrift für deutsche Sprache* 26 (1970): 90–91; cf. C. Berning, "Die
Sprache des Nationalsozialismus," *Zeitschrift für deutsche Wortforschung* 18
(1962): 166–67; Zitelmann, 331ff.

16 W. Wache, "Die Neuordnung Europas durch die Germanen," *SS-Leitheft*
3/3 (1937): 10–15.

17 B. Pätzke, "Die deutsche Wiederbesiedlung des Ostens," *SS-Leitheft* 3/8
(1937): 55–56; Smith, *Politics and the Sciences of Culture*, 219ff.

18 F. Brennecke (ed.), *Handbuch für die Schulungsarbeit in der HJ* (Munich:
Eher, 1937), ch. 8 [= *The Nazi Primer*, trans. H.L. Childs (New York:
Harper & Bros, 1938)]; cf. A. Wolf, *Higher Education in Nazi Germany*
(London: Methuen, 1944), 79–80.

19 E. Hermann, "Sind der Name der Gudden und die Ortsnamen Danzig, Gdingen und Graudenz gotischen Ursprungs?," *NAWG, Phil.-Hist.
Klasse* 1941, no. 8; anon., "Und wieder reiten die Goten ...," *SS-Leitheft*
7/9 (1941): 1–2. Cf., similarly, Hermann, "Was hat die indogermanische
Sprachwissenschaft dem Nationalsozialismus zu bieten?," *GGA* 199
(1937): 49–59.

20 *Zeitschrift für Ortsnamenforschung* 1–13/1 (Munich: Oldenbourg, 1925–37);
thereafter *Zeitschrift für Namenforschung* 31/2–20/1 (Berlin–Dahlem: Ahnenerbe, 1937–44); B. Mees, "Germanising the East through Place-names
and Pots," in S. Atzert and A. G. Bonnell (eds.), *Europe's Pasts and Present*
(Unley: Australian Humanities Press, 2004), 195–211.

21 R. Trautmann, *Die wendische Ortsnamen Ostholsteins, Lübecks, Lauenburgs
und Mecklenburgs* (Neumünster: Wachholtz, 1939 [1950]); Burleigh, 107–
11; Mees, "Germanising the East," 203.

22 M. Vasmer, "Beiträge zur slavischen Altertumskunde, 7," *Zeitschrift für slavische Philologie* 18 (1942/43): 55–59; idem, "Zur Ortsnamen in der Balkanländer," *Zeitschrift für slavische Philologie* 18 (1942/43): 384–87; idem,
"Balkangermanisches," *Arkiv för nordisk filologi* 44 (1944): 87–92; Burleigh,
227–28; cf. M.-L. Bott, "'Deutsche Slavistik' in Berlin?" in R. vom Bruch
and C. Jahr (eds.), *Die Berliner Universität in der NS-Zeit*, 2 vols. (Stuttgart:
Steiner, 2005), II, 287ff.

23 F. Petri, *Germanisches Volkserbe in Wallonien und Nordfrankreich* (Bonn:
Röhrscheid, 1937); Hitler 5.5.42 in Picker (ed.), 263; cf. W. Oberkrome,
Volksgeschichte (Göttingen: Vandenhoeck & Ruprecht, 1993), 208ff.; H.
Derks, *Deutsche Westforschung* (Leipzig: AVA, 2001); idem, "German *West-
forschung*," in I. Harr and M. Fahlbusch (eds.), *German Scholars and Ethnic
Cleansing* (New York: Berghahn, 2004), 175–99.

24 T. Frings, *Germania Romana* (Halle: Niemeyer, 1932); E. Gamillscheg,
Romania Germanica, 3 vols. (Berlin: De Gruyter, 1934–36); idem, *Germanische Siedlung in Belgien und Nordfrankreich* (Berlin: De Gruyter, 1939).

25 Lerchenmueller, *Keltische Sprengstoff*, 400ff.; Hutton, 126ff.

26 A. Rosenberg, *Die Protokolle der Weisen von Zion und die jüdische Weltpolitik*
(Munich: Boepple, 1923); idem, *Der Mythus des XX. Jahrhunderts* (Munich: Hoheneichen, 1930); R. Bollmus, *Das Amt Rosenberg und seiner Gegner* (Stuttgart: Deutsche Verlags-Anstalt, 1970), 17–26.

27 *Nationalsozialistische Monatshefte* 1–15 (Berlin: Eher, 1930–44).
28 A. Baeumler, "Das akademische Männerhaus" (1930), in *Männerbund und Wissenschaft* (Berlin: Junker & Dünnhaupt, 1934), 30–44; idem, *Nietzsche als Philosoph und Politiker* (Leipzig: Reclam, 1931); Taureck, 101–2; R. Mehring, "Tradition und Revolution in der Berliner Universiätsphilosophie," in R. vom Bruch and C. Jahr (eds.), *Die Berliner Universität in der NS-Zeit*, 2 vols. (Stuttgart: Steiner, 2005), II, 206ff.; K.-P. Horn, "Erziehungswissenschaft an der Berliner Friedrich-Wilhelms-Universität in der Zeit des Nationalsozialismus" in Vom Bruch and Jahr (eds.), II, 220ff.
29 H. Reinerth, "Die deutsche Vorgeschichte im Dritten Reich," *Nationalsozialistische Monatshefte* 3 (1932): 256–59; Bollmus, *Amt Rosenberg*, 38.
30 H. Reinerth, *Vorgeschichte der deutschen Stamme*, 3 vols. (Leipzig: Bibliographisches Institut, [1940]).
31 Bollmus, *Amt Rosenberg*, 61ff.
32 Cecil, 11.
33 Bollmus, *Amt Rosenberg*, 154–55.
34 Ibid., 33ff., 156ff.
35 A. Rosenberg, "Germaniche Lebenswerte im Weltanschaungskampf," *Germanen-Erbe* 1 (1936): 198; A. Leube, "Die Ur- und Frühgeschichte an der Friedrich-Wilhelms-Universitäts zu Berlin," in R. vom Bruch and C. Jahr (eds.), *Die Berliner Universität in der NS-Zeit*, 2 vols. (Stuttgart: Steiner, 2005), II, 149ff.
36 Stampfuß, 34; Bollmus, *Amt Rosenberg*, 161ff.
37 B. Kummer, *Midgards Untergang* (Leipzig: Pfeiffer, 1927); L.M. Hollander, review of Kummer, *Journal of English and Germanic Philology* 33 (1934): 255; H. Engster, *Germanisten und Germanen* (Frankfurt a.M.: Lang, 1986), 76; K. von See, "Das 'Nordische' in der deutschen Wissenschaft des 20. Jahrhunderts," *Jahrbuch für interationale Germanistik* 15/2 (1983): 27ff. [= *Barbar, Germane, Arier*, 242ff.].
38 Heusler/Ranisch 8.12.35, no. 183 in Düwel and Beck (eds.), 594.
39 W. Schumann, "Die Universität Jena in der Zeit des deutschen Fachismus," in M. Steinmetz (ed.), *Geschichte der Universität Jena 1548/58–1958* (Jena: Fischer, 1958), 639, 644.
40 Hugin und Munin [i.e. J.O. Plaßmann], "Zur Erkenntnis deutschen Wesens," *Germanien* 9 (1937): 161–68; B. Kummer, "Germanenkunde," *Nordische Stimmen* 7 (1937): 190–91.
41 *Nordische Stimmen* 1–11 (Breslau: Hain, then Erfurt: Verlag Sigrune, 1931–1941); B. Kummer, "Erklärung," *Nordische Stimmen* 8 (1938): 128 [= *Germanien* 10 (1938): 144]; M.H. Kater, *Das "Ahnenerbe" der SS 1935–1945* (Stuttgart: Deutsche Verlags-Anstalt, 1974), 125.
42 B. Kummer (ed.), *Reden und Aufsätze zur nordischen Gedanke* 1–48 (Leipzig: Klein, 1933–39).
43 K.H. Ball, *Germanische Sturmflut* (Karlsbad: Kraft, 1943); Mees, "Germaniche Sturmflut."
44 E.g. H. Kuhn, "Verhütung minderwertigen Nachwuchses im alten Island," *Die Sonne* 12 (1935): 166–68; idem, "Isländisches Bauerntum," *Die Sonne* 12 (1935): 203–7.

45 O. Höfler, "Das germanische Kontinuatätsproblem," *Historische Zeitschrift* 157 (1938): 1–26 [= monograph, Hamburg: Hanseatische Verlagsanstalt, 1938]; idem, "Friedrich Gundolf und das Judentum in der Literaturwissenschaft," *Forschungen zur Judenfrage* 4 (1940): 106–25; H. Heiber, *Walter Frank und sein Reichsinstitut für Geschichte des neuen Deutschlands* (Stuttgart: Deutsche Verlags-Anstalt, 1966), 458, 551–53, 615, 708ff. The subject of the address was Goebbels's teacher Friedrich Gundolf.

46 W. Grønbech, *Kultur und Religion der Germanen*, ed. O. Höfler, trans. E. Hoffmeyer, 2 vols. (Hamburg: Hanseatische Verlagsanstalt, 1937–39).

47 H. Himmler, "Zum Geleit," *Germanien* 8 (1936): 193.

48 H. Himmler, Document 1992(A)-PS, from "National Political Studies for the Armed Forces," January 1937, in International Military Tribunal, *Trial of the Major War Criminals* XXIX (Nuremberg: The Tribunal, 1948), 225–26 [= (partial) trans. D. Kunz, *Inside Hitler's Germany*, ed. B. Sax and D. Kuntz (Lexington, Mass.: Heath, 1992), 376].

49 J. Kostrzewski, *Wielkopolska w czasach przedhistorycznych* (Poznan: Niemierkiewicz, 1914); G. Kossinna, *Die deutsche Ostmark* (Kattowitz: Böhm, 1919); Klejn, 29ff.; McCann, 84–85; Mees, "Germanising the East," 199ff.

50 Ackermann, 35.

51 Kater, *Ahnenerbe*, 80ff.

52 Sandro (A. Langsdorff), *Fluchtnächte in Frankreich* (Stuttgart: Deutsche Verlags-Anstalt, 1920); P. Jacobsthal and A. Langsdorff, *Die Bronzeschabelkannen* (Berlin-Wilmersdorf: Keller, 1929); A. Langsdorf, "Auf den Spuren unserer Ahnen," *Das Schwarze Korps* 10 July 1935, 8 & 24 July 1935, 11; Bollmus, *Amt Rosenberg*, 168; Kater, *Ahnenerbe*, 20–24, 80; W.L. Coombs, *The Voice of the SS* (New York: Lang, 1986), 45, 303, 327, 329.

53 Poliakov and Wulf (eds.), 129ff.; Bollmus, *Amt Rosenberg*, 180ff.

54 A. Langsdorff and H. Schleif, "Die Ausgrabungen der Schutzstaffeln," *Germanien* 8 (1936): 391–99 & 10 (1938): 6–11; H. Schleif, "Die SS-Ausgrabung am 'Kriemhildenstuhl' bei Bad Dürkheim," *Germanien* (10): 1938, 289–96 & 11 (1939): 340–46; idem, "Die SS-Ausgrabung Karnburg," *Germanien* 12 (1940): 63–70; idem, "SS-Ausgrabung Urstätt im Warthegau," *Germanien* 14 (1942): 431–36.

55 H. Jankuhn, "Die SS-Grabung von Haithabu 1939," *Nachrichtenblatt für deutsche Vorzeit* 16 (1940): 103–4; Kater, *Ahnenerbe*, 147–58; McCann, 81–83; C. Hufen, "Gotenforschung und Denkmalpflege," in W. Eichwede and U. Hartung (eds.), *"Betr.: Sicherstellung"* (Bremen: Tremmen, 1998), 75–96; A. Heuß, *Kunst- und Kulturgutraub* (Heidelberg: Winter, 2000), 210ff.; Steuer, art. cit.; H. Pringle, *The Master Plan* (New York: Hyperion, 2006), 211ff.

56 A. Langsdorff, *Verzeichnis und Karte der durch den bevollmächtigten General der deutschen Wehrmacht in Italien geschützten Baudenkmäler* ([s.l., 1945]); Bollmus, *Amt Rosenberg*, 167ff.; L. Klinkhammer, "Die Abteilung 'Kunstschutz' der deutschen Militärverwaltung in Italien 1943–1945," *Quellen und Forschungen aus italienischen Archiven und Bibliotheken* 72 (1992): 483–549.

57 A. Mezynski, *Kommando Paulsen*, trans. A. Hetzer (Cologne: Dittrich, 2000); J. Jacobs, "Peter Paulsen," in A. Leube (ed.), *Prähistorie und Nationalsozialismus* (Heidelberg: Synchron, 2002), 451–60; Pringle, 193ff.

58 H. Jankuhn/W. Sievers 27.5.41, BA PA Jankuhn, cit. in Hufen, 77.

59 B. Arnold, "The Past as Propaganda," *Antiquity* 64 (1990): 464–78.

60 Bollmus, *Amt Rosenberg*, 191.

61 Steuer, 435–45.

62 E. Wahle, "Zur ethnischen Deutung frühgeschichtlicher Kulturprovinzen," *Sitzungsberichte der Heidelberger Akadamie der Wissenschaften, Phil.-Hist. Klasse* 1940/41, no. 2; Klejn, 36ff.; D. Hakelberg, "Deutsche Vorgeschichte als Geschichtswissenschaft," in H. Steuer (ed.), *Eine hervorragend nationale Wissenschaft* (Berlin: De Gruyter, 2001), 199–310.

63 *Das Schwarze Korps* 1–11 (Berlin: Eher, 1935–45); *SS-Leitheft* 1–10/10 (Berlin: Müller & Son, 1935–44); Coombs, passim; M. Zech, *Das Schwarze Korps* (Tübingen: Niemeyer, 2002).

64 "Die Erschließung des germanischen Erbes" (1937), reprinted in Ackermann, 253–55.

65 G. Simon, *Die hochfliegenden Pläne eines "nichtamtlichen Kulturministers"* (Tübingen: GIFT, 1998).

66 Heiber, *Walter Frank*, 862; Bollmus, *Amt Rosenberg*, 183; Ackermann, 42, n. 15; Kater, *Ahnenerbe*, 132.

CHAPTER 6.

Intellectual Prehistory

In pietra od in candido foglio,
che nulla ha dentro, et ervi a ch'io voglio!
Michelangelo

In July 1935, amid some fanfare, the Ahnenerbe was formally instituted within the Race and Resettlement Office of the SS. Its chief researcher was also proclaimed its first president. He was Herman Wirth,
a Dutchman by birth who by that time had achieved renown as the
founder of a new discipline within Germanic historical and philological
discourse. The background of this man and his fate are central to the
understanding of the state and reputation of ideographic studies at the
time they were to reenter the mainstream of German learning. Yet if
Wirth had come to be so strongly identified with ideographic studies,
his later fall from favor did not equally mean the end of *Sinnbildforschung*. On the contrary, the new field of study grew and grew, staking out
a place within both *völkisch* and academic discourse that it was not to
surrender until 1945.

HERMAN WIRTH

The same year as Diesterweg's publishers brought out Höfler's *Secret
Cultic Leagues*, they also published a German translation of the seminal
1927 study of the leading Swedish archeologist Oscar Almgren.[1] His
Rock Carvings and Cultic Practice (Hällristningar och kultbruch), which in
this German translation was entitled *Nordic Petroglyphs as Religious Documents (Nordische Felsbilder als religiöse Urkunden)*, seemed to represent
an opening up of a new view of the earliest history or indeed prehistory
of Germanic religion. Almgren interpreted the rock carvings as records
of sun worship among the early Germanic tribes, a notion favored in
nineteenth-century comparative mythology and which had also been a
tenet of swastika studies since Ludvig Müller's day. It is in this climate,

where the political Germanism of journals such as of *Die Sonne* and the academic mainstream met, that the ideographic studies of Wirth first appeared. One Swedish critic of the day called him "a Germanic cultural prophet,"[2] a contemporary Austrian reviewer described his theories as a kind of radical nationalist gospel,[3] and though it is tempting to dismiss Wirth as a "type of Däniken" (i.e. Erich von Däniken of *Chariots of the Gods* fame)[4] or an "ideologue between the Ahnenerbe and Atlantis,"[5] he clearly was one of several figures investigating the religious aspect of prehistory at the time, and his contribution and its reception in the academic community can only be fairly viewed in the light of the findings of Almgren and others, many of whom were respected and senior scholars.

Born in Utrecht, Holland in 1885, Herman Felix Wirth was the son of a Bavarian academic, a Germanist, and his Dutch wife of West Frisian extraction. Rather short (164 cm or 5' 5½"), the blue-eyed, blond-haired and quite handsome Wirth was usually described by those who knew him as genial, affable and even charismatic. In keeping with his father's example, Wirth had begun an academic career with a position as an adjunct or junior lecturer at the University of Berlin where he gave courses in Dutch philology from 1910. The topic of his doctoral dissertation *On the Decline of the Dutch Folk Song (Der Untergang des niederländischen Volksliedes)* reflected his brief career as a composer of some note, though; after studying under the musicologist Hugo Riemann in Leipzig and the folklorist John Meier at Basel, his dissertation was submitted to the University of Basel in 1910 as a work of folkloric study and was published in Holland in 1911.[6] Specializing at first as a musicologist rather than a philologist or folklorist, Wirth produced three more works on the subject of the Dutch musical tradition, in 1912 and 1920 in Dutch and in 1916 in German. Moreover, as well as planning more publications, he had also founded an orchestral group in 1909 dedicated to performing early Dutch works and continued to produce original music of his own.[7] Yet with the outbreak of World War I, Wirth volunteered for service in the German army; still a Dutch citizen, his role was first restricted only to military transport. He soon found himself near the front, however, serving as a press liaison (censor) for the German 4th Army at Ghent—one of his works on Dutch music and a pamphlet for a "Religious Concert" was published there at the time of the German-sponsored Flemification of the university.[8]

Furthermore, in the winter of 1914–15 he had also become involved with the "Young Flemings" (Jonge Vlaanderen), one of the German-sponsored Flemish groups fighting against (Francophone) Walloon domination in the name of a Greater Netherlands.

Despite his taking out German citizenship in 1915, while on leave recovering from a spate of typhoid fever he was released from service in the middle of 1916 apparently on suspicion he was getting too close to the Flemish groups, although not before reaching officer's rank and earning himself an Iron Cross (2nd class).[9] In the same month in which he was released from the army, though, he married a German woman, Margarette Schmitt (the daughter of the painter E. Vital Schmitt). Moreover, he had also found time to have an edition of old German war songs published by Diederichs's publishing house and produced two German-language works on Flemish culture and language respectively that had appeared by 1916, no doubt due to the success of a Dutch language guide for Germans he had produced three years earlier.[10] He further went on to found the German–Flemish Society (Deutsch–Flämisch Gesellschaft) in Berlin in March 1917, expressing his "Greater Germanic" pan-Germanism in print in the Society's journal *Vlamenland (Fleming-Land)* that year.[11] In December 1916 the Emperor had granted the honorary title professor to all foreigners with teaching posts in Germany who had elected to become German citizens, making him Professor Wirth, but without granting him the right to hold an actual professorship. Yet at the end of the war, Wirth fled Belgium where he had found himself a position at the Brussels Conservatory (although it is not clear whether he was a lecturer there or, as the Belgian Education Ministry records were claimed to show by one of his detractors in 1935, merely an assistant librarian).[12] He did not flee for the new German republic of the Socialists, however, but for Holland instead where he sought work as a high school teacher. By 1919 he had settled in the town of Baarn, less than 20 km northeast of Utrecht.

It is evident that Wirth had already become influenced by *völkisch* thought by the time he left Holland for the last time. A play from his student days has survived (one which he was proud enough to rework and translate into German in 1933) that stresses Nietzschean themes such as rebirth of the spirit.[13] A letter from 1919 has also survived that he wrote to his former colleague Kossinna where he speaks of his aim to found a *Landesgruppe* (rural group) in which he would continue "their" mission to revive the Germanic spirit, this time on Dutch soil.[14] This project culminated later that year with the formation of an organization akin to one of the German Youth Movement groups called the "Rural League of Germanic Migratory Birds" (Landsbond der Dietsche Trekvogels[15]—its description *Dietsch* is a native and decidedly political equivalent of *Germaansch* 'Germanic').[16] He was soon exposed as a former German collaborator, however, and his organization collapsed in 1922. Nevertheless, it was in 1921 while the Landsbond was still active that Wirth seems first to have begun the studies that would lead to his later success. His time in Baarn had not proved as fulfilling as he had hoped, however—he later blamed his failures in Holland on Germanophobia and Jewish interests. Instead he put plans in motion to return to Germany, first sending his wife and children to Marburg in 1922. Wirth later claimed he saw that a truly Netherlandic *Geist* had been surrendered and that the Germanic values lost in Holland were better preserved in Germany. Therefore, a year after his return to Germany in 1924, he decided to throw in his lot with the movement for renewal of Germanic values on German soil. In August 1925 Wirth became a member of the Nazi Party.[17]

Although he kept up his membership for only one year, by this time Wirth's philological interests had become dominated by a *völkisch* approach. He probably left the Party in 1926 fearing his membership might affect his reputation; after the Nazi accession to power Wirth explained that he had come to see his mission in pedagogy not agitation at the time—he felt he could spread his message among the Marxist-influenced masses better by remaining outside the Party, a decision for which he claimed he had Hitler's support.[18] At any rate, from 1924 he had begun to cultivate a circle of disciples of new ideas he was developing in his philological researches and he soon began to receive financial aid from a range of wealthy benefactors. These ideas, presented at first mostly through lectures, were clearly dominated by a religious or philosophical outlook rather than merely historical concerns—a gnosis of a recognizably *völkisch* type. His attempts to rekindle a Germanic consciousness in the Low Countries had been stymied in the aftermath of the German loss in the Great War. Yet after a gap in their association of some years, Diederichs agreed to publish his "Researches on the History of the Religion, Symbolism and Script of the Nordic-Atlantic

Race," which after some delay appeared as *The Emergence of Mankind (Der Aufgang der Menschheit)* in July 1928.[19]

Even before the publication of this work, some of Wirth's ideas had begun to become established in a concrete form. It is clear he had been in contact with Diederichs since at least 1925 and Wirth contributed an essay on Atlantis in a publication celebrating the 30th anniversary of the founding of Diederichs's publishing house in 1926.[20] Moreover, in 1927 plans were first made for the erection of an Atlantis House (Haus Atlantis) in Bremen under the initiative of Wirth's principal benefactor, the coffee magnate Ludwig Roselius. The Atlantis House would serve as a museum and center for the promulgation of Wirth's teachings. It was built from 1930–31 in Bremen's Böttcherstraße and though destroyed by allied bombing in October 1944, it was rebuilt in 1954, and restored and given a new facade in 1963–65. Although its postwar restoration is principally due to its striking expressionist architecture and ornament, in the 1930s it served as a meeting place for Wirth's devotees.[21]

It was also in 1928 upon return to Berlin that he founded the Herman Wirth Society (Herman-Wirth-Gesellschaft), an organization for his followers in which they could discuss his bold new ideas on Germanic antiquity and the Germanic spirit. Yet despite his growing reputation, like many who held doctorates at the time Wirth could not break into German academia, even to reclaim the appointment he had lost with the war. Nevertheless, the Herman Wirth Society was patronized by a number of Nazis and leading members of Berlin society. A foretaste of his future importance in a Hitlerian Reich appeared in 1932 when Walter Granzow, the Nazi premier (Ministerpräsident) of Mecklenburg, realized his plans with the establishment of a Research Institute for Intellectual Prehistory (Forschungsinstitut für Geistesurgeschichte) in Bad Doberan, some 20 km west of Rostock.

Wirth's 1928 work proved a sensation upon publication. Its importance can be gauged by the number of his contemporaries within academia and the public at large who saw fit to comment on it. Literally hundreds of reviews and reactions to it appeared over the next few years. In 1929 Diederichs published a selection of them, both critical and supportive (though clearly with the emphasis on the latter).[22] The interest in Wirth's theories among the public also led a number of prehistorians and Germanists under the leadership of Fritz Wiegers (himself a member of the SA) to respond to Wirth's theories in 1932 in a collection published as *Herman Wirth and German Scholarship (Herman Wirth und die deutsche Wissenschaft)*. Wirth replied in a brief monograph issued by his eponymous society in which he dismissed the scholars' assessments.[23] Yet in 1931 he had published a work that proclaimed his political affiliation in no uncertain terms: the title of his *What is German? (Was heißt deutsch?)* of that year is a reference to the 1924 survey *What is* Völkisch? *(Was heißt völkisch?)* of Max Wundt, a professor of philosophy at Jena.[24] In fact Wirth's 1931 work is mainly a commentary on the meaning of the swastika in the context of Germanic antiquity and was clearly meant as an endorsement of the Nazis. The following year an article signed by Wirth appeared in the *Völkischer Beobachter* explicitly declaring his support for the Hitler movement. Wirth had found his way back to the Nazi Party and less than a year after rejoining in May 1933 was granted his old membership number from 1925–26 again.[25]

It is usually averred today that his studies were nonsense and certainly some of his publications such as his *What is German?* seem quite inane if encountered outside the context of the "intellectual prehistory" expounded in his *Emergence of Mankind*. Wirth's stress on a Nordic-Atlantic race, which he saw as having once inhabited not just Northern Europe, but also North America, even brings the *Atlantica* fantasy of Rudbeck to mind. But a number of Ariosophists had proposed a similar connection between the Nordic-Aryan race and Plato's Atlantis,[26] and by Wirth's time a whole body of "Atlantid" literature had arisen in Germany—most of it mystical and racialist, but usually of a more considered nature than might be assumed from what the picture of Atlantis brings to mind today.[27] Nevertheless, given the emphasis of Wirth on the symbols which also formed the core of some of List's better-known works and indeed his forming an eponymous society just as had List, Wirth could well be accused of descending purely into Ariosophic fantasy.

On the other hand, at the same time as Wirth launched his petroglyph studies, a similar focus on rock carvings had emerged in Scandinavian scholarship. Almgren's 1927 study *Rock Carvings and Cultic Practice* lists over 100 publications on petroglyphs which appeared between 1911 and 1927, and Wirth clearly used a number of these sources in his researches. Moreover, all investigators of the rock carvings agreed that they were religious in intent and contained several religious symbols that recurred over and over again. Wirth's main divergence from the approach of the Scandinavian expert was to link the ideographs from the rock carvings with the swastika and the runes, a relationship which had first been suggested by Swedish antiquarians in the previous centuries and had been taken up by a number of German authors after Liljegren's work had been translated into German in 1848. The theory that the runes had developed from these ideographs of the Bronze Age also appeared in the well-known works of Kossinna and Wilser. Wirth thus seemed to have some basis for his theories in a tradition of scholarship. His emphasis on the timeless, spiritual aspect of these symbols is clear evidence for the influence of mysticism in his thought. Yet there the confluence between Ariosophy and Wirth's theories ends. Although Wirth's Society seems an echo of List's own eponymous group, Wirth did not, for example, employ List's pseudo-runes that often appeared in the works of amateurs and mystics. Nor did he indulge in the construction of secret genealogies of pagan Armanists, Templars, Masons, Rosicrucians and Illuminati, or attempt to rediscover the swastika in bread and cake or medieval German heraldry. Wirth clearly was also aware of the distinctions between the various traditions of runic use of which List appeared oblivious and clearly had a much more empirical approach to matters such as etymology. Plainly any mysticism in Wirth's works is his own and not based on that of List. Of course, many of those who shared his *völkisch* politics recognized the same spiritualism in Wirth as they had encountered in the Germanic Orders and the Thule Society, whose doctrines in part went back to List's books. But these political clubs had had little if any lasting influence on academic Germanic studies—the opposite was more the case. Although Wiegers and his colleagues treated Wirth's theories as foolishness, it is not too surprising to discover that other academics proved less dismissive. In 1932 Gustav Neckel, Heusler's successor as Professor of Old Germanic Philology at the University of Berlin gave a speech to the Herman Wirth Society and later that year a group of Neckel's academic colleagues held a discussion of Wirth's theories under the leadership of Alfred Baeumler, a leading member of Rosenberg's Kampfbund. The papers were published as *What Does Herman Wirth Mean for Scholarship? (Was bedeutet Herman Wirth für die Wissenschaft?)* in the same year as had Wiegers's group.[28] Although many dismissed the more outlandish aspects of Wirth's theories, most contributors praised the scope, pioneering nature and moreover the clearly patriotic spirit of his work. Despite all the signs of obscurantism evident in his scholarship, Wirth had regained an academic audience; by the end of 1932 he had been redeemed. His work was so controversial and so stimulating that he was accepted back into the discourse of Germanic studies. And in 1933 with the coming to power of his beloved National Socialists, he was appointed to a professorship with the *venia legendi* at the University of Berlin.

INTELLECTUAL PREHISTORY

In the introduction to his *Emergence of Mankind*, Wirth makes clear that this work was only meant to serve as a foundation for what would follow in his as then still to be named sequel. Yet the 1928 work was already one of considerable physical size as well as conceptual depth. Its 632 folio-sized pages (along with a booklet of 12 more tables) provide a detailed sketch of his intellectual prehistory, carefully divided into six sections: an introduction, three sections on the characteristics, homeland and migrations of the Nordic race, and the two sections which comprise the bulk of the work (433 pages), an explanation of his prehistoric calendrical system and an outline of the evolution of the language and writing of the Nordic race by means of an analysis of petroglyphs and like symbols.

The mention of the advanced civilization of lost Atlantis in connection with his theories is probably the aspect that most gives his work the appearance of pseudoscience in the manner of a Von Däniken. Wirth traced the origins of the Nordic race to the Arctic continent that the respected geologist Alfred Wegener had argued probably existed in primordial times as part of his theory of plate tectonics: i.e. a land bridge that would once have existed that linked Europe to Greenland and North America.[29] This was Wirth's explanation not only for the clustering of petroglyphs and megaliths about the Atlantic coast of Europe, but also for the many parallels he noted between the symbolic and indeed spiritual beliefs of the American Indians, the Eskimos and the peoples of Northern Europe (including, of course, the use of swastikas). The notion of an Arctic home of the White Race[30] fits into a German tradition going back not only to the ravings of racial fantasists such as Willy Pastor, but more specifically that which Georg Bieden-kapp had derived from the studies of an Indian-nationalist commentary on the Vedas from 1903.[31] In fact, an Anglophonic writer, Ignatius Donnelly, had come to a similar conclusion in 1882, in his theory linking Atlantis, the Aryans and the origin of the alphabet to the evidence of Mayan pictograms.[32] A number of other German *völkisch* authors had developed this Arctic homeland into a well-established tradition, one that had even made its way into a speech of Hitler's and one of Rosenberg's published works.[33] Wirth added his ideas on racial mixture and the establishment of the major blood groups to this picture, giving his work a feeling of mythopoeic completeness. Yet this was not the aspect of his book that attracted the most praise from his academic supporters.

The symbolism of Atlantis does seem in part to have been intended by Wirth as a continuance of a tradition stemming from Rudbeck, the seventeenth-century Gothicist. Wilser had praised Rudbeck, who had connected Jordanes' tradition that Scandinavia was the *vagina gentorum* (womb of nations) with Plato's Atlantis, as a precursor of Kossinna's *ex Septentrione lux*.[34] Rudbeck, of course, was ultimately the origin of all the Atlantid thinking of the time and Atlantid thought, which stressed the origin of Aryan culture in an advanced society independent from and superior to that of the ancient Near East, was clearly another form of rejection of the cultural theory of *ex Oriente lux*. Apart from the Atlantid fantasy, Wirth also specifically employs the imagery of the rejection of the *ex Oriente* on a number of occasions. He even tied it more explicitly to a political agenda late in 1933:[35]

> But the foreign spell—the "*ex Oriente*" that lies upon *Volk* and countryside, state and society, upon spiritual-intellectual as well as economic life—it is broken forever. That is Hitler's doing!

Wirth's Nordic-Arctic Atlantic homeland represented the ultimate unblemished *völkisch* fantasy, a Germanic Eden, racially, culturally and spiritually free from foreign pollution. He even describes it as a verdant, unspoiled paradise, reasoning like other supporters of the Atlantid vision that the wandering of the North Pole over the millennia would at one stage have meant that this homeland enjoyed a much milder climate. The old Norse tradition of *fimbulvetr* (the 1,000 year winter) and several other legendary long winters in Persian, Indian and American Indian belief he assumed were remembrances from the time of a great climactic change that eventually forced the ancestors of the Aryans out of their Arctic home.[36] Yet it was not his Atlantid vision that fascinated and concerned his contemporaries the most: it clearly only served as a backdrop to his theoretical *tour de force*.

The thread connecting Wirth's *Emergence* and later works together was his theory of how petroglyphs and similar ideographs on prehistorical manufactures had derived and developed until historic times. He recounts that this theory dawned on him while visiting Saxon Frisia shortly after the Great War where he saw familial folk symbols on the gables of local farms.[37] As a folklorist, although previously mostly interested in musical tradition, he began to speculate on how such symbols developed—what they meant in a cultural or anthropological sense. Considering other symbols found throughout northern and western Europe, even including those appearing in the French cave murals of the paleolithic, Wirth came to hold that all of these graphic expressions were linked in their purpose and ultimately even their origin. These symbols, which he saw as "spiritual-intellectual" (*geistig-seelisch*) expressions of the Nordic-Atlantic race, could, he believed, be traced back ultimately to the representation of cosmic periods which he theorized would have been of especial significance to a hyperborean people: the day, the year, the seasons. The greatest and presumably earliest of these symbols he connected with a monotheism of the "God of the Year" (*Jahr Gottes*) or "Paternal God" (*Gott-Vater*) which over time had also come to develop cults of the "Son of God" (*Gottessohn*) and "Great Mother" or "Mother Earth" (*Allmutter, Mutter Erde*). The latter of course also implied a level of prehistorical matriarchy, or rather as several nineteenth-century works had stressed, matrilinearity. The symbols, he decided, were in origin a set of religious logograms representing the fundamental references of the solar calendar and these three divinities. His description of them in 1931 as "a cosmic-calendrical hieroglyphic system" illustrates well his tendency to lapse into mumbo-jumbo, one that was common in *völkisch* literature of the time.[38] Nonetheless, as the Germanic peoples had developed a pantheon of figures out of the original monotheism of the God of the Year, the symbols had concomitantly developed from calendrical symbols into ideographs representing all facets of religious life. In 1924 in an article in Kossinna's journal *Mannus*, Ferdinand Bork (a swastika theorist who was later one of Wirth's leading detractors) had linked the names of the runes to a native expression of cosmological principles. In 1928 Wirth went further still.[39]

Espousing an anti-modern, anti-capitalist disdain for the Mammonism of his own age, he thought to recognize a spirituality or gnosis expressed ideographically in the great repertoire of prehistoric symbols, one that had once imbued the entire Nordic race. The primitivism of this expression was not an indication of spiritual poverty, though: after all, as Wirth pointed out, Christianity was not a product of the Roman Empire, but of a group of comparatively primitive Galileans whose religion was eventually to conquer all of Rome.[40] Yet though he stressed the need to treasure the cultural expression of all peoples, even those of the Australian Aborigines (who had for centuries been portrayed as the most degenerate of races in anthropological literature), it was this primitive spirituality which he saw that if recovered and accepted again, would lead to an awakening and rebirth of the Nordic-Atlantic race.[41] It was clearly this mystical aspect to his work that appealed to his publisher, as a spiritual renewal of Germany was the mission of Diederichs's New Romanticism. It also attracted the attention (or rather scorn) of some Protestant theologians.[42] The potential for renewal of the Nordic race was bound to appeal to the more actively politically *völkisch*, especially those like Himmler who had always accepted an overtly mystical brand of nationalism. In this sense, Wirth was a leading proponent of what Jost Hermand calls the "swastika movement."[43] In fact, granted that the swastika was one of the symbols with which Wirth was concerned, his *Sinnbildforschung* might be regarded as the most developed theory of swastika mysticism, the German mythology of blood and race.

Of course Wirth's theories ran counter to what over the preceding few decades had come to be the accepted view of alphabet history. Wirth was critical of "working hypotheses" that he claimed had been accepted as fact rather than mere assertion. After all, the notion worked out essentially by Sir Flinders Petrie that all alphabetic scripts went back to the North Semitic consonantal script and thence back to Egyptian hieroglyphs still had several flaws.[44] For example, the gap between the eleventh-century Semitic script from which the Greek alphabet is held to have sprung and the earliest attestation of the Greek alphabet represents some 300 years.[45] Wirth instead opted for a development of ideographic symbols in the Northwest (already in this sense serving as hieroglyphs, i.e. "priestly language") to syllabary and eventually to an alphabet proper. He also theorized that Egyptian, Sumerian and Semitic writing were all derived from the same Nordic proto-script. Not only does this scheme reverse *ex Oriente* to *ex Septentrione*, it clearly follows the theory first expounded by several nineteenth-century antiquarians that the Germanic runes were a reflection of the most ancient of all scripts and had developed directly out of Nordic or Indo-European symbols such as the fulmen and swastika. Wirth even finishes his *Emergence* with a consideration of the runes. In fact by this stage of the work it becomes clear that most of his theories are underpinned by different uses of the runic script.

The evidence of runic use that he proposes as supportive of his theory is slight, but not entirely specious. Of the European writing systems only the Irish Ogham characters (often misleadingly called the Druidic runes) and those of the old Germanic alphabet had meaningful names. The names of the runes also seem to represent religious and cosmic-calendrical notions: there are runes for 'man,' 'god,' 'year,' 'day' and 'sun' among others. There are even calendrical runes recorded in some Scandinavian manuscripts, though it is usually recognized today that this calendrical usage is quite late.[46] Wirth was also aware that not only were the Frisian gable markings often compared with runes, but that the Frisians at one stage had a lively runic tradition of their own. In fact medieval German hallmarks had been included specifically in the *Urschrift* theory by Müllenhoff and Losch, citing the classic nineteenth-century surveys of German hallmarks by Andreas Michelsen and Carl Homeyer.[47] Wirth's *Sinnbildforschung* in this respect seems a logical outgrowth of the *Urschrift* tradition that Wilser had done so much to promote mixed, of course, with some elements of the swastika mania that culminated most ridiculously in 1931 in Erwin Richter's swastika dance. Wirth's scholarship was poor, but this was true of most of the alphabet history that had emerged in anthropological and archeological discourse since the nineteenth century. In fact his tying of the *Urschrift* theory into a form of racial mysticism can only be judged a success given the response to the *Emergence of Mankind* among his contemporaries.

Yet the religious characters and concepts that Wirth transliterated out of both ancient and medieval sources seemed to have a life of their own. Deities from diverse origins such as Norse Freya and Greek Hera are conflated with Mother Earth, and the names and functions apportioned to the earliest ideographs wander, expand and merge with those of runes. He had even descended into the etymological games common in eighteenth-century philology and held dear by many of the Ariosophists (most ridiculously by List), deriving, for example, the name of the Old Norse deity Baldr (Balder) from that of the Greek god Apollo.[48] Some other linguistic shortcomings, like his etymology of the rune-name Odal, in fact merely mirrored the mistakes of respected nineteenth-century German etymologists, although this was an etymological tradition already prone to nationalistic distortions.[49] His most ridiculous play on Indo-European linguistics, however, was his contention that classes of consonants and even the ablaut (vocalic gradation) series such as are preserved in English *sing sang sung* could be linked to the periodicization of the prehistorical Nordic-Aryan calendar.[50] Even his supporters with linguistic training such as Neckel recognized these flourishes as an amateur "linguistic mysticism."[51] Indeed, Wirth clearly used a German-language work on the Scandinavian rock carvings published in the *Works of the Primordial Teutons (Werke der Urgermanen)* series of a publishing house with the rather *völkisch* name Folkwang (i.e. the Eddic "field of the folk") that had descended into similar grammatical games in 1919. The author, the alternative thinker Ernst Fuhrmann, had taken as his model the sort of etymological fantasies indulged in by medieval Icelandic scholars. In fact Fuhrmann had noted somewhat presciently:[52]

> We have included a short summary of the old grammatical tradition of the North, that although it is rejected by most specialists as nonsensical today, will be crucially important to the language studies of the future.

These obscurantistic and amateurish tendencies were roundly condemned. Yet in other matters many found cause for support. After all, Wirth's theories on the development of Germanic religion, although expressed rather idiosyncratically, were not too dissimilar to those accepted by many scholars at the time. Wirth himself pointed out that he only considered List an influence "not on scientific particularities, but instead in the realm of the intellectual, the spiritual."[53] In fact he was happier to cite academics involved in swastika studies such as Montelius and Bork, and the *"intellectual-historical* prehistory" of Kossinna's journal *Mannus* as his scholarly predecessors.[54] Wirth's monotheism encapsulated in his "God of the Year" was essentially the same as the sunworshipping monotheisms promoted by comparative mythologists and swastika scholars (a year god was defined in essence by the solar calendar). His conception of a "Great Mother" was also mostly identical to the slightly more developed theory of Johann Jakob Bachofen who in the previous century had envisaged a Stone Age European matriarchy.[55] A proof for these theories in the form of an analysis of the prehistorical ideographs would clearly have been well received by prehistorians. Very few academics accepted Wirth's scheme in its entirety. Yet many of the aspects of his *Sinnbildforschung* very quickly came to permeate the writing of his contemporaries. Wirth ranged over a broad selection of scholarship, employing the findings of history of religion, alphabet history, archeology, physical anthropology and even geology, and cited the opinions of a plethora of experts from Britain, North America, France and Scandinavia, as well as the Dutch and German-speaking countries. The very breadth of his scholarship seemed to some to demand respect. Diederichs claimed: "There is probably no scholar in the entire world who has mastered as many disciplines as Herman Wirth."[56] One of the contributors to Baeumler's volume commented similarly:[57]

> The scope of Wirth's research is so great that for the whole work, i.e. in its totality and in all areas drawn upon, no one before has been an expert in the strict sense apart from him.

Wirth repeated a similar claim in his refutations. In 1929 he proudly emphasized:

> *To date no single public, scientific critique has appeared that has truly and objectively tackled the complete complex of my work, in particular my method.*[58]

According to Wirth, even the critics who had contributed to the Wiegers volume only quibbled at the margins of his "cultural-historical synthesis."[59] His work on "paleo-epigraphy" and "prehistorical religion"[60] seemed to have a conceptual consistency that derived no doubt from the decade or more Wirth claims was spent in its gestation, and this, according to Wirth and many of his supporters, was what his critics failed to attend to. Echoing Chamberlain's reply to criticisms of the *Foundations*, no matter what individual flaws were pointed out Wirth maintained his approach to *Sinnbildforschung* was essentially correct. Evidently, many who read his works were unable to separate what was fact from what was merely *völkisch* fantasy—few could claim to be specialists in all the areas he covered. Yet for some of those whose specialization did intersect with Wirth's main area of concern, his ideographic studies offered the possibility of opening up a new approach to the recovery of earlier stages of Germanic gnosis and Weltanschauung. Wiegers claimed Wirth's observations were "false," his conclusions were therefore "wrong" and he dismissed the *Emergence* as "a poem."[61] Yet though there were obviously many faults in Wirth's application of linguistic or comparative cultural method, his main ideas, the basic thrust of his *Geistesurgeschichte*, still earned the respect of many of his contemporaries.

Wirth's 1928 work was groundbreaking in another way too. German scholarship on runes was thin and sporadic before the appearance of his *Emergence*, but after 1928 a welter of German runological works appeared. Königsberg's Wolfgang Krause did not produce his first monograph on the subject until 1932 and the *Handbook of Runic Studies* of the University of Giessen's Helmut Arntz from 1934 was the first substantial assessment to appear since the German translation of Wimmer's originally Danish treatise had appeared in 1887. In fact many sections of Arntz's *Handbook* were prepared in direct response to the growing number of theories advanced by those like Wirth whom he dismisses as fantasists.[62] Clearly, Wirth inspired the rescue of a tradition of runic scholarship in Germany that had mostly lapsed since the appearance of Rudolf Henning's *German Runic Monuments (Die deutsche Runendenk mäler)* in 1889.[63] He certainly refocused Neckel's attention and Konstantin Reichardt's runic handbook of 1936 also owes a debt to Wirth—his reference in his foreword to the criticism that serious scholars were too "narrow-minded" is hard to reconcile with the approach to Germanic antiquity of his late publisher, Diederichs, which was anything but reticent or restrained.[64] Yet to scholars such as Arntz and Krause, Wirth mostly represented the popular runology of *völkisch* nationalists, of the Germanic Orders and the disciples of Ariosophy.

Whereas List's brief attempt to have his own research recognized in Vienna had ended with his rejection by the Imperial Academy of Sciences, Wirth was not treated so dismissively. Some scholars were contemptuous of the upstart, yet others instead after reading his work seemed to become obsessed with the runes and petroglyphs that he had fulminated on. In light of the many eccentricities in Wirth's thought, today his hold upon the minds of his followers both within academia and without seems almost like that of a guru. It is hard to believe that respected and often irascible philologists such as Neckel could have been at all supportive of Wirth's theories. Wirth had encapsulated *völkisch* thought within a world that was a farrago of fact, mythology and mysticism. But the obscurantistic aspect of Wirth's construction did not seem cause enough for all academics to reject it in its entirety. Instead it seems to have liberated some of them from traditional scholarly reserve. It seems no accident that Neckel became a proponent of an *"Urverwandtschaft"* (cognate relationship) between the runes and other ancient alphabets by the middle of 1929 (mirroring the similar claim of Wilser accepted by Wirth). Neckel's acceptance of this form of *ex Septentrione lux* even saw him laud Wirth for being a "troublemaker" in 1932.[65] In fact the next year Neckel visited the Atlantis House in Bremen where he read a paper on the development of the runes from pre-runic ideographs to a conference assembled there by Roselius as the First Nordic *Thing*.[66] Neckel also saw a connection between his own controversial ideas on the role of women in Germanic society (which had first been published in 1932) and Wirth's notion of the Great Mother.[67] In the midst of the development and indeed promulgation of the notion of Germanicness developed by Heusler, Wirth's philosophically speculative approach to antiquity for many evidently represented a breakthrough of the Germanic spirit. What today appear to be eccentric and often woolly notions did not seem so strange given Kossinna's *ex Septentrione lux*, Heusler's Germanicness, Helm's history of religion and the emphasis on the religious aspects of the Scandinavian rock carvings most intelligently expounded by Almgren. The central position given to race in Wirth's studies, an aspect that had become prevalent in historical works since Chamberlain's time, had also become favored in surveys of Germanists such as Neckel and the younger Much. To some, a project to uncover a *Geistesurgeschichte* of the Nordic-Germanic race seemed to have very real prospects given the state and direction of research at the time. Despite criticizing Wirth's linguistic understanding as "unconventional" and his intellectual pre-history as "arbitrary," in 1930 Neckel had claimed Wirth was "a Co-pernicus in the widest sense" and had started giving a two-hour lecture on "Germanic philology in the context of modern intellectual life" to his students at the University of Berlin each semester.[68] "Who harps on about the mistakes of Jacob Grimm?," remarked Baeumler.[69] For his supporters, the folklorist Eugen Fehrle probably summed Wirth's importance up best: "Much I cannot judge at all, other parts I reject. But one thing is certain: this research is a great challenge to the study of religion and *Volkskunde*."[70] Moreover, as Walter Wüst, an Indo-Ira-nist at the University of Munich, concluded at the end of his review of Wirth's *Emergence* in the *Zeitschrift für Missionswissenschaft und Religion-swissenschaft (Journal of Missionary and Religious Studies)* in 1929:[71]

"Praesens Imperfectum
Perfectum Futurum"

HUBRIS

Yet perhaps in overconfidence, in 1933 Wirth overplayed his hand. During the time he had been researching his *Sinnbildforschung*, he had also been wrestling with a work written in a form of the Frisian language known as the *Oera Linda Book*. This work which Wirth had first encountered in 1904[72] was initially published along with a Dutch translation in 1872 and claimed to be the chronicle of a Frisian family, the Over de Lindens, dating back to the thirteenth century.[73] (Oera Linda, which was transliterated by Wirth to Ura Linda in German, was apparently the original form of their family name.) It had, however, almost immediately been revealed as a forgery after its original publica-tion.[74] Philologists had been unearthing medieval German, English and Scandinavian literary treasures throughout the eighteenth and nine-teenth centuries, but little remained of the early narrative traditions of Holland and Frisia. Nonetheless, ever since James MacPherson had sought to fill the similar lack of a great Scots Gaelic tradition with his

Ossian forgeries, like works had turned up periodically throughout Europe, most commonly in regions without outstanding genuine works of medieval literature (quite a number, for example, are also known from Eastern Europe). Wirth accepted part of the *Oera Linda Book* as genuinely antique, however, and in fact sections of the chronicle seem to mirror the direction of the development of his *Sinnbildforschung*. The religion of the authors of the chronicle was monotheistic, embodied in the worship of a divinity known as Wralda (i.e. 'the world'), and Wirth associated the six-spoked wheel symbol so common among the Scandinavian rock carvings with the six-spoked "Yule (winter-solstice) symbol" mentioned in the chronicle as the symbol of Wralda. There were also clear references to ancient matriarchy and the worship of mother goddesses; sections even referred to an ancient Frisian connection with Atlantis (Germanicized in the chronicle as *Atland* or *Altland*, i.e. 'the old country'). In late 1933 Wirth made the mistake of publishing his own German translation of the *Oera Linda Book*. A backlash immediately ensued.[75]

Most of the critics of Wirth's edition of the *Oera Linda Book* were scathing in their reception. Krause perhaps summed up best the disdain that many German philologists felt for the work. It was, according to Krause, simply un-Germanic:[76]

> Only one whose approach to true Germanicness is purely academic and without instinct is capable of finding in the Oera Linda Chronicle, this verbal torrent, rich in moralizing tone, any testament of Germanic tradition.

Linguistic and textual issues aside, many of the scenes from the *Oera Linda Book* did not fit into the notion of Germanicness set out by Heusler. The suggestions of matrilinearity in the chronicle were a feature that especially upset the masculinist picture of Germanic society accepted by most Germanists. A stream of negative reviews continued into 1935. Wirth had accepted that parts of the book were modern—the manuscript, though apparently in an archaic (uncial) script, was even written on machine-made paper. He had instead worked out a complicated scheme whereby although the last recension of the chronicle was compromised, earlier layers could be rescued from within it, some even going back into the pre-Christian era. Evidence that pointed to forgery was tempered in Wirth's view by the consistency of parts of the work with the insights gained in his own research.[77] Not even Neckel could support such an interpretation, however, and the Nordicist openly suspected that the chronicle had been instrumental in the formation of Wirth's *Sinnbildforschung*. Even Wirth's translation appeared merely to have been from Dutch to German, rather than directly from the archaized Frisian pastiche of the manuscript. Neckel withdrew his support for Wirth immediately, although he still refused to admit the influence Wirth had had in his own thinking:[78]

> Wirth's proclamation that sunken Atlantis was the second homeland of the ... White Race, of their beliefs and the role played by the yearly rotation and the eight and six-spoked wheel, these touch on a substantial proportion of the matter of this chronicle; so closely, in fact, that one suspects that they are the source, if not the main source of 1928's *Emergence of Mankind*.
>
> If I was supportive of Wirth to a certain point previously, it was because the general thrust of his approach appealed to me: his critique of the dogma of evolution and of the undervaluing of the cultural achievements of our unbaptized forebears ... I have nothing to retract from my previous statements on the position of women [in old Germanic times] or on the question of runic origins, [however].

Wirth's response was to reject all the criticisms and accuse his detractors of various misdemeanors, from an ivory tower mentality or even to hostility to the National Socialist movement. It was clear that much of the *Oera Linda Book* was influenced by eighteenth and nineteenth-century works and even its language contained anachronistic phrases and terms, *sinnebild* perhaps most notably among them.[79] Moreover, the section that most palpably affected Wirth's *Sinnbildforschung* could be linked directly with a section from a nineteenth-century work by the German folklorist Montanus analyzing festivals where the yuletide festival is connected with:[80]

> ... yule or [the dialectal form] *joel* means the wheel of time by which one makes meaningful the year, old German *ar*. Similarly, one also understands the festival as the *weralt*-festival, after [the Old High German term] *weralt*, that is 'duration,' 'time,' and whence comes our word world.

There is no old German term *ar* meaning 'year.' The term is Old Norse, and is the name of the **A**-rune of the younger, Viking Age runes, the Norse counterpart of the asterisk-like "six spoked" Old English **j**-rune, *gear*, whose name is cognate to Old Norse *ár*. Clearly, Montanus had indulged in a form of visual folk etymology based on the notion that Old Norse is equivalent to Old German. Wralda, the six-spoked yule symbol, Frisian monotheism, the calendrical function of ideographs—all stem from this unfortunate passage. The author of the *Oera Linda Book* had obviously borrowed heavily from nineteenth-century works and occasionally even seemed to show a sense of humor in the way he chose and distorted his sources. Wirth had been completely taken in by the forgery, so deeply in fact that he did not seem aware how dependent he had become upon it. The cover of the *Emergence of Mankind* bears a brown and green yuletide tree-and-wreath emblem, which, somewhat ironically, symbolizes only too well the importance of the identification of the yule-tree with the year-rune and Wralda, the God of the Year, in Wirth's thought. Although in the face of Wirth's denials this connection was not pursued by his detractors, considering his own admission that his *Sinnbildforschung* was linked to Frisian folk-lore, the direction of much of Wirth's ideographic study seems to have grown out of a misguided faith in the testament of the fraudulent *Oera Linda Book*, the half-baked runology of swastika studies and *völkisch* alphabet history, and the worst aspects of Fuhrmann's 1919 work on the Scandinavian rock carvings.

IN THE BLACK

Nonetheless, by 1933 Wirth's situation had been rendered immune to the criticism of his peers. Supported by the Party, his position was unassailable from critics without influence in the movement. Despite the evident opprobrium of many of his colleagues at the University of Berlin, it seemed his battle to reclaim a position in German academia had been won. By this time Wirth's exhibitions had also developed into a more permanent collection, funded by both his private supporters like Roselius as well as the state. He managed to win a new home for his collection in 1934 and his Bad Doberan "Research Institute and Open-Air Museum for Intellectual Prehistory" (which had foundered in 1933 because of Wirth's financial profligacy) was transformed that June into what he dubbed the "Deutsches Ahnenerbe" (German Ancestral Inheritance), the "Open-Air Show and Collection for Intellectual Prehistory and the Study of National Traditions" (Freilichtsschau und Sammlung für Geistesurgeschichte und Volkstums-kunde).[81] In order to fund Wirth's appointment, the university administration had used the money from the chair of archeology left vacant by the retirement of Max Ebert, Kossinna's successor, a move that had sent shivers through the archeological community. Bolko, Baron von Richthofen, a Party member, former student of Kossinna and the head of the Federation of German Prehistorians (Vereinigung deutscher Vorgeschichtsforscher), had mounted a public campaign against Wirth since 1932, which included publishing a letter indicating Kossinna's own low opinion of the Dutchman and his work.[82] Von Richthofen even tried to have Wirth removed from the University of Berlin in 1933 by writing to his contacts within the Party, pointing out that Wirth had accepted Jewish money in 1929 and had lectured to Freemasons in 1932.[83] When these matters had first been revealed the previous year, von Richthofen had managed to turn Rosenberg against Wirth, and the Kampfbund and its Study-Group for Prehistory obviously had no time for the archeological dilettante. But by late 1933 Wirth's backing from other sections of the Party was too strong. The university administration finally appointed Rosenberg's man Hans Reinerth as a replacement for Ebert and used the newly vacated chair in Polish history to fund Wirth's position instead. This stopgap solution at least seems to have satisfied Rosenberg and the archeological community generally. Despite von Richthofen's continuing hostility and the efforts of others within the university to have Wirth removed, political considerations now evidently outweighed any other agendas that could be brought to bear against him.

Wirth had not only survived the concerted attacks of von Richthofen, in the meantime he had accumulated two more important supporters from National Socialist ranks. From mid-1934, at the same time he was playing with the idea of setting up a journal called *Urd* (Old Norse for 'fate') in collaboration with Munich's Wüst, Wirth made the acquaintance of first Darré and then finally Himmler himself.[84] In May 1935 while an exhibition of Wirth's was receiving acclaim in the *völkisch* press and well aware of the criticism of Wirth's Oera Linda translation, Himmler decided to transform Wirth's organization into an arm of the Party.[85] In July, the Deutsches Ahnenerbe, as the "Learned Society for Intellectual Prehistory" (Studiengesellschaft für Geistesurgeschichte) was refounded within the SS, and Wirth, an SS-man since April 1934, was made its president.[86] Officially now a member of the RuSHA, he was set up in official premises in the Berlin suburb of Dahlem, and two research associates and two secretaries were put at his disposal.

The first section established within the SS-Ahnenerbe was devoted solely to Wirth's ideographic studies. Wirth dubbed the sections "Cultivation Posts" (*Pflegstätten*), a term earlier used to refer to civically funded artists' colonies, and his section was called the *Pflegstätte* for Alphabetic and Ideographic Studies (Schrift- und Sinnbildkunde). Other Nazi enthusiasts, none of whom at first was an established academic, soon also joined the ranks of the Ahnenerbe, and the learned society of the SS gradually took over responsibility for first the SS periodical *Nordland* and then *Germanien*, a journal originally founded by a group of amateur *völkisch* antiquarians.[87] A number of amateur Germanists, prehistorians and others had joined the Ahnenerbe by 1936, and a second division, for Germanic Studies (*Germanenkunde*) had been instituted in Detmold under the leadership of one of the amateurs who had founded *Germanien*.

In the year following the refounding of the Ahnenerbe, Wirth had finally completed the second volume of the successor to his *magnum opus* of ideographic studies in the form of a work that had dribbled out in fascicules since 1931. His *Sacred Archaic Alphabet of Humanity (Heilige Urschrift der Menschheit)* subtitled "Symbol-Historical Investigations on Both Sides of the North Atlantic" had been completed after two tours to Scandinavia funded by the SS where he had for the first time been able to view the rock carvings he had studied for the last decade or more at first hand.[88] He took photos, made casts and prepared sketches of the carvings which had inspired him, and began to plan further publications.[89] Some of his designs for works such as a documentary film[90] and more museum exhibitions came to fruition, but his plans for further monographs were never realized. He had announced that the sequel to his *Sacred Archaic Alphabet* would be entitled "Odal" and had even threatened legal proceedings against the legal historian Johann von Leers who had planned a publication under the same name.

Already infamous as a leading Nazi propagandist, von Leers was head of the Society for Germanic Prehistory and Early History (Gesellschaft für Germanische Ur- und Frühgeschichte), the successor to the Herman Wirth Society, and the man who had introduced Wirth to Himmler in the first place. Despite signing a contract with the publishers Koehler and Amelang in July 1935, Wirth's manuscript never made it to the printers and von Leers went on to publish his own study later that year despite Wirth's protestations.[91]

Some members of the Ahnenerbe, including the researchers in his own division, though, soon came to harbor concerns as to Wirth's use of the funds under his control. For example, in May 1936 he had had the SS pay so that his brother Phillip and his family could come out from the Dutch East Indies (Indonesia) to visit him in Berlin.[92] His personal finances were a mess; his requests for more funds neverending. It was the size of the bills for his two research trips to Scandinavia, however, that so shocked the bookkeepers. Increasingly Wirth seemed unable to complete any of his projects; and although Himmler had acted to ensure that year that all criticism of the *Oera Linda Book* would stop, even Wirth's occasional contributions to journals such as *Germanien* had dried up by the end of 1936.[93] Indeed as other members of the Ahnenerbe began to research ideographs, it became apparent that Wirth had not developed his theoretical or methodological approaches since 1928—his *Sacred Archaic Alphabet* had not proven a worthy successor to the *Emergence*. Himmler noted in a letter in October 1936 that Wirth suffered from a "lack of discipline," explaining that he had personally tried to reason with Wirth "not to go on with politically foolish things that in addition will bring us to financial ruin."[94] Hitler had attacked the Atlantid Nordicism of "Böttcherstrasse culture" at the annual Party rally in Nuremberg the previous month; thereafter, amid a rising tide of criticism from within the Ahnenerbe, throughout 1937 Wirth's independence was slowly undermined.[95] He was reduced to the role of honorary president in February 1937 (replaced by his friend Wüst), his status within the structure of the Ahnenerbe was changed to an honorary one early in 1938, and after more promises of ultimately unrealized projects (including another film), finally at the end of the year he was edged out of the organization altogether.[96] Continuing foment at the University of Berlin also prompted the Ministry of Education to resolve to find a way to be rid of him. After receiving numerous

referees' reports from his academic fellows, including ambivalent ones
from Party-aligned scholars like Höfler,[97] the Ministry began to seek
out ways to pension off the now quinquagenarian. Wirth had returned
with his *Pflegstätte* to Marburg in 1937 and the Education Ministry
hoped they had seen the back of him. Nonetheless, late in 1939 with
his other options evidently exhausted, Wirth wrote to the Education
Ministry demanding that they make a professorship available to him.
When it was pointed out to him that he needed to complete a professional thesis first, Wirth agreed to start on a project entitled "The
Runic Calender Fragment from Fossum." He duly received a DFG stipend, but by 1940 had abandoned the project.[98] Inquiries were then
made at the University of Marburg in the hope of providing him with
an honorary curatorship as some academics there had written to the
DFG in support of Wirth's requests for travelling funds. Confront-
ed with the possibility of a closer relationship, the academics quickly
changed their tune, however, and so even the plan to pension Wirth
off in this way came undone.[99] By this time Wirth had lost contact with
his wealthier supporters—he had fallen out with Roselius in 1936 (who
had previously always been the most forthcoming with funds) after the
Third Nordic *Thing* had failed to eventuate[100] and Roselius had become disillusioned further after Hitler's attack on the Atlantis House
(in fact it was closed down in 1937 and only survived demolition after
Hitler's architect Albert Speer had suggested the Böttcherstraße be preserved as a museum of degenerate architecture.)[101] In 1942 Wirth was
still promising Himmler he would complete an atlas of Indo-European
ideographs and he had managed to set up yet another organization of
ideograph enthusiasts in Marburg, the "Germanicdom and Christendom" Association (Arbeitsgemeinschaft "Germanentum und Christentum"). Under instructions from Himmler, the DFG stipend was extended again and again, the last time after Wirth had been forced to
surrender even his precious collection of moulds and casts, albeit at
very generous financial terms.[102] Finally, in 1944 an honorary position
in *Volkskunde* was arranged for him at the University of Göttingen; but
again, his would-be colleagues protested, and the looming German ca-
pitulation meant that he was never able to take up the post.[103]

Wirth had been drawn to *völkisch* thought in the idealism of his youth.
Like several other Nazis, and perhaps mostly in the manner of his fel-

low myth-maker Rosenberg, his marginally German status appears to have led to a patriotic overcompensation. Yet he had always been a marginal figure, whether as a volunteer in the Great War, as a *völkisch* agitator in Holland or in his academic life—and his plans usually fell apart all too readily. His translation of the *Oera Linda Book* had almost led to his complete discrediting, but he had been saved at the last minute by Darré and Himmler. Nevertheless even while he was at the peak of his powers, when as president of the learned society of the SS he was finally in a position to realize the mission he had written of to Kossinna so many years before, he failed. But he did not accept his fate.

In his mind Wirth rejected his culpability for this state of affairs. He had always been caught between worlds—between Holland and Germany, between Party and financial opportunity, and between academia and the wilderness of the *demi-lettré*. Time and again he had proved both irresolute and profligate with other people's money: from Roselius, at Bad Doberan and then in the SS. His written projects were usually published well after they had been scheduled—even the *Emergence* appeared two years later than had originally been advertised. Things had just got worse in the SS. He had done more than merely revert to type; he had grown too comfortable and too greedy. At first he seems to have attempted to blame ill health for his repeated failings. Evidently, on top of his natural predilection for dithering and overspending, soon the responsibility as president of the ever-expanding Ahnenerbe became too much for him. Then once things began to fall apart he fell into a paralysis of indecision and procrastination. But the charade appears not to have ended there. As Höfler's influence had begun to grow in SS circles, and especially in light of the Kummer affair, Wirth tried to claim his dismissal from the Ahnenerbe was due to his disillusionment with the direction in which the Party was headed. In a letter to Himmler from late 1938 (whose authenticity has been called into question), Wirth claimed that the new destructive *Männerbund* ideology of the SS was antipathetic to his own more idealistic, creative conception of National Socialism.[104] Wirth had identified with Kummer and his emphasis on the idyllic aspects of Old Norse religion, although he had obviously not come under any hint of sanction at the time. In fact despite the vehemence directed at Kummer by several SS-aligned academics, Himmler seemed more annoyed than concerned by the Kummer affair.[105] Nonetheless, for Wirth, now everything seemed to be Höfler's fault too.

Yet despite these machinations, unpleasantries and failures, Wolfram Sievers—who had first worked for Wirth at Bad Doberan, but as Ahnenerbe general secretary had dispatched him from the organization—could still indicate his respect for Wirth's intellectual contribution in a letter in 1943. In response to a query about the fate of Wirth he replied:[106]

> We owe Herman Wirth a wealth of seminal stimuli in the area of Indo-European intellectual history. Among other things he may be considered the founder of what today is the serious science of *Sinnbildforschung*.

Wirth's *Sinnbildforschung* was ostensibly based in Atlantid fantasies, swastika studies, the popular antiquarianism of the *völkisch* movement and the Oera Linda forgery. Yet it also reflected in part developments in German scholarship of the previous decades: most patently that of the more radical scholars of antiquity such as Kossinna and the Muchs, and *völkisch* popularizers and historical intuiters such as Wilser. The appearance of his *Emergence of Mankind* in 1928, despite all its amateurish, obscurantist and deliberately ideological trappings had an immediate effect on the German understanding of the past, especially in runological circles; and despite their protestations, many German academics became caught up in the ideas and the spirit of Wirth's *Sinnbildforschung*. It is salutary here to remember that the reaction which the first impulses of Wirth's achievement produced in German antiquarian scholarship predate the coming to power of the National Socialists or even the onset of the Great Depression. Wirth represented the radical fringe of a movement within German and Austrian antiquarian scholarship that had already come to impinge upon academic antiquarian discourse well before the Nazi breakthrough of 1933.

Notes

1 O. Almgren, *Hällristningar och kultbruch* (Stockholm: Wahlström & Widstand, 1927); idem, *Nordische Felsbilder als religiöse Urkunden*, rev. ed., trans. S. Vrancken (Frankfurt a.M.: Diesterweg, 1934).
2 N. Åberg, "Herman Wirth," *Fornvännen* 28 (1933): 246–47.

3 S.F. Nadel, review of P. Hambruch, *Die Irrtümer und Phantasien des Herrn Prof. Dr. Herman Wirth*, *Mitteilungen der Anthropologischen Gesellschaft in Wien* 61 (1931): 384.

4 "Schenkel der Göttlichen," *Der Spiegel* 29 Sept. 1980, 95.

5 I. Wiwjorra, "Herman Wirth," in B. Danckwott et al. (eds.), *Historische Rassismusforschung* (Hamburg: Argument, 1995), 91–112.

6 H. Wirth, *Der Untergang des niederlandischen Volksliedes* (The Hague: Nijhoff, 1911); L. Buning, "Notities betreffende Hermann Felix Wirth," *Wetenschappelijke Tijdingen* 33 (1974): 142–43; Wiwjorra, "Herman Wirth," 91–92; Pringle, 53ff.

7 H. Wirth, *National-Nederlandsche muziek politiek* (Amsterdam: Van Holkema & Warendorf, 1912); idem (ed.), *Orkestcomposities van Nederlandsche meesters van het begin der 17de eeuw* (Amsterdam: Alsbach, 1913); idem (ed.), *Altniederländische Arméemärsche* (Berlin: Bote & Bock, 1914); idem, *Das niederländische Volkslied* (Leipzig: Breitkopf & Härtel, 1916); idem, *Eerste uitvoering van Oud-Nederlandsche toonkunstwerken* (Utrecht: Bosch, 1920); A. Einstein (ed.), *Hugo Riemanns Musik Lexikon*, 10th ed. (Berlin: Hesse, 1922), 1429.

8 H. Wirth, *Das niederländische Volkslied*; idem, *Die niederländichen kirchlichen Meister vom Mittelalter bis zum 19. Jahrhundert* (Ghent: [s.n.,] 1916); M. Lamberty, "Activisme," in E. de Bruyne et al. (eds.), *Winkler Prins encyclopadie*, 18 vols., 6th ed. (Amsterdam: Elsevier, 1947–52), I, 198; idem, "Vlaamse beweging," op. cit., XVIII, 176–77; Wiwjorra, "Herman Wirth," 93.

9 Wirth, resumés/questionnaires, 23.10.35, 7.12.35, 1.4.36, 2.10.37; all BA: SSO 1875; Buning, 141–55.

10 H. Wirth, *Niederländisch-Deutsch* (Berlin: Neufeld & Henius, 1913); idem (ed.), *Ein Hähnlein woll'n wir rupfen* (Jena: Diederichs, 1914); idem, *Flandern und sein Volk*, 2 vols. (Leipzig: Breitkopf & Härtel, [1916]); idem, *Flämisch* (Berlin: Neufeld & Henius, 1916).

11 Wirth in *Vlamenland* 1 (1917): 1.

12 Wirth, resumé, 7.12.35, BA: SSO 1875; P. Braeunlich/REM 24.2.35, BA: REM A114; C. Dachlhaus (ed.), *Riemanns Musik Lexikon*, 12th ed., *Ergänzungsband*, 2 vols. (Mainz: Schott's Sons, 1972–75), II, 917; Wiwjorra, "Herman Wirth," 94.

13 H. Wirth, *Hervoorming en wedergeboorte* (Amsterdam: Van Holkema & Warendorf, 1911) = *Heilige Wende* (Leipzig: Koehler & Amelang, 1933).

14 Wirth/Kossinna 19.8.19, in Schwerin von Krosigk, 162.

15 H. Wirth, *Wat is en wat wil de Dietsche Trekvogel?* (Leiden: Landsbond de Dietsche Trekvogel, 1920).

16 Dutch *Duitsch* is a rendering of German *deutsch*, whereas *Dietsch* is a learned neologism based on the medieval Dutch term *Dietsch*, whence English *Dutch*; N. van Wijk, *Franck's etymologisch woordenboek der Nederlandsche taal*, 2nd ed. (The Hague: Nijhoff, 1912), s.v. *Duitsch*.

17 Wirth, resumé in *Germanien* 1 (1929–30): 40; idem (ed.), *Die Ura Linda Chronik* (Leipzig: Koehler & Amelang, 1933), 139; idem, resumé, 7.12.35,

BA: SSO 1875; cf. Kater, *Ahnenerbe*, 11ff.; U. Hunger, *Die Runenkunde im Dritten Reich* (Frankfurt a.M.: Lang, 1984), 180–81.

18 Wirth, questionnaires, 1.4.36, 11.6.40, BA: SSO, 1875; Poliakov and Wulf (eds.), 243; Kater, *Ahnenerbe*, 13.

19 H. Wirth, *Der Aufgang der Menschheit* (Jena: Diederichs, 1928). The work was originally advertised in 1926 under the title "The Development of European Mankind" in E. Diederichs (ed.), *Das deutsche Gesicht* (Jena: Diederichs, 1926), 60, n. * & 132.

20 H. Wirth, "Die Atlantisproblem," in E. Diederichs (ed.), *Das deutsche Gesicht* (Jena: Diederichs, 1926), 69–79 = *Germanien* 2 (1930/31): 115–22 [with an afterword]; idem (ed.), *Die Ura Linda Chronik*, 135.

21 H. Roselius, *Ludwig Roselius und sein kulturelles Werk* (Brunswick: Westermann, 1954); A. Strohmeyer, *Der gebaute Mythos* (Bremen: Donat, 1993).

22 E. Diederichs (ed.), *Der Fall Herman Wirth* (Jena: Diederichs, [1929]). Diederichs had even attempted to enlist Heusler's support, but Heusler would have none of "this wildness of mysticism"; Heusler/Ranisch 24.3.29, no. 154 in Düwel and Beck (eds.), 515.

23 F. Wiegers (ed.), *Herman Wirth und die deutsche Wissenschaft* (Munich: Lehmann, 1932); H. Wirth, *Um die wissenschaftliche Erkenntnis und den nordischen Gedanken* (Berlin–Steglitz: Herman Wirth Society, [1932]).

24 M. Wundt, *Was heißt völkisch?* (Langensalza: Beyer & Sons, 1924); H. Wirth, *Was heißt deutsch?* (Jena: Diederichs, 1931).

25 H. Wirth, "Prof. Herman Wirth für Hitler," *Völkischer Beobachter* 11th Apr. 1932; Poliakov and Wulf (eds.), 243; Wiwjorra, "Herman Wirth," 98–99.

26 H. Wieland, *Atlantis, Edda und Bibel*, 2nd ed. (Nuremberg: Wuzel, 1922); K.G. Zschaetzsch, *Die Herkunft und Geschichte des arischen Stammes* (Berlin: Arier, 1920); idem, *Atlantis* (Berlin: Arier, 1922).

27 F. Wegener, *Das atlantidische Weltbild* (Gladbeck: Kulturförderverein Ruhrgebiet, 2000).

28 A. Baeumler (ed.), *Was bedeutet Herman Wirth für die Wissenschaft?* (Leipzig: Koehler & Amelang, 1932).

29 A. Wegener, *Die Entstehung der Kontinente und Ozeane* (Brunswick: Vieweg, 1915).

30 Wirth clearly saw the Arctic peoples as pre-Aryan, employing the Medieval Irish description, Tuatha Dé Danann (the first element of which is cognate to the modern term *Deutsch*), to describe this Arctic *Urrasse*; Wirth, *Aufgang*, 166ff.

31 B.G. Tilak, *The Arctic Home in the Vedas* (Poona: Kesari, 1903); G. Biedenkapp, *Der Nordpol als Völkerheimat* (Jena: Costenoble, 1906); W. Pastor, *Der Zug vom Norden* (Jena: Diederichs, 1906); idem, *Aus germanischer Vorzeit* (Berlin: Haessel, 1907); Figueira, 129ff.

32 I. Donnelly, *Atlantis* (London: Samson Low, Marsdon & Co., 1882).

33 A. Hitler, speech of 13.8.1920, apud idem, *Sämtliche Aufzeichnungen 1905–1924*, ed. E. Jäckel (Stuttgart: Deutsche Verlags–Anstalt, 1980), 186–87; Rosenberg, *Mythus*, 20.

34 L. Wilser, *Deutsche Vorzeit*, 4th ed. (Leipzig: Voigtländer, [1934]), VI.

35 Wirth (ed.), *Die Ura Linda Chronik*, 314.

36 Wirth, *Aufgang*, 61ff.

37 Ibid., 15.

38 H. Wirth, *Die heilige Urschrift der Menschheit* (Leipzig: Koehler & Amelang, 1931–36), 93.

39 F. Bork, "Zur Entstehungsgeschichte"; idem, review of Wirth, *Aufgang*, reprinted in E. Diederichs (ed.), *Der Fall Herman Wirth* (Jena: Diederichs, [1929]), 8; idem, "Herman Wirth als Orientalist," in F. Wiegers (ed.), *Herman Wirth und die deutsche Wissenschaft* (Munich: Lehmann, 1932), 61–69. Cf. idem, "Runenstudien," *Archiv für Schreib- und Buchwesen* 3 (1929): 67–81.

40 Wirth, *Aufgang*, 9–10. He would return to this theme in his exhibition of May 1933, "The Savior"; H. Wirth, *Führer durch die erste urreligionsgeschichtliche Ausstellung "Der Heilbringer"* (Berlin: Zentralinstitut für Erziehung und Unterricht, 1933).

41 Wirth, *Aufgang*, 20, 22–23, 46.

42 G. Gloege, "Die Weltanschauung Herman Wirths," in W. Künneth and H. Schreiner (eds.), *Die Nation vor Gott* (Berlin: Im Wichern, 1933), 392–421; Stark, 69ff.

43 Hermand, *Old Dreams*, 88.

44 W.M.F. Petrie, *The Formation of the Alphabet* (London: MacMillan, 1912); Wirth, *Aufgang*, 5–8.

45 J. Naveh, *Early History of the Alphabet* (Jerusalem: Magnes, 1982), 175–86.

46 S.O. Jansson, "Gyllental," in J. Brøndsted et al. (eds.), *Kulturhistorisk leksikon for nordisk middelalder* V (Copenhagen: Rosenkilde & Bagger, 1960), 615–18.

47 A.L.J. Michelsen, *Die Hausmarke* (Jena: Frommann, 1853); C.G. Homeyer, *Die Haus- und Hofmarken* (Berlin: Decker, 1870).

48 Wirth, *Aufgang*, 427ff.

49 E.G. Graff, *Althochdeutscher Sprachschatz*, 7 vols. (Berlin: Nikolai, 1834–46), s.v. *Odal 'patria'*; M.-L. Rotsaert, "Etymologie et idéologie," *Historiographia linguistica* 6 (1977): 311.

50 Wirth, *Aufgang*, 501–14, 520–21, 615–17.

51 G. Neckel, review of Wirth, *Was heißt deutsch?*, *Mannus* 23 (1931): 331–32; cf. L. Wolff, "Herman Wirth als Germanist," in F. Wiegers (ed.), *Herman Wirth und die deutsche Wissenschaft* (Munich: Lehmann, 1932), 49.

52 [E. Fuhrmann,] *Schwedische Felsbilder von Göteborg bis Strömstad* (Hagen i.W.: Folkwang, 1919), 6; cf. A. Windus and H.-G. Winter, *Ernst Fuhrmann* (Herzberg: Traugott Bautz, 2000).

53 H. Wirth, "Deutsche Vorgeschichte und deutsche Geistesgeschichte," *Germanien* 1 (1929/30): 34.

54 Wirth, "Deutsche Vorgeschichte," 36; and cf. Montelius, "Das Sonnenrad"; idem, "Das lateinische Kreuz"; H. Wirth, "Zum Ursprung des Kreuzes," in L. Feiler, *Die Entstehung des Christentums aus dem Geiste des magischen Denkens* (Jena: Diederichs, 1927), 150–52.

55 J.J. Bachofen, *Das Mutterrecht* (Stuttgart: Krais & Hoffmann, 1861); U. Wesel, *Der Mythos vom Matriachat* (Frankfurt a.M.: Suhrkamp, 1985); H.-

J. Heinrichs (ed.), *Das Mutterrecht von Johann Jakob Bachofen in der Diskussion* (Frankfurt a.M.: Campus, 1987); P. Davies, "Ilse Langner's *Amazonen* and the Reception of J.J. Bachhofen's *Das Mutterrecht*," *German Life and Letters* 56 (2003): 223–43.

56 E. Diederichs "Offener Brief an den Staatsminister a.D. Schmidt-Ott," in idem (ed.), *Der Fall Herman Wirth*, 3.

57 E. Jung, "Zu Herman Wirths Forschungen," in A. Baeumler (ed.), *Was bedeutet Herman Wirth*, 65.

58 Wirth, "Deutsche Vorgeschichte," 35.

59 Wirth, *Um die wissenschaftliche Erkenntnis*, 11.

60 Loc. cit.

61 F. Wiegers, "Vorwort," in idem (ed.), *Herman Wirth und die deutsche Wissenschaft*, 4–5.

62 W. Krause, *Beiträge zur Runenforschung*, 2 vols. (Halle a.S.: Niemeyer, 1932–33); H. Arntz, *Handbuch der Runenkunde* (Halle a.S.: Niemeyer, 1935), 4, 69, 317, 321.

63 R. Henning, *Die deutschen Runendenkmäler* (Strasbourg: Trübner, 1889).

64 K. Reichardt, *Runenkunde* (Jena: Diederichs, 1936), 6.

65 G. Neckel, "Herman Wirth und die Wissenschaft," in A. Baeumler (ed.), *Was bedeutet Herman Wirth*, 20.

66 G. Neckel, "Die Herkunft der Runenschrift," in L. Roselius (ed.), *Erstes Nordisches Thing* (Bremen: Angelsachsen, 1933), 60–76 [= *Neue Jahrbücher für Wissenschaft und Jugendbildung* 9 (1933): 406–17].

67 G. Neckel, "Herman Wirth und die Wissenschaft," 14–17; idem, "Liebe und Ehe bei den vorchristlichen Germanen," *Zeitschrift für Deutschkunde* 46 (1932): 193–207, 281–93, 386–412 [= monograph, Leipzig: Teubner, 1932].

68 Neckel, report on Wirth, 8.4.30, BA: REM A144.

69 A. Baeumler, "Vorwort," in idem (ed.), *Was bedeutet Herman Wirth*, 9.

70 E. Fehrle, "Herman Wirth und die Volkskunde," in A. Baeumler (ed.), *Was bedeutet Herman Wirth*, 63.

71 W. Wüst, "Gedanken über Wirths 'Aufgang der Menschheit'," *Zeitschrift für Missionskunde und Religionswissenschaft* 44 (1929): 307.

72 Wiwjorra, "Herman Wirth," 101; cf. also Wirth's letters to Dutch newspapers in 1923 listed in E. Baumann, *Verzeichnis der Schriften, Manuskripte und Vorträge von Herman Felix WIRTH Roper Bosch* (Toppenstedt: Uwe-Berg, 1995), 25.

73 J.G. Ottema (ed.), *Thet Oera Linda Bok* (Leeuwarden: Kuipers, 1872) [= *The Oera Linda Book*, trans. W.R. Sandbach (London: Trübner, 1876)].

74 J. Beckering Vinckers, *De onechtheid van het Oera Linda Bôk aangetoond* (Haarlem: Bohn, 1876); idem, *Wie heeft het Oera Linda Boek geschreven?* (Kampen: Van Hulst, 1877); M. de Jong Hendrikszoon, *Het geheim van het Oera Linda Boek* (Bolsward: Oringa, 1927); idem, *Het Oera-Lind-Boek in Duitschland en hier* (Bolsward: Oringa, 1939); P.C.J.A. Boeles, *De auteur van het Oera Linda Boek* (Leeuwarden: Noord Nederlandsche Boekhandling, 1928).

75 Wirth (ed.), *Die Ura Linda Chronik*; J.O. Plaßmann, "Die Ura Linda-Chronik," *Germanien* 5 (1933): 323–29; Buning, 156–59.

76 W. Krause, "Uralinda Chronik und Germanentum," *Alt-Preußen* 1 (1935): 56–57.

77 Wirth (ed.), *Die Ura Linda Chronik*, 131–300.

78 G. Neckel, "Ist die Ura-Linda-Chr. echt?," *Der Tag* 29 Dec. 1933; idem, "Zur Ura-Linda-Chronik," *Island* 20 (1934/35): 106–7 [= (abridged) *Nationalsozialistische Monatshefte* 5, 1934, 273–75].

79 O. Suffert, "Zum Streit um die Ura-Linda-Chronik," *Germanien* 6 (1934): 49–56; A. Hübner, *Herman Wirth und die Ura Linda-Chronik* (Berlin: De Gruyter, 1934); W. Krogmann, *Ahnenerbe oder Falschung?* (Berlin: Ebering, 1934); T. Stecke, "Die Ura-Linda-Chronik," *Völkischer Beobachter* 11 Jan. 1934; K.H. Jacob-Friesen, "Die Ura-Linda-Chronik," *Vergangenheit und Gegenwart* 24 (1934): 125–28; idem, "Hermann Wirths Ura-Linda-Chronik und die deutschen Vorgeschichtsforscher," *Nachrichtenblatt für deutsche Vorzeit* 10 (1934): 130–35; H.D. Köhler, *Studien zur Ura-Linda-Chronik* (Weimar: Böhlau, 1936); S. Storm, "Die öffentliche Aussprache über Herman Wirths 'Ura-Linda-Chronik' in Berlin (1934)," in B. Almgren (ed.), *Bilder des Nordens in der Germanistik 1929–1945* (Huddinge: Södertörns Högskola, 2002), 79–97.

80 Montanus, *Die deutschen Volksfeste, Volksbräuche und deutscher Volksglaube in Sagen, Märlein und Volksliedern I* (Iserlohn: Bädecker, 1854), apud Hübner, 27–28.

81 Wirth/Roselius 20.6.34, BA: AE B284. By March 1935 the subtitle had changed to the "Collection for People's Beliefs and Primordial Belief" ("Sammlung für Volksglauben und Urglaube").

82 B. Freiherr von Richthoften, "Zur religionsgeschichtlichen Auswertung vorgeschichtlicher Altertümer," *Mitteilungen der Anthropologischen Gesellschaft in Wien* 62 (1932): 110–44; idem, "Eine Entgegnung an Prof. H. Wirth," vol. cit., 228–30; cf. idem, "Um Herman Wirth," *Reichswart* 7 May 1932, H. Wirth, "Zur religionswissenschaftlichen Auswertung vorgeschichtlicher Altertümer," *Mitteilungen der Anthropologischen Gesellschaft in Wien* 62 (1932) 227–28.

83 Rosenberg/Wirth 23.5.32, BA: OPG 1848; von Richthofen/Frick 7.10.33; von Richthofen/Achelis 20.11.33; Reinerth/Achelis 14.11.33; Wiegers/Achelis 23.11.33, all BA: REM A114; and cf. R. Glaser, *Wer ist Herman Wirth?* (Breslau: self published, [1934]), 11; von Richthofen/Plaßmann 5.6.36, BA: OPG 1848.

84 Wirth/Roselius 20.6.34 BA: AE B284; Wirth/Darré 15.6.34; Darré/Wirth 7.7.34; both BA: AE B315.

85 Indeed Hermann Rauschning records that Himmler had asked him to put the "fear of god" into a noted critic of Wirth's acceptance of the forgery; H Rauchning, *Hitler Speaks* (London: Thornton Butterworth, 1939), 225.

86 M. Ziegler, "Der Lebensbaum im germanischen Brauchtum," *Völkischer Beobachter* 17 May 1935; cf. *Germanien* 7 (1935): 128.

87 *Nordland* 1–9 (Düsseldorf: Nordland–Verlag, 1933–41); *Germanien* 1–15 (Bielefeld: Wittekind, then Thomas, 1929–32 and Leipzig: Koehler, 1933–44).

88 Wirth, *Heilige Urschrift*; Pringle, 63ff.

89 "Vereinsnachrichten," *Germanien* 9 (1937): 384.

90 H. Wirth (dir.), *Nordischer Urmythus und die Fleichwerdung Christi* (Berlin 1935 [premiered 7 Apr. 1935, now lost]).

91 J. von Leers, *Juden sehen dich an* (Berlin–Schöneberg: NS Druck & Verlag, 1933); idem, *Odal* (Goslar: Blut und Boden, 1935); contract for "Odal," 5/11.7.35; Wirth/AE 9.7.36; Wirth/Himmler 7.5.36; Galke/Wirth 26.11.36; Sievers, file note, 1.3.40; all BA: AE B315; Buning, 160–61.

92 Wirth/Galke 25.5.36; Galke/P. Wirth 20.7.36; both BA: AE B315.

93 W. Höppner, "Kontinuität und Diskontinuität in der Berliner Germanistik," in R. vom Bruch and C. Jahr (eds.), *Die Berliner Universität in der NS-Zeit*, 2 vols. (Stuttgart: Steiner, 2005), II, 267–68; Baumann, *Verzeichnis*, 35.

94 Himmler/Galke 28.10.36; cf. Sievers/Winzer 5.11.38; Wüst/Himmler 13.7.38; all BA: AE B315; Pringle, 67, 91–93.

95 Pringle, 91–92.

96 Himmler/Wirth 15.2.37; Wirth/Himmler 3.9.37; both BA: AE B315; Kelz/RFSS-PHA 11.6.40; BA: OPG 1875.

97 Höfler supported the direction of Wirth's scholarship but advised he was not suitable for a teaching role; Höfler, reference, 9.10.35, BA: REM A114; and cf. Höfler/Sievers 29.7.1937, BA AE 776.

98 Wirth/Menzel 28.10.39; Menzel, filenote, 15.12.39; Menzel/Wirth 11.11.39; Wirth/Menzel 2.12.39; Wirth/Himmler 15.12.39; Wirth/Menzel 20.12.39; Menzel/Wirth 6.2.40; Himmler/Wirth 13.7.40; Menzel, file note, 21.2.42; all BA: REM A114.

99 Menzel, file note, 21.2.42; Frick/Rector of Phillips-Universität, Marburg 24.4.42; Martin/Rector of Phillips-Universität, Marburg 29.4.42; all BA: REM A114.

100 Wirth/Roselius 8.1.35, BA: AE B284; Sievers/Himmler, 24.9.36, BA: AE B315.

101 Strohmeyer, 69–79.

102 Wirth/Himmler 27.2.42, BA: REM A114; protocol Himmler/Wirth 8.7.42; BA: AE B315.

103 Wiwjorra, "Herman Wirth," 107.

104 Wiwjorra, "Herman Wirth," 107, esp. n. 89.

105 Huth/Sievers 19.11.36, BA AE 556; Hauer/Sievers 29.6.37, H. Naumann/Sievers 4.9.37, both BA PA Kummer; W. Wüst, "Das Bedenkliche und Gefährliche in der Germanenauffassung von Dr. Bernhard Kummer," 3 Nov. 1937, BA AE 763; Wüst, minutes of meeting with Himmler, Wolff and Galke, 5.11.37, BA AE 763.

106 W. Sievers/H.-J. Eitner, 14.10.43, BA: AE B315; cf. Hunger, 203.

CHAPTER 7.

Academic Responses

credo, quia impossibile
Tertullian[1]

> Why should we be so concerned with Germanicness presently? It is
> because in grave times we feel a particular need to reflect upon the
> sources of our strength, so as to ensure that these virtues are not for-
> gotten. Germanic studies and *Volkskunde* were born in the Romantic
> period, in a time of national danger. And there are parallels in the
> post-Great War period. The love for Germanicness and the striving
> for an understanding of it is our principal motivation.[1]

There is no doubt more than a germ of truth in this passage from 1943
where Otto Höfler links the resurgence of interest in Germanic antiquity in the 1920s and 30s to a broadly felt sense of national threat comparable to that of Napoleonic times. Diederichs's "New Romanticism"
and many of the other expressions of cultural and social renewal were
based on a sense that something was very wrong in Germany, both
in the latter years of the Wilhelmine Empire and in the more desper-
ate and turbulent times that followed the loss of the First World War.
This feeling of moral and national crisis (or "internal and external dis-
unity and self-abasement of the German people" as Wirth put it 1931)[2]
strongly informed the master of *Sinnbildforschung*'s gnostic vision of antiquity. It also helps explain why his theories struck such a strong chord
with the German public at large.

Yet however well it might explain the growing Germanophilia of
the day, this sense of threat does not explain the abject Germanomania
that both amateur and professional investigators of the Old Germanic
past exhibited at the time. After all, even before Wirth had been in-
stalled as president of the SS-Ahnenerbe in 1935, a sizeable body of literature had grown up around his ideographic studies. Several members
and associates of his society published their own accounts of Germanic
ideographs and a monograph series named for the society had been

established by 1930 in order to further the reception of his theories. Even two digests of the ideas in Wirth's *Emergence* had appeared by 1933.[3] There were many scholars who were accepting or even enthusiastic promoters of this new scholarship: many German academics had long disdained abject *völkisch* Germanism, but by the 1930s many now recognized that circumstances had changed. On the other hand, several of these works were reviewed by German academics who treated *Sinnbildforschung* like a scourge. In fact as the influence of *völkisch* approaches to Germanic antiquarian discourse became more patent after 1933, vociferous opponents rose up against what they saw as the perversion of their discipline.

Perhaps the most intelligent, impartial and succinct review of Wirth's work from the time appeared in the journal of literary review, *Die Neue Literatur* in 1932, where the reviewer, the novelist Hjalmar Kutzleb summarized the essential features of Wirth's *Emergence*.[4]

> It is difficult not to be annoyed by Wirth's *Emergence of Mankind*: an abundance of knowledge, a superhuman effort, an ideal willingness to make sacrifices ... and the fruit of all this: a colossal fantasy.

Kutzleb also explained how this "syncretism of Nietzsche and Christ, of Brahmanism and the Eddas" should be judged vis-à-vis respectable scholarship:

> The scholasticism of the Middle Ages had its opposite number in [Christian] mysticism, and the Nordic doctrine of salvation has produced its mysticism in much the same manner.

With some justification, he then goes on to compare Wirth's project with that of other creators of fabulous world views popular in *völkisch* circles who were active at the time:

> People in [this] mould ... prefer to speak from intuition and play against the prudent and craftsman-like type of empirical scholarship in a similar manner.

Few reviewers were able to enunciate so insightful a characterization of Wirth's learning—of its gnostic, intuitive and fantastic elements. In

France, Salomon Reinach just reacted savagely, dismissing the thesis of Wirth's *Emergence* as "half-read delirium."[5] Nils Åberg, a Swedish antiquarian, dismissively claimed the *Emergence* was a case of emperor's new clothes, contrasting Wirth's fate under Hitler with that of Albert Einstein (who had just been dismissed from the University of Berlin).[6] The shortcomings of the author of the *Emergence* were patent. But the influence of the renewalistic Germanophile fervor that Kutzleb called the "Nordic doctrine of salvation" was not always so simple to insulate oneself from in the Germany of the time. In fact, it is evident that many excellent scholars chose to temper their critical apparatus when it came to *völkisch* offshoots of antiquarianism and accommodated attitudes very similar to those of Wirth and his *confrères* in academic discourse. Some even surrendered to it.

Many antiquarian Germanists responded to Wirth's *Emergence* publicly and their assessments were often less dismissive than that of Kutzleb. Kutzleb himself would go on to write two books on Arminius which would be lauded in *völkisch* circles.[7] Yet it is the judgement of those who could best be considered experts in early Germanic language and culture, not just enthusiasts, that is most relevant to an understanding of the academic reception of *Sinnbildforschung* and other aspects of basely ideologized scholarship from the time. The selection of responses and contexts that follows, then, has largely been chosen by the antiquarian experts who themselves opted to make their views public.

All of the men whose responses are examined in what follows had upper or upper-middle-class backgrounds and all received the traditional classically focused pre-university education of the German gymnasium school. Nearly half followed their fathers into higher studies, they are roughly representative of broader German academia in terms of religious confession, and half again already held tenured positions at the time they first responded to the writings of Wirth.

It must, of course, also be remembered that the German academic system was experiencing institutional stress at the time of the Nazi accession to power. Increasing casualization of staff over the course of the 1920s had raised the level of competition for senior, tenured positions. Under the new regime, in most disciplines a rash of dismissals due to race or political unsuitability eased these pressures somewhat. Such dismissals, however, were rare in Old Germanic studies; instead, the

Party clearly patronized the study of Germanic antiquity after 1933. In fact the length of time between achieving the doctorate (Promotion), the further study (Habilitation) which is required to attain a teaching post, and again the wait to win tenure, decreased markedly for all disciplines between 1933 and 1938.[8] Such an environment clearly favored junior academics and should no longer have been particularly conducive to an increased level of opportunism among those in search of a permanent post.

Yet in terms of social standing, most of these Germanists stem from the background that Fritz Ringer has dubbed the mandarin elite—gymnasium-trained sons of bureaucrats, lawyers, Lutheran churchmen and the like—in contrast to an overall rate of one in two for German academia in general.[9] Old Germanic studies was evidently a conservative field in terms of the backgrounds of its university proponents. Many of the scholars whose opinions are surveyed here were also senior enough to be at least somewhat removed, if not completely immune from the pressures faced by younger academics at the time. In fact the social background and seniority of the scholars whose responses shall now be assessed seems to have little correlation with, and hence direct bearing on, their assessment of *Sinnbildforschung*. Many took the approach of Höfler to the excesses of *völkisch* antiquarianism—treating it as understandable and often allowable exuberance—although few were as cravenly opportunistic as the man often seen as the chief Germanist in the SS at the time.

PROTEST

The runologist Helmut Arntz was a pupil of the leading German linguist Herman Hirt who, apart from being the originator of the concept of the apophonic zero degree (that Roland Barthes was later to make so much of), was also one of the first and most influential of the proponents within linguistics of a European homeland for the Indo-Europeans.[10] Hirt was lionized in his own lifetime as a giant of Germanic and Indo-European philology, and his student Arntz served as editor of his influential *Festschrift* of 1936.[11] Arntz completed the final volume of Hirt's Indo-European grammar after the author's death and went on to publish two collections of his mentor's papers in 1939 and 1940.[12]

Yet Hirt had not been able to set Arntz up with a tenured position, and after the war Arntz was unable to find a suitable position and left academia to work for the West German government.[13]

Arntz produced a dissertation typical for an Indo-Europeanist of the period, but soon came to focus on the relatively new specialization of runic studies.[14] As a 22-year-old he burst upon the scene of German runology with his *Handbook* of 1935, a work which was soon followed by the publication of his professional thesis on runes and the Irish Ogham letters.[15] Arntz thereafter continued to publish widely on runes and by 1939 had even contributed two articles on runology to encyclopedic collections.[16] He was clearly the leading figure in German runic studies in the 1930s and at the end of that decade founded a journal, *Runenberichte (Runic Reviews)*, which he hoped would develop into the principal organ for runological discourse.[17]

Arntz was also the most critical German reviewer of the development of *Sinnbildforschung*. In 1934 he had only recently completed his doctorate at Giessen when he first came to consider the theories of Wirth and the promoters of the *Urschrift* thesis. In his *Handbook* Arntz sought to provide the first comprehensive review of runology that had appeared in German since the translation of Wimmer's seminal *The Runic Script* had appeared in 1887. The young runologist began with a brief outline of the development of writing such as might be found today in any alphabet history, in his summary rejecting *Sinnbildforschung* out of hand. Arntz dismissed the autochthonous theory as fantastic and in his critical bibliography he labelled all works that employed the *Urschrift* thesis as those of fantasists.

When reviews of Arntz's *Handbook* came out, however, the Königsberg-based runologist Wolfgang Krause pointed out that sections of Arntz's work merely parroted passages from a similar handbook published in Swedish in 1933 by the renowned Swedish runologist Otto von Friesen.[18] Krause also chided Arntz for acting merely as a summarizer of previous scholarship, falling short of actually accusing him of plagiarism. *Völkisch* reviewers, however, were appalled. The retired schoolmaster Edmund Weber whose first foray into practical runology had been spectacularly unsuccessful (the inscription he had verified as runic was in fact Latin), listed the names of authors whom Arntz had criticized in his review of his *Handbook* in *Germanien* in 1936, decrying their treatment at his hands.[19] Though this list merely reads like an enumeration of the more inglorious of the dilettantes who had plagued the field over the previous hundred years, Weber thought this list was good evidence for Arntz's arrogance.

Scornful of the criticisms of Weber, but taking on board those of Krause, Arntz continued to attack the purveyors of *Sinnbildforschung*. Not only did he criticize Neckel's theories, he even sought fit to investigate Wirth's books, declaring them follies.[20] Meanwhile, Weber's criticism of Arntz had led to an investigation of the young runologist by members of the Ahnenerbe. Despite the approval of his publications by senior Party members including Himmler, especially his *Native Runic Monuments of the Continent (Die einheimlichen Runendenkmäler des Festlandes)* coauthored with the Germanophile RGK archeologist Hans Zeiss in 1939,[21] with the aid of secret reports from Ahnenerbe associates, including Krause, Arntz's applications for research grants to the DFG were white-anted. Reinerth had been suspicious of Arntz and his connection with RGK "Romelings" like Zeiss (despite the latter's excellent political credentials)[22] and had discovered in his investigations that Arntz was one-eighth Jewish. Word was eventually passed on to the SS and Arntz's name became tainted. Arntz was an Aryan according to the standards set out in the 1933 Law for the Restoration of the Civil Service (Gesetz zur Wiederherstellung des Berufsbeamtentums) and the more comprehensive Nuremberg Laws from 1935. Yet in the late 1930s he was regularly declaimed as racially suspect in Party and administrative channels.[23] With the outbreak of war, however, Arntz's section of the university was closed and he entered the German army. The second edition of his *Handbook* came out in 1944 with the preface written "in the field" explaining how his military service had hampered the preparation of the volume. The second edition of Arntz's *Handbook* became the principal source for the English and French runological handbooks which appeared in the 1950s and 60s.[24] Nevertheless, Arntz was not offered his old position back when the University of Giessen reopened after the war. His academic career had been ruined, ostensibly because his great-grandmother had been Jewish. As Ulrich Hunger has shown, however, Arntz's attitude to *Sinnbildforschung* in his *Handbook* had been noted by both the Ahnenerbe and the Party's ideological censors, the Parteiämtliche Prüfungskommission zum Schutze des NS-Schrifttums. Rather than a racial taint, it seems more likely that it was his strident criticism of Wirth's ideographic studies that was the real reason for his persecution. After all, in 1936 in light of his public criticisms of Höfler's *Männerbund* theories a similar racial claim had been made against Friedrich von der Leyen's wife. The conservative Cologne folklorist was forced into early retirement rather than divorce her, his treatment sending more serious shockwaves through academic circles than did the fate of Arntz.[25]

PRINCIPLE

Some others who judged the new scholarship in a similarly deleterious light chose to confront it in a manner less likely to render them liable to personal attack. Such was the case with Konstantin Reichardt, a Russian-German by birth whose father had been attached to the German ambassador's court at St Petersburg. With the outbreak of the Great War, young "Kostja" had come to Germany, however, where he received a good Calvinist upbringing. He excelled at languages, specialized in Nordic philology and after completing his doctorate at Berlin succeeded Eugen Mogk in 1931 to the chair in Nordic philology at the University of Leipzig.[26] By the 1930s, though, he had become involved in the *Thule* translations of the Old Norse sagas for Diederichs and was invited by the late publisher's sons to contribute a volume on runology to their scientific series.[27] Reichardt's *Runology (Runenkunde)* of 1936 is a very sober assessment of runology at a time when *völkisch* enthusiasm was becoming ubiquitous in Germanic antiquarian studies.[28] But in 1937 Reichardt did what no other German academic involved in runology or Germanic antiquarian studies in general did. Of his own accord, given the chance while on official university business in Uppsala, Reichardt decided he had had enough of the madness of Nazi Germany. He sought out a new life, at first in Gothenburg where he gave guest lectures for a time, and then finally in the United States. Leaving his mother and brothers behind in Germany, he became a naturalized U.S. citizen during the war, and continued to teach in the U.S. until his retirement from Yale in 1972.[29]

Unfortunately for Reichardt one of his colleagues, his "next-door neighbor" (as Reichardt described him) André Jolles, had become especially enamored of National Socialism. A Netherlander by birth and a former lecturer at Ghent late in the First World War, Jolles had been a Party member since 1931 and had begun working for the SD in 1937 as a specialist in Freemasonry.[30] In his papers, Reichardt singles out Jolles especially as one of the reasons that he left; although Reichardt participated in events such as a "political week" under the auspices of the Nazi Teacher's League in early 1937 (where he gave an address on "the cultural meaning of Old Germanic poetry" in the company of Leo Weisgerber), the official reason Reichardt gave to the German authorities for his resignation was a lack of intellectual freedom.[31] The constant attacks on Jews, the Germanomania and the growing atmosphere of denunciation and intimidation from radical students evidently upset Reichardt's sensibilities at the time. In fact the final straw, he told his daughter Maria after the war, was when a student set off a stink bomb during a lecture being given by a Jewish colleague. His former colleagues at Leipzig treated him like a prima donna after the fact, but he could no longer tolerate the insanity into which his ancestral homeland had descended.[32]

Another critic of the new path mapped out for Germanic studies by *völkisch* academics was Franz Rolf Schröder, Professor of Germanic Philology at the University of Würzburg, and, more prominently, from 1920–71, editor of the *Germanisch–Romanische Monatsschrift* (*Germanic–Romance Monthly*, *GRM*).[33] Although at first (from 1920–36) he shared this duty with *GRM*'s founder, his academic father Heinrich, the younger Schröder was editor of Old Germanic literature and already had published some runological work by 1928.[34] In his 1932 presentation of the collection of essays edited by Wiegers on the *Emergence* "of the so-called prehistorian" Wirth, he describes it as an "abstruse book bereft of any rationality."[35] He also turned on Neckel a number of times for his acceptance of the *Urschrift* thesis (among other distortions) and as late as 1935 explicitly pointed out the influence of Wirth at play in Neckel's thinking.[36]

Yet despite his earlier negative assessment of the contributions of dilettantes and academic Germanomania, Schröder grew increasingly tolerant of other *völkisch* work. In 1936, for example, he wrote a less-than-critical review of the second edition of Bernhard Kummer's *Midgard's Decline* in which Schröder averred that Kummer's work was not strongly empirical and scientific, but in the same breath praised it as "stimulating," lauding its idealism and the courage of the author's convictions.[37] Increasingly, Schröder pandered to the political reality of the time, *GRM* under his editorship even publishing explicit endorsements of the National Socialists.[38] In a review from 1929 he had dismissed the dilettantes who lived under the Tertullian-like maxim "*credo, quia absurdum est*" (I believe because it is impossible).[39] Yet by 1936 he was covering them with faint praise and publishing *völkisch* fancies with themes such as whether the English poet Coleridge was a National Socialist and if *völkisch* and racist terminology was translatable into French.[40] In 1937 Schröder's conversion to the new political orthodoxy was completed when he was accepted for Party membership. Despite his earlier statements, Schröder ultimately found the safest path was the one of no resistance.[41]

STRUGGLE

Another, rather less sober figure also involved in the *Thule* translations was Gustav Neckel, from 1923 Professor of Old Germanic Studies at the University of Berlin. The son of a Prussian industrialist, even before the Nazi accession to power Neckel had adopted an extreme political stance to his research and role at the university; from the middle of the 1920s, a new facet had begun to appear in his work. Some of his better-known scholarship that was published prior to 1925 is of high quality, but little after that date can easily be rescued today, steeped as it increasingly became in polemic and indeed outright fantasy. It is difficult to understand how the author of *The Traditions of the God Balder (Die Überlieferungen vom Gotte Balder)* from 1920 in which he compared the Balder cult with earlier Mediterranean beliefs could come out so strongly in favor of Kossinna's *ex Septentrione lux* scarcely a decade later.[42] Similarly, the author of a solid assessment of the runes and their origin from 1909 seems hard to recognize in the scholar who supported Wirth's *Sinnbildforschung*, argued (against Wimmer) that the Scandinavian runes were older than the common Germanic alphabet and maintained that the runic script developed from an Indo-European *Urschrift*.[43]

One of the first signs of the transformation that had overcome Neckel in the late 1920s was his harrying of Sigmund Feist. Heusler, who had come to the conclusion by 1933 that Neckel had simply gone mad, cites a monograph from 1929 that showed the first evidence for his mental deterioration: this was what Heusler called Neckel's "Celts-book," one that was begun at first as an attack on Feist.[44]

A Jewish linguist and sometime runologist, Feist received his doctorate from the University of Strasbourg for a study of Gothic etymology and had come to Berlin in the early 1900s as headmaster of a Jewish orphan school.[45] At the same time Feist joined Berlin's German Philological Society (Gesellschaft für deutsche Philologie), a collective of German academics and schoolteachers that met once a month to discuss German and Germanic linguistics and literature. He soon became active in the Society's linguistic review journal where he rapidly gained a reputation as a stern critic of amateur excess. He had, for example, been one of the most vociferous opponents of the notion that the Indo-Europeans were native to Europe, declaring by 1915 the notion of indigeneity an "Aryan myth." He was also contemptuous of the *Urschrift* theory and the attempts to bring a racial aspect to linguistic and archeological discussion.[46] He reserved an especially caustic tone for *völkisch* antiquarians, though. When he was not poking fun at them, Wilser's works, for example, were characterized variously as romantic, fantastic and ignorant.[47] As Feist observed in 1916, Wilser seemed to think *"risum teneatis"* that "all that is worthwhile in world civilization is of Germanic origin."[48]

In March 1927, however, Feist journeyed to Paris where he gave a paper to the Société de Linguistique de Paris on the vexed issue of "Celts and Germans," the early historical relationship between the ancient Germanic and Celtic peoples in the period about the birth of Christ. He had been invited out of recognition for his work in promoting the teaching of French in Germany (he had published a successful French course in the 1890s).[49] The focus of Feist's research, though, was antiquity and his contribution to Old Germanic studies had clearly won him the respect of his French peers.[50] The paper he delivered promoted a radical theory that sought to explain the ambiguous (and indeed conflicting) linguistic evidence of the records from classical sources, positing that the "Celts" and "Germans" recorded from about the Rhine were in fact members of a third community of Celto-Germans, neither Celtic nor Germanic in the usual sense, but linguistically similar to both.[51] This, of course, suggested that Arminius was not truly German, but a Celto-German instead. His theory came to be published in monographic form later that year and soon after anti-Semitic and chauvinistic members of the German Philological Society rallied to have him expelled, ostensibly for having impugned national pride.[52] One of his main critics, Rudolf Much, even claimed in print that he was a *"Germanenfeind,"* an enemy of the ancient Germanic peoples.[53] In May 1928 Feist resigned, remarking: "I had always seen myself as a member of a scientific society, not a political club. Now I must recognize my mistake. The Society has changed; I have not."[54]

The ferocity of the attacks by Much and others were clearly motivated in part by Feist's Jewishness. Yet Feist continued to enjoy a degree of critical success and indeed the late 1920s were an especially prolific period for him. Moreover, many of the attacks against Feist cannot at all be construed as anti-Semitic. Most such as Richard Huß merely attacked Feist as *"germanenfeindlich."*[55] Indeed, one of the most chauvinistic attacks was that of Neckel, who besides citing Much even calls on the opinion of his colleague the Austro-Czech Celticist Julius Pokorny (who was later dismissed from the University of Berlin as a non-Aryan) in his monographic attack upon Feist and others whom he judged had represented Germanic antiquity unfavorably.[56] Neckel admitted by 1933, however, that upon closer consideration Feist seems merely to have revived ideas found in much older theories (both French and German, but mostly those of Henri d'Arbois de Jubainville, one of Kossinna's old sparring partners) on the question of the relations between the early Celtic and Germanic peoples.[57] In fact, he must have realized by then that much of his vitriol had been misguided. Yet in the late 1920s, wherever he found them he had treated Feist's theories with contempt. Attacks on Feist continued into the 1930s and soon even led to his demonizing. Feist's scholarship was dismissed as destructive Jewish carping by *völkisch* enthusiasts such as Weber and citation of the Gothicist even became a criterion for the assessment of Arntz by his Ahnenerbe investigators.[58] The work of other Germanists of Jewish extraction such as the linguists Otto Bremer (a renowned radical nationalist) and Hermann Jacobsohn (who committed suicide after his 1933 dismissal from the University of Marburg) escaped this fate.[59] Feist became the representative of the destructive Jew of National Socialist propaganda within the discourse of Old Germanic studies. It is no surprise, then, that Neckel's 1929 revival of the autochthonous theory of the origin of the runes, so important to the acceptance of

Sinnbildforschung among sections of the academic community, was accompanied by an attack on Feist's own theory on the question.[60]

The importance of Neckel for *Sinnbildforschung* was the prestige he enjoyed and the influence that he had been able to muster since succeeding Heusler to the chair of Old Germanic studies at the University of Berlin. In 1934 alone he published three different populist histories of the Germanic peoples; and in all three he included the theory that the runes were developed out of Bronze Age symbols.[61] Neckel's opinions may have been controversial in runological circles, but he was clearly an expert in Germanic antiquities and held the most senior Old Germanic studies chair in the country. Neckel's writings clearly served to legitimize the nascent *Sinnbildforschung* of the late 1920s and early 30s.

Through Neckel's writings, a number of Wirth's contentions that mirrored those developed by philologists in the nineteenth century had been (re)introduced to the mainstream of German scholarship. Neckel pronounced that Wirth had gone too far with his edition of the *Oera Linda Book* in 1933, however, and although he continued to uphold some of Wirth's contentions, by this time Neckel's credibility had begun to be questioned, not just by some of his academic fellows like Heusler, but also by some of the ideologues who moved in Party circles.

In 1935 Neckel was forced out of the University of Berlin by order of the Prussian Ministry of Culture and sent to Göttingen where an inaugural chair in Nordic philology was created especially for him.[62] Ostensibly, he had been forced out because he had pursued an affair with one of his assistants. After two years, though, Neckel returned to Berlin redeemed. Yet he died suddenly in 1940 after contracting a lung infection just as he had recuperated from a nervous condition and only a brief allusion to the happenings of those years appeared in the foreword of his selected essays of 1944.[63]

By the mid-1930s Neckel had managed to accumulate several detractors both within National Socialist circles and without. His predecessor Heusler claimed in the late 1920s he had begun to pursue a "pathological ambition, if not obsession."[64] According to Heusler, Neckel had fallen in with the Kossinnas, Wirths and the *völkisch* amateurs, and produced a similarly "deluded picture of antiquity."[65] Nevertheless, Neckel's "folly"[66] although it had granted him some status among the *völkisch* community was not enough to inure him to attacks from those more surely allied to the new regime.

In 1935 Neckel was accused of plagiarism by Bernhard Kummer who had previously served for some time as Neckel's assistant at Berlin but was now a leading Party-aligned Nordicist. Neckel's 1932 work *Love and Marriage among the Pre-Christian Teutons (Liebe und Ehe bei den vorchristlichen Germanen)* had raised rankles among the researchers of the Amt Rosenberg and early in 1935 Kummer publicly denounced Neckel as a plagiarist (of Kossinna), following this up with the claim that Neckel was having an affair with his new research assistant, Anne Heiermeier.[67] Kummer's allegations had been raised only as an excuse to punish Neckel—as his old friend Wilhelm Heydenreich diplomatically states in the 1944 foreword to Neckel's collected essays, he was a "victim of a hostile current directed against him that he was not a match for given his overworked condition."[68] Kummer's allegations were refuted by Neckel (who claimed he had just omitted a footnote and he upheld the reputation of Heiermeier). But amid all the resultant rancor (and attacks by Nazi students) Neckel was sent away to Göttingen before being brought back at the behest of his dean, Baeumler, two years later in 1937. Neckel's last paper was a review published posthumously in the *Historische Zeitschrift* in 1941 which, despite the attacks of Kummer and his less than happy treatment at the hands of the Party, nevertheless shows Neckel still promoting a decidedly *völkisch* perspective of Germanic antiquity.[69]

AMBITION

After Neckel, the most senior Germanist to support Wirth in print was the folklorist Eugen Fehrle. The son of a village schoolteacher from Baden, Fehrle had been sympathetic to National Socialism for at least as long as Wirth: he had rushed to Munich upon hearing of the attempted Nazi putsch in 1923, but had arrived there too late to join in. Moreover, in keeping with the direction of *Volkskunde* at the time, Fehrle was anti-Christian and obsessed with rediscovering the Germanic *Volksgeist* in folk custom. He did not join the Nazi Party until 1931, but had already found antiquarian research to be an avenue in which he could express his political beliefs.[70]

In the spirit of the topical elasticity for which German *Volkskunde* is renown, Fehrle had become one of the foundation editors of *Volk und Rasse* (Volk *and* Race), a periodical published by the Pan-German and racialist Munich-based publisher Julius Lehmann.[71] *Volk und Rasse* promoted the importance of race in matters of national culture, especially in the manner stressed by *Rassen*-Günther, at that time one of Lehmann's star authors.[72] Fehrle was also director of an editorial team that produced an edition of Tacitus' *Germania* for Lehmann's in 1929.[73] It comes as little surprise, then, to find him coming out in support of Wirth's *Emergence* in 1932. In fact with the accession of the National Socialists in 1933, Fehrle was among the first academics to declare allegiance to Hitler publicly and as a recognized Party specialist on universities became involved in the Nazification of the universities in Baden, which included his own institution, the University of Heidelberg.[74] He was duly rewarded with a professorship there at the beginning of 1934 with the support and encouragement of his friend and fellow Nazi, the *Wörter und Sachen* linguist Hermann Güntert (who from October 1933 had been appointed Dean of the Philosophical Faculty). Even in Party circles Fehrle was recognized for his boundless ambition.[75] He did not contribute much to the intellectual development of ideographic studies, though—he was an enthusiastic consumer rather than a producer of ideographic literature. But he did act to proselytize *Sinnbildforschung* among both the academic and broader community. Fehrle was the most prominent established supporter of ideographic studies in the *Volkskunde* community.

Fehrle's enthusiasm for *Sinnbildforschung* was less important, though, than that of one of Neckel's former students. In the winter of 1938/39, Arntz had managed to gain funding to set up an Institute for Runology at the University of Giessen. Yet early in 1938, Wolfgang Krause had already set up a similar body at the University of Göttingen. Krause, the son of gymnasium professor, had just arrived from Königsberg to succeed his former teacher (and signatory to the 1933 *Vow of Allegiance*) the Gothic place-name enthusiast Eduard Hermann. Krause had written his dissertation, as had Arntz, on Indo-European philology and had come to Göttingen to succeed Hermann to the Indo-European chair.[76] He had also studied Norse literature under Neckel in

Berlin, though, and indeed wrote his professional thesis from 1926 in Nordic studies.[77] But from the late 1920s, Krause had begun to direct his energies toward runology, including some brief flirtations with ideographs.[78] Unlike his contemporary and rival at Giessen, however, Krause refrained from criticizing the runological speculations of figures such as Wirth and especially his former teacher Neckel, reserving his approbation for amateur advocates of ideographic studies.[79] Indeed this faithful former student of Neckel soon came to recognize the benefits of cooperation with the Ahnenerbe; by the end of the war he had published in many of its journals and contributed to its surveillance activities, most notably when he had reported on Arntz. Yet though he embraced some of the theories of Wirth and his disciples, his main contribution to their cause, politics aside, was to legitimize *Sinnbildforschung* once and for all by producing new research into runic ideographs and pre-runic symbols, and accommodating previously amateur adherents to Wirth's theories within German academia.[80]

Almost as if in competition with Arntz's *Handbook*, in the same year Krause published his own manual of runology, *What One Carved in Runes (Was man im Runen ritzte)*.[81] Indeed, in 1937, Krause had preempted Arnzt and Zeiss with his own corpus of inscriptions, *Runic Inscriptions in the Older Futhark (Runenischriften im älteren Futhark)*, the second, postwar edition of which is now a standard work.[82] Krause and Arntz were clearly rivals, and the former's accommodation with the Ahnenerbe might well be explained as opportunistic. Yet Krause went much further than a mere accommodation with the Party and its runomaniacs. More so even than in the cases of Neckel and Fehrle, Krause's ambivalence and even warmth toward *Sinnbildforschung* in the 1930s served to legitimize Wirth's creation. In fact by the late 1930s Krause's warmth had turned to promotion and by the early 1940s he could only be described as a practitioner and cultivator of ideographic studies.

The responses of German scholars to the increasing penetration of *völkisch* imperatives, discourses and modes of thought into their discipline were varied. Some such as Arntz, von der Leyen and Feist attempted to combat its excesses; others remained silent. But it was difficult to remain unaffected by the political situation, especially when the advancement and encouragement of Old Germanic studies was so clearly seen in sections of the *völkisch* community (not the least radical university students) as vital to the project of social renewal. One could take a principled stand such as Reichardt did and go into exile, but the path chosen by too many academics instead was opportunistic. There were some figures who managed to retain their integrity throughout the period, but this seemingly was not a path open to all scholars. Instead the picture of the academic response to the challenge of the *völkisch* dictatorship in Old Germanic studies generally followed an all too familiar pattern. In Lixfeld's survey of the field of *Volkskunde* at the time, a tendency emerges that Bollmus shows was mirrored sometimes also in (West) German archeology: older scholars of a conservative persuasion often greeted the prospect of *völkisch* renewal warmly; younger scholars then undermined their elders and radicalized their scholarship further.[83] Infused already with the *völkisch* affinities of men such as Much and Neckel, established scholars of high calibre such as a Krause could be brought into the ambit of Wirth's *Sinnbildforschung* and justify their accommodation of dilettantism and indeed outright fantasy to themselves through philological sophistry. Many hid behind the notion of the new paradigms such as Kossinna's *ex Septentrione lux* or in the revival of the ideals of Germanic studies first produced in the politically charged Germany of the early nineteenth century.[84] Others like Neckel may even have deluded themselves so completely that they sincerely believed that the excesses and the cavalier attitude to evidence and logic they displayed at the time was intellectually justifiable. In Wilser's day few academics were willing to link their names to the abject Germanomania of *völkisch* amateurs. Yet by the time of the launch of Wirth's *Emergence*, a range of scholars had joined the Kossinnas and the Muchs and had become happy to favor a new Germanic antiquarian scholarship based as equally on patriotism as it was any empirical tradition. For too many Germanists an accommodation with *Sinnbildforschung* and the Ahnenerbe proved just too tempting; as the prestige of the SS in the political system rose in general, Himmler's learned society similarly came to dominate antiquarian studies in the Third Reich.

NOTES

1 O. Höfler, "Probleme der germanenkundlichen Forschung in unserer Zeit," lecture given 26 Feb. 1943 to a conference of the Teaching and Research Post for Germanic-German *Volkskunde* in Salzburg; BA PA Höfler.

2 Wirth, *Was heißt deutsch?*, 7.

3 S. Kadner, *Urheimat und Weg des Kulturmenschen* (Jena: Diederichs, 1930); M. Wieser, *Aufbruch des Nordens* (Berlin: Boll, [1933]).

4 H. Kutzleb, "Scholastik von heute II," *Die Neue Literatur* 33 (1932): 108–11; cf. idem, "Unsere Meinung," *Die Neue Literatur* 33 (1932): 533–34.

5 S. Reinach, review of Wirth, *Aufgang*, *Revue archéologique*, 5ᵉ ser., 3 (1929): 136.

6 Åberg, 249.

7 H. Kutzleb, *Der erste Deutsche* (Brunswick: Westermann [1934]); idem, *Arminius* (Münster i.Wf.: Coppenrath, 1935).

8 F.K. Ringer, *The Decline of the German Mandarins* (Cambridge, Mass.: Harvard University Press, 1969); idem, "A Sociography of German Academics, 1863–1938," *Central European History* 25 (1993): 259–62, 264, 279.

9 Ringer, "Sociography," 268.

10 H.A. Hirt, *Die Indogermanen*, 2 vols. (Strasbourg: Trübner, 1905–7).

11 H. Arntz (ed.), *Germanen und Indogermanen*, 2 vols. (Heidelberg: Winter, 1936).

12 H.A. Hirt, *Indogermanische Grammatik*, 7 vols. (Heidelberg: Winter, 1921–37); idem, *Die Hauptprobleme der indogermanischen Sprachwissenschaft*, ed. H. Arntz (Halle a.S.: Niemeyer, 1939); idem, *Indogermanica*, ed. H. Arntz (Halle a.S.: Niemeyer, 1940).

13 Hunger, 43ff.

14 H. Arntz, *Sprachliche Beziehungen zwischen Arisch und Balto-Slawisch* (Heidelberg: Winter, 1933).

15 Arntz, *Handbuch*; idem, "Das Ogam," *PBB* 59 (1935): 321–413 [= monograph, Halle a.S.: Niemeyer, 1935].

16 H. Arntz, *Die Runen* (Tübingen: Schramm, 1938); idem, "Nordeuropa," in W. Otto (ed.), *Handbuch der Archäologie* I (Munich: Beck, 1939), 329–56.

17 *Berichte zur Runenforschung/Runenberichte* 1/1–4 (1939–42).

18 O. von Friesen (ed.), *Runorna* (Stockholm: Bonnier, 1933); W. Krause, review of Arntz, *Handbuch*, *AfdA* 55 (1936): 1–6.

19 H. Harder and E. Weber, "Ein Runenfund im deutschen Museum zu Berlin," *ZfdA* 68 (1931): 217–25; S. Feist, "Zu den Berliner Runenfunden," *ZfdA* (69): 1932, 136; E. Weber, "Ein Handbuch der Runenkunde," *Germanien* 8 (1936): 257–61.

20 H. Arnzt, "Vom Weltbild der Felsritzer und vom Weltbild Herman Wirths," *Runenberichte* 1 (1941): 91–102; idem, "Die Runen," *ZfdPh* 67 (1942): 121–36.

21 H. Arntz and H. Zeiss, *Die einheimischen Runendenkmäler des Festlandes* (Leipzig: Harrassowitz, 1939).

22 Zeiss, the son-in-law of the racialist publisher J.F. Lehmann and an editor of *Volk und Rasse*, had been a longstanding member of the radical right; H. Fehr, "Hans Zeiss, Joachim Werner und die archäologischen Forschungen zur Merowingerzeit," in H. Steuer (ed.), *Eine hervorrangend nationale Wissenschaft* (Berlin: De Gruyter, 2001), 316–30.

23 Hunger, 45–70.

24 R.W.V. Elliot, *Runes* (Manchester: Manchester University Press, 1959); L. Musset, *Introduction à la runologie* (Paris: Aubier-Montagne, 1965).

25 As von der Leyen pointed out at the time, his wife was Aryan according to the Nuremberg Laws; von der Leyen/REM 28.7.36 in K.O. Conrady, *Völkisch-nationale Germanistik in Köln* (Schernfeld: Süddeutsche Hochschul-Verlag, 1990), 56–58; Engster, 86–87.

26 K. Reichardt, *Studien zu den Skalden des 9. und 10. Jahrhunderts* (Leipzig: Mayer & Müller, 1928); idem, reviews in the *DLZ* 1928–36; idem, contributions to *Jahresbericht* NF 3 (1925 [1928]) - NF 15 (1935 [1939]); E. Mogk and K. Reichardt (eds.), *Sammlung altnordischer Übungstexte* 1–7 (Halle a.S.: Niemeyer, 1934–35).

27 K. Reichardt, *Thule* (Jena: Diederichs, 1934); idem, *Germanische Welt vor tausend Jahren* (Jena: Diederichs, 1936); idem, *Havard, der Mann von Ejsfjord* (Jena: Diederichs, 1940).

28 Reichardt, *Runenkunde*.

29 W.M. Craigie/Reichardt, 7.11.1937, Reichardt papers, Yale: Ser. I, box 1, fol. 1; anon., "Tysk professor blir ny lektor vid Högskolan," *Göteborgs Handels* 23 Dec. 1937; K. Reichardt, résumés, 1938ff., Reichardt papers: Ser. I, box 1, fol. 1, 5 & 25.

30 A. Jolles, *Freimaurerei* ([s.l.], 1944); J. Lerchenmüller and G. Simon, *Im Vorfeld des Massenmords*, 3rd ed. (Tübingen: GIFT, 1997), 33ff.

31 "*Er war einer der zwei, die wußten, daß ich meine Stellung aufgeben würde,*" undated photocopy taken from a letter of Reichardt's, Reichardt papers, Yale: I, 1, 22; W. Becher, "Volkspolitische Woche in Sachsen," *Muttersprache* 52 (1937): 203 and cf. BA AE 21/710.

32 Heusler/Ranisch 28.1.38 and 11.3.38, nos 195 & 196 in Düwel and Beck (eds.), 632 & 635; Schirmer/RSK 26.1.39, BA: RKK 2101, Box 982, File 19; H.A. Strauß and W. Röder (eds.), *International Biographical Dictionary of Central European Emigrés 1933–1945*, 3 vols. (Munich: Saur, 1980–83), II/2, 950; Maria Wilkinson (née Reichardt), personal communication.

33 *Germanisch–Romanische Monatsschrift* 1–31 (Heidelberg: Winter, 1909–43); F.R. Schröder, *Untersuchungen zur Halfdanar Saga Eysteinssonar* (Halle a.S.: Niemeyer, 1917).

34 F.R. Schröder, "Neuere Runenforschung," *GRM* 10 (1922): 4–16; idem, "Zur Runeninschrift auf dem Marmorlöwen im Piräus," *PBB* 47 (1923): 347–50; A. Johanesson, *Grammatik der urnordischen Runeninschriften*, trans. J.C. Poestion, ed. F.R. Schröder (Heidelberg: Winter, 1923).

35 F.R. Schröder, presentation of F. Wiegers (ed.), *Herman Wirth und die deutsche Wissenschaft, GRM* 20 (1932): 313; B. Almgren, *Germanistik und Nationalsozialismus* (Uppsala: Almqvist & Wiksell, 1997), 248–49.

36 F.R. Schröder, presentation of G. Neckel, *Kultur der alten Germanen* (Potsdam, 1934), *GRM* 23 (1935): 230; Almgren, *Germanistik,* 147–49; cf. also the attack on Neckel from later that year provoked by Neckel's unfavorable review of his *Altgermanische Kulturprobleme* (Berlin: De Gruyter, 1929): G. Neckel, review of Schröder, *DLZ* 50 (1929): 521–24; F.R. Schröder, "Neuere Forschungen zur germanischen Altertumskunde und Religionsgeschichte," *GRM* 17 (1929): 418, n. 2.

37 F.R. Schröder, review of Kummer, *Midgards Untergang, GRM* 24 (1936): 150; Almgren, *Germanistik,* 156–59.

38 Almgren, *Germanistik,* 248, 253–55.

39 Schröder, "Neuere Forschungen," 177. The correct expression is "*credo, quia impossibile.*"

40 L.A. Willoughby, "Coleridge und Deutschland," *GRM* 24 (1936): 112–27; A. Kuhn, "Das französische Neuwort," *GRM* 25 (1937): 296–313.

41 Almgren, *Germanistik,* 108, 120, 234–41.

42 G. Neckel, *Die germanischen Relativpartikeln* (Berlin: Meyer & Müller, 1900); idem, *Die Überlieferungen vom Gotte Balder* (Dortmund: Ruhfus, 1920); Von See and Zernack, 124ff.

43 G. Neckel, "Zur Einführung in die Runenforschung," *GRM* 1 (1909): 7–19, 81–95.

44 Heusler/Ranisch 6.4.33 & 11.3.39, nos 173 & 196 in Düwel and Beck (eds), 562–63 & 635.

45 S. Feist, *Grundriß der gotischen Etymologie* (Strasbourg: Trübner, 1888); R. Römer, "Sigmund Feist," *Muttersprache* 91 (1981): 249–308; S. Hank et al. (eds.), *Feldpostbriefe jüdischer Soldaten 1914–1918,* 2 vols. (Teetz: Hentrich & Hentrich 2002).

46 S. Feist, *Europa im Lichte der Vorgeschichte und die Ergebnisse der vergleichenden indogermanischen Sprachwissenschaft* (Berlin: Weidmann, 1910); idem, *Kultur, Ausbreitung und Herkunft der Indogermanen* (Berlin: Weidmann, 1913); idem, "La question du pays d'origine des indo-européens," *Scientia* 14 (1913): 303–314; idem, "Indogermanen und Germanen," in R. Klee (ed.), *Verhandlungen der zweiundfünfzigsten Versammlung deutscher Philologen und Schulmänner* (Leipzig: Teubner, 1914), 153; idem, "Indogermanen und Germanen," *Zeitschrift für den deutschen Unterricht* 28 (1914): 161–77, 261–74; idem, *Indogermanen und Germanen* (Halle a.S.: Niemeyer, 1914); idem, "Das Arierproblem," *Sokrates* 3 (1915): 417–32; idem, "Archäologie und Indogermanenproblem," *Korrespondenz-Blatt* 47 (1916) 61–68; idem, "Runen und Zauberwesen"; idem, "Germanen," in M. Ebert (ed.), *Reallexikon der Vorgeschichte* IV (Berlin: De Gruyter, 1924), 273–89; idem, "Indogermanen," in M. Ebert (ed.), *Reallexikon der Vorgeschichte* VI, 54–66.

47 S. Feist, notice of Wilser, *Zur Runenkunde;* idem, notice of Wilser, *Europäische Völkerkunde, Jahresbericht* 33, (1911 [1913]): I, 23; idem, notice of Wilser, *Die Germanen,* vol. cit., I, 36; idem, notice of Wilser, "Ursprung

und Entwicklung der Buchstabenschrift," *Jahresbericht* 34 (1912 [1914]): I, 146; idem, notice of Wilser, *Deutsche Vorzeit*, *Jahresbericht* 39–40 (1917–18 [1920]): I, 42.

48 S. Feist, notice of Wilser, *Die Germanen*, *Jahresbericht* 36 (1914 [1916]): I, 43.

49 S. Feist, *Lehr- und Lesebuch der französischen Sprache für praktische Ziele*, 3 vols. (Halle a.S.: Waisenhaus, 1895–98).

50 Cf. A. Meillet, *Caractères généraux des langues germanique* (Paris: Hachette, 1917).

51 "Matiérs," *Bulletin de la Société de Linguistique de Paris* 28/2 (1928): ix.

52 S. Feist, *Germanen und Kelten in der antiken Überlieferung* (Halle a.S.: Niemeyer, 1927); idem, "Was verstanden die Römer unter 'Germanen'?," *Teuthonista* 4 (1927/28): 1–12; idem, "Entgegnung," *Wiener prähistorische Zeitschrift* 15 (1928): 65–71; R. Römer, "Sigmund Feist und die Gesellschaft für deutsche Philologie in Berlin," *Muttersprache* 103 (1993): 28–40.

53 R. Much, "Sigmund Feist und das germanische Altertum," *Wiener prähistorische Zeitschrift* 15 (1928): 1–19; idem, "Bemerkung zur Feists 'Entgegnung,'" vol. cit., 72–81.

54 Feist/Gesellschaft, 12.5.38, apud Römer, "Feist und die Gesellschaft," 38.

55 R. Huß, "Die rheinischen Germanen im Altertum," *Teuthonista* 5 (1928/29): 85–92.

56 G. Neckel, *Germanen und Kelten* (Heidelberg: Winter, 1929), 7ff.; P. Ó Dochartaigh, *Julius Pokorny* (Dublin: Four Courts, 2004).

57 G. Neckel, "Germanen und Kelten," *Zeitschrift für Deutschkunde* 47 (1933): 403ff.

58 E. Weber, "Sinnbilder und Runen," *Sigrune* 10 = 12/7–8 (1943): 10; Hunger, 83, n. 50; cf. W. Wüst, "Germanenkunde," *Germanien* 8 (1936): 326 [= "Zur Germanenkunde," *Odal* 5 (1936): 372 = *Indogermanisches Bekenntnis* (Berlin–Dahlem: Ahnenerbe, 1942), 10].

59 Bremer, who like Pokorny, did not consider himself particularly Jewish, died shortly after he lost his emeritus standing at the University of Halle in 1935; A.C. Nagel (ed.), *Die Phillips-Universität Marburg im Nationalsozialismus* (Frankfurt a.M.: Steiner, 2000), 41ff.; and Mees, "Germanising the East."

60 S. Feist, "Zum Ursprung der germanischen Runenschrift," *Acta philologica Scandinavica* 4 (1929): 1–25; G. Neckel, review of M. Hammarström, "Om runeskriftens härkomst," *DLZ* 50 (1929): 1237–39; Römer, "Sigmund Feist"; Mees, "Linguistics and Nationalism," 54ff.

61 G. Neckel, *Altgermanische Kultur*, 2nd ed. (Leipzig: Quelle & Meyer, [1934]); idem, *Kulturkunde der Germanen* (Berlin: Junker & Dünnhaupt, 1934); idem, *Kultur der alten Germanen* (Potsdam: Athenaion, 1934); cf. also idem, "Die Herkunft der Runenschrift"; idem, "Die Herkunft der Runen," *Forschungen und Forschritte* 9 (1933): 293; idem, "Die Runen," *Acta philologica Scandinavica* 12 (1937–38): 102–15 [= idem, *Vom Germanentum*, ed. W. Heydenreich and H.M. Neckel (Leipzig: Harrassowitz, 1944), 423–35].

62 F. Paul, *Fünfzig Jahre Skandinavistik an der Georg-August-Universität Göttingen* (Göttingen: Skandinavisches Seminar der Universität, 1985), 1ff.; Von See and Zernack, 115ff.

63 W. Heydenreich, "Vorwort," in W. Heydenreich and H.M. Neckel (eds.), *Vom Germanentum*, (Leipzig: Harrassowitz, 1944), xxii.

64 Heusler/Ranisch 10.3.35, no. 177 in Düwel and Beck (eds.), 573.

65 Heuser/Ranisch 26.2.33 and 28.1.38, nos 172 & 195 in Düwel and Beck (eds.), 560 & 632.

66 Heusler/Ranisch 6.4.33, no. 173 in Düwel and Beck (eds.), 562.

67 Neckel, "Liebe und Ehe"; Von See and Zernack, 134ff.

68 Heydenreich, xxii; cf. Heydenreich in Heusler/Ranisch 8.12.35, no. 183 in Düwel and Beck (eds.), 594.

69 G. Neckel, review of H. Naumann, *Germanisches Gefolgschaftswesen* (Leipzig 1939), *Historische Zeitschrift* 163 (1941): 124–26; U. Wiggershaus-Müller, *Nationalsozialismus und Geschichtswissenschaft* (Hamburg: Kovacs, 1998), 108.

70 P. Assion, "Was Mythos unseres Volkes ist," *Zeitschrift für Volkskunde* 81 (1985): 224–25 [= J.R. Dow and H. Lixfeld (eds.), *The Nazification of an Academic Discipline* (Bloomington: Indiana University Press, 1994), 116–17]; cf. M. Scharfe, "Einschwörung auf den völkisch-germanischen Kulturbegriff," in J. Tröger (ed.), *Hochschule und Wissenschaft im Dritten Reich* (Frankfurt a.M.: Campus, 1984), 107ff.

71 *Volk und Rasse* 1–19/4–6 (Munich: Lehmann, 1926–44). Other editors of the journal included respected archeologists such as Gero von Merhart and Hans Zeiss; M. Heidler, "Die Zeitschriften des J.F. Lehmanns Verlages bis 1945," in S. Stöckel (ed.), *Die "rechte Nation" und ihr Verleger* (Heidelberg: Lehmanns, 2002), 77–81.

72 Stark, 197–201, 242.

73 P. Cornelius Tacitus, *Germania*, ed. E. Fehrle (Munich: Lehmann, 1929).

74 B. Vezina, *"Die Gleichschaltung" der Universität Heidelberg* (Heidelberg: Winter, 1982), 23, 30.

75 Assion, 225ff. [= Dow and Lixfeld (eds.), 117ff.]; E. Wolgast, *Die Universität Heidelberg, 1386–1986* (Berlin: Springer, 1986), 154.

76 W. Krause, "Die Wortstellung in den zweigliedrigen Wortverbindungen," *KZ* 50 (1920): 74–129.

77 W. Krause, *Die Frau in der Sprache der altisländischen Familiengeschichten* (Göttingen: Vandenhoeck & Ruprecht, 1926).

78 W. Krause, "Runica I," *NAWG, Phil.-Hist Klasse* 1926, 1–7; idem, "Runica II," *NAWG, Phil.-Hist Klasse* 1929, 25–56; idem, "Das Runendenkmal von Kårstad"; idem, *Beiträge zur Runenforschung*; idem, reviews of Hammarström, "Om runeskriftens härkomst," *AfdA* 50 (1931), 9–19 & *Gnomon* 7 (1931): 488–97; Hunger, 70ff.

79 W. Krause, review of K.T.Weigel, *Runen und Sinnbilder*, *Historische Zeitschrift* 152 (1935): 552–56.

80 W. Krause, "Neue Wege zur Runenforschung," *Forschungen und Forschritte* 12 (1936): 443–44; idem, "Sinnbilder und Runen," *Alt-Preußen* 2 (1936): 15–24; idem, "Wesen und Werden der Runen," *Zeitschrift für Deutschkunde*

51 (1937): 281–93, 345–56; idem, "Die Runen als Begriffszeichen," in
K.H. Schlottig (ed.), *Beiträge zur Runenkunde und nordischen Sprachwissen-schaft* (Leipzig: Harrassowitz, 1938), 35–53.

81 W. Krause, *Was man in Runen ritzte* (Halle a.S.: Niemeyer, 1935).

82 W. Krause, *[Die] Runeninschriften im älteren Futhark* (Halle a.S.: Niemeyer, 1937), 2nd ed. (with H. Jankuhn), 2 vols. (Göttingen: Vandenhoeck & Ruprecht, 1966).

83 Bollmus, *Amt Rosenberg*, 191; cf. idem, "Das 'Amt Rosenberg', das 'Ahnenerbe' und die Prähistoriker," in A. Leube (ed.), *Prähistorie und National-sozialismus* (Heidelberg: Sychron, 2002), 31; Lixfeld, 35ff., 55ff.

84 Cf. Almgren, *Germanistik*, synopsis.

CHAPTER 8.

The Expansion of the Ahnenerbe

Die Unvernunft einer Sache ist kein Grund gegen ihr Dasein,
vielmehr eine Bedingung desselben.
Nietzsche

The Herman Wirth Society produced several monographs penned by authors other than Wirth, few being writers with a traditional academic background. Wirth also attracted some younger scholars into his field who, in reflection of the difficulties faced by beginning academics in the university system at the time, had otherwise been unable to find a post. After his ensconcement at the University of Berlin in 1933, even some doctoral candidates sought Wirth out, seemingly eager to break into the new field. Much of the ideographic literature produced, however, remained amateur at first, substantially under the influence of the *völkisch* enthusiasm for things runic which went back to List and the Germanic Orders. Yet gradually, over the course of the 1930s, and despite the eventual fall from grace of Wirth himself, with the help of figures like Fehrle and Krause, *Sinnbildforschung* attained academic respectability. It is perhaps this course marked out by the ideographic studies of the 1930s that is more central to an understanding of how political outlook could come to be more important in the study of Germanic antiquity than remaining true to traditional scholarly methods and concerns. But it can only be seen in light of the broader atmosphere of antiquity enthusiasm and popular runomania of the day too.

The course of the development of *Sinnbildforschung* and the radical *völkisch* antiquarianism of the time also corresponds with the evolution of the Ahnenerbe itself. The SS involvement in Old Germanic studies began as much as a response to calls by *völkisch* antiquarian enthusiasts that their contribution to the nation be recognized as it was to individual archeologists or other antiquarians with Party connections. There was a significant number of enthusiasts from *völkisch* antiquarian groups among the first researchers to be enrolled into the Ahnenerbe. In fact Himmler's learned society grew to incorporate other radical expressions of half-lettered discourse over the course of the late 1930s, but now the half-lettered were increasingly accompanied by respectable scholars as well. A radical refocusing of the activities of the Ahnenerbe occurred shortly after the outbreak of war, too, which led to the involvement of German academics in SS-sponsored crimes against humanity, and finally, after the German defeat, to the trials of Ahnenerbe functionaries and researchers at Nuremberg.

There were in effect, then, three stages of development within the Ahnenerbe; and these stages also reflect the development of ideographic studies. Darré, the Nazi agriculture expert, had first been drawn into the world of *völkisch* antiquarianism during his time in the Nordic Ring. But his enthusiasm for the old Germanic past had become even more pronounced after Wirth developed a rustic aspect to his *Sinnbildforschung*. In the mid-1930s, other antiquarian enthusiasts similarly began to concentrate on the rural aspect of ancient ideographs, and *Sinnbildforschung* became entwined in Darré's vision of blood-and-soil fascism. The research sponsored by the SS also began to reach a larger audience by the late 1930s, which in turn led to the production of even more radical publications, both from amateur and academic sources. Nonetheless, as the Ahnenerbe opened out to other fields of study in the late 1930s, radicals like Wirth were culled and replaced by more respectable figures, much as other "old fighters" were culled and replaced in organizations like the Nazi Women's Group (NS-Frauenschaft).[1] At this time *Sinnbildforschung* was gradually legitimized by academic philologists and prehistorians, almost as if they were encouraged to lend their support to the new field by the removal of Wirth from the scene. But then as Hitler pushed Europe into war, *Sinnbildforschung* was again transformed in a third, more clearly political stage. By 1942 ideographic studies had finally become a respectable academic discipline and had even developed a foreign outpost; the academics drawn into the Ahnenerbe legitimized ideographic studies and the Ahnenerbe then began to use *Sinnbildforschung* as part of its pan-Germanist propaganda in the occupied territories of the Nazi imperium. But *Sinnbildforschung* had begun in amateur circles in the late 1920s before it had come to be adopted by the Party and the theories first raised in these amateur circles clearly influenced the thinking of Party officials such as Himmler and Darré. In fact even as the Third Reich was collapsing all around him Himmler was still talking about ideographs. As late as April 1945, while he was establishing contacts with the Red Cross as part of a plan to win a separate peace with the western Allied powers, the Red Cross's Count Bernadotte discovered that runes and ideographs were still so important to Himmler that he spent an hour ruminating on them at one of their meetings, much to the Swede's bemusement.[2] Yet the Reichsführer-SS was not the only German to be caught in the spell of the *völkisch* vision of antiquity. A mystique had developed around the Old Germanic past, one that fascinated both amateur and academic antiquarians. To understand the mystique of *völkisch* ideography, however, and how it developed to the stage where eventually it even captured university Germanists, it is opportune to turn to those who first called themselves the friends of *völkisch* antiquity.

STANDING STONES

Every midsummer Germans from many walks of life make their way to a natural rock formation in Lower Saxony. Forming a crowd described in press reports as comprising many alternative lifestyle groups, these greenies, mystics, witches, pagans, punks and heavy metal fans are joined in their celebration by Armanists, skinheads and neo-Nazis. The sandstone formations are known as the Extern Stones (*Externsteine*) and their continuing reputation as a holy place of the ancient Germanic tribes is palpably a result of the endeavors of the researchers of the Ahnenerbe.[3]

In the Middle Ages, a relief of Christ's descent from the cross and other religious representations were erected by the banks of a river in niches on a group of natural sandstone pillars which tower over a small meadow. By the baroque period these Agisterstene, later Externsteine, had been incorporated into the hunting park of a local noble. At the same time the stones also came to the attention of the Protestant theologian Hermann Hamelmann who described these fascinating features in a book from 1564. By 1976 more than 670 publications had joined this first offering, and the growth in treatments of these natural monuments shows no sign of abating.[4]

Much of the contemporary fascination with the stones no doubt derives not just from their remarkable form, but from their location, in the Teutoburg Forest, the surviving area of woodland where it was thought until recently that Arminius had routed three Roman legions in A.D. 9, ending the attempt of the Romans to bring all of Germany under their control.[5] The Extern Stones are barely a spear's throw from the Arminius monument (Hermannsdenkmal), erected in the nineteenth century to commemorate the savior of ancient Germany, not to mention the actual site of Arminius' ambush. The first descriptions of the Extern Stones also identified them as the home of Irminsûl, the great sacred column of the pagan Saxons chopped down by the order of Charlemagne in A.D. 772.

The nearest city to the Extern Stones is Detmold, in the tiny former state of Lippe, where in 1927 a group of prehistory enthusiasts came together as the Federation of Friends of Germanic Prehistory (Vereinigung der Freunde germanischer Vorgeschichte). By the early 1930s local branches of the Friends had developed in cities across northern Germany (including Berlin, Bremen, Essen, Hagen, Hanover and Mannheim) and contacts had been set up with similar groups such as that of Wirth. The leading figure among the Detmold Friends was Wilhelm Teudt, who had proclaimed the Extern Stones "the Germanic Stonehenge" in 1926 and from 1929 each year published several leading articles in the Friends' journal *Germanien*.[6] By 1936 Teudt's standing had grown to such an extent that he was rewarded with the leadership of the second division of the Ahnenerbe after that of Wirth, the Division for Germanic Studies (*Germanenkunde*), which was headquartered at Detmold.[7]

It might seem that it was the numinous attraction of the Extern Stones or the approval of the *völkisch* character of the antiquarianism pursued by the Friends that influenced Wirth in Teudt's direction. The early issues of *Germanien* are, after all, full of advertisements for establishments such as the Extern Stones Hotel and Pension, and guided tours of the monuments of the region about Detmold. Wirth had known of the Friends since the late 1920s and had used their journal to explain his views to a wider audience. The very first issue of *Germanien* includes an explanation of a symbol on the wall of a grotto in the Extern Stones by Wirth (prepared in reply to a letter from the editor Friedrich Platz) and subsequent numbers featured articles by and on Wirth and the development of his *Sinnbildforschung*.[8] Wirth even visited the Extern Stones late in 1932 and published an account of some of his observations in *Germanien* in the new year.[9] The Friends and their publication were to be of crucial importance to both the Ahnenerbe and the growth in ideographic literature over the coming years, more so even than were organizations in Berlin such as the Herman Wirth Society and its successor.

Evidently the proximity to the Extern Stones and the Teutoburg Forest as well as the secretariat of the Friends rendered some institutional and symbolic merit for considering Detmold as a center for Ahnenerbe-funded studies. Lippe had also brought out an especially strong National Socialist vote in 1933. Yet there was another reason for the involvement of the SS too: since the years of the Nazi assumption of power, Teudt and his Friends had become part of the struggle between brown and black-sponsored research. The Kampfbund's Kummer had presented a paper at the third annual Pentecost meeting of the Friends in 1931;[10] Rosenberg's prehistory expert Reinerth, however, had at first dismissed them as a bunch of fantasists. Nevertheless, archeological excavations had been carried out at the feet of the Extern Stones by Julius Andrée in 1933–34, who though he was a member of the Kampfbund and was later enrolled in Reinerth's Reich Institute for German Prehistory, had won financial backing from the SS. In March 1934, Himmler had consequently had the Lippe authorities legislate for an Extern Stones Foundation (Externsteine-Stiftung);[11] Reinerth hurriedly responded, offering Teudt's group the protection of his Federation. Yet after the foundation of the SS-Ahnenerbe in 1935, Reinerth was quickly pushed aside by the SS and an Ahnenerbe Division for Germanic Studies under the leadership of Teudt was constituted in Detmold. This move saw the enrollment of both the Extern Stones Foundation and Teudt's Friends as ancillaries of the Detmold division of the Ahnenerbe.[12] The incorporation of the Detmold Friends within the Ahnenerbe seemed a logical extension of the process of consolidation of SS-sponsored antiquarian research activities within a single national body.

Apart from the focus upon Detmold and the Extern Stones, another lasting contribution to the *völkisch* antiquarian tradition developed by the Friends was the image of Irminsûl. A medieval relief depicting Christ's descent from the cross erected on one of the Extern Stones seems to show what Teudt interpreted as a tree being withered by the cross (less imaginative researchers consider it merely to be an elaborate chair). This representation was seen by the Friends as symbolic of the destruction of Irminsûl, the sacred column of the pagan Saxons. The Friends reconstructed an upright form of Irminsûl from this depiction and it soon became one of the icons of *völkisch* antiquity.[13] The felling of Irminsûl apparently represented at the Extern Stones by the medieval relief became a symbol for the destruction of German paganism at the hands of Christian missionaries. It joined the runes and the swastika as one of the foremost symbols of an anti-Christian *völkisch* identity at the time and remains a motif treasured in German neo-pagan circles today. In the late 1930s this image of Irminsûl was also used in official Nazi symbolism: from the *Schulingsbrief*, the journal of the Reich Labor Service (Reichsarbeitsdienst), to SS badges and jewellery and one of the Ahnenerbe's publishing logos. The Detmold Friends were clearly at the forefront of *völkisch* Germanism and as such were favored by both Himmler and the local Gauleiter, Alfred Meyer. In fact they soon came to be a major force in the shaping of the Ahnenerbe itself.

Among the Detmold Friends, Teudt had always been preeminent. Born in 1860, as a Lutheran minister he worked as a pastor in nearby Schaumburg-Lippe from 1885–94. In 1895, however, he left his parish duties and succeeded Friedrich Naumann as leader of the Lutheran Union for the Home Mission (Evangelischer Verein für Innere Mission) in Frankfurt am Main.[14] Yet by 1908 he had left holy orders and had become involved with the Kepler League for the Advancement of the Knowledge of Nature (Keplerbund zur Förderung der Naturerkenntnis) where he published on conservative topics.[15] He arrived in Detmold in 1920, set up the Friends in 1927 and in 1929 his antiquarian monograph, *Germanic Shrines (Germanische Heiligtümer)*, subtitled "Contributions to Uncovering Prehistory, Exploring the Extern Stones, the Source of the Lippe and the Teutoburg," was published by Diederichs.[16] Indeed Teudt's theory that the Extern Stones were the site of early astronomical practice had first been published by Kossinna in *Mannus*.[17] Teudt was well read in archeological matters: he acknowledged Kossinna's death by contributing a review of his legacy to *Germanien* in 1931 and his *Germanic Shrines* received praise from academics such as Neckel.[18] There is even a grovelling but also revealing review by one of the Friends of the flattering review by Neckel of the second edition of *Germanic Shrines* that underlines how sorely these amateur antiquarians craved the respect of their academic counterparts.[19] Yet with the absorption of his Friends by the Ahnenerbe in 1936, Teudt was gradually to be marginalized. Wolfram Sievers, as his control grew throughout the organization, began to undermine the position of Teudt over the course of 1936–37, and in early 1938 oversaw Teudt's exit from the Ahnenerbe, the same year he similarly disposed of Wirth. The by then 77-year-old Teudt had to be satisfied with an honorary professorship and in 1940 a gold Goethe medal.[20] Rosenberg in his memoirs described Teudt's fate:[21]

A certain Dr. Teudt had done some important work in connection with the history of the so-called Externsteine, and had founded an organization for this purpose. Himmler was interested. Through direct pressure, bypassing the Gauleiter, Teudt was induced to incorporate his organization into the Ahnenerbe. Thus, he was eliminated. He turned over his material and became honorary president of his former organization, but was no longer permitted to supervise the investigations, since Himmler's own historians held different opinions than he.

Teudt would not be bowed so easily, however, and soon established an Osningsmark Society (Osningsmarke Gesellschaft), which was duly supported by Reinerth. A collection of Teudt's essays were also published in 1940, some two years before his death, in a manner usually reserved for academics.[22] Teudt's Friends and their journal had been caught up in the struggle between brown and black Nazi antiquarianism: the Friends and *Germanien* were cannibalized by the Ahnenerbe and Himmler's prehistorians discarded Teudt when they no longer needed him.

The leader of the third division of the Ahnenerbe, that for lexical studies (*Wortkunde*), was to enjoy a rather different fate to Teudt. The appointment of its leader, Walther Wüst, represented the first steps towards a transformation of the Ahnenerbe. Wüst already held the title professor before being drawn into the SS's learned society. He had gained the attention of the Party in the early 1930s through the popularity of his courses on Aryan language and culture at the University of Munich and had been appointed Dean of the Faculty of Philosophy there in 1935, a post which made him heir to the Rectorship.[23] Of course, Aryan to Wüst, a philologist of ancient Indic and Iranian, ostensibly was intended only to apply to Aryan proper: the oriental branch of Indo-European peoples who gave their name to Iran. Nevertheless, Wüst's lectures on an ancient oriental culture had become an expression of the prehistory of Germany. As Wüst's forte was Aryan *Wörter und Sachen* studies, his Munich division of the Ahnenerbe became a division for SS *Wörter und Sachen*. By 1938 the Ahnenerbe had assumed responsibility for publishing the flagship of historical semantic studies, Meringer's journal *Wörter und Sachen*, with Wüst acting as a member of the editorial panel before replacing its editorial director Hermann Güntert altogether at the end of 1939 (after differences had arisen over a map). Güntert suffered a stroke soon after his removal from his editorial position and was no longer able to participate in the discourse of Old Germanic studies.[24]

Although Wüst's contribution to Aryan lexicography was not outstanding, his contribution to the Ahnenerbe was unequalled.[25] Wüst had already been approached to be ersatz leader of the Ahnenerbe before Wirth had come into official disfavor, Sievers reasoning that a senior academic would lend credibility to the fledgling organization. Wüst had been a supporter of Wirth's *Emergence*, was one of the minority of academics to have accepted the *Oera Linda Book* as genuine and his field of study was certainly acceptable to Himmler.[26] As president, or rather "curator" of the Ahnenerbe, Wüst would act as go-between between academics and the Party, gradually enticing many to join the Ahnenerbe outright. Wüst's own division was later more cumbersomely renamed the Division for Indo-European–Aryan Linguistic and Cultural Science (*Indogermanisch–Arische Sprach- und Kulturwissenschaft*); he soon also redesignated Wirth's romantically entitled *Pflegstätten* (despite having written in support of the description in 1936), variously as "Research Posts" (*Forschungsstätten*) or both "Teaching and Research Posts" (*Lehr- und Forschungsstätten*), and had the reference to "intellectual prehistory" in the title of the Ahnenerbe deleted.[27]

After giving a series of lectures on "*Mein Kampf* as a mirror of the Aryan Weltanschauung" to senior members of the SS, in early 1937 Wüst was soon rewarded with presidency of the German Academy in Munich that summer and had officially replaced Wirth as head of the Ahnenerbe by March of the same year. Wirth was forced out of the organization altogether at the end of 1938. Wüst had not only added gravitas to the organization, he had shorn it of much of Wirth's idiosyncratic trapping, and finally of the man himself.[28]

Some of Wirth's followers, however, had already managed to establish themselves well enough by 1937 not to require his patronage any more. Rather than merely survive his sidelining, as Wüst and Sievers aimed to professionalize the Ahnenerbe, many instead prospered. Foremost was J. Otto Plaßmann who had first met Wirth in Belgium during the Great War serving as a Flemish specialist. After being wounded on the

Russian front, he had been released from the military late in 1916 and from March 1917 came to work instead for the German civil authority in Brussels. Involved in the Freecorps movement after the war, in 1918 Plaßmann returned to the studies he had begun in 1914, and after obtaining his doctorate in 1920 for an edition of the vernacular works of the medieval Flemish mystic Hadewijch, he had eked out a living writing popular histories (including four of medieval German kings for Diederichs in 1927 and 1928).[29] First becoming involved in Nazi Party activities in 1929, Plaßmann had worked for Wirth in Bad Doberan before joining Rosenberg's and then Darré's staff at the end of 1935. He had also been a member of the Detmold Friends since 1928 and is recorded developing an archive for Germanic prehistory for Teudt's group in March 1929, although his first publication did not appear in *Germanien* until 1932.[30] Nevertheless, his academic and political credentials were excellent. In 1936 his specialization in Germanic studies and religion saw him become Berlin editor of the Friends' *Germanien* and the journal under his editorship became the Ahnenerbe's flagship publication. In fact Plaßmann subsequently became one of the three leading figures in the administration of the Ahnenerbe after Wüst and Sievers, and went on to earn a professional doctorate in 1943 with backing from the SS.[31]

Another enthusiast whom the Friends attracted was Otto Huth. Ten years younger than Plaßmann, Huth had been associated with *völkisch* groups since 1922 and had joined both the Nazi Students' League and the SA in 1928. First making contact with Wirth in 1929, Huth started contributing to *Germanien* from 1931 and even gained a doctorate in classical philology the next year for a study on the cult of Janus, the two-faced Roman god who stands at the beginning and end of the year.[32] An imaginative student, he launched his career of *völkisch* publication pursuing themes such as "Against Ultra-Montanism in Classical Philology" and an acceptance of theories like *ex Septentrione lux* and the Germanic–Aryan *Urschrift* thesis.[33] From 1933 Huth received DFG financial support with Wirth's backing (against the advice of the DFG's academic referees) and finally joined the Ahnenerbe in 1935.[34] He had initially usually written on themes first developed in Wirth's *Emergence*, but by the late 1930s Huth had begun writing on pagan symbols such as the Yule fire or what he saw as the Aryan Christmas Tree. The Yule fire was subsequently adopted as part of the neo-pagan cult which Himmler had replace Christian symbols within the SS. (In fact the receptacle for the Yule fire designed for the SS ersatz Christmas ceremony bears a six-spoked wheel, the symbol of Wralda in the *Oera Linda Book*.)[35] Huth's 1936 work *The Felling of the Tree of Life (Die Fällung des Lebenbaumes)* which argues that Christianity coopted Germanic culture, with its invocation of Irminsûl clearly betrays his past as one of the Friends.[36] Yet by the end of the decade Huth had moved beyond amateur circles and had taken only to citing academics aligned to the SS as his main models in method. After completing his professional thesis on the Aryan fire cult at the University of Tübingen in 1939, he was ultimately rewarded with his own professorship in 1942 at the Reich University of Strasbourg.[37]

After Wirth's exclusion from the Ahnenerbe, the leadership of his section had gone over to his research assistant K. Theodor Weigel who promptly moved the division from Wirth's Marburg to Horn in Lippe (near the Extern Stones, where Plaßmann had set up a "Haus Ahnenerbe" that year). From the mid-1930s Weigel threatened to upstage Wirth as the best known practitioner of ideographic studies. Yet he had a quite different background to the other ideograph enthusiasts such as Plaßmann and Huth. Like Teudt, Weigel had no philological or archeological training. And like both Wirth and Teudt he had a decidedly amateur and speculative approach to the study of Germanic antiquity.

Fascinated by runes since his time in the Youth Movement in the 1910s, by 1929 Weigel had become associated with Teudt's Friends and in 1934 published his first monograph on German ideography.[38] A Party member since 1931, he joined the SS in 1935 and by the end of that year had earned renown as the new expert on *Sinnbildforschung*. In 1936 he successfully applied to the DFG for funds and although he had no research profile let alone formal training was able to set up an independent Center for Ideographic Studies (Hauptstelle für Sinnbildforschung) with the monies so obtained. The responsibility for his activities was taken over by the Ahnenerbe in 1937 and his center merged with that of Wirth. Yet already he had begun to publish a wealth of surveys of symbols he had found throughout the German landscape, his output including some thirteen monographs and many scores of articles besides between 1934 and 1942.[39]

Weigel's first introduction to runes and ideographs, however, was not solely through Wirth, but instead equally through the Listian tradition. The bibliography of his first general survey on *Sinnbildforschung*, his *Runes and Ideographs (Runen und Sinnbilder)* from 1935, features mainly the works of Ariosophists: List, Phillip Stauff, the later rune mysticists such as Siegfrid Kummer and Rudolf John Gorsleben, and even a contribution from Karl Schirmeisen who had produced another fantastic alphabet study in 1924.[40] Apart from the "trail blazer" List,[41] Weigel describes Wilser similarly, notes the support of Neckel and spends some pages considering Wirth's theories in the context of the *völkisch* alphabetic tradition in all its manifold forms.[42] Among all the Ahnenerbe figures, Weigel's approach to *Sinnbildforschung* showed the most patently fantastic side. Yet with its Listian pseudo-runes and other Ariosophical sensibilities Weigel's 1935 work was an immediate success within Party ranks. In it he even criticized the rune-gymnastics of the obscurantist Marby who was soon to be officially persecuted (and incarcerated).[43] Weigel's book captured the radical zeitgeist displayed in the popular approaches to runes and ideographs that had developed in amateur circles so well it ended up going through four editions. He also firmly introduced the theory most strongly put by Stauff of "rune-houses" (*Runenhäuser*) to *Sinnbildforschung*, the notion that runic shapes could be seen in the traditional forms of housing construction.[44] Soon the Listian prerogative for seeing runic designs betrayed in all sorts of native German expressions became a part of *Sinnbildforschung*. Although Weigel eschewed the esoteric aspect of this Listian semiology, in his wake a whole new enthusiasm for ideographic analyses swept through the SS, and Plaßmann eagerly accepted such contributions for inclusion in *Germanien*.[45]

After Weigel had joined the Ahnenerbe, however, he began to realize that *Sinnbildforschung* as he and Wirth had construed it still required some methodological development if it was to establish itself as a proper discipline. Plaßmann, too, worked to rescue a coherent doctrine out of their publications: his two methodological articles from 1933 and 1936 and other similar surveys in *Germanien* from the time attempt to put *Sinnbildforschung* in a more refined and critical light.[46] Although he never lost interest in ideographs, Plaßmann soon moved on to studies more clearly in the realm of *Volkskunde*; in 1939 he contributed yet another work on the Extern Stones and he wrote his professional thesis on the Germanic roots of medieval culture.[47] Nevertheless, it was not Wirth's former associates who had contributed most toward the acceptance of ideographic studies—except in SS circles, Weigel and Plaßmann were mostly ignored by the academic mainstream. More credibility came when those already in academia came to sponsor such research.

Over 1937–38, years of rapid expansion, the Ahnenerbe had begun to influence the DFG and the Research Division of the Education Ministry (which from May 1939 were both headed by Rudolf Mentzel[48]). At the same time it had also lost both Wirth and Teudt, its two best known lay researchers. Other lesser-known fringe dwellers such as Weigel and Plaßmann, at one stage subordinates of Wirth and Teudt, took over their respective research positions. Others still entered the Ahnenerbe after that time setting up new divisions which developed on themes that these two men had focused on. An amateur enthusiast, Karl Konrad Ruppel began a Division for Hallmarks and Kinship Symbols (*Hausmarke und Sippenzeichen*) in autumn 1937; a dialectologist, Bruno Schweizer, who together with Plaßmann briefly replaced Teudt at Detmold, began his own division in early 1938 that would come to be entitled the Division of Locating and Landscape Ideographs (*Ortung- und Landschaftssinnbilder*) later that year; and the erstwhile classicist Huth joined Plaßmann's division for Fairytale and Saga Studies (*Märchen- und Sagakunde*) where he produced numerous papers, not just on *Sinnbildforschung* but also on topics as diverse as the Aryan origins of the Olympic Games,[49] before going on to establish his own division for the History of Indo-European Belief (*Indogermanische Glaubensgeschichte*) in Berlin, probably late in 1938.[50]

BEYOND ATLANTIS

If Wirth's works have not fared well in the esteem of postwar generations, neither has the research of the organization he led from 1935–37. One general survey of the history of the Third Reich assesses the Ahnenerbe in this manner:

> Its task was to investigate all aspects of ancient German tradition. It conducted "research" into earth mysteries by studying the connection of race

with house design; the occult properties of church bells; and runes, a form of ancient German script believed to possess magical properties.[51]

At least two of these areas of investigation ridiculed here by Jackson Spielvogel are clear, albeit somewhat misleading, references to *Sinnbild-forschung*. Ideographic study was not thought so ridiculous at the time, however, but instead was increasingly to be viewed as a very serious concern by some German academics. In fact many areas of research undertaken by members of the Ahnenerbe were considered much more respectable in their day than commentators like Spielvogel would have us believe.

Some research associated with Himmler, however, certainly was not. Wüst and Sievers tried to professionalize the Ahnenerbe in the years after the departure of Wirth. Yet the Reichsführer-SS entertained all manner of interests, from the scholarly, the half-baked to the utterly fantastic. Nonetheless, Wüst and Sievers were usually successful in their aim to keep Himmler's more fantastic pet projects at arms length from official association with the SS's learned society.

A remarkable example of half-baked research carried out in the name of the SS was the Nazi search for the Holy Grail of Arthurian legend. This rather bizarre incident eerily replicates the premise of Steven Spielberg's *Indiana Jones and the Temple of Doom* and more recently served as the lead theme of *Hitler's Search for the Holy Grail*, a documentary on the Ahnenerbe that first screened in Britain in 1999.[52] The chief figure involved was Otto Rahn, who in 1933 had claimed that the medieval Cathars had had possession of the Grail at Montségur in the south of France shortly before their destruction at the hands of the Albigensian crusaders. Rahn was convinced the Cathars were descended directly from the Spanish Visigoths and that their religion represented an Aryan rejection of Judaism. He seemed to be another sort of Wirth and his 1933 work *Crusade against the Grail* (*Kreuzzug gegen den Gral*) had won him comparable success and popular fame.[53] Nonetheless Rahn remained an outsider to the academic world and never had any direct connection with the Ahnenerbe.[54] Nor was this kind of expression of Himmler's credulous approach to the past favored by leading figures of the SS's learned society. There were individual scholars and pseudo-scholars connected to the SS whose schemes are not representative of the range of activities undertaken with the backing of the Ahnenerbe.

Many of the areas of research conducted within the Ahnenerbe today do seem decidedly strange. In their time, however, not all were as
specious as they appear now. The excavations performed under its auspices are generally considered to have been excellent technically, and
with the exception of that of Huth, the classical philology produced by
Ahnenerbe scholars was also generally of a high quality.[55] The Berlin
Associate Professor (Dozent) Rudolf Till had been granted a Division
for Classical Philology and Antiquity (Abteilung für Klassische Philologie und Altertum) in 1938, and even the paleographical investigation of
Tacitus' *Germania* he produced in 1943 from the principal (*Codex Aesi-
nas*) redaction of the *Germania* in Italy has had its admirers.[56] In Till's
case it is probably more the subsequent attempt to steal the *Germania*
manuscript by SS operatives from its private Italian owner after the fall
of Mussolini that has left a mark of opprobrium over his endeavor.[57]
The direction of study pursued in the Ahnenerbe was usually decided
only by the interests of the Reichsführer-SS. Yet Wüst worked to reform the quality of research and personnel in those areas in which he
had some expertise. Other fields of study supported by the Ahnenerbe,
however, were not so easily to be assessed.

One example of a field pursued by Ahnenerbe researchers that
seems decidedly specious today is World Ice Theory (*Welteislehre* or
WEL). Developed by the Austrian engineer and inventor Hanns Hörbiger, *WEL* was an attempt to find a unified answer to the relationship
between the causes of a number of cosmological and celestial features
that astronomy, meteorology and geology at the time had been unable to explain. First appearing in 1913, Hörbiger's *Glacial Cosmogony*
sought to marry the two principal geological theories, Plutonism (vol-
canism) and Neptunism (crystalization), and extend them to cosmogony.[58] Hörbiger's theory did not attempt to balance the two opposing
views, however: instead he had them clashing head on. Hörbiger saw
both geology and cosmogony in terms of an unending struggle between
the forces of ice and heat. In the times before the development of the
atomic pile, the theory of the big bang, radio telescopes and space trav-
el, Hörbiger's view of the universe as some sort of cosmic steam en-
gine had the virtue of explaining many baffling features of astrophysics
through reference to known processes of mechanics and chemistry. By
the time of his death in 1931 Hörbiger had convinced many thousands

of the validity of his theory, not the least of them Hitler and his ideologues Rosenberg and Himmler.[59]

Hörbiger had long been dismissed as a crank by respected cosmologists. Nevertheless, several engineers became enamored of his theory, and all manner of monographs dealing with World Ice Theory appeared both in German-speaking countries and England.[60] Glacial cosmogony also proved to be profound in terms of *völkisch* thought as the Eddic story *Gylfi's Beguiling* (*Gylfaginning*) describes a Nordic cosmogenesis in the meeting of the realms of ice (Niflheim) and heat (Muspelheim), and moreover, the Eddic *Seeress's Prophecy* (*Völuspá*) describes the end of the world when the personified forces of fire and ice return. World Ice Theory was thus a Nordic and Aryan science in the minds of some of his followers and it seemed to represent a cosmological extension of the mythopoesis of the *völkisch* Weltanschauung.

In 1936, Himmler had Sievers contact Hörbiger's collaborator the astronomer Philipp Fauth and one of the sons of the late theorist, Alfred Hörbiger, with the intention of setting up an Ahnenerbe division for *Welteislehre*. A protocol was signed in July by Fauth, Hörbiger and other key supporters of *WEL* which led in February 1937 to the formal institution of a Division for Meteorology (*Wetterkunde*) in Berlin with a Hörbiger enthusiast, the meteorologist Hans Scultetus, as its leader.[61] In March 1938 Fauth was also rewarded with leadership of a similar organization, the Division for Astronomy, upon the transfer of responsibility for the Grünewald Observatory to the SS. Only one division was to be maintained. Nevertheless, the two divisions for *WEL* even led in April 1938 to the foundation of a third *WEL*-inspired division (although it effectively only replaced that of Scultetus) for geology and minerology (later retitled "geophysics"). *Welteislehre* continued to be popular among members of other organs of the Party, but Himmler had quickly moved to enlist nearly all the key figures of *WEL* into his organization.[62] The Ahnenerbe had expanded from an organization for the promotion of Germanic antiquity to one that also encompassed Nordic natural science. This time, however, Himmler had completely trumped Rosenberg, a victory whose completeness only seemed matched by the utter crankiness of the explanation that underlay *WEL*.

Other interests of Himmler were not necessarily reflected by the institution of divisions within the Ahnenerbe, but could, nevertheless, come to impinge upon its researchers. For instance in June 1936 two mystics patronized by Himmler went on a mission to the Murg valley, near Baden Baden, and subsequently declared the area a center of importance to ancient Germany. The more senior of these two, Karl Maria Wiligut, was a former officer of the Imperial Austrian army, and since the collapse of the Hapsburg Empire had retreated into a world of Listian delusion. After being institutionalized in an asylum in the late 1920s, he fled the Austrian Republic for Germany where he became a leading contributor to the Armanist journal *Hagal*, recalling memories of imaginary German and Gothic (Wili-gut, "Vili-Goth") ancestors among whom he even counted Arminius. In 1933 he was introduced to Himmler by a friend and so impressed the Reichsführer-SS that he was given a senior position in the RuSHA in Munich where he was to write down his ancestral fantasies under the assumed name of Weisthor (i.e. 'Wise-Thor'). Wiligut/ Weisthor was responsible for the design of the skull-ring (*Totenkopfring*) worn by SS officers and he also influenced the development of the SS order castle, the Wewelsburg, a museum, library and officer school modelled on the Marienburg in Pommerania, the headquarters of the medieval Teutonic Knights (*Deutsche Orden*). Wiligut was particularly supportive of the Albigensian fantasies of Rahn and hoped the Holy Grail might be recovered and brought one day to the Wewelsburg. Moreover, in August 1934 Wiligut introduced Himmler to the correspondence of another occultist, Günther Kirchhoff, who lived at Gaggenau in the Black Forest. It was Kirchhoff who first interested Wiligut and subsequently Himmler in the nearby valley, and with Himmler's support urged members of the Ahnenerbe to take up a study of the valley that Wiligut had described as the site of a gigantic ancient religious complex apparently of a similar ilk to the Extern Stones.[63]

The reception of Wiligut and Kirchhoff by the researchers of the Ahnenerbe, however, was to prove anything but cordial. Correspondence from Plaßmann belittled the significance of the reports of the mystics, and Hans Schleif (Excavations) was told to obfuscate by Sievers, putting off the proposed excavation of the site indefinitely. Michael Kater even reports that after the war Plaßmann and Wüst still loathed Wiligut, describing him as "grotesque" and an "idiot," respectively in their correspondence with him.[64]

The field of *Sinnbildforschung* must be located somewhere between poor scholarship and the extremes of *Welteislehre* and the researches of Wiligut and Kirchhoff. *Sinnbildforschung* was created by a *völkisch* fantasist, but it had some academic pedigree and sensibility nonetheless. *WEL* and Ariosophy, on the other hand, were based in stubbornly misguided science and the contrivances of *völkisch* obscurantists. *Sinnbildforschung* had no proper empirical basis, but it did represent some sort of outgrowth of an academic tradition. Moreover, with its original focus on symbols like the swastika, *Sinnbildforschung* also was palpably useful politically. Unlike *WEL* or Ariosophy, ideographic studies had both an academic pedigree and an immediately obvious *völkisch* symbolism. In fact the "visual etymology" that the symbols investigated in *Sinnbildforschung* represented to those initiated into Wirth's theories had come to influence the thinking of senior Party officials.

ODAL

As the expansion of the Ahnenerbe continued, another facet to ideographic studies which emerged in the early years of the dictatorship began to be reflected in the development of the SS's learned society. It was one that, once again, developed ostensibly out of swastika studies, but took the focus of ideographic research even further away from the tradition established in the wake of the finds of Schliemann at Troy. The mid-1930s witnessed a major change to the way *Sinnbildforschung* was conceptualized. It remained a discourse based on the theories of Wirth, but developed an entirely new political dimension as other strands of *völkisch* antiquarian endeavor became wedded to ideographic studies.

With the accession of the National Socialists, studies of the swastika developed a previously unheralded importance. Experts such as the Kossinna-school archeologist Jörg Lechler reissued their old studies after suitably reworking them to make their political orthodoxy clear.[65] A new edition of Wilser's study of the swastika was even prepared for Fritsch's Hammer publishing house which had been continued by his son.[66] Yet few of the works on the swastika from the 1930s contributed much new to the body of scholarship developed by Müller, Goblet d'Alviella, Montelius and Déchelette, even though swastika studies was the main intellectual precursor of *Sinnbildforschung*.[67] The exception here, however, was Wirth.

Wirth's ideas on the swastika deviated from the mainstream; he did not follow the traditional interpretation of the symbol that went back ultimately to Schliemann and Müller. He had connected the swastika with the runes, but in a manner quite unlike that which List had divined in the early 1900s. He was the most adventurous and original theorist (*völkisch* or academic) of the swastika in the early 1930s. In fact it seems it was especially his theories on the swastika that won him the interest of Darré and then Himmler, which in turn explains why they made Wirth's private Ahnenerbe the foundation of the SS's learned society in 1935.

In April 1934 Darré, the Reich agriculture chief, renamed his journal *Deutsche Agrarpolitik (German Agricultural Politics)*, the "Monthly for German Rurality," as *Odal*, the "Monthly for Blood and Soil," adopting Odal, the Germanized name of the **o**-rune, not only as title of the journal, but also its emblem.[68] Darré also had *Odal* adopt the old German names of the months, reviving a tradition first adopted by the early pan-Germanist journals such as *Heimdall* that was soon copied by other *völkisch* periodicals such as *Germanien*.[69] Various other runes were similarly adopted by Nazi associations over the next few years, usually under the influence of Wirth's theories. The German Women's Work (Deutsches Frauenwerk), for instance, the new Nazi general women's organization, adopted the (somewhat tree-like) younger **m**-rune (Y) in the mid-1930s even though this rune was thought to signify "man" in Listian tradition.[70] Yet the prehistorical matriarchy-enthusing Wirth had proclaimed this rune the prototype for the Christian cross— and furthermore in his "Tree of Life" exhibition, the *Lebensrune*, the "rune of life," theorizing that it symbolized healing and fecundity.[71] The *Lebensrune* was also adopted by the German Pharmacy Federation (Apothekervereinigung) and the National League for the German Family (Reichsbund deutsche Familie) in this light. It subsequently came to be employed as well as a replacement for asterisks and (in its inverted form) obelisks in bibliographical citations in journals like *Germanien*, and under Himmler's direction the "rune of life" even replaced crosses commemorating fallen members of the SS during the war.[72] Darré was well acquainted with the latest trends in antiquarian scholarship and the renaming of his agricultural journal with a runic letter-name is also clearly to be associated with views Wirth had first put forward in 1931.

It equally reveals an interesting symbolism that remains quite opaque outside the world of Wirth's *Sinnbildforschung*.

In his *What is German?* Wirth delineated a long evolution of the swastika from an Arctic-Atlantean ideograph he called the "year ideogram" which he also claimed was the ultimate ancestor of the o-rune (⊗). This rune's name is rendered *Odal* by German runologists after the name *œðal* "inheritance" or "heritable possession" given to it in medieval English and Wirth claimed that the swastika derived from a variant of the "year ideogram" he labelled the Odal-cross. Moreover, rescuing a nineteenth-century etymology which linked Odal with the concept "fatherland," Wirth maintained this was the answer to the question "what is German?": the swastika was the ancient symbol of German patrimony.[73]

Wirth also argued that the Odal-cross was the ancestor of the Celtic cross—and it was clearly in light of this theory that the Celtic cross (as the Celtic swastika) was adopted by Nazi collaborators in France and the Low Countries during the war.[74] Furthermore, the rune name Odal even became connected to *Allod* (allodial land tenure) in Wirth's system, i.e. *Od-al* became *All-od*. There had been a long tradition of study of a system of land tenure in Scandinavia known as "Odal law" (Danish *Odelsrett*, Germanized as *Odalrecht*) which connected Odal with agriculture—and Darré seems to have been especially taken by this interpretation, stating in 1934 that "Odal is the key to understanding the agricultural life of the Germanic tribes."[75] In fact later that year a monographic analysis by the sometime racial theorist Hermann Gauch of *Germanic Odal or Allodial Tenure (Die germanische Odal- oder Allodverfassung)* was published in conjunction with Darré's journal which developed Wirth's theory in light of the Scandinavian tradition.[76] A similar, although much more substantial publication by Johann von Leers also appeared soon thereafter (also published in conjunction with Darré's *Odal*) that was supposed to delineate the history of Germanic agriculture. Its appearance, though, led to friction between Wirth and von Leers, who was a member of Darré's circle as well as the leader of the successor to the Herman Wirth Society.[77]

The connection between Odal and Allod, however, is clearly etymological nonsense, and in 1934 this Odal scholarship provoked a public refutation by the venerable Germanist Otto Behagel.[78] After first confining his criticisms to newspaper articles, in 1935 Behagel published a detailed attack on the Odal fantasists in one of the *Transactions of the Bavar-*

ian Academy of Sciences.[79] As an octogenarian, Behagel seemed uncon-
cerned by the prospect of retaliation. Ideographic studies had threatened
to produce its own blood-and-soil form of *Wörter und Sachen*. But the
timely attack of Behagel, which coincided with a distancing of the Ahnenerbe from Darré's group in early 1936 (reflecting, among other things,
the growing animosity between Wirth and von Leers), ensured that the
new Odal scholarship did not infiltrate broader Germanistic discourse.[80]

Yet the Wirthian contribution to Nazi blood-and-soil mythology
did not end there. In 1934 Weigel resurrected the Listian idea that
runic designs influenced rural architecture, in the so-called "rune-
houses." In fact proving his blood-and-soil credentials, in his *Runes
and Ideographs*, he even cited Darré as an influence. By this date the
acknowledgement had already been reciprocated by Darré's people,
however: in 1934 one of Darré's writers had explained the notion of
rural rune-houses to the readership of *Odal* in a simple graphic manner, showing the o-rune hidden in one of the simplest of traditional
architectural features, the gable, an explanation that subsequently provoked further comment from both Wirth and Weigel.[81]

Given the growing connection between *Sinnbildforschung* and blood-
and-soil thinking, it comes as no surprise that Darré became one of the
patrons of the SS-Ahnenerbe upon its establishment in 1935. Wirth had
become a de facto blood-and-soil ideologue. His basic premise from 1928
that the ancient ideographs could be read by means of his *Sinnbildkunde*
had not evolved in its essence. But by 1935 the range of expressions to
which his theories could be applied had. His prehistorical religion of
runes and ideographs had now penetrated the rural Teutonic mystique
promoted by Darré and his circle. Wirth and *Sinnbildforschung* had obviously begun to verge again on the territory of Ariosophy. Yet many of
the researchers of the Ahnenerbe accepted this new *Sinnbildforschung* that
had moved on from prehistory into the rural, *völkisch* folkloric present.
Although it was ostensibly founded in prehistorical discourse, *Sinnbildforschung* had become another way in which *völkisch* continuity could be
demonstrated, especially in terms of German *Volkskunde*.

But the purview of *Sinnbildforschung* could be expanded further by
more radical ideograph enthusiasts. Ruppel had announced a new interpretation of medieval hallmarks in an essay published in *Odal* in 1936
and in the following year was assigned a *Pflegstätte* in which to concentrate on these symbols.[82] He produced an introductory survey for the Ah-

nenerbe in 1939 in which he noted that the appearance of Carl Homeyer's classic study on hallmarks from 1870 had quickly been followed by a mania for hallmarks among the public.[83] Homeyer and his correspondents had investigated all sorts of markings on buildings, stones, coats-of-arms, letters and seals. Weigel's take on *Sinnbildforschung* duly inspired a similar clamor to find runic and pre-runic shapes in all manner of rustic arts and architecture. The hallmark frenzy of the Bismarckian period was reenacted in a popular ideograph mania under the dictatorship.

Weigel painstakingly recorded thousands of examples of what he believed were examples of folk-art symbolism and he inspired other authors both inside and outside the SS to produce similar surveys. His ideograph archive survives, housed at the University of Göttingen today, and has since become an object of some mirth among present-day folklorists. The hundreds and thousands of symbols collected and catalogued by Weigel, however, stand as a testament to the enthusiastic reception of *Sinnbildforschung* at the time. Modern-day folklorists may be entitled to their scorn, but ideographic study could not have become more quintessentially folksy than in the specious ideograph mania inspired by Weigel.[84] It was in 1936 while this ideographic mania was still young that an SS lawyer, Kurt Schmidt-Klevenow, came up with the theory that some Chinese characters had developed from Germanic ideographs.[85] His theory was obviously specious, but he managed to win over Himmler who has been recorded musing that if the Japanese characters were related to runes and hallmarks, then the Japanese might one day be proven to be Aryans too.[86] Himmler seems to have turned Chinese into Japanese characters on his own accord, but had clearly, like Schmidt-Klevenow, also been caught up in Weigel's ideographic mania.

The mania that surrounded ideographic studies was most evident in the rune-house and other aspects of the blood-and-soil mystique based in ruminations on the o-rune. First emerging in the mid-1930s, ideograph mania was chiefly the preserve of radical scholars and their enthusiastic amateur followers. The SS-Ahnenerbe had clearly been established to further the studies of the *völkisch* enthusiasts who had gathered around Teudt and Wirth, however, some of whom even held doctorates but had surrendered to ideograph mania just as readily as their untrained fellows nonetheless. By the early 1930s Wirth had also clearly slipped completely into *völkisch* fantasy and both the Reich Agriculture Leader and the head of the SS had similarly become caught up in the runic mystique. But the broadening dissemination of *Sinnbildforschung* did not end with its acceptance by the members of the learned society of the SS and its patrons.

According to Hermann Rauschning, and as was also asserted by Wirth, Hitler was supportive of *Sinnbildforschung*, especially in its gnostic aspect.[87] Copies of *What is German?* and Wirth's Oera Linda translation are still to be found in the remains of Hitler's library in Washington today, but it is evident that the dictator grew increasingly annoyed by Wirth over time.[88] The anti-Christian element of Wirth's form of *Volkskunde* appealed strongly to senior Nazis like Darré, Himmler and, if Rauschning is to be believed, initially Hitler as well. Ideographic studies was at the forefront of the anti-Christian movement in 1930s German folklore—it was the heathenness of the symbols which men like Weigel collected that is so strongly stressed in their work. Traditional practices from the symbols used in harvest festivals, even to those used in games and regional varieties of cakes and breads, could now all be analyzed in the light of Wirth's groundbreaking work. A runomania broke out in the SS where the new theories of Germanic ideography were joined by all sorts of dilletantish speculation. The books of Wirth and Weigel were listed on official reading lists for the SS, and after 1933 various runes became part of official Nazi heraldry.[89] Wirth's theories lay behind the use of some runic symbols; other employments such as the adoption of the **t**-rune (↑, named for Tyr, the Old Norse war god, and thought to represent "eternal struggle") and the **s**-rune (ϟ, with its Listian name Sig, i.e. *Sieg* "victory") reflected the popular runology of the Youth Movement and runic obscurantists instead—thus their employment in the Hitler Youth, to symbolize the Adolf Hitler Schools and eventually even divisions of the Waffen-SS. Darré's later adoption of a complex series of runic ligatures for his blood-and-soil heraldry (his own symbol was a ligature of a **d**-rune and an angular swastika) even seems to indicate the influence of Weisthor—and a mixture of these influences also emerged in the neo-paganism encouraged in SS circles.[90] *Sinnbildforschung* represented one of the most sophisticated of all the antiquarian-enthusing discourses which grew up around the resurgent Germanicness consciousness that had long been associated with the movement for *völkisch* renewal. With the establishment of the Ahnenerbe, all manner of supporters of the gnostic aspect of the national renewal movement, from Wirth, the most radical exponent of Diederichs's New Romanticism, to abject amateurs such as many of the Friends of Germanic Prehistory—all had been brought together in a single, state-funded National Socialist body. But with the intrusion of men such as Wüst, Wirth's academic students and other followers such as Plaßmann and Huth, ideographic studies would soon penetrate the universities too.

NOTES

1 J. Stephenson, *The Nazi Organisation of Women* (London: Croom Helm, 1981), 97ff.

2 F. Bernadotte, *Slutet* (Stockholm: Norstedt & Sons, 1945), 46–47; Trevor Roper, 72.

3 L.P. Eisenhut, "Runen-Freunde, Hippies, Mystiker," *Die Welt* 20 June, 1998; M. Schulz, "Der Kult der Sternenmagier," *Der Spiegel* 25 Nov. 2002, 192–206.

4 H. Hamelmann, *Epitome chronici Osnaburgensis* (Lemgo: [Schuchen,] 1564); F. Hohenschwert et al. "Externsteine," in J. Hoops, *Reallexikon der Germanischen Altertumskunde* VIII, 2nd ed. (Berlin: De Gruyter, 1994), 37–38; cf. M. Schmidt and U. Halle, "On the Folklore of the Externsteine," in A. Gazin-Schwartz and C. Holtorf (eds.), *Archaeology and Folklore* (London: Routledge, 1999), 158–74; U. Halle, "Die Externsteine," in A. Leube (ed.), *Prähistorie und Nationalsozialismus* (Heidelberg: Synchron, 2002), 235–53; and eadem, *"Die Externsteine sind bis auf weiteres germanisch!"* (Bielefeld: Verlag für Regionalgeschichte, 2002).

5 The actual site of Arminius's victory was discovered in 1987 to be by Kalkriese, near Osnabruck; P.S. Wells, *The Battle that Stopped Rome* (New York: Norton, 2003), 45ff.

6 Teudt cit. apud A.A. Lund, *Germanenideologie und Nationalsozialismus* (Tübingen: Niemeyer, 1995), 84, n. 72.

7 W. Teudt, "Bericht über den Stand der Detmolder germanenkundlichen Werkes und der begründenden Pflegstätte," *Germanien* 7 (1935): 257–61; J.O. Plaßmann, "Eröffnung der Pflegstätte für Germanenkunde in Detmold am 5. Oktober 1936," *Germanien* 8 (1936): 328–31.

8 H. Wirth, "Die Rune in der Externsteingrotte," *Germanien* 1 (1929/30): 10–19; idem, "Deutsche Vorgeschichte"; idem, "Das Atlantisproblem," *Germanien* 2 (1930/31): 115–22; anon., biographical sketch of Wirth, *Germanien* 1 (1929/30): 40; Herman Wirth Society report, "Aussprache zwischen Prof. Dr. Herman Wirth und seinen wissenschaftlichen Gegnern," *Germanien* 3 (1931/32): 63–65.

9 H. Wirth, "Das Felsengrab an den Externstein," *Germanien* 5 (1933): 9–15.

10 B. Kummer, "Der germanische Begriff vom Tode," *Germanien* 2 (1930/31): 22–23.

11 Landesregierung Lippe, "Errichtung einer Externsteine-Stiftung," *Germanien* 6 (1934): 129–31; J. Andrée, *Die Externsteine* (Münster i.W.: Coppenrath, 1936); Bollmus, *Amt Rosenberg*, 176–77.

12 F. Platz, "An unsere Mitglieder!," *Germanien* 7 (1935): 161; Kater, *Ahnenerbe*, 55.

13 W. Teudt, *Germanische Heiligtümer*, 2nd ed. (Jena: Diederichs, 1931), 47–55; cf. A. Franssen, "Grundsätzliches zur Frage der Externsteine," *Germanien* 6 (1934): 289–95, 327–42 and Weißmann, 201–2 and table li.

14 J. Latscha and W. Teudt, *Nationale Ansiedelung und Wohnungsreform*, 2nd ed. (Frankfurt a.M.: Ecklin, 1889).

15 W. Teudt, *"Im Interesse der Wissenschaft!"* (Godesberg bei Bonn: Keplerbund, 1909); idem, *Die deutsche Sachlichkeit und der Weltkrieg* (Godesberg bei Bonn: Keplerbund, 1917).

16 W. Teudt, *Germanische Heiligtümer* (Jena: Diederichs, 1929).

17 W. Teudt, "Altgermanischer Gestirndienst," *Mannus* 18 (1926): 349–57; cf. J. Mitchell, *A Little History of Astro-Archaeology* (London: Thames & Hudson, 1977): 58–65.

18 W. Teudt, "Das Werk Gustaf Kossinnas," *Germanien* 3 (1931/32): 73–75; G. Neckel, review of Teudt, 2nd ed., *DLZ* 3. Folge, 2 (1931): 1171–74.

19 O. Suffert, review of Neckel, review of Teudt, *Germanien* 3 (1931/32).

20 Kater, *Ahnenerbe*, 126–27.

21 S. Lang and E. von Schenk (eds.), *The Memoirs of Alfred Rosenberg*, trans. E. Posselt (Chicago: Ziff-David, 1949), 178.

22 R. Bünte (ed.), *Wilhelm Teudt im Kampf um Germanenehre* (Bielefeld: Velhagen & Klasing, 1940); Bollmus, *Amt Rosenberg*, 309, n. 80.

23 Cf. W. Wüst, *Deutsche Frühzeit und arische Geistesgeschichte* (Munich: Deutsche Akademie, 1934); idem, *Das Reich* (Munich: Gässler, 1937); Pringle, 93ff.

24 W. Meid, "Hermann Güntert," in M. Mayrhofer et al. (eds.), *Antiquitates Indogermanicae* (Innsbruck: Institut für Sprachwissenschaft, 1974), 517; Hutton, 39.

25 W. Wüst, "Der Schaltsatz im Rgveda" (dissertation, Munich, 1924); idem, *Stilgeschichte und Chronologie des Rgveda* (Leipzig: Brockhaus, 1928); idem, *Indisch* (Berlin: De Gruyter, 1929); idem, *Vergleichendes und etymologisches Wörterbuch des Altindoiranischen (Altindischen)* I (Heidelberg: Winter, 1935).

26 Wüst, "Gedanken über Wirths 'Aufgang'"; Hübner, 3.

27 Wüst, "Germanenkunde," 324 [= *Odal* 5 (1936): 369 = *Indogermanisches Bekenntnis*, 7].

28 *Germanien* 9 (1937): 98; Kater, *Ahnenerbe*, 43–45, 54, 59–60; K. Poewe, *New Religions and the Nazis* (London: Routledge, 2006), 27.

29 J.O. Plaßmann, *Die Prosawerke der Zuster Hadewych* (Münster i.W. 1920); idem, *Die Geschichte der Stadt Münster in Westfalen* (Münster i.W.: Theissing, 1925); idem, *Das Leben des Kaiser Friedrich II. von Hohenstaufen* (Jena: Diederichs, 1927); idem, *Das Leben Kaiser Ottos des Großen* (Jena: Diederichs, 1928); idem, *Das Leben Kaiser Konrads des Zweiten des Saliers* (Jena:

Diederichs, 1928); idem, *König Heinrich der Vogler* (Jena: Diederichs, 1928); idem, *Orpheus* (Jena: Diederichs, 1928); idem, *Wikingerfahrten und Normannenreiche* (Jena: Diederichs, 1929); Stark, 190; E. Gajek, "Joseph Otto Plaßmann," in K.D. Sievers (ed.), *Beiträge zur Wissenschaftsgeschichte der Volkskunde im 19. und 20. Jahrhundert* (Neumünster: Wachholtz, 1991), 121ff.

30 Plaßmann and Kreyenborg, "Zum Arbeitsplan III," *Germanien* 1 (1929/30): 75–77; J.O. Plaßmann, "Grundfragen zur germanischen Kultur," *Germanien* 3 (1931/32): 76–84.

31 Kater, *Ahnenerbe*, 46, 135; Gajek, 134–37.

32 O. Huth, "Das Roßsymbol und der totenkultliche Charakter der Rennspiele," *Germanien* 2 (1930/31): 122–24 and 142–45; idem, *Janus* (Bonn: Röhrschied, 1932); H. Junginger, *Von der philologischen zur völkischen Religionswissenschaft* (Stuttgart: Steiner, 1999), 248ff.

33 O. Huth, "Wider der Ultramontanismus der Altphilologie," *Germanien* 3 (1931/32): 89–92; idem, "Zur Pferdezucht bei den Germanen," *Germanien* 4 (1932): 21–32; idem, "Astara-Stern," *Germanien* 4 (1932): 32; idem, "Zum Alter der Schriftkenntnis bei den indogermanischen Völkern," *Germanien* 5 (1933): 118–19; idem, "Zur kurzen Runenreihe," *Germanien* 5 (1933): 119; idem, "Der Jahrgott auf dem Stein von Gliende," *Germanien* 8 (1936): 364.

34 Hammerstein, 104ff.

35 O. Huth, "Herkunft und Sinn des Lichterbaums," *Germanien* 8 (1936): 372–76; H. Himmler in *SS-Leitheft* 3/8 (1937): i (and cf. "Das Fest des Lichtes" and "Kunde von Weihnachtsbaum," vol. cit., 36–45).

36 O. Huth, *Die Fällung des Lebensbaumes* (Berlin: Widukind, 1936).

37 O. Huth, "Die Gesittung der Kanarier als Schlüssel zum Ur-Indogermanentum," *Germanien* 9 (1937): 50–54; idem, "Der Lichterbaum," *Germanien* 9 (1937): 357–60; idem, *Der Lichterbaum* (Berlin: Widukind, 1937); idem, "Der Feuerkult der Germanen," *Archiv für Religionswissenschaft* 36 (1939): 108–34; idem, *Vesta* (Leipzig: Teubner, 1943); Lerchenmüller and Simon, *Im Vorfeld*, 70–71.

38 K.T. Weigel, *Lebendige Vorzeit rechts und links der Landstraße* (Berlin: Metzner, 1934); Hunger, 203–220.

39 K.T. Weigel, *Runen und Sinnbilder* (Berlin: Metzner, 1935); Lehmann, art. cit.; U. Nußbeck, *Karl Theodor Weigel und das Göttinger Sinnbildarchiv* (Göttingen: Schmerse, 1993).

40 K. Schirmeisen, "Die Runen als Göttersymbole," *Zeitschrift des deutschen Vereins für die Geschichte Mährens und Schliesens* 26/4 (1926) [n.v].

41 Weigel, *Runen und Sinnbilder*, vii.

42 Ibid., 5, 34, 52–54.

43 Ibid., vii.

44 P. Stauff, *Runenhäuser* (Berlin–Lichterfeld: Scheffer, 1913).

45 K.T. Weigel, "Gibt es Runen im Fachwerk?," *Deutsches Handwerk* 5 (1936): 361–63; idem, "Runen am deutschen Hause," *Nationalsozialistische Monatshefte* 7 (1936): 163–65 and 900–904; idem, "Giebelzeichen und Sinn-

bilder," *Germanen-Erbe* 1 (1936): 122–23; idem, "Sinnbilder am Hause," *Haus und Hof im nordischen Raum* 2 (1937): 111–23; idem, "Dachziegel als Sinnbildträger," *Germanien* 13 (1941): 434–38.
46 J.O. Plaßmann, "Sinnfälliges und Sinnbildliches," *Germanien* 5 (1933): 33–41; idem, "Runenformen in brauchtümlichen Sinnbildern," *Germanien* 8 (1936): 105–14; H. Dingler, "Wege und Grundlagen der Sinnbildforschung," *Germanien* 9 (1937): 36–40, 69–76; Hunger, 240–44.
47 J.O. Plaßmann, *Die Externsteine* (Berlin–Dahlem: Ahnenerbe, 1939); idem, *Ehre ist Zwang genug* (Berlin–Dahlem: Ahnenerbe, 1941); idem, "Das Sinnbild im Märchen," *Germanien* 13 (1941): 201–10; idem, "Odal, Odalrune und Schaub," *Germanien* 15 (1943): 237–46.
48 On Mentzel, see Hammerstein, 130ff.
49 O. Huth, "Die kultischen Wettspiele der Indogermanen," *Germanien* 8 (1936): 235–39.
50 The exact date is unclear: Kater, *Ahnenerbe*, 385, n. 51.
51 J.J. Spielvogel, *Hitler and Nazi Germany*, 2nd ed. (Englewood Cliffs: Prentice Hall, 1992), 108.
52 K. Sim (dir.), *Hitler's Search for the Holy Grail* (London: Channel 4, 1999).
53 O. Rahn, *Kreuzzug gegen den Gral* (Freiburg i.Br.: Urban, 1933); C. Bernadac, *Montségur et le graal* (Paris: France-Empire, 1994); H.-J. Lange, *Otto Rahn* (Engerda: Arun, 1995), idem, *Otto Rahn und die Suche nach dem Gral* (Engerda: Arun, 1999).
54 Bernadac, 302.
55 McCann, 81ff.; B. Arnold and H. Hausmann, "Archaeology in Nazi Germany," in P.L. Kohl and C. Fawcett (eds.), *Nationalism, Politics and Practice of Archaeology* (Cambridge: Cambridge University Press, 1995), 70–81.
56 R. Till, "Die Überlieferung von Tacitus Germania," *Germanien* 15 (1943): 119–29; idem, *Handschriftliche Untersuchungen zu Tacitus Agricola und Germania* (Berlin–Dahlem, Ahnenerbe, 1943); Kater, *Ahnenerbe*, 200; V. Losemann, *Nationalsozialismus und Antike* (Hamburg: Hoffmann & Campe, 1977), 120ff.; Lund, 31.
57 Recreated in Schama, 75–76.
58 H. Hörbiger with P. Fauth, *Glacial-Kosmogonie* (Kaiserslautern: Kayser, 1913); B. Nagel, *Die Welteislehre* (Stuttgart: Verlag für Geschichte der Naturwissenschaften und Technik, 1991); R. Bowen, *Universal Ice* (London: Bellhaven, 1993).
59 Picker, 94.
60 H. Voigt, *Eis, ein Weltenbaustoff* (Berlin–Wilmersdorf: Paeckel, 1920); H. Fischer, *Der Wunder des Welteises* (Berlin–Wilmersdorf: Paekel, 1922); R. Henseling, *Weltentwicklung und Welteislehre* (Potsdam: Die Sterne, 1925); G. Hinzpeter, *Urwissen von Kosmos und Erde* (Leipzig: Voigtländer, 1928); W. Aspendorf, *Die Edda als Welteislehre* (Krefeld: Hons, 1933); H.S. Bellamy, *Moons, Myth and Man* (London: Faber & Faber, 1936); Nagel, 42ff.; Bowen, 71–83.
61 Kater, *Ahnenerbe*, 52; Nagel, 72.

62 Kater, *Ahnenerbe*, 51–53, 86–87; Nagel, 70ff.; Bowen, 130–50.

63 Hunger, 164–68; Goodrick-Clarke, 177–86; H.-J. Lange, *Weisthor* (Engerd: Arun, 1998); cf. S.E. Flowers and M. Moynihan, *The Secret King* (Waterbury Center: Dominion, 2001); Pringle, 46ff.

64 Kater, *Ahnenerbe*, 364, n. 99; Hunger, 169–70.

65 J. Lechler, *Vom Hakenkreuz*, 2nd ed. (Leipzig: Kabitzsch, 1934); idem, "Sinn und Weg des Hakenkreuzes," *Der Schulungsbrief* 2 (1935): 404–13.

66 L. Wilser, *Das Hakenkreuz nach Ursprung, Vorkommen und Bedeutung* (Zeitz: Sis, 1917); D. Bernhardi, *Das Hakenkreuz*, 7th ed. (Leipzig: Fritsch, 1933).

67 W. Scheuermann, *Woher kommt das Hakenkreuz?* (Berlin: Rowohlt, 1933); T. Bieder, *Das Hakenkreuz*, 2nd ed., (Leipzig: Weicher, 1934).

68 *Deutsche Agrarpolitik* 1/1–2/3 (Berlin: NSDAP/Zeitgeschichte, 1932–33); thereafter *Odal* 2/4–11 (Berlin: Zeitgeschichte, then Berlin/Goslar: Blut und Boden, 1933–42); R.W. Darré, "Unser Weg," *Odal* 2 (1934): 690–720; A. D'Onofrio, *Ruralismo e storia nel Terzo Reich* (Naples: Liguori, 1997); Schmitz-Behring, 446–47.

69 K.-H. Schumacher, *Die deutschen Monatsnamen* (Griefswald: Bamberg, 1937), 59ff., 120ff.

70 It was subsequently also adopted by the NS-Frauenschaft after the two organizations merged during the war; Stephenson, 152.

71 Wirth, *Was heißt deutsch?*, 14–15.

72 Weißmann, 202, 208–9 and tab. xlviii, c.

73 Wirth, *Was heißt deutsch?*, 36ff.

74 Weißmann, tab. lix.

75 Darré, 707; K. Robberstad et al., "Odelsrett," in J. Brøndsted et al. (eds.), *Kulturhistorisk leksikon for nordisk middelalder* XII (Copenhagen: Rosenkilde & Bagger, 1967), 493–503; G. von Olberg, "Odal," in A. Erler and E. Kaufmann (eds.), *Handwörterbuch zur deutschen Rechtsgeschichte* II (Berlin: Schmidt, 1982), 1178–84.

76 H. Gauch, *Die germanische Odal- oder Allodverfassung* (Berlin: Blut & Boden, 1934). Gauch is more famously the subject of S. Gauch, *Vaterspuren* (Königsstein i.Ts.: Athenäum, 1979); cf. G. Dahl, *Radikalare än Hitler* (Stockholm: Atlantis, 2006), 243–44.

77 Leers, *Odal*; cf. also idem, "Das Odalsrecht bei den Japanern," *Odal* 2 (1934): 881–88 and A. Bramwell, *Blood and Soil* (Bourne End: Kensel, 1985), 49ff.

78 O. Behagel, "Aussenseiter," *Deutsche Allgemeine Zeitung*, 9 Aug. 1934; H. Strobel, "Allzu 'geheim' Herr Geheimrat!," *Völkischer Beobachter* 12–13 Aug. 1934; R. Olt and H. Ramge, "'Aussenseiter,'" *LiLi* 14 (1984): 194–223.

79 O. Behagel, "Odal," *Sitzungsberichte der Bayrischen Akademie der Wissenschaften, Phil.-Hist. Abt.* 1935, no. 8; idem, "Odal," *Forschungen und Fortschritte* 11 (1935): 369–70; and cf. W. Krause, review of Behagel, *Historische Zeitschrift* 154 (1936): 323–34.

80 Wüst, "Germanenkunde," 327 [= *Odal* 5 (1936): 373 = *Indogermanisches Bekenntnis*, 12]; Kater, *Ahnenerbe*, 39ff. A leading figure in German linguistics as well as *Volkskunde*, Behagel died a year later in 1936.
81 G. Klandor, "Erbhof und Runen," *Odal* 3 (1934): 337–39; K.T. Weigel, "Sinnbilder-Kulturerbe," *Odal* 5 (1936): 720–26; H. Wirth, "Die ältesten Odal-Urkunden des germanischen Bauern," *Odal* 5 (1936): 882–90.
82 K.K.A. Ruppel, "Das Symbol der germanischen Sippe," *Odal* 5 (1936): 391–404.
83 K.K.A. Ruppel, *Die Hausmarke* (Berlin: Metzner, 1939), 12ff.; H. Arntz, "Hausmarken –Sippensymbole," *Runenberichte* 1 (1941): 123–26; Hunger, 250–62.
84 F. Langewiesche, *Sinnbilder germanischen Glaubens im Wittekindsland* (Eberswalde: Langewiesche, 1935); O. von Zaborsky-Wahlstätten, *Urväter-Erbe in deutscher Volkskunst* (Leipzig: Koehler & Amelang, 1936); E.O. Thiele, *Sinnbild und Brauchtum* (Potsdam: Bogenreiter, 1937); M.F. Helmers, "Heilzeichen im Gefüge des niedersächsischen Bauernhauses," *Germanien* 9 (1937): 205–10; idem, *Sinnbilder alten Glaubens in ostfriesischer Volkskunst* (Aurich: Duckmann, 1938); F.H. Hamkens, "Drei Steingräber Schleswig-Holsteins," *Germanien* 9 (1937): 339–42, 360–66; idem, *Sinnbilder auf Grabsteiner von Schleswig bis Flandern* (Brussels: Die Osterlingen, 1942); A. Bode, *Heilige Zeichen* (Heidelberg: Winter, 1938); W. Stief, *Heidnische Sinnbilder an christlichen Kirchen und auf Werken der Volkskunst* (Leipzig: Hase & Koehler, 1938); H. Wühr, *Ewiger Sinn im zeitgebundenen Sinnbild* (Stuttgart: Tuchenmüller, 1938); M. Raschdorff, *Nordische Sinnzeichen- und Bilderschrift durch 4 Jahrtausende* (Finsterwalde: Raschdorff-Viehrig, 1939); A. Schröder, *Ahnenerbe in der Volkskunst der Heide* (Düben: Streubel, 1939); K.S. Kramer, *Die Dingbeseelung in der germanischen Überlieferung* (Munich: Neuer Filser, 1940); Nußbeck, 123ff.
85 K. Schmidt-Klevenow, "Nordische Runen und Hausmarken in der chinesichen Schrift," *Germanien* 8 (1936): 183–84.
86 Trevor Roper, 72.
87 Rauschning, 225; Poliakov and Wulf (eds.), 243.
88 P. Gassert and D.S. Mattern, *The Hitler Library* (Westport, Conn.: Greenwood, 2001), 322–23; Pringle, 92.
89 E.g. in the "Verzeichnis wertvoller Bücher für den SS-Mann," ed. by the RuSHA, Dec. 1935, reprinted in D'Onofrio, 274–85.
90 Hunger, 148ff.; Weißmann, 203ff. and tabs xlvii–l.

CHAPTER 9.

Into the Academy

Ástráð þin ec vil öll hafa
svá lengi, sem ec lifi
Sigurd in the Edda's *Sigrdrífumál*

On the 2nd of September, 1938, I was, for the last time, at the Fiener marshes, with my former Halle colleague Walter Schulz, a place where Indo-European peoples had already settled by the Mesolithic Period. While he and my son looked for pieces of amber in the silted-up lakes, I lay on the edge of the marish on a rise leaning against a pine tree and gazed over the unending marshes ... As in a dream, the life of the former inhabitants emerged before me, and I imagined how it would have been here in the Middle Stone Age ... On the 9th of March, 1942, I gave a presentation in which I first spoke on the contents of this book at a scientific evening in Berlin. That was how I last saw my son who was at that time in an anti-aircraft unit defending the city. A few days later he went to the eastern front as a volunteer.[1]

In 1944 the German linguist Franz Specht saw his *magnum opus* of *Wörter und Sachen* studies appear in print with the blessings of the Ahnenerbe's Wüst. Specht's book was a breakthrough work in comparative linguistics, but concentrating as it does on the origin of the declensional classes of the Indo-European languages, it at first appears a strange publication to be allowed to appear in the year that also saw the liberation of much of Europe from Nazi control. Specht dedicated the book to the memory of his son, Günther, who was missing, presumed dead in the region about Stalingrad. But the publication of Specht's *Origin of the Indo-European Declension* was not only a recognition of his son's sacrifice and his family's loss—it was very much the kind of work that senior Nazi academics like Wüst were keen on patronizing. Not only is Specht's book, with its demonstration that grammatical features can be explained historically in terms of former semantic (and cultural) realities, a brilliant contribution to the *Wörter und Sachen* field, it was also a highly original (if equally impenetrable to the non-specialist) addition to understanding the ancestral inheritance—i.e. the kind of work the Ahnenerbe was founded explicitly in order to promote.

Nonetheless, alongside the studies of figures such as Specht (whose occasional forays into romantic over-interpretation usually did not adversely affect the caliber of his work), the Ahnenerbe had begun as a center for markedly speculative and politicized studies. In fact already by the time Specht last saw his son, and despite the efforts of Germanists like Arntz and Behagel (as well as Wirth's enemies within the academic system), ideographic studies had finally (re)entered respectable academic discourse. It did not do so under the command of Darré or Himmler, however, or any other form of overt coercion. Instead, as Weigel himself pointed out in 1943, although it had been a struggle, by the 1940s *Sinnbildforschung* had finally been accepted within the universities; it had become a respectable academic field.[2] In the second half of the 1930s, the reserved distance maintained by many leading practitioners of Old Germanic studies who had not been as accepting of the new theoretical currents as had Neckel or Fehrle finally gave way to this most radical and often patently fantastic of *völkisch* discourses. Old Germanic studies sank to its nadir at the time, but it was not forces from outside the universities which instigated this decline; at a time when runes were being used symbolically all over the new Germany with meanings developed in ideographic studies, it was brought on instead by scholars from within. This acceptance of *Sinnbildforschung* was not a half-hearted accommodation of dilettantism by established scholars either—on the contrary the enthusiasm of these university men for the new science is often palpable in their publications. The acceptance of ideographic studies by academic Germanists under the dictatorship represented the last victory of the *völkisch* cultural tide. Experts today may shake their heads or even laugh at many of the publications of Ahnenerbe researchers from the period, but much of the radical Germanic studies of the SS was produced by established and even leading scholars who had volunteered to become Himmler's Germanists.

Moreover, these scholars also became part of another expansion of *Sinnbildforschung* and the Ahnenerbe, one that would eventually bring even more shame upon their colleagues than did the base politicization of their researches or their increasing toleration of dilettantes and fantasists. By the 1940s, Wirth's paleo-epigraphy and the rustic expressions of *Sinnbildforschung* most closely associated with Weigel had developed broader Germanic and even Indo-European provinces as well. Symbols from Italy, Iceland and the Low Countries also came into the purview of ideographic studies. But though the associated scholars may have often joined Specht in his antiquarian reverie, many also drank as much from the approach of his son. Following the extraordinary successes of the German Armed Forces, the Ahnenerbe even came to take on a more overt political role as the *völkisch* approach to Germanic antiquarianism was exported west and north too, and SS Germanists became involved in and planned for the control and ethnic and cultural reorganization of the Nazi empire.

GERMANIC PHILOLOGY

In 1938 a *Festschrift* came out in time to celebrate Gustav Neckel's sixtieth birthday. By this date Neckel was a sick man, physically and if we believe his predecessor Heusler, mentally as well. Heusler also remarked, however, that it was strange that the *Festschrift* was entitled *Contributions to Runology and Nordic Linguistics (Beiträge zur Runenkunde und nordischen Sprachwissenschaft)*. Neckel's speciality, like Heusler's, was Old Norse literature. "Does he think most fondly of his *lærisveinar* (students) as runologists?," Heusler asked his friend Wilhelm Ranisch rhetorically in their correspondence.[3]

The Neckel *Festschrift* was a book of its time. Along with Hans Kuhn's *Sinnbildforschung*-inspired *Wörter und Sachen* contribution stood several other essays on topics dear to ideographic studies, one even by Höfler's detractor, the folklorist von der Leyen. Suddenly everyone was a runologist. The appearance of a valueless paper from the pen of the amateur Edmund Weber was merely another sign of how ready the honoree was to sponsor *völkisch* antiquarianism.[4] The contribution most clearly supportive of the Wirthian stance taken by Neckel, however, was by his former student Krause, who had just succeeded Neckel in Göttingen at the end of 1937 (Neckel's position had been merged into Hermann's Indo-European chair and Krause became the Professor of Indo-European Philology and Runology, the first and hopefully last official German professor of runes).[5] In it he investigated the ideographic use of runes in light of two articles from 1936 in which he had come out squarely in favor of ideographic studies.[6]

Perhaps the most telling critique of Wirth's acceptance of the *Oera Linda Book* had been that of Krause when he dismissed the forgery in terms of Heusler's Germanicness. Mindful of the political climate of the time, many of those critical of Wirth no doubt felt it necessary to frame their rejection of the *Oera Linda Book* in terms that would not appear too damning. As Arthur Hübner concluded:[7]

> We do not doubt Wirth's idealism. Nor do we doubt his good intention to help bring about the spiritual renewal of our people either; but we have serious doubts that the intellectual position that obviously lies behind his research, his propaganda and his polemic really can be of much use to our race.

It is also worth noting at the same time, though, that Hübner, the editor since 1930 of the German national dictionary (*Grimms Wörterbuch*) and later a member of the Amt Rosenberg, had already worked to undermine Wirth privately late in 1934, damning any scholastic merit he had in a report to the Education Ministry.[8]

Nevertheless, in 1936 Krause publicly declared himself a supporter of Wirth's *Sinnbildforschung*. In two papers from that year he dealt with the ideographic use of runes. In one of the articles, in the academic magazine *Forschungen und Fortschritte (Research and Progress)* in December, he announced:[9]

> The fact that the runes were also employed as symbols is to be explained in my opinion only in the following way: caused by incidental likeness of form, they amalgamated with the at times much older symbols which are frequently met with on Teutonic soil, on gravestones, weapons, tools, urns and the famous Scandinavian rock-carvings.
>
> What was formerly considered to be exceptional or regarded as the arbitrary whim of a writer of runes has proved to be a very ancient heritage, an older stratum in the runic tradition which appeared rather late (3rd century A.D.), a heritage leading us back to a very remote pre-runic period. If we were to try to interpret these pre-runic symbols in themselves alone, we should be without any firm support and wholly given up to fancy. The meaning of the runes, however, is limited rather definitely

by their names, and as the runes seem to have taken on the heritage of the pre-runic symbols, they bestow the light of scientific methods even on the interpretation of the spiritual contents of many older signs.

That scientific method was the essence of Wirth's *Sinnbildforschung*.

Krause's other publications from the time are similarly enlightening. His 1936 contribution to the prehistorical journal *Altpreußen (Old Prussia)* seems to have been influenced by a brief mention of a work by him from 1935 by the archeologist Hans-Lüitjen Janssen who had pointed out that *Sinnbildforschung* (or rather *Sinnbilderforschung*) had a long academic pedigree before Weigel's popular book had appeared in 1935.[10] But as Krause explained:[11]

> Hardly an area of Germanic antiquarian study has come to concern the widest circles in so strong and so lively a manner than in the rounds of the mysterious symbols that our forefathers first used and which they called runes. In thick books, in the journals of many disciplines and in the pages of the daily press, the question of the secret of the runes is discussed, often in a passionate manner, and hardly a day passes in which the ocean of writings on things runic is not topped up again.

He clearly felt it was time to put a properly academic perspective on things.

Krause had come around to this idea already in 1935 when he had produced his *What One Carved in Runes*, which was clearly aimed at the popular market or rather as he put it "those in whose hearts a newly awoken sympathy for the consideration and the care of our Germanic inheritance lies."[12] Janssen had already noticed that Krause was supportive of *Sinnbildforschung* in this short survey. Krause's contributions from 1936 build further on this clearly enthusiastically *völkisch* sentiment.

Although wary of Wirth's penchant for mega-comparison, Krause was convinced that some of the runes had developed out of earlier symbols. He did not accept that the pre-runic symbols developed directly into a fully fledged and autochthonous script—he was only too well aware that many of the Germanic letters probably had a Mediterranean origin. The question for Krause was how the runes developed their "dual nature"—as ideographs as well as more regular alphabetical characters. Some runes such as **j** (*y*) and η (*ng*) which had no clear Mediterranean forebears he thought were purely Germanic creations. For others, instead he suggested some sort of accommodation. He suggested the **t**-rune (↑) was compared with an arrow by the early Germans; thus its name Tyr, that of the god of victory. The **o**-rune (⊗), Odal "heritable land," he compared with the form of a sling, the modern Danish word for which (*løkke*) is a homonym of that for a fenced-in section of land.[13] In his second article from 1936, however, he came out more strongly in favor of the notion of Wirth that the ideographic values of the runes could be projected back onto the earlier symbols, and thus that the methodology of *Sinnbildforschung* was basically correct. He believed that several of the runes in fact were continuations of the pre-runic symbols, but unlike Wirth and his devotees, probably not all. The more often he restated the premise of his interpretation of *Sinnbildforschung*, the more he came to sound like a Neckel or a Wirth. In fact his enthusiasm for his runological work had soon grown to the point of exuberance. In 1939 in an article suggestively entitled "The Power of the Runes" he observed:[14]

In the new Germany the runes now enjoy a resurgence ... The revival of consciousness among the German people of the deepest changes in their existence and nature has at the same time led the old symbols, the ideographs of the Old Germanic feeling of life, to be filled with new content and new worth. One can reconstruct now the life of every old symbol, from the beginning of Germanicness at the end of the Stone Age to the present of our days, and seek them out in farm and village houses, in monasteries and churches. The runologist ... is pleased by this development, as a kindling spark from that which until now was cherished and trusted only in the restricted circle of his few colleagues, has now spread to his whole people with alacrity.

Krause had clearly become caught up in the spirit of *völkisch* antiquarianism; like Specht his superlative runic vision stretched back to the Stone Age. In 1934 we already find him discovering a form of the word "Aryan" on a Scandinavian rune-stone;[15] and with the endorsement of Krause very soon the tenets of *Sinnbildforschung* came to be accepted by several other academics. The archeologist Karl Hermann Jacob-Friesen, a noted opponent of settlement archeology who had also been one of the leading critics of Wirth's acceptance of the *Oera Linda Book*, responded to the new runological development in June 1937 declaring that he had discovered runic ideographs on an urn at the State Museum of Hanover, explicitly citing Krause's authority.[16] Krause's articles on runic ideographs had become seminal reading. Even Wirth's most vocal critics during the Oera Linda debacle had come to accept the validity of his *Sinnbildkunde*.

Critics in *völkisch* antiquarian circles had long bemoaned that professional runologists neglected the question of the relation of the runes to ideographs. Arntz of course had dismissed this dilletantism in 1934. Reichardt, on the other hand, had responded diplomatically in the foreword of his own *Runology* in 1936: he considered the understanding of this relationship not to be sufficiently established for him to pass any comment or include any survey of other symbols in his book.[17] Even Janssen who regarded himself as a voice of clarity in the area criticized authors like Reichardt for not providing an ideographic aspect to their handbooks.[18] A runological unknown, Bernhard Reiss, had produced a runic handbook for the publishers Reclam in 1936 in which he pointed out that *völkisch* thought made it imperative that such symbols be included in any survey of runology, and even cited Heusler's name in his argument that runes were a creation of primordial Germanic antiquity.[19]

The Ahnenerbe's Huth in his review of Reiss's *Runology (Runenkunde)* for *Germanien* praised the author for precisely this point: accepting *Sinnbildforschung* as part of runic studies.[20] Krause would eventually follow suit, providing a survey of runic ideographs in the second edition of *What One Carved in Runes* in 1943. Arntz, on the other hand, rubbished this section of Krause's work in his review: he had gone to great lengths to combat the *Urschrift* thesis and the *Sinnbildforschung* that had developed around it.[21] Arntz and Arthur Nordén, a Swedish expert in rock carvings, spent much time defending scholarship from these incursions from *völkisch* academia.[22] Arntz stood in marked contrast to his rival at Göttingen who seems to have been overcome with his enthusiasm for the occasionally ideographic nature of the runes.

There was an academic tradition of sorts, however, that had considered the possibility of a relationship between runes and the symbols of prehistoric antiquity. In 1917, for instance, a folklorist Robert Petsch had written an article on the symbols employed in an ancient

Germanic divination ceremony recorded by Tacitus. Petsch built on some ideas found in respectable Germanist circles—most clearly the *Urschrift* fantasies of von Liliencron and Müllenhoff—after all, the description *notae* used by Tacitus in the *Germania* could clearly be translated as "ideograph."[23] Tacitus' description was thought to be too early to refer to runes proper, however, so it had become generally accepted in philological circles that this reference must have been to pre-runic ideographs—swastikas and the like. Commenting on the tendency of both academics and the public to call any ancient symbol a rune and suggesting this confusion extended also to pre-modern sources, Petsch contended that a distinction needed to be made between these symbols (*Zeichenrunen*) and the runic characters (*Schriftrunen*) proper. Reichardt's teacher Mogk had also written a short work on the runes and the swastika in 1921 playing down the possibility of any relationship.[24] Yet there was a tradition in respectable scholarship that linked the pre-runic symbols with the runes by concentrating on the Tacitean passage and contending that word rune itself was once used to refer to both sorts of characters.

Krause seems to have been unaware of Petsch's contribution and unaffected by the scepticism of Mogk. Nevertheless, in 1936 he had come around to essentially the same taxonomy as Petsch, albeit expressed this time in terms of a direct relationship, i.e. under the influence of the *Urschrift* thesis. Krause separated the use of runes as ideographs (*Begriffsrunen*) from the usual alphabetic employment where the runes represented individual sounds (*Lautrunen*) and he restricted primordial antiquity only to the former, not the latter usage of the runes.[25]

Krause's sophistry soon descended into fantasy, however: by the mid-1930s he had developed a predilection for finding runes in all sorts of unclear contexts—any scratch on a prehistoric find could potentially be a runic ideograph.[26] By 1940 Krause had even begun a relationship with the Ahnenerbe that, despite writing a dismissive review of Weigel's *Runes and Ideographs* in 1935, would see him join up with the amateur in early 1943 as Wirth's heir to the leadership of the Division for Alphabetic and Ideographic Studies.[27] Weigel and Krause had already contributed complimentary articles to *Wörter und Sachen* in 1942 (since 1939 an Ahnenerbe-controlled journal) on a symbol discovered by Weigel on a prehistoric urn, Krause's a preposterous contribution where he argued for an indigenous origin for the clearly Latinate **r-**

rune (ᚱ)—his belief in the ideographic theory had clearly become intellectually overriding.²⁸ With Arntz's gradual exclusion from academic
life, Krause remained the only runologist of note within the academic
system. Wirth's *Sinnbildforschung* had begun to subsume mainstream
German runology.

The relationship between Weigel and Krause had begun as early
as 1939 when they had met at Plaßmann's "Haus Ahnenerbe" near
the Extern Stones in Horn. They soon established a working relation-
ship.²⁹ In 1940 Krause had Weigel use his SS connections to try to
ascertain the whereabouts of an ancient spearhead that seemed to bear
some sort of inscription and similar inquiries were made in subsequent
years to Sievers and Jankuhn about items bearing runic texts that had
last been reported in museums in Eastern Europe, but which were now
under German control.³⁰ In 1942 Krause went further still and decided to join the Ahnenerbe outright. He submitted a plan to Wüst to
unite his Institute for Runology at Göttingen with Weigel's division of
the Ahnenerbe as a "Center for Runological and Ideographic Studies"
(Zentralstelle für Runen- und Sinnbildkunde) under his direction, with
him leading the runological section and Weigel the ideographic one.³¹
His suggested wording for the official establishment of the Center begins with the following words:³²

> A center for runological and ideographic studies is created in Germany
> therewith that will serve the needs of research, study and propaganda.
> Runic and ideographic studies, as the scientific development especially in
> the last years has insistently shown, are loosely interconnected; but only
> through a firm and strictly scientific study of both areas might one ex-
> pect to remove the great harm to the reputation of German science done
> by the manifold, often sensational fantasies that unfortunately again and
> again seem to encroach upon this area of study, and with time set down
> truly indisputable results.

There is a querying mark pencilled in red under the word *Propaganda*
on the original of this document, but it is clear from what the Center
produced over the next two years that propaganda was indeed part of
Krause's plan. After all, he was an enthusiastic promoter of Germanic
antiquity and recognized that its promotion to the pubic at large by
1943 served as *völkisch* propaganda. Krause had sold out completely

to the Nazis. His wish to rectify the damage done to the reputation of German scholarship over the preceding decade seems to have been inspired by a review of Arntz's *Handbook* by the Danish runologist Erik Moltke—Krause's words replicate Moltke's warning that "Herman Wirth ... has done irreparable damage to Germany's scholarly reputation."[33] Krause's sentiment would seem worthy enough if it were not that the document also sets down the principle that:

> ... the ideographs of the Germanic and thus from the Indo-European living space, which can be shown to go back to the Stone Age and from about 100 B.C. contributed to the creation of the runic script, live on in part in the traditions of modern and the most recent of times ... The work of the new Teaching and Research Post will contribute in this way: to rediscover and to revive long-buried sources of the beliefs of our people and most of all the spiritual bearing of our kind.

After receiving confirmation from Himmler in early 1943, Krause wrote to Wüst thanking him for his support. He also asked for his help in his mission to clean up runic scholarship, to discourage in the future "any Guido von Lists or Herman Wirths,"[34] and to channel any reports of runic matters through him, evidently so he could vet them. But in accepting *Sinnbildforschung* the would-be runological censor had already legitimized and himself been won over by *völkisch* antiquarianism, albeit not in its most extreme form, but still one that is evidently quite far removed from one based in a dispassionate consideration of the available evidence.

With Krause's acceptance of the mandate of the Ahnenerbe and its *Sinnbildkunde*, it is no surprise to see him publishing articles in *Germanien* after having first been sought out by Plaßmann for a commentary on the fraudulent American Kensington rune-stone in 1937, and moreover in collaboration with Ahnenerbe identities such as Weigel and Plaßmann.[35] An article from 1941 was on the rune-inscribed spearhead from Kovel (now in the Ukraine), which had been looted from a private Polish collection by the archeologist Peter Paulsen, a member of the Ahnenerbe involved in the SS "antiquarian rescue team" (Prähistorische Bergungskommando) assigned to German-occupied Poland in 1939.[36] It was held at Ahnenerbe premises at Dahlem in Berlin, where

Krause travelled in 1940 after being informed of the find by Weigel, and again in the next year, having proper photos made of it for his Göttingen collection. His assessment of the inscription was partly provoked by a fumbled reading from Weber who had always been one of the most respected of the *völkisch* dilettantes—and it was duly invoked subsequently as yet another piece of evidence justifying German eastern ambitions in the *SS-Leithefte* in 1941.[37] Nevertheless, from that year Krause had replaced Weber altogether as runological authority for *Germanien*, the latter moving on to Rosenberg-allied circles, becoming especially involved in *Sigrune*, another *völkisch* antiquarian journal which merged with Kummer's *Nordische Stimmen* in 1942.

Ulrich Hunger also recounts the struggle Krause had stopping the publication of a monograph on a variant of the hieroglyphic thesis in the *Germanien* monographic series in 1943.[38] The author, J. Wilhelm Hauer, Professor of Religious Studies at the University of Tübingen, was the founder of the German Faith Movement (Deutsche Glaubensbewegung), a *völkisch* neo-pagan group. He had also been producing lectures since at least 1932 on modern (i.e. mostly Ariosophic) expressions of Indo-European belief and had long been working on an anthology or "lay breviary" for the Ahnenerbe that would bring together many of the key sources dealing with Indo-European paganism.[39] Straying somewhat outside his field of comparative religious studies, however, Hauer had been publicly promoting a paper in 1942 (later to appear in *Germanien*) on the use of the swastika in which he had traced runic use back to the Bronze Age.[40] Krause, though, dismissed Hauer's Wirth-like theories in a contribution to the German-language *Brüsseler Zeitung (Brussels Newspaper)* in the middle of that year.[41] With the support of Wüst, Krause had decided to attempt to rid the Ahnenerbe of the influence of the worst runic fantasists, and despite his academic credentials, Hauer's ideas were clearly of this ilk. After several sharp letters between Krause, Wüst and Sievers, and another caustic assessment of Hauer's theories by Krause published in the review journal of the Göttingen Academy in 1943, the publication of the book was finally put off indefinitely despite its imminent appearance already having been announced in *Germanien*.[42] Krause thought he could reshape the runological section of the Ahnenerbe along empirical, even Neogrammarian grounds. Yet the Ahnenerbe had been founded to foster the radical research that was ideographic studies and the specter of

Wirth still lay on his former *Pflegstätte* until the time of its dissolution in 1945.

The new *Sinnbildforschung* stripped of Wirth's more incredible fantasies made a strong impression on several academics. Krause himself lauded Weigel's last original work *Carved Symbols of the Threshing Floors of the Black Forest* (*Ritzzeichnungen in Dreschtennen des Schwarzwaldes*, published as a supplement to *Wörter und Sachen* in 1942) as suitable for acceptance as a doctoral dissertation and encouraged Weigel to complete the other studies necessary to achieve the German *Promotion*.[43] Only the loss of the war stopped him from attaining a doctorate. It is clear that ideographic studies had evolved beyond the *völkisch* fringe it had inhabited for many years and returned to the academic sphere in which its seeds had first developed. As an exposition of the latest trends of scholarship, Weber had clearly been correct to devote a chapter or more to ideographic studies in his SS-published *Runological Digest (Kleine Runenkunde)* of 1941, despite the reservations which might be held of judgements he made elsewhere in his runological ditherings.[44] The writings of a number of academics had become flushed with *völkisch* thought over the course of the 1920s and even more specialists in Germanic antiquity had been supportive of Wirth's *Sinnbildforschung* when it had first appeared. Krause, as Neckel's heir at Göttingen, had continued his teacher's legacy, adding to ideographic studies the respectability that allowed other scholars to use *Sinnbildforschung* in their own work. Krause no doubt felt that he had successfully pared ideographic studies of the worst of the obscurantism of Wirth much as Wüst thought he had similarly remodelled the Ahnenerbe in the guise of an academic learned society. The ideographic theory, palpably quite specious outside the context of the *völkisch* revolution, captured many of the leading German scholars of the time, and led to the preparation of scores of publications that today are no longer considered a part of respectable scholarship.

FOLKLORE

With the expansion of *Sinnbildforschung* after its institutional adoption by the SS in 1935, Wirth's theories also soon began to affect the field which at that time was still dominated by his old doctoral supervisor

John Meier. Meier, a man of independent means, had left Basel in 1911 and returned to Germany, to the University of Freiburg in Breisgau where he was granted an honorary professorship in 1913. *Volkskunde* was still largely unrecognized in Germany in terms of chairs at that time—except for Otto Lauffer who held the sole German chair in folklore (which had been created at the University of Hamburg during the early years of the Weimar Republic), most of its practitioners taught courses in music, theology or more commonly Old Germanic languages and literatures instead. Meier, himself a former student of the Neogrammarians Sievers and Paul, proposed that a research institute needed to be set up to promote the establishment of *Volkskunde* as an autonomous discipline within Germanic studies. A League of German Folklore Societies (Verband deutscher Vereine für Volkskunde) already existed and Meier himself had headed it since 1911; but it lacked the gravitas of an institute with secure funding. He also inaugurated a scheme for a *Volkskunde* atlas—an encyclopedic survey of German folklore on the scale of the *Monumenta Germaniae historica*. Meier began to implement the project in 1927 after winning the support of the DFG. Yet it was not until the Nazi accession in 1933 and with Meier approaching his seventieth birthday that he seemed to be about to realize his wish with the foundation of the League for German Folklore (Bund deutscher Volkskunde) which he hoped would lead in due course to the establishment of a central research institute for *Volkskunde*.[45]

Although Meier had the support of the Education Ministry, in 1934 the DFG turned instead to a younger folklorist, Adolf Spamer, then teaching at the Technical University of Dresden, to lead its new folklore section (which included responsibility for the production of the *Volkskunde* atlas). Under Spamer, it looked again for a time that Meier's plans would soon be realized. But then Rosenberg stepped in. Recognizing that German folklore was a field that studied the *Volk* directly, Rosenberg moved to coordinate *Volkskunde* throughout Germany, and his chief folklorist Matthes Ziegler destroyed the plans of Meier and Spamer, and their supporters at the DFG and the Education Ministry. Although he had been given a chair in *Volkskunde* at the University of Berlin in early 1936, Spamer was forced to retire from his DFG posting later that year, and Ziegler became the leader of the folklore division of the new Rosenberg-aligned Working Group on German Folklore (Arbeitsgemeinschaft für deutsche Volkskunde) founded in January 1937. Meier now attempted to win the support of Himmler, but when the SS finally came to the party their action was belated and typically cannibalistic. Himmler had supported Rosenberg's Working Group at first, but friction developed between Ziegler's folklorists and those of the Ahnenerbe, particularly in light of the Kummer affair. Ziegler, an adherent of the Viennese mythologist school, attacked SS-aligned researchers such as Höfler and his *Männerbund* theories, and even attempted to set up a sort of rival to the Ahnenerbe's ideography division. In turn, Heinrich Harmjanz, by then the folklorist responsible for the *Volkskunde* atlas at the DFG, defected from Rosenberg's circle and took the atlas over to the Ahnenerbe. Rosenberg had his revenge, denouncing the traitor Harmjanz for plagiarism in 1942. But eventually, much as in archeology, separate brown and black organizations for German *Volkskunde* were established; and as Europe moved closer to war, German folklore grew to be dependent upon the Party's chief two ideological organs for all manner of institutional support.[46]

The most active supporter of *Sinnbildforschung* within the *Volkskunde* establishment at the time, however, was Eugen Fehrle. Meier had politely declined his former student's request to become involved with Wirth's first intellectual prehistory exhibition in 1933—he thought at the time that Wirth's theories might damage the credibility of *Volkskunde*.[47] But *Sinnbildforschung* had other friends more closely aligned to the Party. Not only did radical Party folklorists like Ziegler clearly approve of the new approach to Germanic studies, in keeping with his earlier indication of support for Wirth's *Emergence* published in the Baeumler volume, from 1934 Fehrle began to assemble a photographic collection of ideographs at Heidelberg as part of the development of a *Volkskunde* archive and went so far as to have copies made of some of the casts Wirth had executed during his Scandinavian tours. Fehrle's own exhibition of *Sinnbildforschung*-inspired *Volkskunde* seemed merely to be an expanded version of those of Wirth; he even chose to include graphic representation of the claim that the Nazi salute was of Aryan (rather than Roman) antiquity, obviously in line with Erwin Richter's argument in his extreme piece of swastika mania from 1931.[48] Fehrle also attracted several young folklorists to Heidelberg, including supporters of eccentricities such as the rune-houses of Stauff and Weigel, by the late 30s making the University of Heidelberg in effect the leading center for *Sinnbildforschung* outside the Ahnenerbe. Fehrle's students produced a two-volume collection of studies entitled a *Handbook of Symbol Studies (Handbuch der Symbolforschung)* in 1941, calling their studies *Symbolforschung* in an apparent attempt to distinguish themselves from the older, and arguably more empirical, epigraphically focused ideographic studies; and Fehrle's *Festschrift* from 1940 (entitled *Brauch und Sinnbild—Custom and Ideograph*) is full of papers on what its contributors no doubt saw as a suitably refined version of folkloric *Sinnbildforschung*.[49]

The focus of the criticism of Fehrle and the other folklorists was the *Sinnbildforschung* developing around the more adventurous studies of Weigel, Plaßmann and Huth. As *Sinnbildforschung* among the less linguistically or prehistorically concerned had begun to move on from ancient ideographs to what are more properly native symbolic expressions such as the Christmas tree or recurrent decorative motifs such as Germanic zoomorphy, *Sinnbildforschung* had more clearly come to trespass on the territory of folklorists. Lauffer, a contributor to Fehrle's *Festschrift*, wrote scornful reviews of the works of some of the worst dilettantes who had been attracted to *Sinnbildforschung*. In fact the circulation of *Germanien* had boomed since 1935, rising from 2,000 at the time of the foundation of the Ahnenerbe to 12,500 by 1937.[50] *Sinnbildforschung* in the form of Weigel's works and as one of the major focuses of *Germanien* had come to reach a broad audience. Many respected folklorists were concerned by this wild new amateurism that was supported by the SS. Yet *Volkskunde* had become dependent on the new regime institutionally—Lauffer's sole folklore chair from 1932 became one of many under the dictatorship—and as good National Socialists, figures like Fehrle actively supported the more mainstream forms of *Sinnbildforschung* developed by Plaßmann, Krause and Huth.

A longstanding and ambitious National Socialist, Fehrle had become the local Party district leader at Heidelberg, and though he had earlier been associated with Baeumler, by the late 1930s he put his former affiliation to Rosenberg's people behind him and as an associate of Meier began to build up contacts with the Ahnenerbe instead. In 1935 he had attempted to have Meier's proposed research institute set up in Heidelberg with help from the Amt Rosenberg, but had only succeeded in alerting Himmler to his ambitions.[51] Werner Haverbeck, a member of the SS and a young friend and private student of Wirth's, was subsequently assigned to Fehrle as an assistant. Himmler no doubt

had thought Haverbeck would keep an eye on the ambitious Party folklorist, while at the same stroke cleaning up some of the unfinished matters left behind by Wirth after he had relocated to Marburg. Haverbeck
is perhaps more remarkable because of his postwar career as a leading
purveyor of racist mysticism, but like Huth and Weigel represents well
what the right kind of connections and academic taste could win someone under the Nazis.

A former member of the Nazi Students' League and the Hitler
Youth, Haverbeck had been involved with Wirth and his *Sinnbildforschung* since 1930, although by 1933 the budding young ideographist
had returned to Munich. With the Nazi accession, however, Haverbeck
had found favor with Hess, and with his support founded the Reich
League for National Tradition and Homeland (Reichsbund Volkstum und Heimat) within the PO. This body, associated with the KdF,
worked to promote folk customs such as traditional music and dance,
and both Plaßmann and Huth had also been involved with Haverbeck's group from an early stage. The League had come under suspicion in 1934 as a haven for Strasserites, however, and was taken over
by Spamer in 1936 (Haverbeck had since approached Spamer to supervise him in Berlin after Wirth had assumed other duties). But under
Fehrle's tutelage Haverbeck eventually attained a doctorate at Heidelberg later that year, a doctorate in *Sinnbildforschung*.[52] Haverbeck even
completed a professional thesis at Heidelberg entitled "German Folk
Belief in Ideography" ("Deutscher Volksglaube im Sinnbild") in 1938,
making him (unlike Wirth) a full Professor.[53] The journal of the Reich
League for National Tradition and Homeland became a new organ for
ideographical speculation, and Fehrle's students and other associates
especially lent their names to the new discipline, one paper in Fehrle's
Festschrift even trying to reconcile Wirth's "rune of life" theory with
the "man rune" of Listian tradition by postulating the influence of a
"woman" ideograph (Υ) based on the shape of a woman's pudenda.[54]
But Haverbeck's academic career was put on hold when war broke out,
albeit not ended altogether.

In 1939 Fehrle finally left the SA for the SS and four years later
was duly awarded the Pro-Rectorship of the University of Heidelberg.
Fehrle's acceptance of ideographic studies was clearly not merely opportunistic—it was consistent with the *völkisch* aspect he had always
brought to his *Volkskunde*. Over the course of the 1930s he produced

papers on ideographic concerns such as the swastika, all the while building up his own ideography collection which formed the basis of his department's permanently exhibited folklore archive.[55] Fehrle did not add to the literature on ideographs-cum-folk symbols in as significant a manner as did the other SS-aligned scholars. Haverbeck aside, his other students only came to the new field somewhat belatedly. But it is clear what kind of folkloric research they would have continued to produce if it had not been for the loss of the war. Nevertheless, Fehrle's accommodation of ideographic studies did add to the impression prevalent after 1945 (especially promoted by Lauffer) that there had been two folklores in Germany at the time. One *Volkskunde* was thought to be a credible continuation of the tradition of cultural analysis of the *Volk* represent in the Grimms' collection of fairytales. The other was incredible, most patently in the example of Huth, Weigel, Fehrle and the other folk symbol-focused purveyors of *Sinnbildforschung*.[56] Yet as the reassessment of *Volkskunde* that began with the studies of Hermann Bausinger and Wolfgang Emmerich has shown, there was no such twofold distinction.[57] By the 1930s *Volkskunde* had become riddled with ideological concerns and owed most of its institutional development to Party support. With the rise of a radical political movement that took its very name from the *Volk*, *Volkskunde*—as *Volk*-lore—itself became infested with reactionary ideas. The poor *Volkskunde* of the day was not just misgiven, it was ideologically driven. *Sinnbildforschung* merely represented the most extreme expression of what *völkisch* thought wrought on the folkloric studies of the day.

CLASSICAL ANTIQUITY

The *Symbolforschung* of Fehrle and the other folklorists was only a side issue in contemporary *Volkskunde* generally, though, given the influence of the Much school and the more traditional folkloric researches of figures like Spamer and Lauffer. The area of Germanistic inquiry most influenced by *Sinnbildforschung* remained runic studies. Yet perhaps the most striking contribution to *Sinnbildforschung* remains in the works produced by the classicist Franz Altheim, one which maps out territory that, as was recognized by Wüst, suggested that there was a broader Indo-European aspect to the study of traditional ideography. In the late

1930s, Altheim and his archeologist-mistress Erika Trautmann (later Trautmann-Nehring) won a stipend from the Ahnenerbe to investigate the rock carvings of the Camonica Valley in northern Italy.[58]

These rock carvings had become linked to the runes through several odd coincidences. First, the pictorial representations were clearly of a late Bronze–early Iron Age date and a number of archeologists had previously compared them with the similarly vivid and contemporary Scandinavian pictographs. Second, in 1925 Rudolf Much had put forward (spurious) philological evidence to argue that ancient Germanic tribes had been active in the Alpine region as early as the sixth century B.C., at least 400 years previous to their first classical attestation in the region.[59] This theory of early Alpine Germanic tribes (*Alpengermanen*) became focused by the decipherment in 1925 by the Norwegian linguist Carl Marstrander of an inscription on a helmet found in Schöniak, Negau (now Slovenian Ženjak, Negova) in southwestern Styria in 1811.[60] The inscription on the helmet was clearly Germanic in language and as the script in which the helmet inscription was written was one of the pre-Roman, so-called North Etruscan alphabets of the Alpine region, the inscription seemed to represent evidence for Germanic speakers living in the region in about the third century B.C. Moreover, three years later, Marstrander came to the conclusion that the runes had developed from this very script (or one very much like it).[61] Marstrander's North Etruscan thesis of the origin of the runes had become the dominant one in established runological circles by the early 30s, perhaps as represented most comprehensively in the first edition of Arntz's *Handbook*. The importance of Schöniak/Ženjak to Germanic antiquarianism saw the village renamed Harigast by the National Socialists after the invasion of Yugoslavia, Harigast being the Germanic name inscribed on the helmet. After an inconclusive excavation in late 1942 by Walter Schmid (an Austrian archeologist of Slovenian extraction whom it seems the locals had purposefully pointed to the wrong location), the site was established as an archeological park, much as were the Extern Stones.[62]

The North Etruscan inscriptions found near the Camonica Valley seemed to be the closest in form to runes. The inscriptions of this region had still not been deciphered, however. Yet if they could be shown to be Germanic, it could be demonstrated exactly where these shadowy early Alpine Germans had lived. The eminent German paleographer (and Party member) Georg Baesecke had focused attention on the evidence for ancient Germanic tribes in this region in 1934 in an article in Schröder's *Germanisch-Romanische Monatsschrift*, linking the origin of the runes with the wanderings of the early Germanic tribe of the Cimbri who had campaigned in this region at the end of the second-last century B.C.[63] In fact Baesecke subsequently described this putative Cimbrian discovery of the runes in a moment of *völkisch* hyperbole as "a master deed of the Germanic, the Cimbrian spirit, one unparalleled in the whole of the oriental experience."[64] Much's Alpine Germans had become rune-bearing Germans. Consequently, the connection between pictorial rock carvings and runes would clearly be of concern to ideographic studies. Altheim's expedition was duly judged suitable for Ahnenerbe sponsorship.

Altheim, however, was first and foremost a classicist and quite prominent academically. His fame rested on his *History of Roman Religion (Römische Religionsgeschichte)*, a work valued highly enough to be translated subsequently both into English and French.[65] Since archeologists such as Oscar Almgren had attempted to elucidate the religious motivation behind the Scandinavian rock carvings, Altheim would naturally have been drawn to attempt a similar interpretation of the comparable carvings from Italy. Yet by the late 1930s, it seems he had become obsessed not just by the Camonica Valley, but also with runes.

On his expedition Altheim did make an important discovery: he uncovered a number of inscriptions in the Camonica Valley that he judged to be of great importance. These Camunic inscriptions he thought might prove to be sensational in terms of *Sinnbildforschung* and the question of the origin of the runes. He first announced his findings to the academic world in 1937 and although he disagreed with much of what Wirth and Neckel had theorized about the runes, Altheim's findings also subsequently appeared as the second offering of the Germanic studies monographic series of the Ahnenerbe. His 1939 study *From the Origin of the Runes (Vom Ursprung der Runen)*, also saw him granted his own division within the Ahnenerbe and with it he began a new phase in the evolution of *Sinnbildforschung*.[66]

Although seemingly concerned principally with the iconography of the rock carvings, from the very beginning Altheim had dabbled with runes. He had first proclaimed the rock carvings Celtic, based on a rather specious attempt to link some of the iconography with Gaulish

representations.[67] The discovery at the same time of Camunic inscriptions, however, soon led him to make another connection very much
in line with *Sinnbildforschung*. The second edition of his ostensibly collaborative work (Trautmann, although she had first put Altheim on to
the Camonica Valley, provided mostly only the pictures) he entitled
The Cimbri and the Runes. Although the autochthonous thesis of the
origin of the runes is rejected in this work (Altheim, of course, followed
Marstrander's North Etruscan thesis), much like Krause he still managed to accommodate *Sinnbildforschung* within his investigations. His
aim became to establish a link between the carvings of the Camonica
Valley and those Swedish petroglyphs which had fascinated previous
generations of prehistorians, but at the same time to explain both the
clear evidence for a North Etruscan origin of the runes and retain elements of the *Urschrift* theory promoted by Wirth and Neckel.[68]

Yet instead of looking for an Alpine Germanic identity in these
carvings (à la Much), Altheim's philological training pointed to evidence that these inscriptions belonged to the Italic group of languages.
They evidently were not Latin. Instead, they appeared to him to be
related to the language of the ancient neighbours of the early Latins:
the Faliscans.[69] If the rock carvings were also to be associated with the
early Italic tribes (from which, of course, the Romans and Faliscans
had sprung), the early Italic peoples must have shared an iconographi-
cal repertoire with that of the Swedish rock carvers.

Altheim contrasted the similarities shared by the south and north
with other comparable carvings from the rest of Europe (and even
Egypt): yet he found no other iconography so Germanic as that of the
Camonica Valley. He also sought to give his speculations linguistic
credibility by pointing out the many similarities shared by the Germanic and Italic languages. He further claimed this relationship was also
betrayed by a number of similarities in the religious lives of Rome and
ancient Germany. Most of all, however, he argued for a shared iconography and repertoire of early ideographs.

Over the next few years, he expanded his theory to connect the
figurative rock paintings, the symbols, the inscriptions and the runes
more comprehensively. He came to see the runes as borrowed from
ancient Italic peoples by the Germanic Cimbri, but with important intrusions from the ideographic repertoire of the Camonica Valley. Although his theory did not ascribe an origin for the runes as purely Ger-

manic as had Neckel, in his opinion the northern Italic and Germanic
tribes were so close in terms of culture that this did not matter. Indeed,
Altheim clearly sought to show that the energy and brilliance of Rome
was a reflection of that same superlative Aryan spirit that was equally (if not more) manifest in Germanic experience. By the late 1930s,
Altheim had managed to enlarge the Germanic identity to encompass
that of Rome. Yet he did not stop there. In *Italy and Rome (Italien und
Rom)*, his *tour de force* from 1941, Altheim extended this Italo-Ger-
manic identity to include the Celts, the Illyrians and finally also the
Greeks.[70] *Sinnbildforschung* had now become truly Aryan.

Altheim's interpretations of the rock carvings of the Italian Alps
had descended into Germanomania. In 1937 he thought he had discovered Celtic images among the Italian rock carvings; by 1941 he
was finding runic ideographs and depictions of Odin there too.[71] His
own descent into Germanomaniacal fantasy is probably signposted by
an essay from 1938 that appeared in *Klio*, a respectable journal of ancient history, where he argued runic symbols could be seen depicted
in the standards of Germanic troops in Roman service from the period
of the late Empire.[72] Not only had he come around to essentially the
same conclusion as Krause with respect to the ideographic origin of the
runes, he had put a novel Italian perspective on his *Sinnbildforschung*-
based theory, and had even begun to broaden the focus of academic
Sinnbildforschung to incorporate heraldry and other forms of historical
iconography much as had List and his Ariosophical followers.

A more broadly Aryan approach to ideographic studies was developed in articles by other Ahnenerbe researchers and only the imminent
loss of the war prevented the appearance of several other ideograph-
based accounts of aspects of Germanic and Aryan culture. Wirth had
been working on an atlas of Indo-European ideographs and Hauer had
wanted to publish a survey with a similar theme. Wüst had even contributed an article on Aryan ideographs to *Germanien* in 1940.[73] Not
only had *Sinnbildforschung* survived the debacle of the *Oera Linda Book*,
with Krause, Fehrle and Altheim it had clearly achieved full academic
status. Given time Weigel would obviously have been habilitated into
a more properly scholarly tradition and Hauer, Huth and Wüst were
also talking about the broader Indo-European aspects of ideographic
studies. In fact doctoral students of *Sinnbildforschung* such as Haverbeck had emerged—a new generation of ideographists had begun to

pass through the academic system. A *völkisch* mania had infected academic antiquarian studies and had been legitimized in the form of the academic ideographic studies of the early 1940s. But the expansion of ideographic studies did not stop there. A further, grimmer stage was yet to come.

EMPIRE

Altheim and Wirth were not the only members of the Ahnenerbe to win funding for international research trips. In 1938 the Detmold-based dialectologist Bruno Schweizer made a study tour of Iceland and its Germanic *Thing*-places, temples and traditionally constructed buildings, observing its folk beliefs, customs and practices apparently untouched by modernization.[74] The fantasist Rahn, although not a member of the Ahnenerbe, had also won money for similar trips searching for hints of the final resting place of the Holy Grail, and a zoologist, Ernst Schäfer, in company with an SS anthropologist Bruno Beger, even managed to win Ahnenerbe backing for a trip to Tibet in 1938–39—the Ahnenerbe's Research and Teaching Post for Inner Asia and Expeditions (and its associated Sven Hedin Tibet Institute) was clearly founded in light of claims (which had become part of Nazi folklore) that a secret community of Aryans was hidden somewhere in the Himalayas.[75] But political events soon intervened that would radicalize the SS's learned society further.

The *Anschluß* of Austria in 1938 had once again led to an expansion of the Ahnenerbe. The SS quickly took over responsibility for several prominent Austrian antiquarian journals, perhaps most notably the *Wiener prähistorische Zeitschrift (Viennese Prehistorical Journal)*.[76] Otto Höfler again showed his willingness to be of use to the regime by reporting on the suitability of scholars in what was now the Nazi Ostmark and SS scholars were despatched to Salzburg and Vienna to ensure that the new developments in Germanic studies were suitably represented.[77] Ahnenerbe functionaries such as Plaßmann and Sievers even became involved in planning for the resettlement of German speakers from Italian Alto Adige as part of Himmler's role in the solution to the "South Tyrolian question" concluded with the Italian ambassador in June 1939, Himmler subsequently being appointed by Hit-

ler as the Reich Commissar for the Consolidation of German Nation-
hood (Reichskommissar für die Festigung deutschen Volkstums).[78] But
with the outbreak of war later that year, the Ahnenerbe threatened to
implode. Some of its researchers such as Ruppel (who, given that hallmarks were usually held to be the domain of legal historians had since
become involved with Eckhardt's German Law Institute at Bonn) had
their relationship terminated, others joined the Armed Forces. Sievers resolved to reform the Ahnenerbe in order to make it more clearly
useful to the war effort. The SS Ancestral Inheritance organization expanded its role from one of supporting studies of the national heritage
to altogether more sinister purposes. Under Sievers's direction, from
1939 the learned society expanded into anatomical, physiological and
entomological research, developments in which now scholarship too
could join in the National Socialist project to plumb ever more lows in
the annals of European inhumanity.[79]

The outbreak of war thus led to another period of rapid expansion for the Ahnenerbe. After all, the year 1939 had seen the institution of the War Operation of the German Humanities (Kriegseinsatz
der Deutschen Geisteswissenschaften) by the Education Ministry, an
organ for supplying specialist academic help to the German Armed
Forces, and in 1940 a similar accommodation was reached between the
German Archeological Institute and the Army to aid in the protection
of monuments and works of art in lands under German occupation.[80]
The Ahnenerbe's own publishing house, the Ahnenerbe-Stiftung (Ahnenerbe Foundation), was also founded in 1939 in Dahlem, and SS
academics like Plaßmann now found they could contribute to the war
effort in direct, Army-connected ways. Moreover, with the invasions
of Denmark, Norway and the Low Countries, suddenly the minds at
Ahnenerbe headquarters realized they had new audiences of German-
ic-speaking academics and public to cater for. The old, antiquarian
Ahnenerbe quickly moved to expand its operations, most notably into
Holland where an outpost of the Ahnenerbe was established at The
Hague in 1940. Soon several Dutch scholars found themselves being
courted by their German colleagues and the Netherlanders were introduced to *Sinnbildforschung* SS-style.

The only runologist in Holland of any note at the time was the University of Groningen's Johannes M.N. Kapteyn. Local runic finds had

been known since the nineteenth century and over the course of the 1930s Kapteyn, a Frisian language specialist, had published a handful of articles on the local inscriptions (and even a recent Swiss runic discovery).[81] As was often the case with his German colleagues, though, Kapteyn's interest in things runic seemed concomitant with Germanomania and extreme right-wing political views. His offering on the origin of the runic script that appeared in a German journal in 1936, for instance, saw Kapteyn attempting to ascribe a second millennium B.C. pedigree to the earliest runic inscriptions, using some scratches on a piece of Bronze Age amber as his evidence.[82] His investigations of other finds are similarly prone to overzealousness and are not held in much regard today. Kapteyn's political contribution, on the other hand, was far more significant. By the 1930s he had become renown for his hatred of all things Hollandic—i.e. those associated with the province of Holland proper, the main region of Dutch political and industrial power. A folk traditions-enthusing, starchy old conservative, he became a champion of a local form of pan-Germanism focused on the "Saxon" characteristics of the northeastern Dutch, a political stance which obviously made him potentially rather useful to the German occupying power.

The main Dutch prewar fascist party, however, the Nationaal-Socialistische Beweging (National-Socialist Movement), was strongly in favor of Netherlandic autonomy and unity. In contrast, Kapteyn rejected "Holland" and instead hailed Germany as the savior of rural Dutch and especially Frisian tradition. In 1939 he had helped found a bimonthly academic journal *Saxo-Frisia* that promoted the Frisian and the Dutch Saxon patrimony (i.e. that of the Dutch speakers of the Northern Netherlands). After the German invasion, though, heeding the call of the new regime he became involved with the Dutch outpost of the Ahnenerbe.[83] Kapteyn set up a Saxo-Frisia Foundation (Stichting Saxo-Frisia) in 1941 which published a popular spin-off of *Saxo-Frisia* called *Het Noorder Land* (*The Northern Land*) that promoted northern Netherlandic particularism, and he gave lectures on similar themes in both Holland and Germany.[84] In fact when Sievers put plans together for a conference of "black" Germanic studies in Hanover in 1943 (the Tagung der Germanischen Arbeitsgemeinschaft), only four invitations were sent to figures not officially in the SS. Two of the four went to Dutch nationals. Kapteyn, by this stage with German help the Rector of the University of Groningen, was the most senior of the Dutch academics in the orbit of the Ahnenerbe.[85] Nonetheless, Kapteyn was a septuagenarian by the 1940s, and although he was especially interested in folklore and German–Dutch friendship he did not become involved in SS-sponsored *Sinnbildforschung* in Dutch territory.[86] Yet not only were there others of his countrymen willing to offer themselves to the service of the new science, Wirth's shadow had returned to Holland.

Kapteyn's organization was only one of several Netherlandic groups that the invading Germans thought they could make use of, although the Nazi planners were careful not to be seen to be favoring regional particularists over the much more numerous Hollanders. The main interest of the SS just seemed at first to be the recruitment of Dutch Nazis, after all, an ambition that required some sort of accommodation between the local fascists and particularist groups like Kapteyn's.

The first suggestion that a Dutch branch of the Ahnenerbe might be founded appeared in October 1939. Plaßmann, like several other Germanists had volunteered for military duty, but for many of them their age ensured this service was mostly performed in non-combatant roles. Like Arntz, Plaßmann still found time to continue on with his philological work while undertaking his military service. But Plaßmann had other ideas as well. Late in 1939 he mooted an involvement of the Ahnenerbe in the creation of propaganda in the Netherlands. In 1940, come the invasion, plans were set in motion for the erection of an imperial arm of the Ahnenerbe under the control of the young SS-Germanist Hans Ernst Schneider.[87]

Schneider has gained more notoriety in recent years for his postwar activities.[88] In the late 1930s he was known as the editor of the literary journal *Die Weltliteratur* (*World Literature*), however, and more infamously, in the last years of the war the leader of a new, imperial branch of the Ahnenerbe, the Germanischer Wissenschaftseinsatz (Germanic Studies Operation, GWE), an organ set up to coordinate Germanic studies in the occupied territories of Hitler's Reich.

Like Huth, Schneider was somewhat younger than the Plaßmanns and Sievers's; in fact the Königsberg-born East Prussian had only completed his dissertation (on the German reception of the Russian writer Turgenev) in 1935. His doctoral studies bridged the cataclysmic years of 1928–35 and despite his specialization in modern literature, he had already deeply imbibed the spirit of *völkisch* antiquarianism. Schneider

had read German folklore and prehistory during the course of his studies, and after joining the SA late in 1933, he had briefly been a member of the KdF's Reich League for National Tradition and Homeland,
the folk song and dancing-enthusing organization that Wirth's student
Haverbeck had once led.[89] But Schneider's true calling seemed to be
as an organizer. He switched from brown shirt to black in the spring of
1937, and after spending much of that year unemployed (save for one
of two short stints in the army, the earlier in late 1936), he won a position in the RuSHA under Darré and subsequently joined the Ahnenerbe in October 1938. After a posting in the Ahnenerbe-Stiftung which
often saw him flitting between Berlin and Vienna, in 1940 Schneider
was dispatched to the occupied Netherlands where he became responsible for setting up the first official imperial outpost of the Ahnenerbe.

There had been contacts between *völkisch* antiquarians in Germany
and Holland before the May 1940 invasion though. A Dutch group had
been associated with the Detmold Friends since the early 30s, and in
Wirth and Plaßmann the Ahnenerbe and the Friends had long had enjoyed a Netherlandic accent. But the first suggestion of a Dutch outpost
of the Ahnenerbe had been inaugurated in Dutch fascist circles some
years before the invasion. An organization patronized by members of
the Nationaal-Socialistische Beweging had been founded in 1937 by a
group of activists who had previously had no ties to the German antiquarian scene. It was called the Vaderen Erfdeel (Ancestral Inheritance), which was clearly a Dutch calque on *Ahnenerbe*, and some of
its members, including its leader, the industrialist Frans Farwerck, had
been in contact with Sievers and Plaßmann since at least late 1939.[90]

Schneider had at first been supposed merely to accompany Plaßmann to The Hague, but the older Nazi Germanist pulled out at the
last minute (hurrying off to newly occupied Paris instead) leaving Schneider to arrive in Holland alone in July 1940.[91] He quickly set about
his task of organizing local antiquity enthusiasts, only to be informed
by Hanns Rauter, the SS's head man in the Netherlands, that the leader of the Vaderen Erfdeel had formerly been a high-ranking mason.
This was a time of intense work for both Rauter and Schneider: amid
the scramble to find collaborators who would remain independent of
Arthur Seyß-Inquart's official Netherlandic satrapy, a Dutch form of
the SS, the SS-Standart "Westland," was set up within the Nationaal-Socialistische Beweging. Schneider also set out to form a separate

group of antiquity enthusiasts free from any masonic taint and a selection of Dutch Nazis, most of whom belonged to the Dutch SS, were roped in to form a rival to the Vaderen Erfdeel. This organization, the Volksche Werkgemeenschap (*Völkisch* Study Group), did not become an official branch of the Ahnenerbe until 1943, but it had already been substantially a German expression from the date of its inception in August 1940.[92]

Farwerck soon saw the writing on the wall, however, and by October 1940 had reached an accommodation with Schneider. He rolled his group and its publishing house (which used Teudt's Irminsûl as its emblem) into the Volksche Werkgemeenschaap, delivering Schneider control of their antiquity-enthusing journal *Volksche Wacht* (*Völkisch Watch*) that had formerly been named after the wolf hook (*Wolfsangel*), a medieval protective symbol (often called a rune) which had been adopted by the Nationaal-Socialistische Beweging.[93] Schneider had already begun preparations for a rival to the Vaderen Erfdeel's *Volksche Wacht* that August, however, and the Volksche Werkgemeenschaap's new journal *Hamer*—a glossy quarter-monthly—soon became the flagship publication of the Dutch Ahnenerbe.[94]

Schneider was so happy with *Hamer* he organized a sister Flemish publication that first appeared early in 1943. Himmler, too, seemed especially to like it and after some delay a German version of *Hamer* was produced in 1944 (Fritsch's longstanding *völkisch* journal of the same name, after all, had been wound up in 1940).[95] Indeed Danish and Norwegian editions of *Hamer* were also part of Schneider's plans. The Dutch journal was much more magazine-like than *Germanien*, and with a print run of up to 9,000, it proved a great success. *Hamer* also became, even more so than *Germanien*, an important organ for the promotion of *Sinnbildforschung*.

Hamer featured articles written by local staff on Dutch manufactures and customs, always stressing the ideographs hidden in all aspects of Dutch folk life, much as had been the diet of the amateur contributions to *Germanien*. Nearly every issue seems to have an offering dealing with Dutch ideographs in it. Translations of, most of all, Weigel's ideographic musings also appeared regularly in *Hamer*.[96] The eponymous publishing house in Amsterdam that produced *Hamer* also issued a monographic series which included a work on Dutch ideographs by one of the local *völkisch* enthusiasts (cowritten by one of the Van

Houten brothers who ran Hamer publishing) and a book by Kapteyn, by now an SS captain, on the topic of the Frisian and Saxon inheritances. These appeared alongside the *Hamer* Series's translations of the major studies of regular Ahnenerbe identities such as Plaßmann.[97] Yet a more clearly Dutch academic pedigree was given to the journal by commissioning Jan de Vries, Holland's most famous Nordicist of the time, to contribute articles on Old Germanic culture.

De Vries had first come into contact with the Volksche Werkgemeenschaap while Seyß-Inquart had been planning his own research foundation.[98] The Leiden philologist had no links with the Nationaal-Socialistische Beweging and seems to have been a reluctant collaborator at first. But his early reticence soon left him; within a year De Vries had embraced the new opportunities afforded by the invasion.

The Dutch philologist already had a substantial scholarly profile in Germany as his contributions to Nordic studies had been well received by all manner of German academics. Neckel, for instance, had reviewed one of his works in 1931 at the same time as Teudt's *Germanic Shrines*, praising them both as examples of what the spirit of the new Heuslerian notion of Germanicness could achieve.[99] By 1943 De Vries had become so close to the Ahnenerbe that he had been the other Dutch academic invited by Sievers to the "black" Hanover conference along with Kapteyn. De Vries had started acting the same way as many of his German colleagues had done faced with the new agenda in Germanic studies, penning articles on runic topics despite never having written in this area before.[100] Moreover, his better-known works from this period such as his *Intellectual World of the Germanic Peoples (Geistige Welt der Germanen)* and *Gods of the Teutons (De Goden der Germanen)* similarly ooze with *völkisch* sentiment, and though clearly expressions of the Germanicness consciousness stressed by Heusler, they can only be seen as statements of his intellectual and political pan-Germanism.[101] Like Kapteyn, De Vries had become politically tainted through his collaboration, in fact so much so that he fled the Allied armies in September 1944 and a position was found for him back at what was now his spiritual home, at Leipzig where he was supported by DFG grants. De Vries and Kapteyn had stood by unmoved by the Aryanizing of Dutch universities and the continuing strikes and other unrest that by 1943 had seen over 600 Dutch, Belgian and French students imprisoned at the concentration camp at Vught.[102] Kapteyn had even

become complicit in the death of one of his Jewish colleagues, Leo Polak, at Sachsenhausen concentration camp, after he had denounced
Polak to the SD in 1941.[103] Schneider, in turn, was involved in the
procurement of medical instruments for use in the gruesome physiological experiments of the SS researcher Sigmund Rascher at Dachau
in 1943.[104] In keeping with Nazi propaganda which promoted Hitler as
"Führer of all the Germanic peoples" (*Führer aller Germanen*),[105] however, the main role of the Dutch outpost of the Ahnenerbe remained
to promote *Sinnbildforschung* and the study of other shared expressions
from Germanic antiquity that fostered a sense of greater Germanic
unity in occupied Holland.

Nevertheless, quite another role was assumed by the Ahnenerbe
with the German invasions of Denmark and Norway, not that the SS's
Scandinavian policy was ever set out in a programmatic way. Jankuhn
had quickly won permission to extend his excavations at Haithabau
across to the other side of the Danish frontier and Wirth's SS-funded
tours of Scandinavia were now followed by those of better-established
academics. Both Höfler and Krause visited Denmark as GWE guest
professors during the "protectorate," Höfler's visit as part of a broader
book-buying Scandinavian tour. Both seemed shocked at the anti-German sentiment they encountered at the time. Höfler, recognizing that
in the Nordic countries "a common Germanic conception of history
is seen as merely a disguised thesis of German propaganda," reported
to his SS masters that the Scandinavian universities were "perhaps our
most dangerous and toughest opponents in the North."[106] Even their
northern runological brethren seemed less than happy to see them.

This hostility was exposed most publicly in 1941 when continued
anti-German foment at the University of Oslo was responded to by
forceful German action. The Norwegian Rector, the Nordicist Didrik
Arup Seip, was judged part of the problem and arrested along with over
a thousand members of the staff and student body (the first professor
arrested had been the runologist Marstrander). By 1943, the university had been closed down and Seip and about 700 of the students imprisoned in German concentration camps where, apart from suffering
the usual physical abuses, they were subjected to efforts from Ahnenerbe identities such as Wüst and Huth to reeducate them.[107] Unlike the
case of the brutal suppression of the Jagiellonian University in Cracow,
however, some of Seip's German colleagues went further than merely

protesting this cruelty.[108] Seip had, after all, been awarded an honorary doctorate by the University of Hamburg some years before and the incident was not only causing shock and disgust throughout Scandinavia. Mustering what influence they had, Finnish scholars, in the light of similar entreaties from some of Seip's German colleagues, successfully had him released at the end of 1942 after Seip had signed an undertaking no longer to engage in anti-German activities. In a development Sievers fraudulently claimed after the war had all been down to him, Seip was first required to remain under Wüst's watchful eye at Munich, then later to be supervised by Plaßmann and Hans Kuhn in Berlin.[109] The Norwegian students, on the other hand, were released during the last days of the war as part of Count Bernadotte's dealings with the still rune-obsessed Himmler. In fact Jankuhn was sent to Norway on one of his antiquarian trips for Himmler soon after the first Oslo arrests as Norwegian scholars had refused to comply with one of the Reichsführer's archeological requests, Jankuhn taking the opportunity at the time to write a security report for the Ahnenerbe on his antiquarian Oslo colleagues (despite his postwar obfuscations to the contrary).[110] Most of the official activities of the Ahnenerbe in the Scandinavian countries, though, were performed through the GWE and the provision of guest professors. Höfler, who had given a paper to an SS conference on the origin of Scandinavian Germanophobia in 1942, was even sent to Copenhagen to lead a German Scientific Institute there the next year, one whose main mission was to ensure that a proper awareness of Germanic commonality would be reinvested in the North.[111]

The Ahnenerbe also looked east as well as north and in many aspects much more grimly. Many of the crimes of SS medical specialists were perpetrated in concentration camps established in occupied Poland, although not all were organized under the Ahnenerbe's official Institute for Military Science-Focused Research (Institut für Wehrwissenschaftliche Zweckforschung). This arm of Himmler's learned society saw hundreds of imprisoned Jews, Russians and others killed as part of experiments with mustard gas, pressure chambers and refrigeration. The activities of Ahnenerbe antiquarians in the less fully Germanic countries, however, were generally restricted to more quotidian matters of security and exploitation. The SS archeologists Paulsen and Jankuhn competed in occupied Poland and the Soviet Union with Rosenberg's prehistorians to see who could secure the contents of the most museums and libraries, and even (enlisting Soviet POW forced labor) archeological sites, sending their spoils back to clearing houses in Germany such as the Ahnenerbe's offices in Berlin. In fact Jankuhn was evidently so excited by the prehistorical potentials in the occupied East he mooted the erection of a local branch of the Ahnenerbe on the Crimea at the time, this being the last known outpost of speakers of Gothic.[112] On the other hand, in the less clearly Germanic West, Plaßmann's call to Paris had been to advise the Army and the German embassy on the reconstitution of the French National Library and National Archives (which had been scattered as a war-time precaution), while Jankuhn's French sojourns involved excavations in Brittany and an investigation of the Bayeux Tapestry, in Paris (rather than Bayeux), whither it had been taken under the auspices of the German Army's "art protection."[113] In fact in a similar manner to Höfler, an SS-aligned University of Bonn archeologist, Kurt Tackenberg, ran a German Scientific Institute in Brussels from 1942 as a center for coordinating Germanophile research and promoting Germanicness.[114] Nonetheless, most involvement of German academics in occupied Belgium and France was through branches of the Nazi authority other than the Ahnenerbe—from the Celticist Leo Weisgerber's propaganda trips to Rennes under the auspices of the SD, to the involvement of Helmut Arntz's one-time collaborator, the RGK archeologist Hans Zeiss, in investigations of Frankish-era cemeteries in France under the guise of the Army's "art protection." Indeed Zeiss and his RGK protégé Joachim Werner clearly saw their archeology in terms of a cultural mission to reclaim territory that had once been home to Frankish (i.e. Germanic) speakers.[115] With the establishment of the Reich University of Strasbourg in 1941, though, with SS help Werner and Huth took up professorships alongside one of the most infamous of all Ahnenerbe researchers, the biologist August Hirt, parts of whose ghoulish Strasbourg anatomy collection were selected while his incarcerated Jewish and Russian victims were still alive.[116]

Yet the main mission of the Ahnenerbe in these new territories was not one of espionage, plunder, archeological exploitation or the facilitation of medical crimes. Instead it was one enunciated most clearly in the case of a manuscript penned in collaboration by Weigel and Krause in the early 1940s.

In 1943 Krause and Weigel put together a manuscript intended for publication as a monograph under the title "Runic Primer" ("Runenfibel"). The title seems to be a deliberate reference to two Ariosophical publications from 1935 which Krause wanted to critique and since his conversion to a more academic mode of thinking, Weigel too.[117] Their editor at Dahlem sought two referees to look at the manuscript, not from scholars with academic posts, but rather senior Party members instead. One, written by Rudolf Brandt, Himmler's personal secretary, complained that the work did not do enough to make clear the ideographic meanings of the runes, not citing those Krause had deduced more or less empirically, but referring instead to those which had developed among List's followers.[118] Krause and Weigel wrote a reply to the issues raised, complaining that this sort of ignorant amateurism stemming from the "false interpretations that first appeared with the "researches" of Guido von *List* and his followers" was exactly what their section of the Ahnenerbe was there to combat.[119] The other reviewer, the GWE's Hans Schneider, loved the work, however, and commented to the editor:[120]

> But shouldn't we get used to having our authors think of the entire Germanic area? I think it's clear that catering only for the purely German view in many ways can mean a sacrifice and a loss. Now that we are responsible for the entire Germanic region, shouldn't we consider this also with regards to this small manuscript?

Schneider further suggested that Norwegian and Dutch translations also be made of the work to cater for this broader Germanic perspective that had been created with the aid of the Wehrmacht.

The work was never published, however. The manuscript was proofed and corrected and a selection of suitable photographs was assembled,[121] but in a letter from Ahnenerbe headquarters in Dahlem from October 1944, it was explained to Krause that all publications had ceased "for the moment" due to the exigencies of the (faltering) war effort.[122] October 1944 also saw the last issue of the *SS-Leithefte* and other similar Party journals. Krause had remained faithful to the Ahnenerbe until what in publishing terms represented the bitter end.

Krause's project to make *Sinnbildforschung* academically respectable had succeeded in official channels. The amateur ideographic studies that had characterized Weigel's early works were still popular among some elements of the Party, however, and both the old *Sinnbildforschung* and the new were clearly judged useful to the imperial propaganda of the Reich. Although half-blind, it is perhaps no surprise, then, to find Krause contributing an article at this time to *European Science Service*, the new journal established for Germans running the academic sections of the Nazi Empire in foreign countries, laying down the official word on runes, ideographs and their origin.[123]

The empirical tradition of Germanic antiquarianism had been founded by the Grimms and their fellows in the heady nationalistic days of the *Kulturnation* and the Frankfurt Diet. The patriotism of the Grimms and their successors had long been recognized to have led on occasion to an overvaluing and misinterpretation of the sources from which they worked. The Müllenhoffs and the Muchs who followed had been tolerated in antiquarian circles but had been respected in the main for their scholarship, not the more fantastic aspects of their work. Many antiquarians under the Nazis contended that they only followed in the steps of this chauvinistic expression of the empirical tradition. As Plaßmann commented in an editorial in *Germanien* in 1943:[124]

> The gestative, productive balance between individual and community is knowledge of the Germanic peoples and the Germanic period ... Here is the battlefield upon which we forge a measured, so-called natural-scientific nationalism, and take up the fight ... In essence, this objective bears no difference to that taken up by each of the early Germanic studies periodicals that appeared in the time of Jacob Grimm, and whose inner drive was to awaken a love of German prehistory in the entire thinking German world. We recognize that in this respect the period of scientific specialization has impoverished the sphere of activity of these journals ... We have assigned ourselves the task to reawaken the sympathy for the old valuing of our national traditions ...

Nationalism under the Nazis had taken on a shriller, darker tone than had the patriotism of the time of the Grimms. Antiquarian scholarship under National Socialism beat out a similar path. The Ahnenerbe, through its periodicals, sought to popularize Germanic antiquity, yet at the same time it was also required to be scientific and progressive.

It was not, like the Amt Rosenberg, a place for reform of the educational system, or of propaganda or ideological pedagogy of a more explicit form. Instead, it was supposed to rekindle the drive of the time of Goethe and the Grimms, the seminal decades of the *Kulturnation*. According to Plaßmann this drive had been diluted by the increasing specialization of the sciences: the Ahnenerbe was to be a mechanism through which this effort could be refocused. Krause perhaps expressed the plan of the academics of the Ahnenerbe in a more revealing manner, however: its task was to make more accessible the secret treasures of Germanic philology, to broaden the eligibility requirements for access to the greater German Germanophile, if not outright Germanomaniacal *völkisch* antiquarian garden of delights.

Yet unlike the case with the Grimms, the Müllenhoffs and the Muchs, the researchers of the Ahnenerbe legitimized and expanded upon notions developed in the works of amateurs who in previous times had mostly only been influential in the world of the *völkisch* fringe. It was plainly not only figures like the seemingly unwell Neckel who had succumbed to this appropriation of academic inquiry by a political-ideological agenda at the time. A catalogue of the leading Austrian and German names in Germanic antiquarian studies of the day responded favorably to this new discourse that had developed first in the realm of *völkisch* studies of antiquity. The archeologist Kossinna had been the first senior academic to accommodate figures such as Wilser, Schirmeisen and Teudt, and now his call had resounded in Germanic philology too. Although the enthusiasts represented by the Ariosophists and the Federation of Friends of Germanic Prehistory had been kept more or less at arms length, a similar distance was not maintained from the other manifestation of *völkisch* antiquarianism. The Friends had been founded by Teudt and Platz, two patriotic sexagenarian antiquarian fantasists. They soon attracted a body of younger and often better educated Germanists to them, and most of these young enthusiasts joined the Nazi Party at the same time as they joined the Friends—Plaßmann, Huth and Weigel were all "old fighters." *Sinnbildforschung*, the most radical form of *völkisch* antiquarianism, had captured first *völkisch* enthusiasts such as the Friends; then it made its way up through Party ranks until it captured Darré and Himmler. The radical politicized *völkisch* antiquarian tradition best represented in Wilhelmine times by the work of Wilser had finally found its way now also into the academy.

The mixed academic reception to the studies of Wirth in the late 1920s had been an early sign—many of the academics who accepted his contribution were radical conservatives if not "old fighters." Over time acceptance broadened and criticism developed into refinement, sophistry, sycophancy and legitimization. The Ahnenerbe had evolved from an expression of the Herman Wirth Society and the Detmold Friends into a place where *völkisch* enthusiasts, *völkisch* Germanism and professionals met. A decade or more after the release of *The Emergence*, the twilight world of Wilser, Wirth and Teudt had grown to cast its half-light over the academic mainstream in the form of the research of the Ahnenerbe. Moreover with the outbreak of war, the project of rescuing the national inheritance had itself developed: the radical spirit of pan-Germanist antiquarians such as Kossinna and the Muchs had transformed into a project of pan-Germanic renewalism that saw scholars like Specht descend into Germanomaniacal fantasy even as their sons died in their millions in the name of an imperialism of incomparable brutality that their research clearly served and had helped validate.

NOTES

1 F. Specht, *Der Ursprung der Indogermanischen Deklination* (Göttingen: Vandenhoeck & Ruprecht, 1944), foreword.
2 K.T. Weigel, *Beiträge zur Sinnbildforschung* (Berlin: Metzner, 1943), foreword.
3 Heusler/Ranisch 21.9.37, no. 192 in Düwel and Beck (eds.), 623; K.H. Schlottig (ed.), *Beiträge zur Runenkunde und nordischen Sprachwissenschaft* (Leipzig: Harrassowitz, 1938).
4 H. Kuhn, "Das Zeugniss der Sprache über Alter und Ursprung der Runenschrift," in Schlottig (ed.), 54–73; F. von der Leyen, "Zur Überlieferung der Abecedarium Nordmannicum," in Schlottig (ed.), 103–5; E. Weber, "Ein alemannischer Runenbrief?," in Schlottig (ed.), 106–7.
5 From 1938 the title of this double *venia* was modified to "Indo-European Philology and Old Nordic Cultural Studies"; Paul, op. cit.
6 Krause, "Die Runen als Begriffszeichen"; and cf. A. Mentz, "Die notae der Germanen bei Tacitus," *Rheinisches Museum für Philologie* 86 (1937): 193–205.
7 Hübner, 39f.
8 Hübner/REM 12.10.34, BA: REM A114; Lerchenmüller and Simon, *Im Vorfeld*, 29.
9 W. Krause, "Neue Wege," 443–44 [= "New Ways," 122].

10 Janssen, "Grundsätzliches," 183.

11 Krause, "Sinnbilder und Runen," 15.

12 Krause, *Was man in Runen ritzte*, foreword.

13 Krause, "Sinnbilder und Runen," 18–24.

14 W. Krause, "Runenmacht," *Geistige Arbeit* 6/19 (1939): 4.

15 W. Krause, "Germanisch *arja*- 'vornehm' auf dem Stein von Tune," *Forschungen und Fortschritte* 10 (1934): 217–18 [= *Nordische Welt* 2/11–12 (1934): 46–47].

16 K.H. Jacob-Friesen, "Odalrunen auf einer altsächsischen Buckelurne," *Forschungen und Fortschritte* 13 (1937): 217–18.

17 Reichardt, *Runenkunde*, 6.

18 H.-L. Janssen, "Der heutige Stand der Runenkunde," *Das Volk* (1936/37), 554–55.

19 B. Reiss, *Runenkunde* (Leipzig: Reclam, [1936]), 3, 10–11, 29ff.

20 O. Huth, review of Reiss, *Runenkunde*, *Germanien* 9 (1937): 160.

21 H. Arntz, review of Krause, *Was man in Runen ritzte* (2nd ed.), *Beiblatt zur Anglia* 54/55 (1943/44): 244–47.

22 A. Nordén, "Die Frage nach den Ursprung der Runen im Lichte der Val Camonica-Funde," *Berichte zur Runenforschung* 1 (1939), 25–34; idem, "Felszeichnungen und Runenschrift," *Runenberichte* 1 (1941), 51–75; Arntz, "Vom Weltbild der Felsritzer," idem, "Die Runen."

23 E. Mogk, "Über Los, Zauber und Weissagen bei den Germanen," in *Kleinere Beiträge zur Geschichte von Dozenten der Leipziger Hochschule* (Leipzig: Duncker & Humblot, 1894), 81–90; R. Petsch, "Über Zeichenrunen und Verwandtes," *Zeitschrift für den deutschen Unterricht* 31 (1917): 433–49; cf. B. Mees, "Runes in the First Century," in M. Stoklund et al. (eds.), *Runes and Their Secrets* (Copenhagen: Museum Tusculanum, 2006), 208–10.

24 E. Mogk, *Über Runen und Hakenkreuz* (Leipzig: Der Ritter vom Hakenkreuz, 1921).

25 Krause, "Sinnbilder und Runen"; K. Düwel, "Begriffsrunen," in J. Hoops, *Reallexikon der Germanischen Altertumskunde* II, 2nd ed. (Berlin: De Gruyter, 1976), 150–53.

26 W. Krause, "Ein neuer Runenfund aus Oberschlesien," *Forschungen und Fortschritte* 11 (1935): 110–11 [= *Nordische Welt* 3 (1935): 347–49]; cf. also W. Krause, "Die Inschrift auf der Urne von Niesdrowitz," *Altschlesien* 6 (1936): 232–38; G. Dechend, "Hütet die Runen, das Weistum eurer Ahnen!," *Nordische Welt* 3 (1935): 642.

27 W. Krause, review of Weigel.

28 K.T. Weigel, "Ein vorrunisches Begriffzeichen aus der Mark," *Wörter und Sachen* 22 (1941–42): 207–10; W. Krause, "Zu der scheinbaren *r*-Rune auf dem früheisenzeitlichen Gefäß von Börnicke," *Wörter und Sachen* 22 (1941–42): 211–17.

29 Weigel/Krause 7.6.39; Weigel/Krause 16.6.39, both BA: AE B264.

30 Weigel/Krause 19.6.40; Krause/Sievers 25.6.40; Krause/Sievers 8.12.40; Weigel/Thaerigen 10.9.41; Krause/Sievers 17.11.41, all BA: AE B264.

31 Krause/Wüst 15.5.42; Wüst/Himmler 5.2.43; Himmler/Krause 10.2.43, all BA: AE B264.

32 W. Krause, "Eine Zentralstelle für Runen- und Sinnbildkunde" (undated): BA: AE B264.

33 E. Moltke, review of Arntz, *Handbuch der Runenkunde*, *Arkiv för nordisk filologi* 53 (1937): 363–64.

34 Krause/Wüst 29.7.43, BA: AE B264.

35 W. Krause, "Runen in Amerika," *Germanien* 9 (1937): 231–36; idem, "Der Speer von Kowel," *Germanien* 13 (1941): 450–64; J.O. Plaßmann and W. Krause, "Die Hrabanische Runenreihe," *Germanien* 15 (1943): 171–88. The collaboration with Plaßmann has its origin in an exchange of letters from 1940: Krause/Plaßmann 25.5.40; Weigel/Krause 31.5.40, both BA: AE B264.

36 Mezynski, passim.

37 Krause/Sievers 8.12.40; Krause/Komanns 10.1.41; Weigel/Krause 18.8.41; Krause/Sievers 27.2.43, Sievers/Brandt 8.7.43; all BA: AE B264; anon., "Der Runenspeer von Kowel" *SS-Leithefte* 7/2 (1941): 6–10; E. Weber, "Ein wiedergefundenes Runendenkmal," *Sigrune* 11 (1944): 8–9; Kater, *Ahnenerbe*, 147–48; Hunger, 229–31.

38 Hunger, 232–37.

39 J.W. Hauer, *Die Religionen* (Berlin: Kohlhammer, 1923); idem, *Was will die deutsche Glaubensbewegung?* (Stuttgart: Hirschfeld, 1934); idem, *Glaubensgeschichte der Indogermanen* (Stuttgart: Kohlhammer, 1937); W. Hauer et al., *Germany's New Religion*, trans. T.S.K. Scott-Craig and R.E. Davies (London: Allen & Unwin, 1937); M. Dierks, *Jakob Wilhelm Hauer 1881–1962* (Heidelberg: Lambert Schneider, 1986); U. Nanko, *Die Deutsche Glaubensbewegung* (Marburg: Diagonal, 1993); Junginger, 49ff.; S. Baumann, *Die Deutsche Glaubensbewegung und ihr Gründer Jakob Wilhelm Hauer*, trans. A. Lessing (Marburg: Diagonal, 2005); Poewe, passim.

40 J.W. Hauer, "Über die ältesten Hakenkreuze, ihre Herkunft und ihre Sinn," *Germanien* 15 (1943): 88–100.

41 W. Krause, "Woher stammen die Runen?," *Brüsseler Zeitung* 2 Aug. 1942, 3.

42 J.W. Hauer, "Die Herkunft der Runen und der westeurasischen Alphabets aus den indogermanischen Heilszeichen und Sinnbildern" (1942/43) [= *Schrift der Götter* (Kiel: Orion Heimreiter, 2004)]; W. Krause, "Zum Stand der Runenforschung," *GGA* 205 (1943): 240.

43 K.T. Weigel, *Ritzzeichnungen in Dreschtennen des Schwarzwaldes* (Heidelberg: Winter, 1942); Hunger, 219.

44 E. Weber, *Kleine Runenkunde* (Berlin: Nordland, 1941).

45 Lixfeld, 1ff.

46 Lixfeld, 33ff., 117–19; Hunger, 117ff.; L. Scholze-Irrlitz, "Universitätsvolkskunde im Nationalsozialismus," in R. vom Bruch and C. Jahr (eds.), *Die Berliner Universität in der NS-Zeit*, 2 vols. (Stuttgart: Steiner, 2005), II, 133ff.

47 Lixfeld, 189–90; A. Oesterle, "John Meier und das SS-Ahnenerbe," in H. Gerndt (ed.), *Volkskunde und Nationalsozialismus* (Munich: Münchener Vereinigung für Volkskunde, 1987), 83 [= eadem, "The Office of Ancestral Inheritence and Folklore Scholarship," in J.R. Dow and H. Lixfeld (eds.), *The Nazification of an Academic Discipline* (Bloomington: Indiana University Press, 1994), 203].

48 Richter, 15–16; J.R. Dow and H. Lixfeld, "National Socialist Folklore and Overcoming the Past in the Federal Republic of Germany," *Asian Folklore Studies* L-1 (1991), 137 [= eidem (eds.), *The Nazification of an Academic Discipline* (Bloomington: Indiana University Press, 1994), 287].

49 F. Herrmann and W. Treutlein (eds.), *Brauch und Sinnbild* (Karlsruhe: Sudwestdeutsche Druck- und Verlags-Gesellschaft, 1940); F. Herrmann (ed.), *Handbuch der Symbolforschung*, 2 vols. (Leipzig: Hierseman, 1941).

50 O. Lauffer, review of Langewiesche, *Sinnbilder germanischen Glaubens im Wittekindsland, Zeitschrift für Volkskunde* 45 (1937): 179–81; idem, review of von Zaborsky-Wahlstätten, *Urväter-Erbe in deutscher Volkskunst, Zeitschrift für Volkskunde* 45 (1937): 326; idem, "Wunderbäume und Wunschbäume im Schrifttum und in der bildenden Kunst," in F. Herrmann and W. Treutlein (eds.), *Brauch und Sinnbild* (Karlsruhe: Sudwestdeutsche Druck- und Verlags-Gesellschaft, 1940), 161–78; Kater, *Ahnenerbe*, 109.

51 Lixfeld, 44; Hammerstein, 189–90.

52 Wirth/Roselius 20.6.34, BA: REM B284; *Volkstum und Heimat* 1–7 (Kampen auf Sylt: Volkstum und Heimat, 1934–40); W. Haverbeck, *Volkstum und Heimat als Bekenntnis jungen Kulturwollens* (Berlin: Reichsbund Volkstum und Heimat, 1935); idem, *Deutscher Mai* (Berlin: Phoenix, 1935); Bollmus, *Amt Rosenberg*, 47–50; H. Bausinger, "Volkskunde und Volkstumsarbeit im Nationalsozialismus," in H. Gerndt (ed.), *Volkskunde und Nationalsozialismus* (Munich: Münchener Vereinigung für Volkskunde, 1987), 131–41 [= J.R. Dow and H. Lixfeld (eds.), *The Nazification of an Academic Discipline* (Bloomington: Indiana University Press, 1994), 87–96]; Lixfeld, 41–42; A. Ferch, *Viermal Deutschland in einem Menschenleben* (Dresden: Zeitenwende, 2000), 15ff.

53 The outbreak of war prevented its publication by Diedrichs's sons who lost their publishing license in 1939; Ferch, 34.

54 F. Kolbrand, "Eine krasser Widerspruch," *Volkstum und Heimat* 46 (1937): 297–300; anon., "Lebendiges Brauchtum," *Volkstum und Heimat* 48 (1939): 283–89; F. Pfister, "Brauch und Sinnbild," in F. Herrmann and W. Treutlein (eds.), *Brauch und Sinnbild* (Karlsruhe: Sudwestdeutsche Druck- und Verlags-Gesellschaft, 1940), 40; Hunger, 362.

55 E. Fehrle, "Das Hakenkreuz," *Oberdeutsche Zeitschrift für Volkskunde* 8 (1934): 5–38, idem, "Zur Entwicklung des Sinnbildes," *Oberdeutsche Zeitschrift für Volkskunde* 12 (1938): 165; Assion, 226ff. [= Dow and Lixfeld (eds.), 118ff.].

56 O. Lauffer, "Volkswerk," in W.-E. Peukert and O. Lauffer, *Volkskunde* (Bern: Francke, 1951), 262–335; R. Bollmus, "Zwei Volkskunden im Drit-

ten Reich," in H. Gerndt (ed.), *Volkskunde und Nationalsozialismus* (Munich: Münchener Vereinigung für Volkskunde, 1986), 49–60.

57 H. Bausinger, "Volksideologie und Volksforschung," *Zeitschrift für Volkskunde* 61 (1965): 177–204 [= J.R. Dow and H. Lixfeld (eds.), *The Nazification of an Academic Discipline* (Bloomington: Indiana University Press, 1994), 11–33]; W. Emmerich, *Germanistische Volkstumsideologie* (Tübingen Schloß: Tübinger Vereinigung für Volkskunde, 1968).

58 Pringle, 145ff.

59 Much, *Der Eintritt der Germanen.*

60 C.J.S. Marstrander, "Les inscriptions des casques de Negau, Styrie," *Symbolae Osloenses* 3 (1925): 37–64; idem, "Remarques sur les inscriptions des casques en bronze de Negau et de Watsch," *Avh. utgitt av Det Norske Videnskaps Akademi i Oslo, Hist.-filos. Klasse* 2 (1926), no. 2.

61 C.J.S. Marstrander, "Om runene og runenavnenes oprindelse," *Norsk tidsskrift for sprogvidenskap* 1 (1928): 85–188; B. Mees, "The North Etruscan Thesis of the Origin of the Runes," *Arkiv för nordisk filologi* 115 (2000), 33ff.

62 Markey, 76.

63 G. Baesecke, "Die Herkunft der Runen," *GRM* 22 (1934): 413–17; P. Boden, "Universitätsgermanistik in der SBZ/DDR. Personal- und Berufungs-politik 1945–1958," *Zeitschrift für Germanistik* NF 5 (1995), 374; cf. H. Hempl, "Der Ursprung der Runenschrift," *GRM* 23 (1935): 401–26.

64 G. Baesecke, *Vor- und Frühgeschichte des deutschen Schrifttums* I (Halle a.S.: Niemeyer, 1940), 125.

65 F. Altheim, *Römische Religionsgeschichte*, 2 vols. (Berlin: De Gruyter, 1931–33), idem, *A History of Roman Religion*, trans. H. Mattingly (London: Methuen, 1938); idem, *La Religion romaine antique*, trans. H.E. Medico (Paris: Payot, 1955).

66 F. Altheim and E. Trautmann, *Vom Ursprung der Runen* (Frankfurt a.M.: Klostermann, 1939); F. Altheim and E. Trautmann-Nehring, *Kimbern und Runen*, 2nd ed. (Berlin: Ahnenerbe, 1942); Losemann, 123ff.; Hunger, 263–78.

67 F. Altheim and E. Trautmann, "Nordische und italische Felsbildkunst," *Die Welt als Geschichte* 3 (1937): 83–113; eidem, "Keltische Felsbilder der Val Camonica," *Mitteilungen des Deutschen Archäologischen Instituts, Römische Abteilung* 54 (1939): 1–13.

68 Cf. F. Altheim and E. Trautmann, "Neue Felsbilder aus der Val Camonica," *Wörter und Sachen* NF 1 (1938): 12–45; idem, "Gründsatzliches zur Runen- und Felsbildforschung," *Germanien* 11 (1939): 449–56.

69 He was clearly wrong, however; A. Morandi, "Epigrafia camuna," *Revue belge de philologie et d'histoire* 76 (1998): 99–124.

70 F. Altheim, "Die Felsbilder der Val Camonica und die altitalischen Kultur," in *Bericht über den VI. Internationalen Kongreß für Archäologie* (Berlin: De Gruyter, 1940), 442–43; idem, *Italien und Rom*, 2 vols. (Amsterdam: Pantheon, 1941), I, 15–30.

71 F. Altheim and E. Trautmann, "Die Elchrune," *Germanien* 13 (1941): 22–30; eidem, "Die älteste Darstellung des Woden?," *Germanien* 14 (1942): 369–82.

72 F. Altheim, "Runen als Schildzeichen," *Klio* 31 (1938): 51–59.

73 W. Wüst, "Arisches zur Sinnbildforschung," *Germanien* 12 (1940): 212–19.

74 G. Simon, "Die Island-Expedition des 'Ahnenerbe' der SS," <homepages. uni-tuebingen.de/gerd.simon/ nordistik1.htm>, 2002; Pringle, 187ff.

75 Kater, *Ahnenerbe*, 79–80, 211ff; R. Greve, "Tibetforschung im SS-Ahnenerbe," in T. Hauschild (ed.), *Lebenslust und Fremdenfurcht* (Frankfurt a.M.: Suhrkamp, 1995), 168–99; C. Hale, *Himmler's Crusade* (London: Bantam, 2003); Pringle, 145ff.

76 *Wiener prähistorische Zeitschrift* 25–30 (Berlin: Die Gesellschaft, 1938–43).

77 Kater, *Ahnenerbe*, 83.

78 Kater, *Ahnenerbe*, 159ff.; M. Wedekind, "The Sword of Science," in I. Haar and M. Fahlbusch (eds.), *German Scholars and Ethnic Cleansing* (New York: Berghahn, 2004), 123ff.

79 Kater, *Ahnenerbe*, 83ff.; 227ff.

80 F.-R. Hausmann, *"Deutsche Geisteswissenschaft" im Zweiten Weltkrieg* (Dresden: Dresden University Press, 1998); Fehr, 339ff.

81 J.M.N. Kapteyn, "Twee runeninscripties uit de terp van Westeremden," *Jaarverslag van de Vereeniging voor Terpenonderzoek* 1930/31 [= "Zwei Runeninschriften aus der Terp Westeremden," *PBB* 57 (1933): 160–226]; idem, "Neue Runenfunde," *PBB* 58 (1934): 299–312; idem, "Eine altalemannische Runeninschrift," *Anzeiger für schweizerische Altertumskunde* NF 37 (1935): 210–12; idem, "Friesche runenvondsten en hedendaagsche runologie," *Frysk jierboek* 1938 [n.v.].

82 J.M.N. Kapteyn, "Ursprung und Herkunft der germanischen Runenschrift im Lichte neuer Funde," *Korrespondenzblatt des Vereins für niederdeutsche Sprachforschung* 49 (1936): 23–25.

83 *Saxo-Frisia* 1–4/4 (Assen: Van Gorcum, 1939–44); G.A. Zondergeld, "Hans Ernst Schneider und seine Bedeutung für das SS-Ahnenerbe," in H. König et al. (eds.), *Vertuschte Vergangenheit* (Munich: Beck, 1997), 25ff.

84 *Het Noorder Land* 1–3/9 (Groningen: Stichting Saxo-Frisia, 1941–44); J.M.N. Kapteyn, *Friezen, Saksen* (Amsterdam: Hamer, 1941); idem, *Friesland und die Friesen in den Niederlanden* (Bonn: Scheur, 1942).

85 Kater, *Ahnenerbe*, 182, n. 334; cf. Burleigh, 239. The others were the Swedish archeologist, Eric Count Oxenstierna, who had completed his doctorate under Reinerth in 1942 and had since won Ahnenerbe funds for an excavation in Flanders, and a Fleming, Jef van de Wiele, the leader of the Flemish–German Working Group DeVlag, "The Flag" (Vlaamsch-Duitsche Arbeidsgemeenschap); J. van de Wiele, *Op zook naar een Vaderland* (Brussels: Steenlandt, 1942) [= *Flandern wird Leben* (Brussels: Steenlandt, 1944)]; W. Pape, "Zur Entwicklung des Faches Ur- und Frühgeschichte in Deutschland bis 1945," in A. Leube (ed.), *Prähistorie und Nationalsozialismus* (Heidelberg: Synchron, 2002), 183f.; Derks, "German *Westforschung*," 185–87.

86 For his other activities see L. van Hasselt, "'De zaken moeten nu eenmaal loopen,'" *Groniek* 144 (1999): 311–19.

87 J. Lerchenmüller and G. Simon, *Maskenwechsel* (Tübingen: GIFT, 1999), 177–79.

88 See pp. 259–60.

89 B.-A. Rusinek, "Ein Germanist in der SS," in G. Jasper (ed.), *Ein Germanist und seine Wissenschaft* (Erlangen: Friedrich-Alexander Universität Erlangen-Nürnberg, 1996), 29ff.; Zondergeld, pp.17ff.

90 Farwerck/Sievers 9.11.39, in N.K.C.A. in 't Veld (ed.), *De SS in Nederland* (The Hague: Nijhoff, 1976), no. 12.

91 Sievers/Rauter 1.7.40, in In 't Velde (ed.), no. 37.

92 Filenote Schneider 7.8.40, in In 't Velde (ed.), no. 42; Zonderfeld, 19ff.

93 *De Wolfsangel* 1–2/10 (Utrecht: Nederlandsche Nationaal-Socialistische Uitgeverij, 1936–38); thereafter *Der Vaderen Erfdeel* 2/11–3/12 (Leiden: Der Vaderen Erfdeel, 1938–39); and then *Volksche Wacht* 4/1 – 9/[4] (Amsterdam: Der Vaderen Erfdeel, then The Hague, Hamer, 1939–44). Filenote, Schneider 4.10.40, in In 't Velde (ed.), no. 51

94 *Hamer* 1–4/11 (The Hague, Amsterdam: Hamer, 1940–44).

95 *Hamer* 1–2/8 (Antwerp: De Burcht, 1943–44); *Hammer* 1 (Berlin–Dahlem: Ahnenerbe, 1944); cf. Kater, *Ahnenerbe*, 179–80.

96 E.g. K.T. Weigel, "Gedachten over volkskunst," *Hamer* 2/4 (1942): 21–24; idem, "Lichtmis," *Hamer* 2/6 (1942): 18–19; idem, "Zinnebeelden in zand gestrooid," *Hamer* 2/11 (1942).

97 W.F. van Heemskerk-Düker and H.J. van Houten, *Zinnebeelden in Nederland* (Amsterdam: Hamer, 1941); Kapteyn, *Friezen, Saksen*; J.O. Plaßmann, *Ehr is dwang gnog*, trans. A.E.C. Vuerhard-Berkhort (Amsterdam: Hamer, 1944).

98 L. de Jong, *Het Koninkrijk der Nederlanden in de Tweede Wereldoorlog*, 14 vols. (The Hague: Staatsdrukkerij- en Uitgeverijbedrif, 1969–91), V, 271–82.

99 G. Neckel, review of De Vries, *De germaansche oudheid* and Teudt, *Germanische Heiligtümer* (2nd ed.).

100 J. de Vries, "Über neuere Runenforschung," *Geistige Arbeit* 9/8 (1942): 3–4; idem, "Germanische goden," *Hamer* 2/5–12 (1942); idem, "Het raadsel der runen," *Hamer* 3/5–10 (1943).

101 J. de Vries, *Die geistige Welt der Germanen* (Halle a.S.: Niemeyer, 1943); idem, *De Goden der Germanen* (Amsterdam: Hamer, 1944); and cf. idem, "Over Germaanse wereldbeschouving," *Algemein Nederlands Tidschrift voor Wijsbegeerte en Psychologie* 34 (1941): 185–204; K. Heeroma, "Vorwort," in J. de Vries, *Kleine Schriften*, ed. K. Heeroma and A. Kylstra (Berlin: De Gruyter, 1965), v–vii.

102 G. Hirschfeld, "Die nationalsozialistischen Neuordnung Europas und die 'Germanisierung' der westeuropäischen Universitäten," in H. König et al. (eds.), *Vertuschte Vergangenheit* (Munich: Beck, 1997), 80–93.

103 Zonderfeld, 29–30; Van Hasselt, 317–18.

104 Kater, *Ahnenerbe*, 100–4, 231–45; idem, *Doctors under Hitler* (Chapel Hill: University of North Carolina Press), 90, 125–26; L. Jäger, *Seitenwechsel* (Munich: Fink, 1998), 132–50.
105 See the title page of the Dutch SS journal *Vormingsbladen*, reproduced in Lund, table 1.
106 Höfler, "Die Entwicklung der geistigen Lage in Skandinavien," lecture given 23 Nov. 1942 to an RSHA conference; BA PA Höfler 240–74; Höfler/RFSS 24.3.42, BA AE K86; cf. Hunger, 338f., n. 32.
107 D.A. Seip, *Hjemme og i fiendeland 1940–45* (Oslo: Gyldendal, 1946), 220ff.; Kater, *Ahnenerbe*, 185–86, 327–28; Junginger, 264.
108 Burleigh, 227f.
109 Sievers in International Military Tribunal, *Trial of the Major War Criminals* (Nuremberg: The Tribunal, 1948), vol. XX, 605; Kater, *Ahnenerbe*, 314.
110 O.S. Johansen, "Anmerkungen zur archäologischen Tätigkeit in Norwegen in den Jahren 1940–1945," in A. Leube (ed.), *Prähistorie und Nationalsozialismus* (Heidelberg, Synchron, 2002), 619–20; cf. Steuer, 433.
111 Höfler, "Entwicklung" (cit. supra n. 106); M. Jakubowski-Tiessen, "Kulturpolitik im bestzten Land," *Zeitschrift für Geschichtswissenschaft* 42 (1994): 129–38; Jäger, 197ff.; 219, n. 374.
112 Hufen, passim; Mezynski, passim; Heuß, 224–43.
113 Heuß, 218–24.
114 Jäger, 234–44. The Berlin *Westforscher* Ernst Gamillscheg, on the other hand, ran the Bucharest DWI; F.-R. Hausmann, *"Vom Strudel der Ereignisse verschlungen"* (Frankfurt a.M.: Klostermann, 2000), 577–616; Bott, 278.
115 Fehr, 329–30, 340–41, 359ff.
116 F.H. Kasten, "Unethical Medicine in Annexed Alsace–Lorraine," in G.O. Kent (ed.), *Historians and Archivists* (Fairfax: Rowman & Littlefield, 1991), 173–208; Pringle, 239ff.
117 G.G. Engelkes, *Runenfibel* (Langensalza: Beltz, [1935]); K. Renck-Reichert, *Runenfibel* (Heilbronn: Salzer, 1935).
118 Filenote, Sievers 26.11.43; Schmitz-Kahlmann/Brandt 17.3.44; Brandt/Schmitz-Kahlmann 6.4.44, all BA: AE B264.
119 Undated copy of a response to Brandt, probably from Weigel, BA: AE B264.
120 Schneider/Schmitz-Kahlmann 22.5.44, BA: AE B264.
121 Sievers/Krause 7.7.44; Krause/Sievers 11.8.44; Krause/Sievers 14.8.44, all BA: AE B264.
122 Sievers/Krause 6.10.44, BA: AE B264.
123 W. Krause, "Über die Anfange der Runenschrift," *Europäischer Wissenschafts-Dienst* 3/3 (1943): 16–18; cf. idem, "Die Herkunft der Runen," *Jahrbuch des Auslandamtes der deutschen Dozentschaft* 1943, 102–10.
124 J.O. Plaßmann, "Rückblick und Ausblick," *Germanien* 15 (1943): 2–3.

CHAPTER 10.

Epilogue, Aftermath

On doit des égards aux vivants;
on ne doit aux morts que la verité
Voltaire

In 1992, an American Romanist was in Berlin with his researcher-wife and while there decided to do a favor for a Belgian friend, a professor at the Technical University at Aachen, by chasing up some Nazi-era archival material for him. His good will was to turn into shock, though, when his friend told the Romanist, Earl Jeffery Richards, about an old photo the American had sent him of the GWE's Hans Ernst Schneider. The young man in the photo bore an uncanny resemblance to the former Rector of the University of Aachen. Richards had stumbled across one of the strangest cases of reinvention by a former SS academic. Schneider's postwar doppelganger, Hans Schwerte, had become a noted critic of the conservative academic establishment in the 1960s and was even seen in some quarters as a hero from the days of the student protests of 1968. His duplicity was breathtaking; Schwerte's former colleagues were variously dumbfounded and horrified.[1]

The Schneider/Schwerte affair did not become public in Germany until 1995, though, when Dutch journalists became aware of rumors that had arisen in the wake of the discovery that Schwerte was the same man who had led the Dutch outpost of the Ahnenerbe during the war. Uproar soon ensued in Germany, Schneider/Schwerte lost his pension rights, emeritus standing and finally even his doctorates. He had completely reversed his public wartime persona: in 1943—in light of the losses at Stalingrad—Schneider had penned an article lauding the German embrace of tragedy; in his 1962 study of the Faustian, a similarly popular conservative theme, as Schwerte he had concluded that it was an invention of the German national right.[2] False names, Schwerte subsequently claimed, had been common in the postwar years, and it had just seemed pointless to him to take his old name back. He had gone to great lengths to reinvent himself, having himself declared dead, doing a new doctorate, remarrying his wife and adopting their daughter—as well, in time, as establishing a completely new politics. His former Dutch colleagues had been severely punished for their dealings with him, but Schneider/Schwerte now seemed to think that the wartime skeletons in his closet could now all be forgotten.

Much like Hans Schneider, *Sinnbildforschung* as a discipline disappeared in 1945. Its former practitioners did not, however, and nor did many of the other attendant expressions of *völkisch* Germanism, or what a Swedish scholar writing in 1944 called "the absurdity of the extreme applied antiquarian studies of the German philologists."[3] This, however, was the last frank academic assessment of *Sinnbildforschung* and the excesses of German antiquarianism of the National Socialist period to appear until 1982. The *völkisch* antiquarian past had proved a very difficult topic in the immediate postwar years for a variety of reasons.

Marburg fell within the American sector of the postwar Allied Military Government and Wirth was denounced and interned from 1945–47 by the Americans. But after adding his mother's maiden name Roeper Bosch to the end of his own, he managed to pass himself off as a Dutchman and a victim of Nazism. He was released and left Germany for Holland as a displaced person.

In 1949 Wirth then went to Sweden, where he became involved with the Institute of Color Photography in Lund. He returned to Germany upon his retirement, settled in Marburg again and revived the Herman Wirth Society.[4] In 1953 he was even able to get the casts he had made in his Ahnenerbe days back. His first postwar exhibition premiered in December 1960 and the decade that followed saw the appearance of several new works on *Sinnbildkunde* and *Geistesurgeschichte*.[5] In the 1970s his *Holy Sacred Script* was reissued by his Society's publishing house and reprints of his *Emergence* and *What is German?* duly followed in 1993. The Herman Wirth Society exists to this day, although it has been subsumed by the group Primordial Europe (Ur-Europa), which was formerly known as the Society for the Study of Early European Society (Gesellschaft für europäische Urgemeinschaftskunde). In 1980 Wirth devotees even managed to solicit a promise of funding for a museum of intellectual prehistory from the government of the state of Rhineland-Palatinate, although Wirth was eventually exposed by the press as a former Nazi and racist theorizer.[6] The master of *Sinnbildforschung* died in 1981, but his legacy lives on today in the form of his Society and other similar groups who inhabit the extreme-right European fringe, as well as a private museum in Spital am Pyhrn in Austria which has inherited his collection of casts.[7]

Theodor Weigel disappeared into obscurity after 1945. He some-how managed to prove to the postwar authorities that he too had been a victim of Nazism and after being released from internment in late 1947, he produced a handful of studies for local newspapers and magazines on antiquarian themes. He also attempted to get support from Wolfgang Krause in the 1950s, hoping to win some sort of return to academic life. Unsuccessful, he died, somewhat symbolically, in Detmold in 1953.[8]

At the end of 1945, Otto Plaßmann was forced to retire at the age of 50 from the position in Bonn he had won as a leading figure in the Ahnenerbe. He protested after the war that he had never actu-ally joined the Nazi Party and despite all the evidence to the contrary, had distanced himself from the SS after 1937. During the early 1950s he published a version of his professional thesis and a handful of ar-ticles on medieval Germany, and the University of Bonn granted him emeritus status in 1958.[9] By this time he had also become involved in veterans' affairs, however, and by 1954 had become leader of a Ger-man veterans' group, the Bund deutscher Kriegsverschädigter und Hinterbliebener, Bonn, and even served on the presidium of a similar international body, the Fédération Européenne des Anciens Combat-tants, founded in 1955.[10] He died in 1964, his past as a leading Nazi functionary seemingly forgotten.

Otto Huth fled Strasbourg in autumn 1944 in the face of the Al-lied tide and was found a place at the Institute for *Volkskunde* at the University of Tübingen. After losing his position in 1945, he soon slipped into obscurity, only to resurface in 1961 as a specialist librarian at the University of Tübingen, a position he held until his retirement in 1971.[11] He also published several articles on symbol studies in the Swiss *Jahrbuch für Symbolforschung* (*Yearbook for Symbol Studies*) during the early 60s and resurfaced again in the 1980s when he wrote a book on the novelist Wilhelm Raabe.[12]

An institutionally more marginal fate was visited on Otto Höfler's former whipping boy, the Nordicist Bernhard Kummer. Kummer es-caped from Jena—where the Soviet administration had dismissed him—to the West, and in the 1950s published a German translation of the *Edda*, a book on the Extern Stones and a handful of other Nordic works of no note.[13] Unable to win any sort of institutional accommodation at all, in Bremen in 1954 he also founded a journal, *Forschungsfragen unserer Zeit (Research Questions of our Time)*—it continued on for some years after his death in 1962 and the associated publishing house even issued a new edition of his *Midgards Decline* in 1972.[14]

A similar destiny was in store for the Amt Rosenberg's other leading antiquarian. Hans Reinerth had been expelled from the Party in 1945 in light of Herbert Jankuhn's claim that Rosenberg's archeology chief had associated with Jews like Gerhard Bersu. Further ostracized by the Romelings, after being released from internment in the late 1940s Reinerth renewed his acquaintance instead with a private prehistorical foundation called the Association for Stilt-Building and Homeland Studies (Verein für Pfahlbau- und Heimatkunde) on the shores of Lake Constance that he had been involved with during his time in the Amt Rosenberg. Reinerth had written a work on the prehistoric stilted lake dwellings of the area in 1922 which he continued to rework a number of times after the war and as president of the Association he edited their journal *Vorzeit (Prehistory)* from 1952–78 as well as guides to their museum.[15] Reinerth's involvement with the Association ended only with his death in 1990.

Some other figures associated with Wirth and the *völkisch* antiquarian project lived long enough to get involved in rightist environmentalist circles. A leading example is Werner Haverbeck, the former leader of the Reich League for National Tradition and Homeland, who had received a doctorate in *Sinnbildforschung* in 1936. After disappearing for a time into the priesthood of a radical protestant group and then returning to academic life at the newly established Bielefeld University of Applied Sciences, Haverbeck renewed his association with the *völkisch* project, joining up again with Wirth in the 1960s, and was still active as late as the early 1990s in radical environmental circles. A holocaust denier, Haverbeck has even fulfilled one prewar theologian's suspicion that Wirth's *Emergence* was a sort of paleo-anthroposophy by becoming a leading figure in the revival of the racist anthroposophy of the prewar years. His former followers still advertise conferences and publish monographs and journals today where anthroposophy, neo-paganism and Neo-Nazism meet in a whirl of anti-Semitism, anti-capitalism, anti-Americanism and outright *völkisch* fantasy.[16]

Of all the academics who were caught up in *Sinnbildforschung* that did not owe their positions to Party influence, only Holland's Jan de Vries suffered any long-term censure for collaborating with the Nazi regime. The other leading Dutch Germanist collaborator, Johannes Kapteyn, was tried and convicted by a Dutch court in 1948; but he was in his late 70s by the time and died in 1949.[17] As an active associate of the Ahnenerbe's Volksche Werkgemeenschap and its successor the Germaansche Institut, however, De Vries had fled the advancing Allied forces for Germany and had been set up with DFG funding at Leipzig in 1944.[18] In 1945 he was handed over to the Dutch authorities, interned and subsequently forbidden to hold an academic position within Holland. De Vries published his best material after the war and now stands as the most influential Nordicist Holland has ever produced. Nevertheless, in the 50s and 60s his books were banned and the Dutch state even went so far as to put up barriers to his participation at international conferences. His fate stands in stark contrast to that of his German contemporaries.

Despite all the evidence for involvement with the SS, Krause was able to maintain his position after 1945 as he had never technically joined the Party. Undoubtedly he was too old and too visually impaired to be made a regular member of the SS. His Institute for Runology was officially dissolved in 1950, but his section of the University of Göttingen retained its position as the center for runic studies in Germany and remains so under his successors today.[19] Krause's runological *magnum opus*, the revised edition of his *Runic Inscriptions in the Older Futhark*, appeared in 1966 with archeological contributions prepared by his old Ahnenerbe compatriot Herbert Jankuhn. Jankuhn had declined an offer from the Communist East to take back the chair he had won at Rostock in 1943; despite having to restart his career in the more liberal West, he was eventually able to win back his preeminent place in German archeology nonetheless in time for the "Issues concerning the Teutons" conference of 1982. Recent research has laid out in full Jankuhn's involvement in the mass pillaging of artifacts from collections in Eastern Europe, though, his personal association with Himmler, and how his political career had even culminated by 1942 in his enrolment in the Waffen-SS.[20]

Helmut Arntz, however, was unable to regain his academic position at the University of Giessen at the end of the war. Krause had won. Arntz had attempted some sort of accommodation with the dictates of the Party by cozying up to the Amt Rosenberg late in 1942 and produced a poster of runes and ideographs he hoped would appear in German classrooms.[21] Instead, the most vociferous German opponent of *Sinnbildforschung* had been edged out of academic life. He did take his case to the West German government and won a settlement that included a brief return to runological study at the University of Cologne in the late 1940s.[22] But runology thereafter proved only an interlude to his postwar working life. Instead Arntz worked for the Press and Information Bureau of the FRG at Wiesbaden for much of the 1950s through to the 70s where he prepared government publications such as *Germany Today (Deutschland heute)* and *Facts about Germany (Tatsachen über Deutschland)*,[23] serving as president of the German Society for Documentation (Deutsche Gesellschaft für Dokumentation) from 1962–72 (which he had helped found during the dictatorship). He also served on several UNESCO committees on archival and library documentation in the 1970s, and is currently honorary president of the German Society for the History of Wine (Gesellschaft für Geschichte des Weines) as well as remaining a member of the German Indo-Europeanists' Society (Indogermanische Gesellschaft), the leading body of historical linguists in Germany today.

A 65-year-old in 1945, Eugen Fehrle was interned from 1946–48, but during an appeal to the verdict in his original de-Nazification trial somehow managed to convince the court that he had only worked with the regime in order to minimize the harm that a more radical appointee might have wrought upon the University of Heidelberg.[24] Despite the widespread opprobrium his colleagues felt for him he was granted emeritus status by the university in 1950 and continued to produce a very *völkisch* folklore up until the time of his death seven years later. His collection of copies of Wirth's casts and photos of other expressions of *völkisch* folklore was dispersed in the 1960s and 70s as his successors tried to rid themselves of the legacy of his obsequiously National Socialist form of *Volkskunde*.[25]

The Ahnenerbe's second and last leader Walter Wüst was interned and lost his position at the University of Munich at the end of the war. The Ahnenerbe's secretary Wolfram Sievers was condemned to death at Nuremberg for his role in coordinating the horrific medical experiments performed by Ahnenerbe researchers on the unwilling inmates of concentration and POW camps in the occupied East. Wüst's treatment by the postwar authorities was surprisingly lenient by comparison. He clearly had been responsible at the time of the earliest of these forays into scientific inhumanity, although he had lost his command over the natural science activities of the Ahnenerbe in 1943. He had, strangely enough, also been handed a pretext to escape postwar censure by Rosenberg whose distaste for Wüst is clear in his Nuremberg memoir.[26] Rosenberg had finally got the chance to revenge himself on Wüst in 1944 by closing down parts of his university in the wake of the White Rose affair. Yet instead, Rosenberg probably saved Wüst's life by inadvertently making him a victim of Nazi intrigues.[27] As Rector, Wüst had been responsible for calling in the Gestapo when the Scholl siblings and their friends had begun distributing anti-Nazi propaganda early in 1943. Yet despite the odium associated with the Ahnenerbe, especially after Nuremberg, and the status that the White Rose have achieved as the most romantic of all German resistance groups, Wüst was, nevertheless, not shunned by his former colleagues. Franz Altheim used his help in his *History of the Huns (Geschichte der Hunnen)* in 1961, a number of new monographic studies of Wüst's on Indo-Iranian philology appeared in the 50s and 60s, and he was still reviewing books for a respected Viennese linguistic journal as late as 1974.[28]

Altheim himself moved on to other topics after the war. He did not retreat from his ideographic speculations in his subsequent works and indeed some of his opinions resurface from time-to-time in antiquarian literature today.[29] The second edition of his *From the Origin of the Runes* remained a much-quoted work into the 50s and 60s despite the preface addressing his thanks to Himmler for enabling his research. Nevertheless, none of the studies by his students in Altheim's *Festschrift* from 1969–70 touch upon matters associated with his earlier foray into *Sinnbildforschung*.[30]

Otto Höfler was another matter entirely. Described as one of the Germanist "fanatics" by Heusler in 1937,[31] Höfler soon regained his position at Munich after de-Nazification—one that he had first won on the insistence of Wüst—and continued on his project of *völkisch* antiquarianism, eventually returning to Vienna in time to give his Arminius oration of 1959. An intensely stubborn man, he did not consider recanting. By the 1970s Höfler had even decided he was an expert in runology and even went so far as to link his *Männerbund* theories with the question of the origin of the runes. Honored with two *Festschriften*, Höfler's Nazi legacy is still papered over by his former students today.[32]

The fate of former Nazi academics underlines the lack of resolve in postwar Germany to punish professionals who had collaborated with the regime. The Americans had dealt firmly with those involved in the medical outrages of the Ahnenerbe. But once responsibility was handed over to the German judiciary, the de-Nazification process was clearly compromised. Those Germanistic scholars who lost their positions were generally those whose universities had fallen under Soviet military administration. After de-Nazification, however, even many of those whom the Soviets had dismissed were able to find themselves employment again in the more tolerant West. Only the most compromised academics such as Reinerth and Wüst or those who had won their positions through Party connections rather than proper academic channels were unable to find publicly funded posts again. Even senior Nazi Germanists such as Plaßmann and Fehrle were able to win emeritus status at universities in the West and it is no wonder that Nazi show ponies such as Jankuhn and Höfler were quickly able to find themselves new positions after de-Nazification. Wüst was even accepted back into academic discourse in the late 1950s, albeit in a limited manner, and if the Romelings had not been concentrated in the West, Reinerth might not have had to hide in an obscure private archeological foundation. Only the Dutchman De Vries felt any long-term censure for his active dalliance with National Socialism, though he probably proved himself in his publications after the war to have been the most gifted of all the *völkisch* Germanists.

It is no surprise then to see that some expressions of the worst of *völkisch* Germanism continued on after 1945. In a similar manner to the half-hearted de-Nazification of academic personnel, postwar Germanistic scholarship was similarly only partly reformed. In folklore there was a denial of the effect *völkisch* thought had had on the discipline: the worst scholarship was scapegoated, the rest was legitimized in the myth of the two *Volkskunden*. In archeology instead there was perhaps an overreaction, although the prewar split between the settlement school and the Romelings made the reform of the discipline somewhat simpler. Few German linguists seemed to think that their approach needed to change, however, until the advent of generative grammar in the 1960s when most of the old school were swept away. Not all German and Austrian academics found it easy to recant their allegiance to the *Volk*. The most notable case of malingering, though, is probably that of the Much school which in the person of Höfler enjoyed a second wind after 1950. *Völkisch* Germanism has retained an especially clear influence in postwar German runology and in studies of Old Germanic ideology or religious belief.

NOTES

1　A. Allen, "Open Secret," *Lingua Franca* March/April 1996, 28–41; E.J. Richards, "Dr. Schneider gen. Dr. Schwerte," in *Ungeahntes Erbe* (Aschaffenburg: Alibri, 1998), 212–33.

2　H.E. Schneider, "Das Tragische," *Das Reich* 7 Febr. 1943; H. Schwerte, *Faust und das Faustische* (Stuttgart, Klett [1962]); Rusinek, 37ff.; Jäger, 24ff., 128–32.

3　F. Askeberg, *Norden och kontinenten i gammal tid* (Uppsala: Almqvist & Wiksells, 1944), 86.

4　Wiwjorra, "Herman Wirth," 107–10; S. von Schnurbein, *Religion als Kulturkritik* (Heidelberg: Winter, 1992), 115–18; Dahl, 129; Pringle, 300–2.

5　H. Wirth Roeper Bosch, "Die symbolhistorische Methode," *Zeitschrift für Missionswissenschaft und Religionswissenschaft* 39 (1955): 127–39 [= monograph, Münster: Aschendorff, 1983]; idem, *Um die Ursinn des Menschseins* (Vienna: Volkstum, 1960); idem, *Allmutter* (Marburg a.L.: Eccestan, 1974); idem, *Führer durch die Ur-Europa-Museum* (Marburg a.L: Eccestan, 1975).

6　Anon., "Schenkel der Göttlichen," *Der Spiegel* 29 Sept. 1980.

7　F. Mandl, "Das Erbe der Ahnen," *Mitteilungen der ANISA* 19/20 (1999): 41–67.

8　Nußbeck, 117–22.

9　J.O. Plaßmann, "Widukinds Sachsengeschichte im Spiegel altsächsischer Sprache und Dichtung," *Niedersächsisches Jahrbuch für Landesgeschichte* 24 (1952): 1–35; idem, "Widukind von Corvey als Quelle für die germanische Altertumskunde," *PBB* 75 (1953): 191–228; idem, *Princeps und Populus* (Göttingen: Göttinger Verlagsanstalt, 1954).

10　W. Habel (ed.), *Wer ist wer?*, 13th ed. (Berlin-Grunewald: Arani, 1958), s.v. Plaßmann, J.O.; Gajek, "Plaßmann," 140; W. Killy (ed.), *Deutsche biographische Enzyklopaedia* VII (Munich: Saur, 1998), 686–87.

11　Lerchenmüller and Simon, *Im Vorfeld*, 71.

12　O. Huth, "Der Glasberg," *Jahrbuch für Symbolforschung* 2 (1961): 15–32; idem, "Das Mandäerproblem," *Jahrbuch für Symbolforschung* 3 (1962): 18–38; idem, "Raabe und das Neue Testament," *Jahrbuch der Raabe Gesellschaft* 1965, 103–11; idem, *Raabe und Tieck* (Essen: Blaue Erde, 1985).

13 B. Kummer, *Brünnhild und Ragnarök* (Lübeck: Schiller, 1950); idem, *Die Kampf um ein Heiligtum* (Pähl i.Obb.: Hohe Warte von Bebenburg, 1953); idem, *Gefolgschaft, Führertum und Freiheit* (Zeven: Forschungsfragen unserer Zeit, [1956]); idem, *Die Lieder des Codex Regius und verwandte Denkmäler*, 2 vols. (Zeven: Forschungsfragen unserer Zeit, 1959–61).

14 *Forschungsfragen unserer Zeit* 1–19 (Zeven: Forschungsfragen unserer Zeit, 1954–1973); B. Kummer, *Midgards Untergang*, 5th ed. (Zeven: Forschungsfragen unserer Zeit, 1972).

15 H. Reinerth, *Pfahlbauten am Bodensee* (Augsburg: Filser, 1922), 14th ed. (Überlingen am Bodensee: Feyel, 1986); idem, *Pfahlbauten Unteruhldingen am Bodensee um 2200 und 1100 v. d. Ztr*, 14th ed. (Überlingen am Bodensee: Feyel, 1957); *Vorzeit am Bodensee* 1–10 (Überlingen am Bodensee: Feyel, 1952–62); *Vorzeit* 11–36 (Singen am Hohentwiel: Hegau, 1963–87); Bollmus, "Das 'Amt Rosenberg', das 'Ahnenerbe' und die Prähistoriker," 32–35; G. Schöbel, "Hans Reinerth," in A. Leube (ed.), *Prähistorie und Nationalsozialismus* (Heidelberg: Synchron, 2002), 321–96.

16 Gloege, 482; W.G. Haverbeck, *Das Ziel der Technik* (Olten: Walter, 1965); idem, *Die andere Schöpfung* (Stuttgart: Urahhaus, 1978); idem, *Rudolf Steiner* (Munich: Langen–Müller, 1989); F.-W. Haack, *Wotans Wiederkehr* (Munich: Claudius, 1981), 170–76; von Schnurbein, *Religion als Kulturkritik*, 63–79, 253–57; J. Biehl and P. Staudenmaier, *Ecofascism* (Edinburgh: AK Press, 1995); Ferch, 39ff.

17 Hasselt, 311–12.

18 Kater, *Ahnenerbe*, 187.

19 Paul, "Fünfzig Jahre."

20 Krause with Jankuhn, *Die Runeninschriften im älteren Futhark*; H. Jankuhn, *Haithabu*, 8th ed. (Neumünster: Wachholtz, 1986), 78; Steuer, art. cit.; Pringle, 311–13.

21 Hunger, 59–60.

22 Ibid., 60–61, n. 67.

23 H. Arntz, *Tatsachen über Deutschland* (Wiesbaden: Informations- und Presseamt der BRD, 1957); idem, *Deutschland heute* (Wiesbaden: Informations- und Presseamt der BRD, 1959).

24 Assion, 220, 243–44 [= Dow & Lixfeld (eds.), 112, 129–30].

25 E. Fehrle, *Sagen aus Deutschland* (Vienna: Ueberreuter, 1952); idem, *Feste und Volksbräuche im Jahreslauf europäischer Völker* (Kassel: Hinnenthal, 1955).

26 Lang and von Schenk (eds.), 179.

27 Kater, *Ahnenerbe*, 275ff.; Lerchenmüller and Simon, *Maskenwechsel*, 141, 255–57, 261–64; Pringle, 313–15.

28 W. Wüst, "Goten in Indien?," in F. Altheim, *Geschichte der Hunnen* 3 (Berlin: De Gruyter, 1961), 141–89 [= *AfdA* 73 (1961), 45–74]; idem, review of A. Kammenhuber, *Die Arier in vorderen Orient*, *Die Sprache* 20 (1974), 136–63.

29 F. Altheim, "Runenforschung und die Val Camonica," *La Nouvelle Clio* 1–2 (1949–50): 166–85; idem, *Geschichte der lateinischen Sprache* (Frankfurt

a.M.: Klostermann, 1951); idem, *Aus Spätantike und Christentum* (Tübingen: Niemeyer, 1951); P. MacCana, *Celtic Mythology* (Feltham: Hamlyn, 1970), 54–55.

30 R. Stiehl and H.E. Stier, *Beiträge zur Alten Geschichte und deren Nachleben*, 2 vols., Berlin: De Gruyter, 1969–70; Pringle, 304–5.

31 Heusler/Ranisch 24.1.37, no. 189 in Düwel and Beck (eds.), 613.

32 H. Birkhan and O. Gschwantler (eds.), *Festschrift für Otto Höfler* (Vienna: Notring, 1967); H. Birkhan (ed.), *Festgabe für Otto Höfler* (Vienna: Universität-Verlag-Buchhandel, 1976).

CONCLUSION:

The Secret Garden

It is indeed a desirable thing to be well descended,
but the glory belongs to our ancestors
attributed to Plutarch

Two short years after the fall of Berlin an exchange of correspondence was published in the *Göttinger Universitäts-Zeitung (Göttingen University News)* between the Swiss theologian Karl Barth and its editor Erich von Holst, a senior zoologist. In it Barth recounted his first-hand experience of academic life in prewar Germany and lamented the state of denial still prevalent in the German university system at the time. Roy Pascal, who had been in a delegation of British university teachers to the occupied British sector, published Barth's comments in *German Life and Letters*, remarking that they were representative of what the delegation to the universities in their sector had also found:[1]

Between 1921 and 1933 I found that the professors I got to know socially, or met in common rooms or at meetings of the senate and elsewhere, were, with few exceptions, fully occupied with the then fashionable struggle against Versailles and the poor Weimar Republic. They were far from giving the latter a fair chance, and I can still only call their attitude sabotage. Not only did they offer no resistance to the political nonsense to which large numbers of students of the period used to devote themselves, but rather bestowed on it their paternal benevolence and sometimes their direct encouragement... Pray where were your eyes, dear colleague, if you today assert you have never seen that type of professor?

Then you saw what happened in 1933 ... You saw how, with a few honourable exceptions, they all changed their colours; they readjusted themselves and began to pipe loudly or softly, as the case may be, their modulation of the latest tune. What somersaults were then to be seen! What interpretations and re-interpretations were to be heard! ... I had always considered this catastrophe of the spirit to be an obvious consequence of the German-nationalist (*deutschnational*) attitude which had

not been dropped in 1918, but on the contrary had won more devoted
adherents than before ...

And today? Today I note that no one admits to having had anything
to do with this ... deep down—in those depths from which the National-
Socialist evil arose—they remain the same, having learnt nothing and forgotten nothing, and continue to be able to combine the quality of being
very decent with the quality of being very reactionary.

The editor, von Holst, replied, attempted to explain away Barth's criticisms and recounted the experience of a friend, now in internment because of his SA and Party membership:[2]

> He was one of the many who joined the party out of pure idealism in the
> years around 1933, i.e. at the time when the "movement" still contained
> valuable, productive forces ... Afterwards he became embittered by what
> he saw and did endless good by sheltering persecuted people (at the risk
> of his own life) and by keeping his own work strictly clear of any taint of
> Nazi ideology (as indeed only a party member was able to do).

Von Holst seemed surprised that Barth thought that the Weimar Republic had any good in it and continued to attempt to explain away
any blame that might be thought to be attached to his generation of
academics. Pascal commented that the British delegation had heard
similar pleadings from other academics in the British sector. Von Holst
claimed that most of his colleagues had buried themselves in their work
and had remained apolitical. Barth would have none of this.[3]

> It was so in 1933, when members of the German universities were able to
> interpret National Socialism with such consummate skill, such profundity
> and such idealism, and, as a result of all these excellent interpretations,
> most certainly furthered the cause of National Socialism.
>
> A man can never educate German students to become "free men" if
> he can today, in 1947, look back to 1918 and ruminate over the German
> defeat and Versailles, instead of seeing that the German people were then
> for the first time given the opportunity of shaping their own future among
> the other nations as a free people.

Since the nineteenth century German academics had come to see
themselves as the guarantors of German *Kultur*. As Ringer has argued,

by the dawn of the new century they had built themselves up as a new elite.[4] Although in the time of the Grimms German scholars had represented the liberal aspirations of the nation, by the early twentieth century they had become part of a new reactionary elite. This elite by its nature was resistant to change and like other sections of the German mandarin class was antipathetic to the Weimar Republic. The reactionary nature of German academia was revealed both in the sham "un-political" stance claimed by the majority of scholars in the 1920s (which in fact meant "anti-parliamentary politics," or rather "anti-democracy") and in the veritable self-coordination (*Gleichschaltung*) of the universities in 1933.[5] The academies were already full of German-Nationalist Hagens well before the brown-shirted Huns first appeared in their halls.

In the example of the Germanists, the most extreme of their colleagues, the German-Nationalist attitude was revealed by an acceptance of *völkisch* thought in their work. For some Germanists this acceptance seems at first glance no more than an occasional flourish, pandering to the realities of the times. But the acceptance of *völkisch* approaches to the study of antiquity ran much deeper and more pervasively in Old Germanic studies than it did in other disciplines. Barth witnessed mental acrobatics first in 1933, but it is clear they have a much longer pedigree in academic Germanic studies.

In 1936, Plaßmann wrote of the need to establish "the correct relationship between *völkisch* will and exact method."[6] This Nazi Germanism was the most developed form of the *völkisch* antiquarianism that had its seeds in the nineteenth century. But it did not have its immediate origin in the nationalist distortions of the Grimms or the spirit of Herder and Humboldt as Plaßmann seemed to think. It had its origin instead in the new post-empirical thought of Chamberlain and Wilser who themselves garnered their wisdom from the *völkisch* literary tradition of men such as Lagarde and Wagner. Klaus von See, a noted postwar critic of *völkisch* Nordicism, links the new Germanic ideology of the interwar period to events after 1918 (much as did Höfler in 1943), but it clearly had a longer pedigree than that.[7] This post-empirical tradition inspired Rosenberg and many other *völkisch* thinkers who are dismissed as half-read literati today. Similarly, Chamberlain and Wilser were at first held at arms length from the academic establishment. But, as we have seen, *völkisch* post-empiricism gradually came to influence the academic tradition and finally to conquer it. A line of scholars from

Kossinna and the Muchs and through to the more opportunist academics of the 1930s had encouraged and cultivated a radical nationalist academic antiquarianism. By 1944, a Germanist like Krause could
attack the extreme dilettantism of List and even Wirth, but still incorporate more respectable *völkisch* Germanism within his work without
qualms. This process of influence and ultimately arrogation is clearest
in the development of *Sinnbildforschung* as it came to be established as
a proper academic discipline in the late 1930s.

Over the course of the nineteenth century, Old Germanic studies
had been strongly influenced by the discourses of German nationalism.
In fact for some thinkers they had become central to it. Some of the
theories that were formed in light of this nationalist context, such as
the Humboldtian approach to language, have survived in respectable
academic discourse to the present day. Some, such as the notion of
the "*mirage oriental*," have dropped out of use altogether, while others
still, such as Aryanism, have mostly receded only into the background.
In the early decades of the twentieth century, new similarly nationalist discourses arose, ones which this time were more clearly *völkisch* in
their formulation or employment. The cultural concept of Germanicness and the *Wörter und Sachen* manifesto were clearly conceived in
pan-Germanistic and renewalistic terms, and soon became wedded to
the growing *völkisch* antiquarian project. The first *völkisch* antiquarians
such as Wilser were easily recognized and dismissed as such. But as
critics such as Feist were silenced as the Weimar Republic lurched towards oblivion, a new discourse arose that rescued the more respectable *völkisch* approach to antiquity. In archeological circles it was the
figure of Kossinna that the new *völkisch* academia grew up around most
patently. His journal *Mannus* became an organ for the dissemination of
increasingly radical prehistorical scholarship. Heusler and his Germanicness played a similar role, as a new generation of philologists became
ever more adventurous in their attempt to rescue the Germanic spirit
apparently surrendered in the face of modernity. The Much school
with its *völkisch* continuities and cavalier regard for empirical logic was
the most radical form of *völkisch* philology, but its leading exponent
Höfler was not alone in his Germanist fanaticism. The linguistic philologists had their Germanomaniacs among them at the time too and in
the figures of Trier and Weisgerber had even managed to wed *völkisch*
philological content to a framework of linguistic structuralism. *Völkisch*

antiquarianism, like National Socialism, was very anti-modern and culturally pessimistic but also very modern and renewalistically optimistic at one and the same time.

It was in this atmosphere of growing *völkisch* academic Germanomania that Wirth's *Sinnbildforschung* appeared. Decried at the time by many of his erstwhile colleagues as fantastic, he was, nevertheless, still supported by others, Neckel and Fehrle perhaps being the most notable among the Germanist community proper. The acceptance of Wirth's scholarship by Himmler led in due course to the establishment of the SS-Ahnenerbe. But it was at first an organization chiefly for amateurs who were so excited by Wirth's *Emergence* and the new *völkisch* antiquarianism of Kossinna and Neckel. A whole body of popular ideographic thought developed and the ideographs of Wirth and Weigel inaugurated an ideographic mania similar to the hallmark frenzy of the late nineteenth century. Slowly but surely, however, university academics began to be drawn into the SS. The archeologists were first, in a reflection of the earlier surrender of Kossinna to the *völkisch* half-light. But then philologists were inducted too. By the late 1930s, Germanists like Krause were moving in SS circles and soon they were claimed by the radical spirit of *völkisch* Germanism that had produced *Sinnbildforschung*. The entomologists and physiologists were not far behind and they transformed an organization established to promote *völkisch* Germanism into an institute of inhumanity. The SS-Ahnenerbe was born as an expression of radical Germanic antiquarianism and became an organ not just for propaganda, but also surveillance, torture and plunder. Few of the Germanists applied for access to concentration camps, but as the intellectual accomplices to the crimes of Nazism most managed to debase themselves in other ways instead.

The runomania and swastika mysticism of the day was expressed in all sorts of antiquarian endeavor: from the abjectly obscurantist, to the empiricist, the two extremes separated by a *völkisch* middle ground. Other forms of Germanic antiquarian studies had followed suit: in archeology with the settlement method, in philology and linguistics with its Germanicness and neo-Humboldtian wholeness, and in *Volkskunde* with the rootedness of the *völkisch* continuities. By the early 1940s, the *völkisch* middle ground had often swallowed up the empiricist, a development most clearly represented by the academic acceptance of ideographic studies. Other academics in Germanistic fields—the archeologists, the literary philologists, the linguists and the ethnographical philologists cum folklorists—had made their peace with *völkisch* Germanism at different times and in different ways. But the most revealing of all the cases of surrender to *völkisch* Germanism is that of the acceptance of *Sinnbildforschung*, which had as its seminal text the decidedly non-empirical studies of Herman Wirth, an activist of the mind whose main claim to be a serious scholar by the late 1920s was that he thought he understood the history of the symbols which had come to be the emblems of the *völkisch* movement.

Old Germanic studies underwent a revolution during the Wilhelmine autumn and the Weimar spring that followed. This revolution was influenced from its inception by *völkisch* Germanism. The intrusion of *völkisch* thought into Germanic antiquarian studies at the time transformed it and, with the *völkisch* revolution of 1933, radicalized Old Germanic studies further still. For some, evidently, Germanic antiquarian studies became the key to an empire of the Germanic spirit, to a hidden garden of *völkisch* fantasy. Even those who shied away from the racial imperative that was rife in the scholarship of the most radical Germanists could succumb to the lure of this illusory empire of Germanicness. The effort to rescue the Germanicness of the past, or in fact to invent a fantastic Old Germanic delusion, seems to represent a positive, creative foil to the otherwise overwhelmingly destructive nature of German fascism. Rosenberg recognized that Germanic antiquarian study could be enrolled as part of his project to achieve a sophisticated and mature *völkisch* Weltanschauung he hoped to use in schooling new generations of Nazis. A proper understanding of Germanicness, and especially its tales and symbols, would serve as the core of an elaborated *völkisch* ideology that had long accepted that the vision of the distant Germanic past legitimized its racism and imperialism. Yet no matter how deeply they had fallen under the spell of *völkisch* Germanism, the Krauses of the day could still see what was just around the corner for the academic community if the Nazis had won the war.

In the face of the prospect of exile, some of the German literati who remained in the Reich claimed that they reacted to the creation of the *völkisch* tyranny by entering an inner emigration (*innere Emigration*).[8] Whatever we make of this defense against the criticisms of those who did go physically into exile, the academic Germanists under the dictatorship seem to have responded in a similar, though converse manner. From among the ranks of the antiquarian Germanists in the universities, only Konstantin Reichardt followed Thomas Mann into exile. His solitary antiquarian fellow to depart the fatherland was the schoolmaster Sigmund Feist, although as the only Jewish antiquarian Germanist of note still in the country, Feist's departure in 1939 was a matter of necessity rather than conscience. At the end of their sketch of the activities of Germanists under Nazism Joachim Lerchenmüller and Gerd Simon seek to show some balance by including Germanists who resisted Nazism.[9] Sadly, they were only able to list intellectuals from other fields who strayed into Germanistic discourse—an especially telling testimony to the politicized state of Germanic studies at the time, given that rates of dismissal and (physical) emigration were so high in most other academic fields. German *Volkskunde* has its martyrs who were imprisoned or even executed for political resistance and there was similarly a handful of Germanists like the conservative Von der Leyen whose careers were cut short in the 1930s for being outspokenly critical of the perversion of their discipline. But these cases are vanishingly small if we compare them to the losses of about 15 percent of academic staff in other disciplines.[10] Feist's daughter, who carved out an academic career for herself after her family escaped to the U.S. (Feist died in Denmark shortly before the rest of his family were spirited off to Sweden), comments that it was well known how political Germanists were in general in the late 1920s.[11] When they were not actively collaborating with the regime (and even for many such as Krause who were), for the overwhelming majority of academic antiquarian Germanists the only emigration they made was into the secret garden of *völkisch* delights, an emigration from the empirical tradition of scholarship into a radical world of reactionary post-empirical renewalistic delusion.

The collective emigration of Germanistic scholars from the reserved heights of the ivory towers into the caverns and cellars of a world of *völkisch* delirium began with the appearance of the new paradigms—*ex Septentrione lux*, Germanicness and the holistic linguistic cult of the German mother tongue. There were precursors, German voices in the desert such as Kossinna, Wilser and their contemporaries the Muchs in Austria, whose "Teuton-books" proved significant in stoking *völkisch* sentiment in the broader community. But the collective decline and prostitution of the discipline to political concerns began, rather, at the

time it was to be transformed so thoroughly by the philologist followers
of Heusler, Much, Meringer and Helm. The level of Party membership among academic Germanists might not be so remarkable given
the generally high levels among German and Austrian civil servants in
general. But the number of "old fighters" and early supporters of Nazi-
allied groups (many of whom already held senior positions within the
discipline before 1933) is extraordinary. Clearly, right-wing students
were attracted to Germanistic study and hence younger Germanists
were the most likely of their fellows at the universities to become Nazi
idealists. But the number and the influence of those who indulged in
völkisch Germanism in the 1920s points to the infiltration of not just
conservative, but radical reactionary and indeed fascist thought into
senior Austrian and German academic circles well before the time it
seemed to have become mandatory to be a *völkisch* Germanist. The
lack of a concerted resistance to the new *völkisch* discourse that rapidly became ubiquitous in Germanic philology, in contrast to, say, the
attacks on the settlement method in archeology, is especially telling.
Archeologists have written of the "Faustian bargain" entered into by
figures such as Jankuhn and a similar sentiment is displayed in the Romanist Leo Spitzer's description of an academic "collaboration with
Baal."[12] The pact was often much less personal in Germanic philology
and with the strange emigration undertaken by many of its proponents
became as much Gylfi's beguiling as it was an understanding made
with Mephistopheles. By the late 1920s most Germanistic scholars in
Austria and Germany were already supporters of the radical forces of
reaction. Over the course of the 1920s and into the 30s, practitioners
of Old Germanic studies in Germany and Austria went enthusiastically
and *en masse* into the service of the *völkisch* revolution and two generations of Germanistic scholars became intellectual accessories to the
crimes of National Socialism.

Sinnbildforschung began in studies of the swastika, but is itself symbolic more generally of the surrender of the scholars of Germanic antiquity to the challenge mounted by *völkisch* idealists. The dumb ideography of the ancient Germanic past proved to be a canvas upon which
völkisch beliefs could be mapped. This was also the case for many other
aspects of Old Germanic studies. But it was in *Sinnbildforschung*, the
most radical form of Germanic antiquarian discourse, that this process
is most palpable. A tenet or a belief that reflected a prevailing ideol-

ogy or Weltanschauung lay at the core of ideographic studies. It looked for a golden age of Germanicness and aimed to reveal and to cultivate awareness of the continuing legacy of this superlative ancient Germanic spirit. Its practitioners recognized that a complementary project had become manifest at the political level in the Nazi project to reform German society, to re-awaken Germans to past Germanic glories and to re-energize them and make them heroes again. The case of *Sinnbildforschung* shows that the *völkisch* ideal could shape the thinking of those who were immersed in it in a manner now mostly opaque to those who stand outside it. The *völkisch* ideal may seem only worthy of scorn in the face of the complexity of Marxism or liberal positivism, but like other forms of right-wing thought it could command as powerful a grip on its adherents nonetheless. The effects of social dislocation and economic collapse are often stressed as the principal explanations for the rise of National Socialism and the acceptance of its ideals is usually credited to propaganda or baseness. The hold that *völkisch* thought had on German intellectuals in the late 1920s and onwards into the years of the dictatorship, however, has not been well explained by those who stress factors external to the *völkisch* tradition such as political disenchantment and economic misery. Ideology is the key to a proper explanation of the behavior of academic Germanists under National Socialism and it is perhaps only those scholars who treat ideology as the preserve of progressive expressions in political thought who cannot accept its fundamental role in the attraction of the German people to Nazism. Only the acceptance of the ideals of *völkisch* thinking explains the rise and ultimate academic acceptance of *Sinnbildforschung*. The gradual permeation of society with the new radical nationalist thought led German scholars increasingly to accept a *völkisch* viewpoint as normal and natural, and in the end allowed them to recast their scholarship in a deliberated, sophistic *völkisch* guise. No better example of the power of this Weltanschauung cum ideology exists than in the world of *Sinnbildforschung*; a world of ancient Germanic and German utopia where the essential mores of that past life were communicated to the present by those who could read their runes; a world where research fed fantasy and fantasy fed research and some of the brightest minds of the country lost their way in the woods of the ancestral Germanic past.

NOTES

1 K. Barth/E. von Holst, *Göttinger Universitäts-Zeitung* 4.7.47, apud R. Pascal, "A Controversy in the German Universities," *German Life and Letters* NS 1 (1947–48): 142; cf. W. Abendroth, "Die deutschen Professoren und die Weimarer Republik," in J. Tröger (ed.), *Hochschule und Wissenschaft im Dritten Reich* (Frankfurt a.M.: Campus, 1984), 11–25.

2 E. von Holst/Barth, 6.6.47, apud Pascal, 144–45.

3 Barth/von Holst, 23.6.47, apud Pascal, 148 & 149.

4 Ringer, *Decline*.

5 W. Abendroth, "Das Unpolitische als Wesensmerkmal der deutschen Universität," in *Nationalsozialismus und die deutsche Universität* (Berlin: De Gruyter, 1966), 189–223; idem, "Die deutschen Professoren," 11–25; B. W. Reimann, "Die 'Selbst-Gleichschaltung' der Universitäten 1933," in J. Tröger (ed.), *Hochschule und Wissenschaft im Dritten Reich* (Frankfurt a.M.: Campus, 1984), 38–52.

6 J.O. Plaßmann, "'Ir sult sprechen willekommen,'" *Germanien* 8 (1936): 161; cf. idem, "Völkisches Wollen und exaktes Forschen," *Germanien* 8 (1936): 130–33.

7 Von See, *Deutsche Germanen-Ideologie*, 73ff.

8 R. Schnell, *Literarisch Innere Emigration 1933–45* (Stuttgart: Metzler, 1976); idem, "Innere Emigration," in W. Killy (ed.), *Literatur Lexikon* XIII (Gütersloh: Bertelsmann, 1992), 436–38.

9 Lerchenmüller and Simon, *Im Vorfeld*, 85ff.

10 Hutton, 59; Ringer, "Sociography," 259, 279; H.A. Strauss, "Wissenschaftler in der Emigration," in J. Tröger (ed.), *Hochschule und Wissenschaft im Dritten Reich* (Frankfurt a.M.: Campus, 1984), 54–55.

11 E. Feist Hirsch, "Mein Vater Sigmund Feist," in H.A. Strauss and K.A. Grossmann (eds.), *Gegenwart im Rückblick* (Heidelberg: Stiehm, 1970), 272.

12 L. Spitzer/H. Friedrich 8.10.46 in G.O. Oexle, "'Zusammenarbeit mit Baal,'" *Historische Anthropologie* 8 (2000): 1; Arnold and Hausmann, "Archaeology in Nazi Germany."

Abbreviations

AfdA	*Anzeiger für deutsches Altert(h)um und deutsche Lit(t)eratur* (published as a supplement to the *ZfdA*).
BDM	Bund Deutscher Mädel. The girls section of the Hitler Youth.
Correspondenz-Blatt	*Correspondenz-Blatt (Korrespondenz-Blatt) der deutschen Gesellschaft für Anthropologie, Ethnologie und Urgeschichte.*
DFG	Deutsche Forschungsgemeinschaft. The German national research council.
DLZ	*Deutsche Literaturzeitung.*
FRG	Federal Republic of Germany.
GGA	*Göttingische gelehrte Anzeigen.*
GRM	*Germanisch-Romanische Monatsschrift.*
GWE	Germanischer Wissenschafteinsatz. The branch of the Ahnenerbe responsible for matters in countries under German occupation.
Jahresbericht	*Jahresbericht über die Erscheinung auf dem Gebiete der germanischen Philologie.*
KdF	Kraft durch Freude. The leisure activities organization of the Nazi Party.
Korrespondenzblatt	see *Correspondenz-Blatt.*
KZ	*Zeitschrift für vergleichende Sprachforschung (auf dem Gebiete der indogermanischen Sprachen)* (founded by Adalbert Kuhn).

NAWG	*Nachrichten (von) der Akademie der Wissenschaften in Göttingen.*
PBB	*Beiträge zur Geschichte der deutschen Sprache und Literatur* (founded by Hermann Paul and Wilhelm Braune).
PO	Politische Organisation. The regular section of the Nazi Party.
RGK	Römisch-Germanische Kommission. A branch of the German Archeological Institute that concentrates on Roman remains.
RuSHA	Rasse- und Siedlungshauptamt. The part of the SS responsible for cultural matters.
SA	Sturmabteilung. The paramilitary wing of the Nazi Party.
SD	Sicherheitsdienst. The security apparatus of the SS.
SS	Schutzstaffel. Hitler's bodyguard, led by Himmler.
WEL	*Welteislehre.*
ZfdA	*Zeitschrift für deutsches Altert(h)um (und deutsche Lit(t)eratur).*
ZfdPh	*Zeitschrift für deutsche Philologie.*

Picture Credits

Figure 1. J. Magnus, *Historia ... de omnibus Gothorum Suenumque regibus* (1554).

Figure 2. H. Arntz and H. Zeiss, *Die einheimischen Runendenkmäler des Festlandes*, (1939).

Figure 3. The author.

Figure 4. The author.

Figure 5. *Der Schulungsbrief* 2/3 (1935).

Figure 6. *Der Schulungsbrief* 2 (1935), Anglified digitally by the author.

Figure 7. *Revue archéologique* 4ième serie 13 (1909).

Figure 8. *Mannus* 23 (1931).

Figure 9. *Heimdall* 5 (1900).

Figure 10. R. Ströbel, *Führer durch die Ausstellung 'Lebendige Vorzeit' im Lichthof der Technischen Hochschule Berlin-Charlottenburg, vom 15. Febr bis 15. April 1937* (1937).

Figure 11. *Germanen-Erbe* 1 (1936).

Figure 12. H. Wirth, *Der Aufgang der Menschheit* (1928).

Figure 13. H. Wirth, *Der Aufgang der Menschheit* (1928).

Figure 14. *Das Schwarze Korps* 21 Aug 1935.

Figure 15. J.O. Ottema (ed.), *The Oera Linda Book*, trans. W.R. Sandbach (1876).

Figure 16. E. Fuhrmann, *Schwedische Felsbilder von Göteborg bis Strömstad* (1919).

Figure 17. J. Andrée, *Die Externsteine* (1936).

Figure 18. *Germanien* 8 (1936).

Figure 19. R. Bünte (ed.), *Wilhelm Teudt im Kampf um Germanenehre* (1940).

Figure 20. W. Wüst, *Indogermanisches Bekenntnis* (1942).

Figure 21. *Germanien* 6 (1934).

Figure 22. *SS-Leitheft* 3/8 (1937).

Figure 23. *Germanien* 7 (1935).

Figure 24. *Odal* 3/3 (1933).

Figure 25. K.T. Weigel, *Sinnbilder in der fränkischen Landschaft* (1938).

Figure 26. *Germanien* 5 (1933).

Figure 27. *Germanien* 8 (1936), Anglified digitally by the author.

Figure 28. *Germanien* 8 (1936).

Figure 29. *Germanien* 9 (1937).

Bibliography

UNPUBLISHED SOURCES:

BA: Bundesarchiv Berlin-Lichterfelde (incorporating the former Berlin Document Center).

AE: Das Ahnenerbe (NS 21).
OPG: Oberstes Parteigericht der NSDAP (NS 36).
PK: Partei-Kanzlerei (NS 6).
REM: Reichsministerium für Wissenschaft, Erziehung und Volksbildung (R 4901).
RKK: Reichskulturkammer (R 5005).

Reichardt papers, Yale University Library, New Haven, Conn.

LITERATURE:

Abendroth, Wolfgang, 'Das Unpolitische als Wesensmerkmal der deutschen Universität,' in *Nationalsozialismus und die deutsche Universität (Universitätstage 1966: Veröffentlichung der Freien Universität Berlin)* (Berlin: De Gruyter, 1966), 189–223.
———— 'Die deutschen Professoren und die Weimarer Republik,' in Jörg Tröger (ed.), *Hochschule und Wissenschaft im Dritten Reich* (Frankfurt a.M.: Campus, 1984), 11–25.
Åberg, Nils, 'Herman Wirth: En germansk kulturprofet,' *Fornvännen* 28 (1933): 246–47.
Ackermann, Joseph, *Heinrich Himmler als Ideologe* (Göttingen: Musterschmidt, 1970).
Adorno, Theodor W., *In Search of Wagner*, trans. Rodney Livingstone (London: NLB, 1981).
Ahlzweig, Claus, 'Die deutsche Nation und ihre Muttersprache,' in Konrad Ehlich (ed.), *Sprache im Faschismus*, Suhrkamp-Taschenbuch Wissenschaft 760 (Frankfurt a.M.: Suhrkamp, 1989), 35–57.
Allen, Arthur, 'Open Secret. A German Academic Hides His Past—In Plain Sight,' *Lingua Franca* March/April (1996): 28–41.

Almgren, Birgitte, *Germanistik und Nationalsozialismus: Affirmation, Konflikt und Protest. Traditionsfelder und zeitgebundene Wertung in Sprach- und Literatur wissenschaft am Beispiel der Germanisch-Romanischen Monatsschrift 1929–1943*, Acta Universitatis Upsaliensis. Studia Germanistica Upsaliensia 36 (Uppsala: Almqvist & Wiksell, 1997).

Almgren, Oscar, *Hällristningar och kultbruch: Bidrag till belysning av de nordiska bronsålders-ristningarnas innebörd*, Kungliga Vitterhets Historie och Antikvitets Akademiens handlingar 35 (Stockholm: Wahlström & Widstand, 1927) [= *Nordische Felsbilder als religiöse Urkunden*, rev. ed., trans. Sigrid Vrancken (Frankfurt a.M.: Diesterweg, 1934)].

Altenbockum, Jasper von, *Wilhelm Heinrich Riehl 1823–1897: Sozialwissenschaft zwischen Kulturgeschichte und Ethnographie*, Münster historische Forschungen 6 (Cologne: Böhlau, 1994).

Altheim, Franz, *Römische Religionsgeschichte*, 2 vols. (Berlin: De Gruyter, 1931–33) [2nd ed., 1956 = *A History of Roman Religion*, trans. Harold Mattingly (London: Methuen, 1938) = *La Religion romaine antique*, trans. H.E. del Medico, Bibliothèque historique (Paris: Payot, 1955)].

——— 'Runen als Schildzeichen,' *Klio* 31 (1938): 51–59.

——— 'Die Felsbilder der Val Camonica und die altitalischen Kultur,' in *Bericht über den VI. Internationalen Kongreß für Archäologie, Berlin 21–26 Aug. 1939* (Berlin: De Gruyter, 1940), 442–43.

——— *Italien und Rom*, 2 vols. (Amsterdam: Pantheon, 1941).

——— 'Runenforschung und die Val Camonica,' *La Nouvelle Clio* 1–2 (1949–50): 166–85.

——— *Geschichte der lateinischen Sprache* (Frankfurt a.M.: Klostermann, 1951).

——— *Aus Spätantike und Christentum* (Tübingen: Niemeyer, 1951).

Altheim, Franz and Erika Trautmann(-Nehring), 'Nordische und italische Felsbildkunst,' *Die Welt als Geschichte* 3 (1937): 83–118.

——— 'Neue Felsbilder aus der Val Camonica: Die Sonne in Kult und Mythos,' *Wörter und Sachen* 19, NF 1 (1938): 12–45.

——— 'Keltische Felsbilder der Val Camonica,' *Mitteilungen des Deutschen Archäologischen Instituts, Römische Abteilung* 54 (1939): 1–13.

——— 'Gründsatzliches zur Runen- und Felsbildforschung,' *Germanien* 11, NF 1 (1939): 449–56.

——— *Vom Ursprung der Runen*, Deutsches Ahnenerbe Reihe B. Arbeiten zur Germanenkunde [2] 3 (Frankfurt a.M.: Klostermann, 1939).

——— 'Die Elchrune,' *Germanien* 13, NF 3 (1941): 22–30.

——— 'Die älteste Darstellung des Woden?,' *Germanien* 14, NF 4 (1942): 369–82.

——— *Kimbern und Runen: Untersuchungen zur Ursprungsfrage der Runen*, Germanien Beiheft 1, 2nd ed. (Berlin: Ahnenerbe, 1942).

Andree, Christoph, *Rudolf Virchow als Prähistoriker* (Cologne: Böhlau, 1976).

——— *Rudolf Virchow: Leben und Ethos eines grossen Arztes* (Munich: Langen Müller, 2002).

Andree, Julius, *Die Externsteine: Eine germanische Kultstätte* (Münster i.W.: Coppenrath, 1936).

Anon., [biographical sketch of Wirth], *Germanien* 1 (1929/30): 40.

Anon., 'Das Fest des Lichtes' and 'Kunde von Weihnachtsbaum,' *SS-Leitheft* 3/8 (1937): 36–45.

Anon., 'Lebendiges Brauchtum,' *Volkstum und Heimat* 48 (1939): 283–89.

Anon., 'Der Runenspeer von Kowel. Der Siedler im Osten ist kein "Kolonist,"' *SS-Leitheft* 7/2 (1941): 6–10.

Anon., 'Schenkel der Göttlichen,' *Der Spiegel* 34/40, 29 Sept. 1980.

Anon., 'Sonnenwende,' *Heimdall* 13, 14 Apr. 1899, 95.

Anon., 'Tysk professor blir ny lektor vid Högskolan,' *Göteborgs Handels* 23 Dec., 1937.

Anon., 'Und wieder reiten die Goten... Unser Kampf im Osten—unsere Pflicht vor Geschichte und Reich,' *SS-Leitheft* 7/9 (1941): 1–2.

Arbois de Jubainville, [Mary-]Henry d', 'Unité primitive des Italo-celtes, relations de l'empire celtique avec les Germains antérieurement au second siècle avant notre ère,' *Comptes rendus des séances de l'Académie des Inscriptions et Belles-Lettres* 13 (1885): 316–25 [= *Celtes et Germains, étude grammatical* (Paris: Imprimérie National, 1886)].

———— 'Les témoignages linguistique de la civilisation commune aux Celtes et aux Germains pendant le Ve et le IVe siècle avant J.-C.,' *Revue archéologique* 17 (1891): 187–213.

———— 'Recherches sur la plus ancienne histoire des Teutons,' *Revue celtique* 12 (1891): 1–19.

Arnold, Bettina, 'The Past as Propaganda—Totalitarian Archaelogy in Nazi Germany,' *Antiquity* 64 (1990): 464–78.

Arnold, Bettina, and Henning Hausmann, 'Archaeology in Nazi Germany: The Legacy of the Faustian Bargain,' in Philip L. Kohl and Clare Fawcett (eds.), *Nationalism, Politics and Practice of Archaeology* (Cambridge: Cambridge University Press, 1995), 70–81.

Arntz, Helmut, *Sprachliche Beziehungen zwischen Arisch und Balto-Slawisch,* [dissertation] (Heidelberg: Winter, 1933).

———— *Handbuch der Runenkunde*, Sammlung kurzer Grammatiker germanischer Dialekte, B: Erganzungsreihe 3 (Halle a.S.: Niemeyer, 1935); 2nd ed., 1944 [= Faksimile-Edition 14 (Horn: Weeke, 1993)].

———— 'Das Ogam,' *Beiträge zur Geschichte der deutschen Sprache und Literatur* 59 (1935): 321–413 [= monograph, Halle a.S.: Niemeyer, 1935].

———— (ed.), *Germanen und Indogermanen; Volkstum, Heimat, Kultur: Festschrift für Herman Hirt*, 2 vols. (Heidelberg: Winter, 1936).

———— *Die Runen*, Internationale Gesellschaft für Schrift- und Buchkunde. Weltschriften-Atlas 1 (Tübingen: Schramm, 1938).

———— 'Nordeuropa. A. Vermutete frühe Schriftsysteme. Symbolische Zeichen. B. Die germanischen Runen. C. Das altirische Ogom,' in Walter Otto (ed.), *Handbuch der Archäologie* I (Munich: Beck, 1939), 329–56.

———— 'Vom Weltbild der Felsritzer und vom Weltbild Herman Wirths [review of Max Raschdorff, *Nordische Sinnzeichen*],' *Runenberichte* 1 (1941): 91–102.

———— 'Hausmarken—Sippensymbole [review of Karl Konrad Ruppel, *Die Hausmarke*],' *Runenberichte* 1 (1941): 123–26.

———— 'Die Runen: Urschrift der Menschheit?,' *Zeitschrift für deutsche Philologie* 67 (1942): 121–36.

———— review of Wolfgang Krause, *Was man im Runen ritzte*, 2nd ed., *Beiblatt zur Anglia* 54/55 (1943/44): 244–47.

———— *Tatsachen über Deutschland* (Wiesbaden: Informations- und Presseamt der BRD, 1957).

———— *Deutschland Heute* (Wiesbaden: Informations- und Presseamt der BRD, 1959).

Arntz, Helmut, and Hans Zeiss, *Die einheimischen Runendenkmäler des Festlandes*, Gesamtausgabe der älteren Runendenkmäler I (Leipzig: Harrassowitz, 1939).

Arviddson, Stefan, *Aryan Idols: Indo-European Mythology as Ideology and Science*, trans. Sonia Wichmann (Chicago: University of Chicago Press, 2006).

Aschheim, Steven E., *The Nietzsche Legacy in Germany 1890–1990*, Weimar and Now: German Cultural Criticism 2 (Berkeley: University of California Press, 1992).

Askeberg, Fritz, *Norden och kontinenten i gammal tid: Studier i forngermansk kulturhistoria* (Uppsala: Almqvist & Wiksells, 1944).

Aspendorf, Wilhelm, *Die Edda als Welteislehre* (Krefeld: Hons, 1933).

Assion, Peter, '"Was Mythos unseres Volkes ist": Zum Werden und Wirken des NS-Volkskundlers Eugen Fehrle,' *Zeitschrift für Volkskunde* 81 (1985): 220–44 [= James R. Dow and Hannjost Lixfeld (eds.), *The Nazification of an Academic Discipline* (Bloomington: Indiana University Press, 1994), 112–34].

Aynesley, Jeremy, *Graphic Design in Germany, 1890–1945* (London: Thames & Hudson, 2000).

Bachofen, Johan Jakob, *Das Mutterrecht* (Stuttgart: Krais & Hoffmann, 1861).

Baeumler, Alfred, *Nietzsche als Philosoph und Politiker* (Leipzig: Reclam, 1931).

———— (ed.), *Was bedeutet Herman Wirth für die Wissenschaft?* (Leipzig: Koehler & Amelang, 1932).

———— *Männerbund und Wissenschaft* (Berlin: Junker & Dünnhaupt, 1934).

Baesecke, Georg, 'Die Herkunft der Runen,' *Germanisch-Romanische Monatsschrift* 22 (1934): 413–17.

———— *Vor- und Frühgeschichte des deutschen Schrifttums* I (Halle a.S.: Niemeyer, 1940).

Ball, Kurt Herwath, *Germanische Sturmflut: Kleine Geschichte der Wikinger*, Volksdeutsche Reihe 10 (Karlsbad: Kraft, 1943).

Baumann, Eberhard, *Verzeichnis der Schriften, Manuskripte und Vorträge von Herman Felix WIRTH Roper Bosch von 1908 bis 1993 sowie der Schriften für, gegen und über die Person und das Werk von Herman Wirth von 1908 bis 1995*, Toppenstedter Reihe 13 (Toppenstedt: Uwe-Berg, 1995).

Baumann, Shaul, *Die Deutsche Glaubensbewegung und ihr Gründer Jakob Wilhelm Hauer (1881–1962)*, trans. Alma Lessing, Religionswissenschaftliche Reihe 22 (Marburg: Diagonal, 2005).

Bausinger, Hermann, 'Volksideologie und Volksforschung: Zur national-sozialistischen Volkskunde,' *Zeitschrift für Volkskunde* 61 (1965): 177–204 [= James R. Dow and Hannjost Lixfeld (eds.), *The Nazification of an Academic Discipline* (Bloomington: Indiana University Press, 1994), 11–33].

———— 'Volkskunde und Volkstumsarbeit im Nationalsozialismus,' in Helge Gerndt (ed.), *Volkskunde und Nationalsozialismus: Referate und Diskussionen einer Tagung der Deutschen Gesellschaft für Volkskunde, München, 23. bis 25. Oktober 1986*, Münchener Beiträge zur Volkskunde 7 (Munich: Münchener Vereinigung für Volkskunde, 1987), 131–41 [= James R. Dow and Hannjost Lixfeld (eds.), *The Nazification of an Academic Discipline* (Bloomington: Indiana University Press, 1994), 87–96].

Beatus (Bildius) Rhenanus, *Beati Rhenani ... Rerum Germanicarum libri tres. Adiecta est incalce Epistola ad D. Philippu(m) Puchaimeru(m), de locis Plinij per St. Aquæum attactis, ubi mendæ quædam eiusdam autoris emanculantur* (Basel: Froben, 1533).

Becher, Wilhelm, 'Volkspolitische Woche in Sachsen,' *Muttersprache* 52 (1937): 203.

Beck, Friedrich Alfred, *Der Aufgang des germanischen Weltalters* (Bochum: Feldmüller, 1944).

Beck, Heinrich (ed.), *Germanenprobleme in heutiger Sicht*, Ergänzungsbände zum Reallexikon der Germanischen Altertumskunde 1 (Berlin: De Gruyter, 1986).

———— 'Andreas Heuslers Begriff des "Altgermanischen,"' in Heinrich Beck (ed.), *Germanenprobleme in heutiger Sicht*, Ergänzungsbände zum Reallexikon der Germanischen Altertumskunde 1 (Berlin: De Gruyter, 1986), 396–412.

———— 'Andreas Heusler (1865–1940),' in Helen Damico (ed.), *Medieval Scholarship: Biographical Studies on the Formation of a Discipline; Volume 2: Literature and Philology* (New York: Garland, 1998), 283–96.

Becker, Peter Emil, *Wege ins Dritte Reich*, 2 vols. (Stuttgart: Thieme, 1988–90).

Beckering Vinckers, J., *De onechtheid van het Oera Linda Bôk aangetoond* (Haarlem: Bohn, 1876).

———— *Wie heeft het Oera Linda Boek geschreven?* (Kampen: Van Hulst, 1877).

Behagel, Otto, 'Aussenseiter—Eine Phillippika,' *Deutsche Allgemeine Zeitung*, 9 Aug., 1934.

———— 'Odal,' *Forschungen und Fortschritte* 11 (1935): 369–70.

———— 'Odal,' *Sitzungsberichte der Bayrischen Akademie der Wissenschaften, Phil.-Hist. Abt.* 1935, no. 8.

Behrenbeck, Sabine, *Der Kult um die toten Helden: Nationalsozialistische Mythen, Riten und Symbole 1923 bis 1945*, Kölner Beiträge zur Nationforschung 2 (Vierow bei Greifswald: SH-Verlag, 1996).

Bell, William, 'On the Discoveries of Runic Characters on Spears, etc.,' *Journal of the British Archaeological Association* 23 (1867): 385–87.

Bellamy, Hans S., *Moons, Myth and Man: A Reinterpretation* (London: Faber & Faber, 1936).

Berg, Leo, *Henrik Ibsen und das Germanenthum in der modernen Literatur* (Berlin: Eckstein, 1887).

Bergmann, Peter, *Nietzsche, "The Last Antipolitical German"* (Bloomington: Indiana University Press, 1987).

Bernadac, Christian, *Montségur et le graal: Le mystère Otto Rahn* (Paris: France-Empire, 1994).

Bernadotte, [Greve] Folke, *Slutet: Mina humanitära förhandlingar i Tyskland vären 1945 och deras politiska följder* (Stockholm: Norstedt & Sons, 1945).

Bernhardi, Dietrich, *Das Hakenkreuz: Seine Geschichte, Verbreitung und Bedeutung* (Leipzig: Fritsch, 1935).

Berning, Cornelia, 'Die Sprache des Nationalsozialismus,' *Zeitschrift für deutsche Wortforschung* 18 (1962): 108–18 and 180–72.

Bessel, Richard, 'The "Front" Generation and the Politics of Weimar Germany,' in Mark Roseman (ed.), *Generations in Conflict: Youth Revolt and Generation Formation in Germany, 1770–1968* (Cambridge: Cambridge University Press, 1995), 121–36

Biddiss, Michael D., *Father of Racist Ideology: The Social and Political Thought of Count Gobineau* (London: Weidenfeld & Nicholson, 1976).

Biedenkapp, Georg, *Der Nordpol als Völkerheimat. Nach den Ergebnissen der prähistorischen, etymologischen und naturwissenschaftlichen sowie ins besondere der Veda- und Avesta-Forschungen TILAKs dargestellt* (Jena: Costenoble, 1906).

Bieder, Theobald, *Das Hakenkreuz*, 2nd ed. (Leipzig: Weicher, 1934).

Biehl, Janet, and Peter Staudenmaier, *Ecofascism: Lessons from the German Experience* (Edinburgh: AK Press, 1995).

Birkhan, Helmut (ed.), *Festgabe für Otto Höfler zur 75. Geburtstag*, Philologica Germanica 3 (Vienna: Universität-Verlag-Buchhandel, 1976).

———— 'Vorwort,' in Otto Höfler, *Kleine Schriften*, ed. Helmut Birkhan (Hamburg: Buske, 1982), IX – XVI.

Birkhan, Helmut, and Otto Gschwantler (eds.), *Festschrift für Otto Höfler* (Vienna: Notring, 1967).

Blackbourn, David, *The Fontana History of Germany 1780–1918: The Long Nineteenth Century* (London: Fontana, 1997).

Blavatsky, Helena Petrovna, *The Secret Doctrine: The Synthesis of Science, Religion, and Philosophy*, 2 vols. (London: The Theosophical Publishing Company, 1888) [= *Die Geheimlehre*, trans. R. Frobe (Leipzig: Vollrath, 1900)].

Bockhorn, Olaf, 'Der Kampf um die "Ostmark": Ein Beitrag zur Geschichte der nationalsozialistischen Volkskunde in Österreich,' in Gernot Heß, Siegfried Mattl, Sebastian Meissl, Edith Saurer and Karl Stuhlpfarrer (eds.), *Willfährige Wissenschaft: Die Universität Wien 1938–1945*, Österreichische Texte zur Gesellschaftskritik 43 (Vienna: Verlag für Gesellschaftskritik, 1989), 17–38 [= James R. Dow and Hannjost Lixfeld (eds.), *The Nazification of an Academic Discipline* (Bloomington: Indiana University Press, 1994), 135–55].

———— 'Von Ritualen, Mythen und Lebenskreisen: Volkskunde im Umfeld der Universität Wien,' in Wolfgang Jacobeit, Hannjost Lixfeld and Olaf Bockhorn (eds.), *Völkische Wissenschaft: Gestalten und Tendenzen der deutschen und österreichischen Volkskunde in der ersten Hälfte des 20. Jahrhunderts* (Vienna: Böhlau, 1994), 477–526.

Bode, August, *Heilige Zeichen: Vom Stammbaum der Sinnbilder zu einer vorchristlich-germanischen Wissenschaft und zum arisch-germanischen Weltbild* (Heidelberg: Winter, 1938).

Boden, Petra, 'Universitätsgermanistik in der SBZ/DDR. Personal- und Berufungs-politik 1945–1958,' *Zeitschrift für Germanistik* NF 5 (1995): 373–83.

Boeles, P.C.J.A., *De auteur van het Oera Linda Boek* (Leeuwarden: Noord Nederlandsche Boekhandling, 1928) [= *De vrije Fries* 28 (1928): 437–71)].

Bollmus, Reinhard, *Das Amt Rosenberg und seiner Gegner: Studium zum Machtkampf im nationalsozialistischen Herrschaftssystem*, Studien zur Zeitgeschichte (Stuttgart: Deutsche Verlags-Anstalt, 1970).

————— 'Zwei Volkskunden im Dritten Reich. Überlegung eines Historikers,' in Helge Gerndt (ed.), *Volkskunde und Nationalsozialismus: Referate und Diskussionen einer Tagung der Deutschen Gesellschaft für Volkskunde, München, 23. bis 25. Oktober 1986*, Münchener Beiträge zur Volkskunde 7 (Munich: Münchener Vereinigung für Volkskunde, 1987), 49–60.

————— 'Alfred Rosenberg: National Socialism's "Chief Ideologue"?,' in Ronald Smelser and Rainer Zitelmann (eds.), *The Nazi Elite*, trans. Mary Fischer (London: MacMillan, 1993), 183–93.

————— 'Das "Amt Rosenberg", das "Ahnenerbe" und die Prähistoriker: Bemerkungen eines Historikers,' in Achim Leube (ed.), *Prähistorie und Nationalsozialismus: Die mittel- und osteuropäische Ur- und Frühgeschichtsforschung in den Jahren 1933–1945*, Studien zur Wissenschafts- und Universitätsgeschichte 2 (Heidelberg: Synchron, 2002), 21–48.

Bönisch, Michel, 'Die "Hammer" Bewegung,' in Uwe Puschner, Walter Schmitz and Justus H. Ulbricht (eds.), *Handbuch zur "Völkischen Bewegung" 1871–1918* (Munich: Saur, 1996), 341–65.

Bopp, [E.] Franz, *Über das Conjugationssystem der Sanskritsprache in Vergleichung mit jenem der griechischen, lateinischen, persischen und germanischen Sprache* (Frankfurt a.M.: Andreä, 1816).

Bork, Ferdinand, 'Zur Entstehungsgeschichte des Futharc,' *Mannus* 16 (1924): 127–37.

————— review of Herman Wirth, *Der Aufgang der Menschheit*, reprinted in Eugen Diederichs (ed.), *Der Fall Herman Wirth oder Das Schicksal des Schöpfertums: Ein Bericht* (Jena: Diederichs, [1929]), 8.

————— 'Herman Wirth als Orientalist,' in Fritz Wiegers (ed.), *Herman Wirth und die deutsche Wissenschaft* (Munich: Lehmann, 1932), 61–69.

————— 'Runenstudien,' *Archiv für Schreib- und Buchwesen* 3 (1929): 67–81.

Bott, Marie-Luise, '"Deutsche Slavistik" in Berlin? Zum Slavischen Institut der Friedrich-Wilhelms-Universität zu Berlin 1933–1945' in Rüdiger vom Bruch and Christoph Jahr (eds.), *Die Berliner Universität in der NS-Zeit*, 2 vols. (Stuttgart: Steiner, 2005), II, 277–98.

Bowen, Robert, *Universal Ice: Science and Ideology in the Nazi State* (London: Belhaven, 1993).

Boyer, John W., *Political Radicalism in Late Imperial Vienna: Origins of the Christian Social Movement* (Chicago: Chicago University Press, 1981).

Bramwell, Anne, *Blood and Soil: Richard Walther Darré and Hitler's 'Green Party'* (Bourne End: Kensel, 1985).

Brather, Sebastian, 'Wilhelm Unverzagt und das Bild der Slawen,' in Heiko Steuer (ed.), *Eine hervorragend nationale Wissenschaft: Deutsche Prähistoriker zwischen 1900–1995*, Ergänzungsbände zum Reallexikon der Germanischen Altertumskunde 29 (Berlin: De Gruyter, 2001), 475–504.

Brennecke, Fritz (ed.), *Handbuch für die Schulungsarbeit in der HJ: Vom deutschen Volk und seinem Lebensraum* (Munich: Eher, 1937) [= *The Nazi Primer: Official Handbook for Schooling the Hitler Youth*, trans. Harwood L. Childs (New York: Harper & Bros, 1938)].

Breuer, Stefan, *Anatomie der Konservativen Revolution* (Darmstadt: Wissenschaftliche Buchgesellschaft, 1993).

————— *Ordnungen der Ungleichheit: Die deutsche Rechte im Widerstreit ihrer Ideen 1871–1945* (Darmstadt: Wissenschaftliche Buchgesellschaft, 2001).

————— *Grundpositionen der deutschen Rechten* (Tübingen: Niemeyer, 1999).

————— *Nationalismus und Faschismus* (Darmstadt: Wissenschaftliche Buchgesellschaft, 2005).

Broszat, Martin, *German National Socialism, 1919–1945,* trans. Kurt Rosenbaum and Inge P. Boehm, Twentieth Century Series 1 (Santa Barbara: Clio, 1966).

————— 'Soziale Motivation und Führer-Bindung des Nationalsozialismus,' *Vierteljahreshefte für Zeitgeschichte* 18 (1970): 392–409.

————— *The Hitler State: The Foundations and Development of the Internal Structure of the Third Reich*, trans. John W. Hiden (London: Longmann, 1981).

Buchholz, Kai, Rita Latocha, Hilke Pechmann und Klaus Wolbert (eds.), *Die Lebensreform: Entwürfe zur Neugestaltung von Leben und Kunst um 1900*, 2 vols. (Darmstadt: Häusser, 2001).

Buning, Lammert, 'Notities betreffende Hermann (sic) Felix Wirth,' *Wetenschappelijke Tijdingen* 33 (1974): 141–66.

Bünte, Rudolf (ed.), *Wilhelm Teudt im Kampf um Germanenehre: Auswahl von Teudts Schriften* (Bielefeld: Velhagen & Klasing, 1940).

Bureus, Johannes, [Runakänslanås lära-span unde runr], *seu verae veter. Gotorum literae* (Uppsala: [s.n.,] 1599).

————— *Runa ABC-boken* (Stockholm: Gutterwitz, 1611).

————— *Monumenta lapidum aliquot Runicorum* (Uppsala: Curio, 1664).

Burleigh, Michael, *Germany Turns Eastwards: A Study of Ostforschung in the Third Reich* (Cambridge: Cambridge University Press, 1988).

Burleigh, Michael, and Wolfgang Wippermann, *The Racial State: Germany, 1933–1945* (Cambridge: Cambridge University Press, 1991).

Burnouf, Emile, (ed.), *Le Lotus de la bonne Loi, traduit du Sanscrit* (Paris: Imprimérie Nationale, 1837).

————— *Dictionaire classique sanscrit-francais* (Paris: Maisonneuve, 1866).

————— *La Science des religions*, 2nd ed. (Paris: Maisonneuve, 1872).

Büsching, Johan Gustav G., *Abriß der deutschen Alterthums-Kunde: Mit eine Charte des alten Germaniens* (Weimar: [s.n.,] 1824).

[Caesar, C. Julius,] *[G]ay Iulij caesaris dictoris exordia. Vt plera(sque) moraliu(m) fragilia ... .vij. libros de bello gallico ...* ([Esslingen: Fyner,] 1473).

Casper von Lohenstein, Daniel (Daniel Casper), *Grossmütiger Feldherr Arminius oder Hermann, als ein tapffere Beschirmer der deutschen Freyheit nebst seiner durchlauchtigen Thusnelda in einer sinnreichen Staats-Liebes- und Helden-Geschichte*, 2 vols. (Leipzig: Bleditschen, 1689–1690).

[Cassiodorus,] *Antiqua regum Italiae Gothicae gentis rescripta: ex 12 libris Epistolarum Cassiodori ad Eutharicum*, ed. Johannes Cochlaeus (Dobneck), ([Leipzig: Schmidt], 1529).

Cecil, Robert, *The Myth of the Master Race, Alfred Rosenberg and Nazi Ideology* (London: Batsford, 1972).

Celtes, Conradus, *Protucij ... quator libri amorum secundum quatuor latera Germaniæ feliciter incipiunt (Conradi Celti de origine situ moribus et institutis Norimbergae libellis incipit)* (Nuremberg: [s.n.,] 1502).

——— *Cornelii Taciti veridie Historici: de situs Germanie & incolaru: vt secla olim fereba(n)t: moribus libellus lectu dignissimus. Conradi Celtis Protucii: Poeta fragme(n)ta queda(m): de iisdem scitu admodu(m) vttilia Omnibus dilige(n)ter reuisis et castigatis* (Vienna: Singren, 1515).

Chamberlain, Houston S., *Die Grundlagen des neunzehnten Jahrhunderts*, 2 vols. (Munich: Bruckmann, 1899; 14th ed. 1922) [= *Foundations of the Nineteenth Century*, trans. John Lees, 2 vols. (London: Lane, 1910)].

——— *Lebenswege meines Denkens*, 2nd ed. (Munich: Bruckmann, 1922).

Châtellier, Hildegard, 'Wagnerism in der Kaiserzeit,' in Uwe Puschner, Walter Schmitz and Justus H. Ulbricht (eds.), *Handbuch zur 'Völkischen Bewegung' 1871–1918* (Munich: Saur, 1996), 575–612

Chickering, Roger, *We Men Who Feel Most German: A Cultural Study of the Pan-German League 1886–1914* (Boston: Allen & Unwin, 1984).

Cochlaeus (Dobneck), Johannes, *Vita Theoderici, regis quondam Ostrogothorum et Italiae, qurela item de reipublicae statu sub Justiniano... nunc primum evulgata* (Ingolstad: Weissenhorn, 1544).

Conrady, Karl Otto, *Völkisch-nationale Germanistik in Köln: Eine unfestliche Erinnerung* (Schernfeld: Süddeutsche Hochschul-Verlag, 1990).

Coombs, William L., *The Voice of the SS: A History of the SS Journal 'Das Schwarze Corps,'* American University Studies, Series IX: History 1 (New York: Lang, 1986).

Cotta, Bernhard von, *Deutschlands Boden: Sein Bau und dessen Einwirkung auf das Leben der Menschen* (Leipzig: Brockhaus, 1853).

Dachlhaus, Carl (ed.), *Riemanns Musik Lexikon*, 12th ed., *Ergänzungsband*, 2 vols. (Mainz: Schott's Sons, 1972–75).

Dahl, Göran, *Radikalare än Hitler: De esoteriska och gröna Nazisternas insperationskällor, pionjärer, förvaltare och släktingar* (Stockholm: Atlantis, 2006).

Dahn, Felix, *Ein Kampf um Rom*, 4 vols. (Leipzig: Breitkopf & Härtel, 1876–78).

Daim, Wilfried, *Der Mann, der Hitler die Ideen gab: Jörg Lanz von Liebenfels*, 3rd ed. (Vienna: Ueberreuter, 1994).

Daniel, Glyn E., *A Short History of Archaeology* (London: Thames & Hudson, 1981).

Darnton, Robert, *The Literary Underground of the Old Regime* (Cambridge, Mass.: Harvard University Press, 1982).

Darré, R. Walter, 'Unser Weg,' *Odal* 2 (1934): 690–720.

Davies, Peter, 'Ilse Langner's *Amazonen* and the Reception of J.J. Bachhofen's *Das Mutterrecht*,' *German Life and Letters* 56 (2003): 223–43.

Déchelette, Joseph, 'Le culte du soleil aux temps préhistoriques,' *Revue archéologique* 4ième serie 13 (1909): 305–57.

Dechend, Gabriele, 'Hütet die Runen, das Weistum eurer Ahnen!,' *Nordische Welt* 3 (1935): 642.

Degener, Hermann A.L., *Wer ist's? Unsere Zeitgenossen*, 3rd ed. (Leipzig: Degener, 1908), 7th ed., 1914.

Derks, Hans, *Deutsche Westforschung: Ideologie und Praxis im 20. Jahrhundert*, Geschichtswissenschaft und Geschichtskultur im 20. Jahrhundert 4 (Leipzig: AVA-Akademische Verlagsanstalt, 2001).

——— 'German *Westforschung*, 1918 to the Present: The Case of Franz Petri, 1903–1993,' in Ingo Harr and Michael Fahlbusch (eds.), *German Scholars and Ethnic Cleansing* (New York: Berghahn, 2004), 175–99.

Diederichs, Eugen (ed.), *Das deutsche Gesicht; Ein Weg zur Zukunft: Zum xxx. Jahr des Verlags Eugen Diederichs in Jena* (Jena: Diederichs, 1926).

——— *Der Fall Herman Wirth oder Das Schicksal des Schöpfertums: Ein Bericht* (Jena: Diederichs, [1929]).

Dierks, Margarete, *Jakob Wilhelm Hauer 1881–1962: Leben – Werk – Wirkung* (Heidelberg: Lambert Scheider, 1986).

Dieterich, Franz, *Über die Aussprache des Gothischen während der Zeit seines Bestehens* (Marburg: Elwert, 1862).

Dilthey, Wilhelm, *Einleitung in die Geisteswissenachften: Versuch einer Grundlegung für das Studium der Gesellschaft und der Geschichte* (Leipzig: Duncker & Humblot, 1883) [= *Introduction to the Human Sciences*, ed. Rudolf A. Makkreel and Frithjof Rodi (Princeton: Princeton University Press, 1989)].

Dingler, Hugo, 'Wege und Grundlagen der Sinnbildforschung (Zur Methode der Paläoepigraphik),' *Germanien* 9 (1937): 36–40, 69–76.

Donnelly, Ignatius, *Atlantis: The Antediluvian World* (London: Samson Low, Marsdon & Co., 1882).

D'Onofrio, Andrea, *Ruralismo e storia nel Terzo Reich: Il caso 'Odal,'* Università degli Studi, Pubblicazioni del Dipartimento di Disciplini Storische 6 (Naples: Liguori, 1997).

Döring, Jürgen, 'Beispiele englischer Buchkunst,' in Joseph Lammers and Gerd Unverfehrt (eds.), *Vom Jugendstil zum Bauhaus: Deutsche Buchkunst 1895–1930* (Münster i.W.: Westfälisches Landesmuseum für Kunst & Kulturgeschichte, 1981), 18–33.

Dow, James R., and Hannjost Lixfeld, 'National Socialist Folklore and Overcoming the Past in the Federal Republic of Germany,' *Asian Folklore Studies* L-1 (1991): 117–53 [= James R. Dow and Hannjost Lixfeld (eds.), *The Nazification of an Academic Discipline* (Bloomington: Indiana University Press, 1994), 265–96].

────── (eds.), *The Nazification of an Academic Discipline* (Bloomington: Indiana University Press, 1994).

Düwel, Klaus, 'Begriffsrunen,' in Johannes Hoops, *Reallexikon der Germanischen Altertumskunde* II, 2nd ed. (Berlin: De Gruyter, 1976), 150–53.

Düwel, Klaus, and Heinrich Beck (eds.), *Andreas Heusler an Wilhelm Ranisch: Briefe aus den Jahren 1890–1940* (Beiträge zur nordischen Philologie 18), Basel: Helbing & Lichtenhahn, 1989.

Düwel, Klaus, and Harro Zimmermann, 'Germanenbild und Patriotismus in der Literatur des 18. Jahrhunderts,' in Heinrich Beck (ed.), *Germanenprobleme in heutiger Sicht*, Ergänzungsbände zum Realleikon der Germanischen Altertumskunde 1 (Berlin: De Gruyter, 1986), 358–95.

Ebeling, Christoph Daniel, 'Kurze Geschichte der deutschen Dichtkunst,' *Hannoverische Magazin* 5 (1767): 81–92, 97–128 and 6 (1768): 81–94, 97–118, 353–84, 401–58, 529–44, 545–52.

Echternkamp, Jörg, *Der Aufstieg des deutschen Nationalismus (1770–1840)* (Frankfurt a.M.: Campus, 1998).

Einstein, Alfred (ed.), *Hugo Riemanns Musik Lexikon*, 10th ed. (Berlin: Hesse, 1922).

Eisenhut, Lutz P., 'Runen-Freunde, Hippies, Mystiker: Sonnenwendfeier an den Externsteinen im Teutoburger Wald,' *Die Welt*, 20 June 1998.

Eley, Geoff, *Reshaping the German Right: Radical Nationalism and Political Change after Bismarck* (New Haven: Yale University Press, 1980).

Elliot, Ralph W.V., *Runes, An Introduction* (Manchester: Manchester University Press, 1959).

Emmerich, Wolfgang, *Germanistische Volkstumsideologie: Genese und Kritik der Volksforschung im Dritten Reich*, Volksleben: Untersuchungen des Ludwig-Uhlands-Instituts für Volkskunde 20 (Tübingen Schloß: Tübinger Vereinigung für Volkskunde, 1968).

Engelkes, Gustav G., *Runenfibel* (Langensalza: Beltz, [1935]).

Engster, Hermann, *Germanisten und Germanen: Germanenideologie und Theoriebildung in der deutschen Germanistik und Nordistik von den Anfängen bis 1945 in exemplarischer Darstellung*, Texte und Untersuchungen zur Germanistik und Skandinavistik 16 (Frankfurt a.M.: Lang, 1986).

Ergang, Robert R., *Herder and the Foundations of German Nationalism* (New York: Columbia University Press, 1933.

Faulmann, Karl, *Ilustrirte Geschichte der Schrift: Popular-wissenschaftliche Darstellung der Enstehung der Schrift, der Sprache und der Zahlen sowie der Schriftsysteme aller Völker der Erde* (Vienna: Hartleben, 1880).

Feder, Gottfried, *Das Programm der N.S.D.A.P. und seine weltanschaulichen Grundgedanken*, Nationalsozialistische Bibliothek 1 (Munich: Eher, 1927).

Fehr, Hubert, 'Hans Zeiss, Joachim Werner und die archäologischen Forschungen zur Merowingerzeit,' in Heiko Steuer (ed.), *Eine hervorragend nationale Wissenschaft: Deutsche Prähistoriker zwischen 1900–1995*, Ergänzungsbände zum Reallexikon der Germanischen Altertumskunde 29 (Berlin: De Gruyter, 2001), 311–415.

Fehrle, [J.] Eugen, (ed.), Publius Cornelius Tacitus, *Germania* (Munich: Lehmann, 1929).

—— 'Herman Wirth und die Volkskunde,' in Alfred Baeumler (ed.), *Was bedeutet Herman Wirth für die Wissenschaft?* (Leipzig: Koehler & Amelang, 1932), 62–63.

—— 'Das Hakenkreuz—Von seinem Sinn und seiner Geschichte,' *Oberdeutsche Zeitschrift für Volkskunde* 8 (1934): 5–38.

—— 'Zur Entwicklung des Sinnbildes,' *Oberdeutsche Zeitschrift für Volkskunde* 12 (1938): 165.

—— *Sagen aus Deutschland* (Vienna: Ueberreuter, 1952).

—— *Feste und Volksbräuche im Jahreslauf europäischer Völker* (Kassel: Hinnenthal, 1955).

Ferch, Andreas, *Viermal Deutschland in einem Menschenleben: Werner Georg Haverbeck Genie der Freundschaft* (Dresden: Zeitenwende, 2000).

Feist, Sigmund, *Grundriß der gotischen Etymologie* [dissertation] (Strasbourg: Trübner, 1888).

—— *Lehr- und Lesebuch der französischen Sprache für praktische Ziele*, 3 vols. (Halle a.S.: Waisenhaus, 1895–98).

—— notice of Ludwig Wilser, *Zur Runenkunde*, *Jahresbericht über die Erscheinungen auf dem Gebiete der germanischen Philologie* 27 (1905 [1907]): I, 67.

—— *Europa im Lichte der Vorgeschichte und die Ergibnisse der vergleichenden indogermanischen Sprachwissenschaft: Ein Beitrag zur Frage nach dem Ursitzen der Indogermanen*, Quellen und Forschungen zur alten Geschichte und Geographie 19 (Berlin: Weidmann, 1910).

—— notice of Ludwig Wilser, *Europäische Völkerkunde*, *Jahresbericht über die Erscheinungen auf dem Gebiete der germanischen Philologie* 33 (1911 [1913]): I, 23.

—— notice of Ludwig Wilser, *Die Germanen*, 2nd ed., *Jahresbericht über die Erscheinungen auf dem Gebiete der germanischen Philologie* 33 (1911 [1913]): I, p. 36.

—— *Kultur, Ausbreitung und Herkunft der Indogermanen* (Berlin: Weidmann, 1913).

—— 'La question du pays d'origine des indo-européens,' *Scientia* 14 (1913): 303–314.

—— 'Indogermanen und Germanen,' in Rudolf Klee (ed.), *Verhandlungen der zweiundfünfzigsten Versammlung deutscher Philologen und Schulmänner in Marburg vom 29. September bis 3. Oktober 1913* (Leipzig: Teubner, 1914), 153.

—— 'Indogermanen und Germanen,' *Zeitschrift für den deutschen Unterricht* 28 (1914): 161–77 and 261–74.

—— notice of Ludwig Wilser, 'Ursprung und Entwicklung der Buchstabenschrift' (*Mannus* 4, 1912), *Jahresbericht über die Erscheinungen auf dem Gebiete der germanischen Philologie* 34 (1912 [1914]): I, 146.

—— *Indogermanen und Germanen: Ein Beitrag zur europäischen Urgeschichtsforschung* (Halle a.S.: Niemeyer, 1914).

—— 'Das Arierproblem,' *Sokrates* 3 (1915): 417–32.

—— 'Archäologie und Indogermanenproblem,' *Korrespondenz-Blatt der Deutschen Gesellschaft für Anthropologie, Ethnologie und Urgeschichte* 47 (1916): 61–68.

—— notice of Ludwig Wilser, *Die Germanen*, 2nd ed., *Jahresbericht über die Erscheinungen auf dem Gebiete der germanischen Philologie* 36 (1914 [1916]): I, 43.

—— 'Runen und Zauberwesen im germanischen Altertum,' *Arkiv för nordisk filologi* 35, 1919, 243–87.

—— notice of Ludwig Wilser, *Deutsche Vorzeit* (2nd ed.), *Jahresbericht über die Erscheinungen auf dem Gebiete der germanischen Philologie* 39–40 (1917–18 [1920]): I, 42

—— 'Germanen,' in Max Ebert (ed.), *Reallexikon der Vorgeschichte* IV (Berlin: De Gruyter, 1924), 273–89.

—— 'Indogermanen,' in Max Ebert (ed.), *Reallexikon der Vorgeschichte* VI (Berlin: De Gruyter, 1926), 54–66.

—— *Germanen und Kelten in der antiken Überlieferung*, Neue Germanen forschungen 1 (Halle a.S.: Niemeyer, 1927).

—— 'Was verstanden die Römer unter "Germanen"?,' *Teuthonista* 4 (1927/28): 1–12.

—— 'Entgegnung [zu Much, *WPZ* 15/1],' *Wiener Prähistorische Zeitschrift* 15 (1928): 65–71.

—— 'Zum Ursprung der germanischen Runenschrift,' *Acta philologica Scandinavia* 4 (1929): 1–25.

—— 'Zu den Berliner Runenfunden,' *Zeitschrift für deutsches Altertum und deutsche Literatur* 69 (1932): 136.

Fichte, Johann Gottlieb, *Reden an die deutsche Nation*, Berlin: Realschulbuchhandlung, 1808 [= *Johann Gottlieb Fichtes sämtliche Werke*, ed. Immanuel Hermann Fichte, 8 vols. (Berlin: Veit, 1845–46), VII, 257–516].

Field, Geoffery G., 'Nordic Racism,' *Journal of the History of Ideas* 38 (1977): 523–40.

—— *The Evangelist of Race: The Germanic Vision of Houston Stewart Chamberlain* (New York: University of Columbia Press, 1981), 17–50.

Figueira, Dorothy M. *Aryans, Jews, Brahmins: Theorizing Authority Through Myths of Identity*, SUNY series The Margins of Literature (Albany, N.Y.: State University of New York Press, 2002).

Fischer, Hanns, *Der Wunder des Welteises* (Berlin-Wilmersdorf: Paekel, 1922).

Fischer, Jens Malte, *Richard Wagners 'Das Judentum in der Musik': Eine kritische Dokumentation als Beitrag zur Geschichte des Antisemitismus*, Insel Taschenbuch 2617 (Frankfurt a.M.: Insel, 2000).

Fischer-Dieskau, Dietrich, *Wagner and Nietzsche*, trans. Joachim Neugroschel (New York: Seabury, 1976).

Flowers, Stephen E., and Michael Moynihan, *The Secret King: Karl Maria Wiligut; Himmler's Lord of the Runes* (Waterbury Center, VY: Dominion, 2001).

Franssen, A., 'Grundsätzliches zur Frage der Externsteine (3. Teil): Die Kreuzabnahme,' *Germanien* 6 (1934): 289–95 and 327–42.

Frecot, Janos, Johann Friedrich Geist and Diethart Kerbs, *Fidus 1868–1948: Zur ästhetischen Praxis bürgerlicher Fluchtbewegungen* (Munich: Rogner & Bernhard, 1972).

Friesen, Otto von, 'Om runeskriftens härkomst,' *Språkvetenskapliga sällskaps i Uppsala förhandlingar* 2 (1904–1906): 1–55 [= monograph, Uppsala: Akademika, 1904].

———— 'Runes,' in Walter Yust (ed.), *Encyclopædia Britannica*, 24 vols., 14th ed. (London: The Encyclopædia Co., 1929), XVII, 659–64.

———— (ed.), *Runorna, Nordisk Kultur* VI (Stockholm: Bonnier, 1933).

Frings, Theodor, *Germania Romana*, Mitteldeutsche Studien 2 = Teuthonista Beiheft 4 (Halle a.S.: Niemeyer, 1932).

Fritsch, Theodor, *Antisemitische Katechismus* (Leipzig: Hammer, 1887).

———— *Handbuch der Judenfrage: Die wichtigsten tatsachen zur Beurteilungen des jüdischen Volkes*, 49th ed. (Berlin: Hammer, 1944).

[Fuhrmann, Ernst,] *Schwedische Felsbilder von Göteborg bis Strömstad*, Werke der Urgermanen: Schriften zum Wiederaufbau der alten nordischen Kulturen 1 (Hagen i.W.: Folkwang, 1919).

Gajek, Esther, 'Joseph Otto Plaßmann Eine akademische Laufbahn im Nationalsozialismus,' in Kai Detlev Sievers (ed.), *Beiträge zur Wissenschaftsgeschichte der Volkskunde im 19. und 20. Jahrhundert* (Neumünster: Wachholtz, 1991), 121–55.

Gall, Lothar, *Bismarck: The White Revolutionary*, trans. J. A. Underwood, 2 vols. (London: Allen & Unwin, 1986).

Gamble, William T. M., *The Monument Germaniae historica: Its Inheritance in Source-Valuation and Criticism* (Washington: The Catholic University of America, 1927).

Gamillscheg, Ernst, *Romania Germanica: Sprach- und Siedlungsgeschichte der Germanen auf dem Boden des alten Römerreiches*, Grundriss der germanischen Philologie 11, 3 vols. (Berlin: De Gruyter, 1934–36).

————, *Germanische Siedlung in Belgien und Nordfrankreich*, Abhandlungen der Preußischen Akademie der Wissenschaften, Phil.-hist. Klasse 1937, no. 12 (Berlin: De Gruyter, 1939).

Gasman, Daniel, *The Scientific Origins of National Socialism: Social Darwinism in Ernst Haeckel and the German Monist League* (London: MacDonald, 1971).

Gassert, Phillip, and Daniel S. Mattern, *The Hitler Library: A Bibliography* (Westport, Conn.: Greenwood, 2001).

Gauch, Hermann, *Die germanische Odal- oder Allodverfassung* (Berlin: Blut & Boden, 1934).

Gauch, Sigfrid, *Vaterspuren: Eine Erzählung* (Königsstein i.Ts.: Athenäum, 1979).

Gerstenhauer, Max R., *Der volkische Gedanke in Vergangenheit und Zukunft: Aus der Geschichte der völkischen Bewegung* (Leipzig: Armanen, 1933).

Gilbhard, Hermann, *Die Thule-Gesellschaft: Vom okkulten Mummenschanz zum Hakenkreuz* (Munich: Kesseling, 1994).

Gilch, Eva, Carmen Schramka and Hildegard Prütting, *Volkskunde an der Münchener Universität 1933–1945*, Münchener Beiträge zur Volkskunde 6 (Munich: Münchener Vereinigung für Volkskunde, 1986).

Glaser, Herman, *The Cultural Roots of National Socialism*, trans. Ernst A. Menze (London: Croom Helm, 1978).

Glaser, Rudolf, *Wer ist Herman Wirth? Volkstümliche Aufsätze über die Forschungen Herman Wirths* (Breslau: self-published, 1934).

Gloege, Gerhard, 'Die Weltanschauung Herman Wirths,' in Walter Künneth and Helmuth Schreiner (eds.), *Die Nation vor Gott: Zur Botschaft der Kirchen im Dritten Reich* (Berlin: Im Wichern, 1933), 392–421.

Glunk, Rolf, 'Erfolg und Mißerfolg der nationalsozialistischen Sprachlenkung,' *Zeitschrift für deutsche Sprache* 26 (1970): 84–97.

Gobineau, Arthur Cmpte de, *Essai sur l'inégalité des races humaines*, 4 vols. (Paris: Firmin Didot, 1853–54) [= *Versuch über die Ungleichheit der Menschenracen*, trans. Ludwig Schemann, 4 vols. (Stuttgart: Frommanns, 1898–1901)].

Goblet d'Alviella, Eugène Cmpte, *La Migration des symbols* (Paris: Leroux, 1891).

Gollwitzer, Heinz, 'Zum politischen Germanismus des 19. Jahrhunderts,' in Josef Fleckenstein, Sabine Krüger and Rudolf Vierhaus (eds.), *Festschrift für Hermann Heimpel zum 70. Geburtstag*, Veröffentlichungen des Max-Planck-Instituts für Geschichte 36/I–III, 3 vols. (Göttingen: Vandenhoeck & Ruprecht 1971–72), I, 282–356.

Goodrick-Clarke, Nicholas, *The Occult Roots of Nazism: The Ariosophists of Austria and Germany 1890–1935* (Wellingborough: Aquarian, 1985).

Göpfert, Arthur, et al., *Bekenntnis der Professoren an den deutschen Universitäten und Hochschulen zu Adolf Hitler und dem nationalsozialistischen Staat* (Dresden: Limpert, 1933).

Goschler, Constantin, *Rudolf Virchow: Mediziner, Anthropologe, Politiker* (Cologne: Böhlau, 2002).

Graff, Eberhard G., *Althochdeutscher Sprachschatz*, 7 vols. (Berlin: Nikolai, 1834–46).

Gräslund, Bo, *The Birth of Prehistoric Chronology: Dating Methods and Dating Systems in Nineteenth-Century Scandinavian Archaeology*, trans. Neil Tomkinson and Jacquelline Taffinder (Cambridge: Cambridge University Press, 1987).

Green, Martin, *Mountain of Truth: The Counterculture Begins. Ascona, 1900–1920* (Hanover, NH: University Press of New England, 1986).

Greg, Robert P., 'On the Meaning and Origin of the Fylfot and Swastika,' *Archaeologia* 48 (1884): 293–326.

Gregor-Dellin, Martin, *Richard Wagner: His Life, His Work, His Century*, trans. J. Maxwell Brownjohn (London: Collins, 1983).

Greve, Reinhard, 'Tibetforschung im SS-Ahnenerbe,' in Thomas Hauschild (ed.), *Lebenslust und Fremdenfurcht: Ethnologie im Dritten Reich*, Suhrkamp Taschenbuch Wissenschaft 1189 (Frankfurt a.M.: Suhrkamp, 1995), 168–99.

Griffin, Roger, *The Nature of Fascism* (London: Pinter, 1991).

——— 'The Primacy of Culture: The Current Growth (or Manufacture) of Consensus within Fascist Studies,' *Journal of Contemporary History* 37 (2002): 21–43.

Grimm, Jacob, *Deutsche Grammatik*, 4 vols. (Göttingen: Dieterich, 1819–37).

———— *Deutsche Rechts-Alterthümer* (Göttingen: Dieterich, 1828).

———— *Deutsche Mythologie*, 2 vols. (Göttingen: Dieterich, 1835) [= *Teutonic Mythology*, trans. James Steven Stallybrass, 4 vols. (London: Bell & Sons, 1888–1900)].

Grimm, Jacob & Wilhelm, *Deutsches Wörterbuch*, 33 vols. (Leipzig: Hinzel, 1854–1971).

Grimm, Wilhelm, *Ueber deutsche Runen* (Göttingen: Dieterich, 1821).

———— 'Zur Literatur der Runen,' *Jahrbücher der Literatur* (*Wiener Jahrbücher*) 43 (1828): 1–42 [= *Kleinere Schriften*, ed. Gustav Hinrichs, 4 vols. (Berlin: Dümmler, 1881–87), III, 85–131].

Grønbech, Vilhelm, *Vor folkeæt i oldtiden*, 4 vols. (Copenhagen: Pios, 1909–12) [= *The Culture of the Teutons*, trans. W. Worster, 2 vols. (Oxford: Clarendon, 1932) = *Kultur und Religion der Germanen*, ed. Otto Höfler, trans. Ellen Hoffmeyer, 2 vols. (Hamburg: Hanseatische Verlagsanstalt, 1937–39)].

Grünert, Heinz, *Gustaf Kossinna (1858–1931): Vom Germanisten zum Prähistoriker; ein Wissenschaftler im Kaiserreich und in der Weimarer Republik*, Vorgeschicht liche Forschungen 22 (Rahden i.W.: Leidorf, 2002).

Güntert, Hermann, 'Die Ursache der germanischen Lautverschiebung,' *Wörter und Sachen* 10 (1927): 1–22.

———— 'Zum heutigen Stand der Sprachforschung,' *Wörter und Sachen* 12 (1929): 386–97.

———— *Deutscher Geist: Drei Vorträge* (Bühl: Concordia, 1932).

———— *Der Ursprung der Germanen*, Kultur und Sprache 9 (Heidelberg: Winter, 1933).

———— 'Runen, Runenbrauche und Runeninschriften der Germanen,' *Oberdeutsche Zeitschrift für Volkskunde* 8 (1934): 51–102.

———— 'Neue Zeit—neues Ziel,' *Wörter und Sachen* 19, NF 1 (1938): 1–11.

Günther, Hans F.K., *Rassenkunde des deutschen Volkes* (Munich: Lehmann, 1922).

Gutman, Robert W., *Richard Wagner: The Man, His Mind and His Music* (Harmondsworth: Penguin, 1971).

Haack, Friedrich-Wilhelm, *Wotans Wiederkehr: Blut-, Boden- und Rasse- Religion* (Munich: Claudius, 1981).

Habel, Walther (ed.), *Wer ist Wer*, 13th ed. (Berlin: Arani, 1958).

Haeckel, Ernst, *Natürliche Schöpfungsgeschichte: Gemeinverständliche wissenschaftliche Vorträge über die Entwicklungslehre im Allgemeinen und diejenige von Darwin, Goethe, und Lamarck im Besonderen* (Berlin: Reimer, 1868).

———— *Anthropogenie, oder, Entwicklungsgeschichte des Menschen: Gemein verständliche wissenschaftliche Vorträge über die Grundzüge der menschlichen Keimes- und Stammesgeschichte* (Leipzig: Engelmann, 1874).

Hafner, Ulrike, *"Norden" und "Nation" un 1800: Der Einfluß skandinavischer Geschichtsmythen und Volksmentalitäten auf deutschsprachige Schriftsteller zwischen Aufklärung und Romantik (1740–1820)*, Hesperides: Letterature e culture occidentale 1 (Trieste: Parnaso, 1996).

Hakelberg, Dietrich, 'Deutsche Vorgeschichte als Geschichtswissenschaft – Der Heidelberger Extraordinarius Ernst Wahle in Kontext seiner Zeit,' in Heiko Steuer (ed.), *Eine hervorragend nationale Wissenschaft: Deutsche Prähistoriker zwischen 1900–1995*, Ergänzungsbände zum Reallexikon der Germanischen Altertumskunde 29 (Berlin: De Gruyter, 2001), 199–310.

Hale, Christopher, *Himmler's Crusade: The True Story of the 1938 Nazi Expedition into Tibet* (London: Bantam, 2003).

Halle, Ute, 'Die Externsteine Symbol germanophiler Interpretation,' in Achim Leube (ed.), *Prähistorie und Nationalsozialismus: Die mittel- und osteuropäische Ur- und Frühgeschichtsforschung in den Jahren 1933–1945*, Studien zur Wissenschafts- und Universitätsgeschichte 2 (Heidelberg: Synchron, 2002), 235–53.

———— *"Die Externsteine sind bis auf weiteres germanisch!": Prähistorische Archäologie im Dritten Reich*, Sonderveröffentlichungen des Naturwissen schaftlichen und Historischen Vereins für das Land Lippe 68 (Bielefeld: Verlag für Regionalgeschichte, 2002).

Hamann, Richard, and Jost Hermand, *Naturalismus*, Deutsche Kunst und Kultur von der Gründerzeit bis zum Expressionismus 2 (Berlin: Akademie, 1959).

———— *Gründerzeit*, Deutsche Kunst und Kultur von der Gründerzeit bis zum Expressionismus 1 (Berlin: Akademie, 1965).

Hamelmann, Hermann, *Epitome chronici Osnaburgensis a … Ertwino Ertmanno consule … urbis Osnaburgae* (Lemgo: [Schuchen,] 1564).

Hamkens, Freerk Haye, 'Drei Steingräber Schleswig-Holsteins,' *Germanien* 9 (1937): 339–42 and 360–66.

———— *Sinnbilder auf Grabsteiner von Schleswig bis Flandern: Versuch einer Deutung* (Brussels: Die Osterlingen, 1942).

Hammerstein, Notker, *Die Deutsche Forschungsgemeinschaft in der Weimarer Republik und im Dritten Reich: Wissenschaftspolitik in Republik und Diktatur 1920–1945* (Munich: Beck, 1999).

Hank, Sabine, Hermann Simon et al. (eds.), *Feldpostbriefe jüdischer Soldaten 1914–1918: Briefe ehemaliger Zöglinge an Sigmund Feist, Direktor des Reichenheimschen Waisenhauses in Berlin*, Jüdischer Memoiren; Sonderausgabe, 2 vols. (Teetz: Hentrich & Hentrich 2002).

Harder, Hermann, and Edmund Weber, 'Ein Runenfund im deutschen Museum zu Berlin,' *Zeitschrift für deutsches Altertum und deutsche Literatur* 68 (1931): 217–25.

Hartmann, Silvia, *Fraktur oder Antiqua: Der Schriftstreit von 1881 bis 1941*, Theorie und Vermittlung der Sprache 28 (Frankfurt a.M.: Lang, 1998).

Hartung, Günter, 'Völkische Ideologie,' *Weimarer Beiträge* 33 (1987): 1174–85.

———— 'Völkische Ideologie,' in Uwe Puschner, Walter Schmitz and Justus H. Ulbricht (eds.), *Handbuch zur "Völkischen Bewegung" 1871–1918* (Munich: Saur, 1996), 22–41.

Hasselt, Laura van, '"De zaken moeten nu eenmaal loopen": Kapteyn als rector van de Groningse universiteit (1940–1942),' *Groniek* 144 (1999): 311–19.

Hauer, Jacob Wilhelm, *Die Religionen* (Berlin: Kohlhammer, 1923).

―――― *Was will die Deutsche Glaubensbewegung?*, Flugschriften zum geistigen und religiösen Durchbruch der deutschen Revolutions 5 (Stuttgart: Hirschfeld, 1934).

―――― *Glaubensgeschichte der Indogermanen* (Stuttgart: Kohlhammer, 1937).

―――― 'Über die ältesten Hakenkreuze, ihre Herkunft und ihre Sinn,' *Germanien* 15, NF 5 (1943): 88–100.

―――― *Schrift der Götter: Vom Ursprung der Runen* (Kiel: Orion Heimreiter, 2004).

Hauer, [J.] Wilhelm, Karl Heim and Karl Adam, *Germany's New Religion: The German Faith Movement*, trans. T.S.K. Scott-Craig & R.E. Davies (London: Allen & Unwin, 1937).

Haus Ecklöh, *Runenschmuck. Werbeschrift* [S. l., n. d.].

Hausmann, Frank-Rutger, *"Deutsche Geisteswissenschaft" im Zweiten Weltkrieg: Die "Aktion Ritterbusch" (1940–1945)*, Schriften zur Wissenschafts- und Universitätsgeschichte 1 (Dresden: Dresden University Press, 1998).

Haverbeck, Werner G., *Volkstum und Heimat als Bekenntnis jungen Kulturwollens* (Berlin: Reichsbund Volkstum und Heimat, 1935).

―――― *Deutscher Mai: Sinn und Festgestaltung* (Berlin: Phoenix, 1935).

―――― *Das Ziel der Technik* (Olten: Walter, 1965).

―――― *Die andere Schöpfung* (Stuttgart: Urahhaus, 1978).

―――― *Rudolf Steiner, Anwalt für Deutschland: Ursachen und Hintergründe des Welt-Krieges unseres Jahrhunderts* (Munich: Langen-Müller, 1989).

Heemskerk-Düker, W.F. van, and H.J. van Houten, *Zinnebeelden in Nederland* (Amsterdam: Hamer, 1941).

Heeroma, Klaas, 'Vorwort,' in Jan de Vries, *Kleine Schriften*, ed. Klaas Heeroma and Andries Kylstra, Kleinere Schriften zur Literatur und Geistesgeschichte (Berlin: De Gruyter, 1965), v–vii.

Heiber, Helmut, *Walter Frank und sein Reichsinstitut für die Geschichte des neuen Deutschlands*, Quellen und Darstellungen zur Zeitgeschichte 13 (Stuttgart: Deutsche Verlags-Anstalt, 1966).

Heidler, Irmgard, *Der Verleger Eugen Diederichs und seine Welt 1896–1930*, Mainzer Studien zur Buchwissenschaft 8 (Wiesbaden: Harrassowitz, 1998).

Heidler, Mario, 'Die Zeitschriften des J.F. Lehmanns Verlages bis 1945,' in Sigrid Stöckel (ed.), *Die "rechte Nation" und ihr Verleger: Politik und Popularisierung im J.F. Lehmanns Verlag 1890–1979* (Heidelberg: Lehmanns, 2002), 47–101.

Hein, Annette, *'Es ist viel "Hitler" in Wagner': Rassismus und antisemitische Deutschtumsideologie in den 'Bayreuther Blättern' (1878–1938)*, Conditia Judaica 13 (Tübingen: Niemeyer, 1996).

Heinrichs, Hans-Jürgen (ed.), *Das Mutterrecht von Johann Jakob Bachofen in der Diskussion* (Frankfurt a.M.: Campus, 1987).

Heller, Dorothee, *Wörter und Sachen: Grundlagen einer Historiographie der Fachsprachenforschung*, Forum für Fachsprachenforschung 43 (Tübingen: Narr, 1998).

Helm, Karl, *Altgermanische Religionsgeschichte*, Germanische Bibliothek, Reihe V: Handbücher und Gesamtdarstellungen zur Literatur- und Kulturgeschichte 2, 2 vols. (Heidelberg: Winter, 1913–53).

Helmers, Menne Feiken, 'Heilszeichen im Gefüge des niedersächsischen Bauernhauses,' *Germanien* 9 (1937): 205–10.

——— *Sinnbilder alten Glaubens in ostfriesischer Volkskunst* (Aurich: Duckmann, 1938).

Hempel, Hermann, 'Der Ursprung der Runenschrift,' *Germanisch-Romanische Monatsschrift* 23 (1935): 401–26.

——— notice of Otto Höfler, *Kultische Geheimbünde der Germanen I*, *Jahresbericht über die Erscheinungen auf dem Gebiete der germanischen Philologie* 56, NF 14 (1934 [1938]): 161.

Henning, Rudolf, *Die deutschen Runendenkmäler* (Strasbourg: Trübner, 1889).

Henseling, Robert, *Weltentwicklung und Welteislehre* (Potsdam: Die Sterne, 1925).

Herder, Johann Gottfried von, *Auch eine Philosophie der Geschichte zur Bildung der Menschheit: Beytrag zu vielen Beytragen des Jahrhunderts* ([Riga: s.n.,] 1774) [= *Werke*, ed. Bernhard Suphan, 33 vols. (Berlin: Weidmann, 1877–1913), V, 475–586].

Hermand, Jost, *Old Dreams of a New Reich: Volkish Utopias and National Socialism*, trans. Paul Levesque with Stefan Soldovieri (Bloomington: Indiana University Press, 1992).

——— *Geschichte der Germanistik* (Reinbek bei Hamburg: Rowohlt, 1994).

Hermann, Eduard, 'Was hat die indogermanische Sprachwissenschaft dem Nationalsozialismus zu bieten?,' *Göttingische gelehrte Anzeigen* 199 (1937): 49–59.

——— 'Sind der Name der Gudden und die Ortsnamen Danzig, Gdingen und Graudenz gotischen Ursprungs?,' *Nachrichten von der Akademie der Wissenschaften in Göttingen, Phil.-Hist. Klasse* 1941, NF 3, no. 8.

Herrmann, Ferdinand (ed.), *Handbuch der Symbolforschung*, 2 vols. (Leipzig: Hierseman, 1941).

Herrmann, Ferdinand, and Wolfgang Treutlein (eds.), *Brauch und Sinnbild: Eugen Fehrle zum 60. Geburtstag* (Karlsruhe: Sudwestdeutsche Druck- und Verlags-Gesellschaft, 1940).

Hertz, Martin, *Karl Lachmann: Eine Biographie* (Berlin: Hertz, 1851).

Heusler, Andreas, 'Antrittsrede in der Preußischen Akademie der Wissenschaften,' *Sitzungsberichte der Preußischen Akademie der Wissenschaften, Phil.-Hist. Klasse* (1908): 712–14 [= *Kleine Schriften*, ed. Helga Reuschel and Stefan Sonderegger, 2 vols. (Berlin: De Gruyter, 1942–69), II, 14–15].

——— *Nibelungensage und Nibelungenlied: Die Stoffgeschichte des deutschen Heldenepos* (Dortmund: Ruhfus, 1921).

——— *Die altgermanische Dichtung*, Handbuch der Literaturwissenschaft 1 (Berlin: Athenäum, 1923).

——— *Deutsche Versgeschichte: Mit Einschluss des altenglischen und altnordischen Stabreims* (Berlin: De Gruyter, 1925–29).

—————— 'Von germanischer und deutscher Art,' *Zeitschrift für Deutschkunde* 39 (1925): 746–54 [= *Germanentum: Vom Lebens- und Formgefühl der alten Germanen*, Kultur und Sprache 8 (Heidelberg: Winter, 1934), 79–88 = *Kleine Schriften*, ed. Helga Reuschel and Stefan Sonderegger, 2 vols. (Berlin: De Gruyter, 1942–69), II, 598–607].

—————— 'Altgermanische Sittenlehre und Lebensweisheit,' in Hermann Nollau (ed.), *Germanische Wiedererstehung: Ein Werk über die germanischen Grundlagen unserer Gesittung* (Heidelberg: Winter, 1926), 156–204 [= *Germanentum: Vom Lebens- und Formgefühl der alten Germanen*, Kultur und Sprache 8 (Heidelberg: Winter, 1934), 7–62].

—————— *Germanentum: Vom Lebens- und Formgefühl der alten Germanen*, Kultur und Sprache 8 (Heidelberg: Winter, 1934).

—————— *Kleine Schriften*, ed. Helga Reuschel and Stefan Sonderegger, Kleinere Schriften zur literatur- und Geistesgeschichte, 2 vols. (Berlin: De Gruyter, 1942–69).

Heuß, Anja, *Kunst- und Kulturgutraub: Eine vergleichende Studie zur Besatzungspolitik der Nationalsozialisten in Frankreich und der Sovietunion* (Heidelberg: Winter, 2000).

Heydenreich, Wilhelm, 'Vorwort,' in *Vom Germanentum. Ausgewählte Aufsätze und Vorträge von Gustav Neckel*, ed. Wilhelm Heydenreich and Hannah M. Neckel (Leipzig: Harrassowitz, 1944).

Hickes, George, *Linguarum Vett. Septentrionalium Thesaurus Grammatico-Criticus et Archaeologicus* (Oxford: Sheldon Theatre, 1705).

Hillebrecht, Frauke, *Skandinavien—die Heimat der Goten? Der Götizismus als Gerüst eines nordisch-schwedischen Identitätsbewußtseins*, Arbeitspapiere "Gemeinschaften" 7 (Berlin: Humboldt-Universität zu Berlin, 1987).

Himmler, Heinrich, 'Zum Geleit,' *Germanien* 8 (1936): 193–94.

—————— Document 1992(A)-PS, from 'National Political Studies for the Armed Forces' (January 1937), in International Military Tribunal, *Trial of the Major War Criminals* XXIX (Nuremberg: The Tribunal, 1948), 206–34.

Hinzpeter, Georg, *Urwissen von Kosmos und Erde: Die Grundlagen der Mythologie im Licht der Welteislehre* (Leipzig: Voigtländer, 1928).

Hirsch, Elizabeth Feist, 'Mein Vater Sigmund Feist: Erinnerungen an das Reichenheimische Waisenhaus,' in Herbert A. Strauss and Kurt A. Grossmann (eds.), *Gegenwart im Rückblick: Festgabe für die Jüdische Gemeinde zu Berlin 25 Jahre nach dem Neubeginn* (Heidelberg: Stiehm, 1970), 265–73.

Hirschbigel, Jan, 'Die "germanische Kontinuitätstheorie" Otto Höflers,' *Zeitschrift der Gesellschaft für Schleswig-Holsteine Geschichte* 117 (1992): 181–98.

Hirschfeld, Gerhard, 'Die nationalsozialistischen Neuordnung Europas und die "Germanisierung" der westeuropäischen Universitäten,' in Helmut König, Wolfgang Kuhlmann and Klaus Schwabe (eds.), *Vertuschte Vergangenheit: Der Fall Schwerte und die NS-Vergangenheit der deutschen Hochschulen*, Beck'sche Reihe 1204 (Munich: Beck, 1997), 79–102.

Hirt, Herman A., 'Die Deutung der germanischen Völkernamen,' *Beiträge zur Geschichte der deutschen Sprache und Literatur* 18 (1894): 511–19.

——— 'Nochmals die Deutung der germanischen Völkernamen,' *Beiträge zur Geschichte der deutschen Sprache und Literatur* 21 (1896): 125–59.

——— *Die Indogermanen: Ihre Verbreitung, ihre Urheimat und ihre Kultur*, 2 vols. (Strasbourg: Trübner, 1905–7).

——— *Indogermanische Grammatik*, Indogermanische Bibliothek: 1. Abt. Sammlung indogermanischer Lehr- und Handbücher, 1. Reihe: Grammatiken 13, 7 vols. (Heidelberg: Winter, 1921–37).

——— *Die Hauptprobleme der indogermanischen Sprachwissenschaft*, ed. Helmut Arntz (Halle a.S.: Niemeyer, 1939).

——— *Indogermanica: Forschungen über Sprache und Geschichte Alteuropas*, ed. Helmut Arntz (Halle a.S.: Niemeyer, 1940).

Hitler, Adolf, *Mein Kampf*, 44th ed. (Munich: Eher, 1933) [= trans. Ralph Mannheim (Boston: Houghton Mifflin, 1943)].

——— *Sämtliche Aufzeichnungen 1905–1924*, ed. Eberhard Jäckel (Stuttgart: Deutsche Verlags-Anstalt, 1980).

Höfler, Otto, *Kultische Geheimbünde der Germanen I* (Frankfurt a.M.: Diesterweg, 1934) [= Faksimile-Edition 10 (Horn: Weeke, 1993)].

——— 'Der germanische Totenkult und Sagen vom Wilden Heer,' *Oberdeutsche Zeitschrift für Volkskunde* 10 (1936): 33–49.

——— 'Über germanische Verwandlungskulte,' *Zeitschrift für deutsches Altertum und deutsche Literatur* 73 (1936): 109–15.

——— 'Antwort,' *Oberdeutsche Zeitschrift für Volkskunde* 11 (1937): 97–102.

——— 'Das germanische Kontinuatätsproblem,' *Historische Zeitschrift* 157 (1938): 1–26 [= monograph, Schriften des Reichsinstitüts für die Geschichte des neuen Deutschlands 29 (Hamburg: Hanseatische Verlagsanstalt, 1937)].

——— 'Die politische Leistung der Völkerwanderungszeit,' *Kieler Blätter* (1938): 282–97 [= *Kleine Schriften*, ed. Helmut Birkhan (Hamburg: Buske, 1982), 1–16].

——— 'Friedrich Gundolf und das Judentum in der Literaturwissenschaft,' *Forschungen zur Judenfrage* 4, 1940 [= *Sitzungsberichte der Vierten Münchener Arbeitstagung des Reichsinstitüts für Geschichte des neuen Deutschlands vom 4.–6. Juli 1939* (Hamburg: Hanseatische Verlagsanstalt 1940).]

——— 'Siegfried, Arminius und die Symbolik,' in Wolfdietrich Rasch (ed.), *Festschrift für Franz Rolf Schröder* (Heidelberg: Winter, 1959), 11–121 [= monograph, Heidelberg: Winter, 1961].

——— *Kleine Schriften*, ed. Helmut Birkhan (Hamburg: Buske, 1982).

Hohenschwert, Friedrich, Heinrich Beck, Jürgen Udolph and Wolfhard Schlosser, 'Externsteine,' in Johannes Hoops, *Reallexikon der Germanischen Altertumskunde* VIII, 2nd ed. (Berlin: De Gruyter, 1994), 37–38.

Hollander, Lee M., review of Bernhard Kummer, *Midgards Untergang*, *Journal of English and Germanic Philology* 33 (1934): 255–69.

Homeyer, Carl Gustav, *Die Haus- und Hofmarken* (Berlin: Decker, 1870).

Höppner, Wolfgang, 'Kontinuität und Diskontinuität in der Berliner Germanistik,' in Rüdiger vom Bruch and Christoph Jahr (eds.), *Die Berliner Universität in der NS-Zeit*, 2 vols. (Stuttgart: Steiner, 2005), II, 257–76

Hörbiger, Hanns, with Philipp Fauth, *Glacial-Kosmogonie: Eine neue Entwick-elungsgeschichte des Weltalls und des Sonnensystems, auf Grund der Erkenntnis des Widerstreites eines kosmischen Neptunismus mit einem ebenso universellen Plutonismus* (Kaiserslautern: Kayser, 1913).

Horn, Klaus-Peter, 'Erziehungswissenschaft an der Berliner Friedrich-Wilhelms-Universität in der Zeit des Nationalsozialismus' in Rüdiger vom Bruch and Christoph Jahr (eds.), *Die Berliner Universität in der NS-Zeit*, 2 vols. (Stuttgart: Steiner, 2005), II, 2215–28.

Hübinger, Gangolf, *Versammlungsort moderner Geister: Der Eugen-Diederichs-Verlag–Aufbruch ins Jahrhundert der Extreme* (Munich: Diederichs, 1996).

Hübner, Arthur (ed.), *Herman Wirth und die Ura Linda-Chronik* (Berlin: De Gruyter, 1934).

Hufen, Christopher, 'Gotenforschung und Denkmalpflege: Herbert Jankuhn und die Kommandounternehmen des "Ahnenerbe" der SS,' in Wolfgang Eichwede and Ursula Hartung (eds.), *'Betr.: Sicherstellung': NS Kunstraub in der Sowjetunion* (Bremen: Tremmen, 1998), 75–96.

Hugin und Munin [J. Otto Plaßmann], 'Zur Erkenntnis deutschen Wesens: Widersagst Du dem Wodan?,' *Germanien* 9 (1937): 161–68.

Humboldt, K. Wilhelm von, *Über die Verschiedenheit des menschlichen Sprachbaues und ihren Einfluß auf die geistige Entwicklung des Menschengeschlechts* (Berlin: Dümmler, 1836) [= *On Language: On the Diversity of Human Language-structure and its Influence on the Mental Development of Mankind*, trans. Peter Heath, Texts in German Philosophy (Cambridge: Cambridge University Press, 1988)].

Hummel, Bernhard Friedrich, *Bibliothek der deutschen Alterthümer: Systematische geordnet und mit Anmerkungen*, 2 vols. (Nuremberg: Grattenauer, 1781–91).

Hunger, Ulrich, *Die Runenkunde im Dritten Reich: Ein Beitrag zur Wissenschafts- und Ideologiegeschichte des Nationalsozialismus*, Europäische Hochschulschriften 227 (Frankfurt a.M.: Lang, 1984).

Huß, Richard, 'Die rheinischen Germanen im Altertum,' *Teuthonista* 5 (1928/29): 85–92.

Huth, Otto, 'Das Roßsymbol und der totenkultliche Charakter der Rennspiele,' *Germanien* 2 (1930/31): 122–24 and 142–45.

———— 'Wider der Ultramontanismus der Altphilologie: Die Italiker als ausgewanderte Urgermanenstämme,' *Germanien* 3 (1931/32): 89–92.

———— *Janus: Ein Beitrag zur altrömischen Religion* [dissertation] (Bonn: Röhrschied, 1932).

———— 'Zur Pferdezucht bei den Germanen,' *Germanien* 4 (1932): 21–32.

———— 'Astara-Stern,' *Germanien* 4 (1932): 32.

———— 'Zum Alter der Schriftkenntnis bei den indogermanischen Völkern,' *Germanien* 5 (1933): 118–19.

———— 'Zur kurzen Runenreihe,' *Germanien* 5 (1933): 119.

———— 'Die kultischen Wettspiele der Indogermanen,' *Germanien* 8 (1936): 235–39.

———— 'Der Jahrgott auf dem Stein von Gliende,' *Germanien* 8 (1936): 364.

———— 'Herkunft und Sinn des Lichterbaums,' *Germanien* 8 (1936): 372–76.

———— *Die Fällung des Lebensbaumes: Die Bekehrung der Germanen in völkischer Sicht*, Das deutsche Leben 2, 2 (Berlin: Widukind 1936).

———— 'Die Gesittung der Kanarier als Schlüssel zum Ur-Indogermanentum,' *Germanien* 9 (1937): 50–54.

———— review of Bernhard Reiss, *Runenkunde, Germanien* 9 (1937): 160.

———— 'Der Lichterbaum,' *Germanien* 9 (1937): 357–60.

———— *Der Lichterbaum: Germanischer Mythos und deutscher Volksbrauch*, Deutsches Ahnenerbe, Abt. B: Fachwissenschaftliche Untersuchungen 9 (Berlin: Widukind 1937).

———— 'Der Feuerkult der Germanen,' *Archiv für Religionswissenschaft* 36 (1939): 108–34.

———— *Vesta: Untersuchung zur indogermanischen Feuerkult*, Archiv für Religionswissenschaft Beiheft (Leipzig: Teubner, 1943).

———— 'Der Glasberg (1955),' *Jahrbuch für Symbolforschung* 2 (1961): 15–32.

———— 'Das Mandäerproblem—das Neue Testament im Lichte der mandäischen und essenischen Quellen,' *Jahrbuch für Symbolforschung* 3 (1962): 18–38.

———— 'Raabe und das Neue Testament,' *Jahrbuch der Raabe Gesellschaft* (1965): 103–11.

———— *Raabe und Tieck*, Wilhelm Raabe Studien 1 (Essen: Blaue Erde, 1985).

Hutten, Ulrich von, *Arminius ... quo homo patriae amantissimus, Germanorum laudem celabravit* (Hagenau: Secerius, 1529).

Hutton, Christopher M., *Linguistics and the Third Reich: Mother-Tongue Fascism, Race and the Science of Language*, Routledge Studies in the History of Linguistics 1 (London: Routledge 1999).

Iggers, Georg G., *The German Conception of History*, 2nd ed. (Middleton, Conn.: Wesleyan University Press, 1983).

Ihre, Johan, *Dissertatio de runarum patria et origine* (Uppsala: Stenberg, 1770).

International Military Tribunal, *Trial of the Major War Criminals before the International Military Tribunal, Nuremberg, 14 November 1945–1 October 1946*, 42 vols. (Nuremberg: The Tribunal, 1947–49).

Irenicus, Franciscus, *Germaniae Exegesos volumina duodecim* (Hagenau: Koberg, 1518).

Ivo, Hubert, *Muttersprache—Identität—Nation: Sprachliche Bildung im Spannungsfeld zwischen einheimisch und fremd* (Opladen: Westdeutscher Verlag, 1994).

Jäckel, Eberhard, *Hitler's Weltanschauung*, trans. Herbert Arnold (Middletown, Conn.: Wesleyan University Press, 1972).

Jacob-Friesen, Karl Hermann, 'Die Ura-Linda-Chronik,' *Vergangenheit und Gegenwart* 24 (1934): 125–28.

———— 'Hermann Wirths Ura-Linda-Chronik und die deutschen Vorgeschichts-forscher,' *Nachrichtenblatt für deutsche Vorzeit* 10 (1934): 130–35.

———— 'Odalrunen auf einer altsächsischen Buckelurne,' *Forschungen und Fortschritte* 13 (1937): 217–18.

Jacobs, Jörn, 'Peter Paulsen: Eine Wanderer zwischen zwei Welten,' in Achim Leube (ed.), *Prähistorie und Nationalsozialismus: Die mittel- und osteuropäische Ur- und Frühgeschichtsforschung in den Jahren 1933–1945*, Studien zur Wissenschafts- und Universitätsgeschichte 2 (Heidelberg: Synchron, 2002), 451–60.

Jacobsthal, Paul, and Alexander Langsdorff, *Die Bronzeschabelkannen: Ein Beitrag zur Geschichte des vorrömischen Imports nördlich der Alpen* (Berlin–Wilmersdorf: Keller, 1929).

Jäger, Ludwig, *Seitenwechsel: Der Fall Schneider/Schwerte und die Diskretion der Germanistik* (Munich: Fink, 1998).

Jakubowski-Tiessen, Manfred, 'Kulturpolitik im bestzten Land. Das Deutsche Wissenschaftliche Institut in Kopenhagen 1941 bis 1945,' *Zeitschrift für Geschichtswissenschaft* 42 (1994): 129–38.

Jankuhn, Herbert, 'Gemeinschaftsformen und Herrschaftsbildung in frühgermanischer Zeit' *Kieler Blätter* (1938): 270–381.

——— 'Die SS-Grabung von Haithabu 1939,' *Nachrichtenblatt für deutsche Vorzeit* 16 (1940): 103–4.

——— 'Politische Gemeinschaftsformen in germanischer Zeit,' *Offa* 6/7 (1941/42): 1–39.

——— 'Das Germanenproblem in der älteren archäologischen Forschung (bis Tode Kossinnas),' in Heinrich Beck (ed.), *Germanenprobleme in heutiger Sicht*, Ergänzungsbände zur Reallexikon der Germanischen Altertumskunde 1 (Berlin: De Gruyter, 1986), 298–309.

——— *Haithabu: Ein Handelsplatz der Wikingerzeit*, 8th ed. (Neumünster: Wachholtz, 1986).

Janssen, Hans-Lüitjen, 'Vom Wesen nationalsozialisticher Sinnbilder,' *Altpreußen* 1 (1935): 36–41.

——— 'Grundsätzliches zur vor- und frühgeschichtlichen Sinnbilderforschung,' *Altpreußen* 1 (1935): 183–85.

——— 'Der heutige Stand der Runenkunde,' *Das Volk* (1936/37): 553–55.

Jansson, Sam Owen, 'Gyllental,' in Johannes Brøndsted et al. (eds.), *Kulturhistorisk leksikon for nordisk middelalder* V (Copenhagen: Rosenkilde & Bagger, 1960) 615–18.

Jensen, Hans, *Geschichte der Schrift* (Hanover: Lafaire, 1925).

Johanesson, Alexander, *Grammatik der urnordischen Runeninschriften*, trans. Josef Calansz Poestion, ed. Franz Rolf Schröder (Heidelberg: Winter, 1923).

Johannesson, Kurt, *The Renaissance of the Goths in Sixteenth-century Sweden: Johannes and Olaus Magnus as Politicians and Historians*, trans. James Larson (Berkeley: University of California Press, 1982).

Johansen, Olav Sverre, 'Anmerkungen zur archäologischen Tätigkeit in Norwegen in den Jahren 1940–1945,' in Achim Leube (ed.), *Prähistorie und National sozialismus: Die mittel- und osteuropäische Ur- und Frühgeschichtsforschung in den Jahren 1933–1945*, Studien zur Wissenschafts- und Universitätsgeschichte 2 (Heidelberg: Synchron, 2002), 619–22.

Johnson, Samuel, *A Dictionary of the English Language: In Which The Words are deduced from their Originals, And Illustrated in their Different Significations By*

Examples from the Best Writer, To Which Are Prefixed, A History of the Language, And An English Grammar, 2 vols. (London: Knapton et al., 1775).

Jolles, André, *Freimaurerei. 1. Die Entstehung der Freimaurerei* ([S.l.: s.n.,] 1944).

Jomard, Edme-Françoise et al., *Description de l'Egypte ou Recueil des observations et des recherches qui ont été faites en Egypte pendant l'expédition de l'armée française,* 20 vols. (Paris: Imprimérie impériale/royale, 1809–22).

Jones, William, *The Works of Sir William Jones,* ed. John Shore, Baron (Lord) Teignmouth, 13 vols. (London: Stockdale, 1807).

Jong, Louis de, *Het Koninkrijk der Nederlanden in de Tweede Wereldoorlog,* 14 vols. (The Hague: Staatsdrukkerij- en Uitgeverijbedrif, 1969–91).

Jong Hendrikszoon, Murk de, *Het geheim van het Oera Linda Boek* (Bolsward: Oringa, 1927).

——— *Het Oera-Lind-Boek in Duitschland en hier* (Bolsward: Oringa, 1939).

[Jordanes and Paul the Deacon] *Iornandes de rebus Gothorum. Paulus Diaconus Forojuliensis de gestis Langobardorum,* ed. Conrad Peutinger (Augsburg: Miller, 1515).

Jung, Carl Gustav, *Nietzsche's* Zarathustra: *Notes of the Seminar Given in 1934–1939,* ed. James L. Jarrett, Bollingen series 99, 2 vols. (Princeton: Princeton University Press, 1989).

Jung, Erich, 'Zu Herman Wirths Forschungen,' in Alfred Baeumler (ed.), *Was bedeutet Herman Wirth für die Wissenschaft?* (Leipzig: Koehler & Amelang, 1932), 64–66.

Junginger, Horst, *Von der philologischen zur völkischen Religionswissenschaft: Das Fach Religionswissenschaft an der Universität Tübingen von der Mitte des 19. Jahrhunderts bis zum Ende des Dritten Reiches,* Contubernium 51 (Stuttgart: Steiner, 1999).

Junius, Franciscus (François du Jon, the younger) (ed.), *Gothicum glossarium, quo pleraque Argentei codicis vocabula explicantur, atque ex linguis cognatis illustratur: Praemittuntur ei gothicum, runicum, anglo-saxoricum, aliaque alphabeta* (Dordrecht: Junius, 1665).

Kadner, Siegfried, *Urheimat und Weg des Kulturmenschen: Eine allgemeine verständliche zusammenfassende Einführung in die von Herman Wirth u.a. gewonnenen urgeschichtlichen, sprachlichen und völkerkundlichen Forschungsergebnisse, zugleich eine Darstellung der Enstehung der Rassen und der Entwicklungsstufen des nordisch-atlantischen Menschen,* Veröffentlichung der Herman-Wirth-Gesellschaft (Jena: Diederichs, 1931).

Kapteyn, Johannes M.N., 'Twee runeninscripties uit de terp van Westeremden,' *Jaarverslag van de Vereenigung voor Terpenonderzoek* (1930/31) [= 'Zwei Runeninschriften aus der Terp Westeremden,' *Beiträge zur Geschichte der deutschen Sprache und Literatur* 57 (1933): 160–226].

——— 'Neue Runenfunde,' *Beiträge zur Geschichte der deutschen Sprache und Literatur* 58 (1934): 299–312.

——— 'Eine altalemannische Runeninschrift,' *Anzeiger für schweizerische Altertumskunde* NF 37 (1935): 210–12.

―――― 'Ursprung und Herkunft der germanischen Runenschrift im Lichte neuer Funde,' *Korrespondenzblatt des Vereins für niederdeutsche Sprachforschung* 49 (1936): 23–25.

―――― 'Friesche runenvondsten en hedendaagsche runologie,' *Frysk jierboek* (1938).

―――― *Friezen, Saksen: Twee loten van den Germaanschen stam. Rede uitgespr. tot inledning der stichting Saxo-Frisia* (Amsterdam: Hamer, 1941).

―――― *Friesland und die Friesen in den Niederlanden,* Kriegsvorträge der Rheinischen Friedrich-Wilhelms-Universität Bonn a.Rh. 71 (Bonn: Scheur, 1942).

Karbaum, Michael, *Studien zur Geschichte der bayreuther Festspiele, 1876–1976* (Regensberg: Bosse, 1976).

Kasten, Frederick H., 'Unethical Medicine in Annexed Alsace–Lorraine: The Strange Case of Nazi Anatomist Dr. August Hirt,' in George O. Kent (ed.), *Historians and Archivists: Essays in Modern German History and Archival Policy* (Fairfax, Virg.: George Mason University Press, 1991), 173–208.

Kate, Lambert ten, *Gemeenschap tussen de gottische spraeke en de nederduytsche* (Amsterdam: Rienwertsz, 1710).

Kater, Michael H., *Das "Ahnenerbe" der SS 1935–1945: Ein Beitrag zur Kulturpolitik des Dritten Reiches,* Studien zur Zeitgeschichte (Stuttgart: Deutsche Verlags-Anstalt, 1974).

―――― *The Nazi Party: A Social Profile of Members and Leaders 1919–1945* (Cambridge, Mass.: Harvard University Press, 1983).

―――― *Doctors under Hitler* (Chapel Hill: University of North Carolina Press, 1989).

Kaufmann, Walter, *Nietzsche: Philosopher, Psychologist, Anti-Christ,* 4th ed. (Princeton: Princeton University Press, 1975).

Kelley, Donald R., '*Tacitus Noster*: The *Germania* in the Renaissance and Reformation,' in T. James Luce and Anthony J. Woodman (eds.), *Tacitus and the Tacitean Tradition,* Magie Classical Publications (Princeton: Princeton University Press, 1993), 152–67.

Kelly, Alfred, *The Descent of Darwin: The Popularization of Darwinism in Germany, 1860–1914* (Chapel Hill: University of North Carolina Press, 1981).

Kerbs, Detlev, and Jürgen Reulecke (eds.), *Handbuch der deutschen Reformbewegungen 1880–1933* (Wuppertal: Hammer 1998).

Kershaw, Ian, *The 'Hitler Myth'* (Oxford: Clarendon, 1987).

―――― '"Working Towards the Führer": Reflections on the Nature of the Nazi Dictatorship,' *Contemporary European History* 2/2 (1993): 103–18 [= Ian Kershaw and Moshe Lewin (eds.), *Stalinism and Nazism: Dictators in Comparison* (Cambridge: Cambridge University Press, 1997), 75–87].

―――― 'Hitler and the Uniqueness of Nazism,' *Journal of Contemporary History* 39 (2004): 239–254.

Kiefer, Annegret, *Das Problem eine "jüdischen Rasse": Eine Diskussion zwischen Wissenschaft und Ideologie (1870–1930),* Marburger Schriften zur Medizingeschichte 29 (Frankfurt a.M.: Lang, 1991).

Killy, Walther (ed.), *Deutsche biographische Enzyklopaedia*, 12 vols. (Munich: Saur, 1995–2000).

Kipper, Rainer, *Der Germanenmythos im Deutschen Kaiserreich: Formen und Funktionen historischer Selbstthematisierung*, Formen der Erinnerung 11 (Göttingen: Vandenhoeck & Rupprecht, 2002).

Kittler, Wolf, *Die Geburt des Partisanen aus dem Geist der Poesie: Heinrich Kleist und die Strategie des Befreiungskriege* (Freiburg: Rombach, 1987).

Klandor, G., 'Erbhof und Runen,' *Odal* 3 (1934): 337–39.

Klejn, Leo S., 'Kossinna im Abstand von vierzig Jahren,' *Jahresschrift für mitteldeutsche Vorgeschichte* 58 (1974): 7–55.

Klemm, Gustav Friedrich, *Handbuch der germanischen Alterthumskunde* (Dresden: Walther, 1836).

Klindt-Jensen, Ole, *A History of Scandinavian Archaeology* (London: Thames & Hudson, 1975).

Klinkhammer, Lutz, 'Die Abteilung "Kunstschutz" der deutschen Militärverwaltung in Italien 1943–1945,' *Quellen und Forschungen aus italienischen Archiven und Bibliotheken* 72 (1992): 483–549.

Klopstock, Friedrich Gottlieb, *Oden und Elegien* (Darmstadt: Wittich, 1771; 2nd ed., Hamburg: Bode, 1771) [= *Klopstocks sämmtliche Werke* IV, V (Leipzig: Göschen, 1844)].

——— *Die deutsche Gelehrtenrepublik: Ihre Einrichtung, ihre Gesetze, Geschichte des letzten Landtages* I (Hamburg: Bode, 1774) [= *Klopstocks sämmtliche Werke* VIII (Leipzig: Göschen, 1844)].

Knobloch, Clemens, 'Sprachwissenschaft,' in Frank-Rutger Hausmann (ed.), *Deutsche Geisteswissenschaften im Nationalsozialismus*, Schriften des Historischen Kollegs, Kolloquien 53 (Munich: Oldenbourg, 2002), 305–27.

Koch, Hannsjoachim W., *The Hitler Youth: Origins and Development 1922–1945* (New York: Stein & Day, 1976).

Köhler, Heinz Dieter, *Studien zur Ura-Linda-Chronik* [dissertation] (Weimar: Böhlau, 1936).

Kohn, Hans, *The Mind of Germany: The Education of a Nation*, 2nd ed. (London: MacMillan, 1962).

Kolbrand, Franz, 'Eine krasser Widerspruch … Gegen die Bestattungs-Unwesen,' *Volkstum und Heimat* 46 (1937): 297–300.

Koselleck, Reinhard, Fritz Gschnitzler, Karl Ferdinand Werner and Bernd Schönemann, 'Volk, Nation, Nationalismus, Masse,' in Otto Brunner, Werner Conze and Reinhard Koselleck (eds.), *Geschichtliche Grundbegriffe: Historisches Lexikon zur politisch-sozialischen Sprache in Deutschland* VII (Stuttgart: Klett-Cotta, 1992), 141–431.

Kossinna, [H.] Gustaf, *Die ältesten hochfränkischen Sprachdenkmäler: Ein Beitrag zur Grammatik der Althochdeutschen*, Quellen und Forschungen zur Sprach- und Kulturgeschichte der germanischen Völker 46 [dissertation] (Strasbourg: Trübner, 1881).

——— 'Die Sueben im Zusammenhang den ältesten deutschen Völkerbewegungen,' *Westdeutsche Zeitschrift für Geschichte und Kunst* 9 (1890): 199–216.

——— 'Über die vorgeschichtliche Ausbreitung der Germanen in Deutschland,' *Correspondenz-Blatt der Deutschen Gesellschaft für Anthropologie und Urgeschichte* 26 (1895): 109–12.

——— 'Die vorgeschichtliche Ausbreitung der Germanen in Deutschland,' *Zeitschrift des Vereins für Volkskunde* 6 (1896): 1–14.

——— review of Ludwig Wilser, *Die Germanen*, 1st ed., *Archiv für Rassen- und Gesellschaftsbiologie* 1 (1904): 780–85.

——— 'Die indogermanische Frage archäologisch beantwortet,' *Zeitschrift für Ethnologie* 34 (1902): 161–222 [= Anton Scherer (ed.), *Die Urheimat der Indogermanen* (Darmstadt: Wissenschaftliche Buchgesellschaft, 1968), 25–109].

——— 'Die Grenzen der Kelten und Germanen in der La Tène Zeit,' *Correspondenzblatt der Deutschen Gesellschaft für Anthropologie, Ethnographie und Urgeschichte* 38 (1907): 57–62

——— 'Vorbemerkung,' *Mannus* 3 (1911): 97–98.

——— 'Die deutsche Vorgeschichte, eine hervorragend nationale Wissenschaft, Kurzer Auszug,' *Mannus* 4 (1912): 17–19.

——— *Die deutsche Vorgeschichte: Eine hervorragend nationale Wissenschaft*, Mannus Bibliothek 9 (Würzburg: Kabitzsch, 1912; 6th ed., Leipzig: Kabitzsch, 1936).

——— *Die deutsche Ostmark: Ein Heimatboden der Germanen* (Kattowitz: Böhm Bros., 1919).

Kostrzewski, Józef, *Wielkopolska w czasach przedhistorycznych*, Biblioteka Wielkopolska 2/3 (Poznan: Niemierkiewicz, 1914).

Krabbe, Wolfgang R. *Gesellschaftsveränderung durch Lebensreform: Strukturmerkmaler einer sozialreformerischen Bewegung im Deutschland der Industrialisierungsperiode*, Studien zum Wandel von Gesellschaft und Bildung im neunzehnten Jahrhundert 9 (Göttingen: Vandenhoeck & Ruprecht, 1974).

Kramer, Karl Sigismund, *Die Dingbeseelung in der germanischen Überlieferung* [dissertation], Beiträge zur Volkstumsforschung 5 (Munich: Neuer Filser, 1940).

Krapf, Ludwig, *Germanenmythus und Reichsideologie: Frühhumanistische Rezeptionsweisen der taciteische 'Germania'*, Studien zur deutsche Literatur 59 (Tübingen: Niemeyer, 1979).

Krause, Wolfgang, 'Die Wortstellung in den zweigliedrigen Wortverbindungen,' [dissertation] *Zeitschrift für vergleichende Sprachforschung* 50 (1920): 74–129.

——— *Die Frau in der Sprache der altisländischen Familiengeschichten*, Zeitschrift für vergleichende Sprachforschung Ergänzungsheft 4 (Göttingen: Vandenhoeck & Ruprecht, 1926).

——— 'Runica I,' *Nachrichten der Akadamie der Wissenschaften zu Göttingen, Phil.-Hist Klasse* 1926, no. 1, 1–7.

——— 'Runica II,' *Nachrichten der Akadamie der Wissenschaften zu Göttingen, Phil.-Hist Klasse* 1929, 25–56.

——— 'Das Runendenkmal von Kårstad,' *Zeitschrift für deutsches Altertum und deutsche Literatur* 66 (1929): 247–56.

—— *Beiträge zur Runenforschung,* Schriften der Königsberger Gelehrten Gesellschaft 1932, no. 2 & 1933, no. 1, 2 vols. (Halle a.S.: Niemeyer, 1932–33).

—— review of Magnus Hammarström, 'Om runeskriftens härkomst,' *Studier i nordisk filologi* 20 (1929), *Anzeiger für deutsches Altertum und deutsche Literatur* 50 (1931): 9–19 [= *Gnomon* 7 (1931): 488–97].

—— 'Germanisch *arja-* "vornehm" auf dem Stein von Tune,' *Forschungen und Fortschritte* 10 (1934): 217–18 [= *Nordische Welt* 2/11–12 (1934): 46–47].

—— review of Karl Theodor Weigel, *Runen und Sinnbilder,* *Historische Zeitschrift* 152 (1935): 552–56.

—— *Was man in Runen ritzte* (Halle a.S.: Niemeyer, 1935; 2nd ed. 1943).

—— 'Uralinda Chronik und Germanentum,' *Altpreußen* 1 (1935): 56–57.

—— 'Ein neuer Runenfund aus Oberschlesien,' *Forschungen und Fortschritte* 11 (1935): 110–11 [= *Nordische Welt* 3 (1935): 347–49].

—— 'Neue Wege zur Runenforschung,' *Forschungen und Fortschritte* 12 (1936): 443–44 [= 'New Ways of Runic Research,' *Research and Progress* 3 (1937): 119–22].

—— review of Otto Behagel, 'Odal,' *Historische Zeitschrift* 154 (1936): 323–34.

—— review of Helmut Arntz, *Handbuch der Runenkunde,* 1st ed., *Anzeiger für deutsches Altertum und deutsche Literatur* 55 (1936): 1–6.

—— 'Sinnbilder und Runen,' *Altpreußen* 2 (1936): 15–24.

—— 'Die Inschrift auf der Urne von Niesdrowitz,' *Altschlesien* 6 (1936): 232–38.

—— *Runeninschriften im älteren Futhark,* Schriften der Königsberger Gelehrten Gesellschaft 13, 4 (Halle a.S.: Niemeyer, 1937), 2nd ed. (with Herbert Jankuhn), Abhandlungen der Akadamie der Wissenschaften in Göttingen, Phil.-Hist. Klasse III, 65, 2 vols. (Göttingen: Vandenhoeck & Ruprecht, 1966).

—— 'Runen in Amerika,' *Germanien* 9 (1937): 231–36.

—— 'Wesen und Werden der Runen,' *Zeitschrift für Deutschkunde* 51 (1937): 281–93 and 345–56.

—— 'Die Runen als Begriffszeichen,' in Kurt H. Schlottig (ed.), *Beiträge zur Runenkunde und nordischen Sprachwissenschaft. Gustav Neckel zum 60. Geburtstag* (Leipzig: Harrassowitz, 1938), 35–53.

—— 'Runenmacht,' *Geistige Arbeit* 6/19 (1939): 1–4.

—— 'Der Speer von Kowel: Ein wiedergefundenes Runendenkmal,' *Germanien* 13, NF 3 (1941): 450–64.

—— 'Zu der scheinbaren *r*-Rune auf dem früheisenzeitlichen Gefäß von Börnicke,' *Wörter und Sachen* 22, NF 4 (1941–42): 211–17.

—— 'Woher stammen die Runen?,' *Brüsseler Zeitung* 2 Aug., 1942.

—— 'Über die Anfange der Runenschrift,' *Europäischer Wissenschafts-Dienst* 3/3 (1943): 16–18.

—— 'Die Herkunft der Runen,' *Jahrbuch des Auslandamtes der deutschen Dozentschaft* (1943): 102–10.

────── 'Zum Stand der Runenforschung,' *Göttingische gelehrte Anzeigen* 205 (1943): 231–68.

Krogmann, Willy, *Ahnenerbe oder Falschung? Eine Klarstellung im Sachen der Ura-Linda-Chronik* (Berlin: Ebering, 1934).

Kroll, Frank-Lothar, *Utopie als Ideologie: Geschichtsdenken und politisches Handeln im Dritten Reich* (Paderborn: Schöningk, 1998).

Kuehnemund, Richard, *Arminius, or the Rise of a National Symbol in Literature* (Chapel Hill: University of North Carolina Press, 1953).

Kuhn, Alwin, 'Das französische Neuwort (auch im Hinblick auf die nationalsozialistische Terminologie): Ein Auswahl,' *Germanisch-Romanische Monatsschrift* 25 (1937): 296–313.

Kuhn, Hans, 'Verhütung minderwertigen Nachwuchses im alten Island,' *Die Sonne* 12 (1935): 166–68.

────── 'Isländisches Bauerntum,' *Die Sonne* 12 (1935): 203–7.

────── 'Das Zeugniss der Sprache über Alter und Ursprung der Runenschrift,' in Kurt H. Schlottig (ed.), *Beiträge zur Runenkunde und nordischen Sprachwissenschaft. Gustav Neckel zum 60. Geburtstag* (Leipzig: Harrassowitz, 1938), 54–73.

Kummer, Bernhard, *Midgards Untergang: Germanischer Kult und Glaube in der letzten heidnischen Jahrhunderten* [dissertation], Veröffentlichungen der Forschungsinstitüt für Vergleichende Religionsgeschichte an der Universität Leipzig 2, 7 (Leipzig: Pfeiffer, 1927), 3rd ed. (Leipzig: Klein, 1937), 5th ed. (Zeven: Verlag der "Forschungsfragen unserer Zeit" Lienau, 1972).

────── 'Der germanische Begriff vom Tode,' *Germanien* 2 (1930/31): 22–23.

────── 'Germanenkunde,' *Nordische Stimmen* 7 (1937): 190–91.

────── 'Erklärung,' *Germanien* 10 (1938): 144.

────── *Brünnhild und Ragnarök: Die Gestaltung der isländischen Brunhilddichtung aus dem Erlebnis des Glaubenswechsels* (Lübeck: Schiller, 1950).

────── *Die Kampf um ein Heiligtum: Der Irminsulgedanke und die religionsgeschichtliche Bedeutung der Externsteine* (Pähl i.Obb.: Hohe Warte von Bebenburg, 1953).

────── *Gefolgschaft, Führertum und Freiheit: Vom Grundgesetz der Demokratie in alter Zeit* (Zeven: Verlag der "Forschungsfragen unserer Zeit" Lienau, [1956]).

────── *Die Lieder des Codex Regius und verwandte Denkmäler*, 2 vols. (Zeven: Verlag der "Forschungsfragen unserer Zeit" Lienau, 1959–61).

Kutzleb, Hjalmar, 'Scholastik von heute II: Herman Wirth,' *Die Neue Literatur* 33 (1932): 108–11.

────── 'Unsere Meinung,' *Die Neue Literatur* 33 (1932): 533–34.

────── *Der erste Deutsche, Roman Hermann des Cheruskers* (Brunswick: Westermann [1934]).

────── *Arminius: Held der Teutoburger Schlacht* (Münster i.Wf.: Coppenrath, 1935).

Lagarde (Boetticher), Paul A. de, *Deutsche Schriften* (Göttingen: Dieterich, 1878).

Lamberty, Max, 'Activisme,' in E. de Bruyne, G.B.J. Heltermann and H.R. Hoetink (eds.), *Winkler Prins encyclopadie*, 18 vols., 6th ed. (Amsterdam: Elsevier, 1947–52), I, 198.

—— 'Vlaamse beweging,' in E. de Bruyne, G.B.J. Heltermann and H.R. Hoetink (eds.), *Winkler Prins encyclopadie*, 18 vols., 6th ed. (Amsterdam: Elsevier, 1947–52), XVIII, 176–77

Lang, Serge, and Ernst von Schenck (eds.), *The Memoirs of Alfred Rosenberg*, trans. Eric Posselt (Chicago: Ziff-David, 1949).

Lange, Hans-Jürgen, *Otto Rahn: Leben und Werk* (Engerda: Arun, 1995).

—— *Weisthor: Karl-Maria Wiligut—Himmlers Rasputin und seine Erben* (Engerd: Arun, 1998).

—— *Otto Rahn und die Suche nach dem Gral* (Engerda: Arun, 1999).

Langewiesche, Friedrich, *Sinnbilder germanischen Glaubens im Wittekindsland* (Eberswalde: Langewiesche, 1935).

Langsdorff, Alexander (Sandro), *Fluchtnächte in Frankreich* (Stuttgart: Deutsche Verlags-Anstalt, 1920) [later edn published as *Flucht aus Frankreich: Kriegserlebnisse eines jungen Soldaten* (Munich: Langen, 1934)].

—— 'Auf den Spuren unserer Ahnen: Die Erdenburg bei Köln, eine germanische Wallberg,' *Das Schwarze Korps* 1/19, 10 July, 1935, 8 and 1/21, 24 July 1935, 11.

—— *Verzeichnis und Karte der durch den bevollmächtigten General der deutschen Wehrmacht in Italien geschützten Baudenkmäler* [S.l.: s.n., 1945].

Langsdorff, Alexander, and Hans Schleif, 'Die Ausgrabungen der Schutzstaffeln,' *Germanien* 8 (1936): 391–99 and 10 (1938): 6–11.

Laquer, Walter Z., *Young Germany: A History of the German Youth Movement* (London: Routledge & Keegan Paul, 1962).

Large, David C., 'Wagner's Bayreuth Disciples,' in David C. Large and William Weber (eds.), *Wagnerism in European Culture and Politics* (Ithaca: Cornell University Press, 1984), 72–133.

Latham, Robert Gordon, *The Germania of Tacitus, with Ethnological Dissertation and Notes* (London: Taylor, Walton & Marberly, 1851).

Latscha, Jakob, and Wilhelm Teudt, *Nationale Ansiedelung und Wohnungsreform: Grundgedanken und Vorschläge*, 2nd ed. (Frankfurt a.M.: Ecklin, 1899).

Lauffer, Otto, *Deutsche Sitte*, Deutschkundliche Bücherei 10 (Leipzig: Quelle & Meyer, 1920).

—— 'Die Entwicklungsstufen der germanischen Kultur: Umwelt und Volksbrauch in altgermanischer Zeit,' in Hermann Nollau (ed.), *Germanische Wiedererstehung: Ein Werk über die germanischen Grundlagen unserer Gesittung* (Heidelberg: Winter, 1926), 17–155.

—— review of Friedrich Langewiesche, *Sinnbilder germanischen Glaubens im Wittekindsland*, *Zeitschrift für Volkskunde* 45 (1937): 179–81.

—— review of Oskar von Zaborsky-Wahlstätten, *Urväter-Erbe in deutscher Volkskunst*, *Zeitschrift für Volkskunde* 45 (1937): 326.

—— 'Wunderbäume und Wunschbäume im Schrifttum und in der bildenden Kunst,' in Ferdinand Herrmann and Wolfgang Treutlein (eds.), *Brauch und Sinnbild: Eugen Fehrle zum 60. Geburtstag* (Karlsruhe: Sudwestdeutsche Druck- und Verlags-Gesellschaft, 1940), 161–78.

———— 'Volkswerk,' in Will-Erich Peukert and Otto Lauffer, *Volkskunde: Quellen und Forschungen seit 1930*, Wissenschaftliche Forschungsberichte: Geisteswissenschaftliche Reihe 14 (Bern: Francke, 1951), 262–335.

Lechler, Jörg, *Vom Hakenkreuz: Die Geschichte eines Symbols*, Vorzeit: Nachweise und Zusammenfassungen aus dem Artbeitsgebiete der Vorgeschichtsforschung 1 (Leipzig: Kabitzsch 1921, 2nd ed., 1934).

———— 'Sinn und Weg des Hakenkreuzes,' *Der Schulungsbrief* 2 (1935): 404–13.

Leers, Johann von, *Juden sehen dich an* (Berlin–Schöneberg: NS Druck & Verlag, 1933).

———— 'Das Odalsrecht bei den Japanern,' *Odal* 2 (1934): 881–88.

———— *Odal: Das Lebengesetz eines ewigen Deutschlands* (Goslar: Blut und Boden, 1935).

Lehmann, Siegfried, 'Der Kampf um die Sinnbildforschung,' *Nationalsozialistische Monatshefte* 7 (1936): 832–35.

Lerchenmüller, Joachim, 'Arbeiten am Bau Europa? Zur Wissenschaftspolitik der SS in den "germanischen Randländern,"' in Gotthard Jasper (ed.), *Ein Germanist und seine Wissenschaft: Der Fall Schneider/Schwerte*, Erlangen Universitätsreden, 53/3 (Erlangen: Friedrich-Alexander Universität Erlangen-Nürnberg, 1996), 47–74.

———— *'Keltischer Sprengstoff': Eine wissenschaftliche Studie über die deutschen Keltologie von 1900 bis 1945* (Tübingen: Niemeyer, 1997).

Lerchenmüller, Joachim, and Gerd Simon, *Im Vorfeld des Massenmords*, 3rd ed. (Tübingen: Gesellschaft für Interdisziplinäre Forschung Tübingen, 1997).

———— *Masken-Wechsel: Wie der SS-Hauptsturmführer Schneider zum BRD-Hochschulrektor Schwerte wurde und andere Geschichten über die Wendigkeit deutscher Wissenschaft im 20. Jahrhundert* (Tübingen: Gesellschaft für Interdisziplinäre Forschung Tübingen, 1999).

Leroy, Esther, *Konstruktionen des Germanen in bildungsbürgerlichen Zeitschriften des deutschen Kaiserreiches*, Imaginatio Borealis: Bilder des Nordens 6 (Frankfurt a.M.: Lang, 2004).

Leube, Achim, 'Die Ur- und Frühgeschichte an der Friedrich-Wilhelms-Universitäts zu Berlin,' in Rüdiger vom Bruch and Christoph Jahr (eds.), *Die Berliner Universität in der NS-Zeit*, 2 vols. (Stuttgart: Steiner, 2005), II, 149–63.

Levy, Richard S., *The Downfall of the Anti-Semitic Political Parties in Germany*, Yale Historical Publications. Miscellany 106 (New Haven: Yale University Press, 1975).

Leyen, Friedrich von der, review of Otto Höfler, *Kultische Geheimbünde der Germanen I*, *Anzeiger für deutsches Altertum und deutsche Literatur* 54 (1935): 153–65.

———— 'Erwiderung auf Otto Höfler: "Der germanische Totenkult und Sagen vom Wilden Heer"', *Oberdeutsche Zeitschrift für Volkskunde* 11 (1937): 94–97.

———— 'Zur Überlieferung der Abecedarium Nordmannicum,' in Kurt H. Schlottig (ed.), *Beiträge zur Runenkunde und nordischen Sprachwissenschaft. Gustav Neckel zum 60. Geburtstag* (Leipzig: Harrassowitz, 1938), 103–5.

Lichtenberg, Reinhold Frieherr von, 'Beiträge zur Schriftgeschichte,' *Mitteilungen der Allgemeinen der Schriftverein* NF 3/4 (1911).

—— 'Das Alter der arischen Buchstabenschrift, ihre Entwicklung und ihre ferneren Einflüße,' *Mannus* 4 (1912): 295–305.

Liliencron, Rochus von, review of Johan G. Liljgren, *Die nordischen Runen* and Adolf Kirchhoff, *Das gothische Runenalphabet, Allgemeine Monatsschrift für Wissenschaft und Literatur* (1852): 169–93 [= Rochus von Liliencron and Karl Müllenhoff, *Zur Runenlehre: Zwei Abhandlungen* (Halle a.S.: Schwetschke & Son, 1852), 1–25].

Liliencron, Rochus von, and Karl Müllenhoff, *Zur Runenlehre: Zwei Abhandlungen* (Halle a.S.: Schwetschke & Son, 1852).

Liljegren, Johan G., *Run-Lära* (Stockholm: Norstedt & Sons, 1832) [= *Die nordischen Runen*, trans. Karl Oberleitner (Vienna: Haas, 1848)].

Lincoln, Bruce D., *Theorizing Myth* (Chicago: University of Chicago Press, 1999).

Lindenschmidt, Ludwig, *Die Alterthümer unserer heidnischen Vorzeit: Nach den öffentlichen und Privatsammlungen befindlichen Originalien*, 5 vols. (Mainz: von Zabern, 1858–1911).

Landesregierung Lippe, 'Errichtung einer Externsteine-Stiftung,' *Germanien* 6 (1934): 129–31.

List, Guido (von), *Deutsch-Mythologische Landschaftsbilder* (Berlin: Haus Lüstenöder, 1891).

—— 'Die esoterische Bedeutung religiöser Symbole,' *Gnosis* 1 (1903): 323–27.

—— *Das Geheimnis der Runen*, Guido von List-Bücherei 1, 1 (Gross Lichterfelde: Zillman, [1907]) [rev. ed. (Leipzig: Steinacker, 1908) = *The Secret of the Runes*, trans. Stephen E. Flowers (Rochester, Vermont: Destiny Books, 1988)].

—— *Die Armanenschaft der Ario-Germanen*, Guido von List Bücherei 1, 2–2a, 2 vols. (Leipzig: Steinacker, 1908–11).

—— *Die Rita der Ario-Germanen*, Guido von List Bücherei 1, 3 (Leipzig: Steinacker, 1908).

—— *Die Namen der Völkerstämme Germaniens und deren Deutung*, Guido von List Bücherei 1, 4 (Leipzig: Steinacker, 1909).

—— *Die Bilderschrift der Ario-Germanen: Ario-Germanische Heiroglyphik*, Guido von List Bücherei 1, 5 (Leipzig: Steinacker, 1910).

—— *Die Religion der Ario-Germanen in ihrer Esoterik und Exoterik* (Zurich: Bürddecke, 1910).

—— *Der Übergang von Wuotanstum zum Christentum* (Zurich: Bürdecke, 1911).

—— *Die Ursprache der Ario-Germanen und ihre Mysteriesprache*, Guido von List Bücherei 1, 6 (Leipzig: Steinacker, 1914).

Lixfeld, Hannjost, *Folklore and Fascism: The Reich Institute for German Volkskunde*, trans. James R. Dow (Bloomington: Indiana University Press, 1994).

Lohalm, Uwe, *Völkischer Radikalismus: Die Geschichte des Deutschvölkischen Schutz- und Trutzbundes 1919–1923*, Hamburger Beiträge zur Zeitgeschichte 6 (Hamburg: Leibnitz, 1970).

Lord, William O., *The Teutonic Mythology of Richard Wagner's* The Ring of the Nibelung, Studies in the History and Interpretation of Music 16–18A/B, 3 vols. (Lewiston: Mellen, 1989–1991).

Losch, Friedrich, 'Zur Runenlehre,' *Germania: Vierteljahrsschrift für deutsche Alterthums-Kunde* 34 (1889): 397–405.

Losemann, Volker, *Nationalsozialismus und Antike: Studien zur Entwicklung des Faches Alte Geschichte 1933–1945*, Historische Perspektiven 7 (Hamburg: Hoffmann & Campe, 1977).

Lougee, Robert W., *Paul de Lagarde, 1827–1891: A Study of Radical Conservatism in Germany* (Cambridge, MA: Harvard University Press, 1962).

Lund, Allan A., *Germanenideologie und Nationalsozialismus: Zur Rezeption der 'Germania' des Tacitus im "Dritten Reich"* (Tübingen: Niemeyer, 1995).

Lunn, Eugene, *Prophet of Community: The Romantic Socialism of Gustav Landauer* (Berkeley: University of California Press, 1973).

Lutzhöft, Hans-Jürgen, *Der Nordische Gedanke in Deutschland 1920–1940*, Kieler historische Studien 14 (Stuttgart: Klett, 1971).

MacCana, Prionsias, *Celtic Mythology* (Feltham: Hamlyn, 1970).

McCann, W.J., '"Volk und Germanentum": The Presentation of the Past in Nazi Germany,' in Peter Gathercole and David Lowenthal (eds.), *The Politics of the Past*, One World Archaeology 12 (London: Unwin Hyman, 1990, 74–88).

Magnus (Store), Johannes, *Historia ... de omnibus Gothorum Sueonumque regibus qui unquam ab initio nationis extitere, eorumque memorabilibus bellis late varieque per orbem gestis* (Rome: De Viotti, 1554).

Magnus (Store), Olaus, *Historia de gentibus septentionalibus earumque diversis statibus, conditionibus, moribus .... necnon universis pene animalibus in Septentrione degentibus, eorumque natura* (Roma: De Viotti, 1555).

Mallet, Paul Henri, *Introduction à l'Histoire de Dannemarc II: Monuments de la mythologie et la poésie des Celtes particuliérements des anciens Scandinaves* (Copenhagen: Phillibert, 1756).

——— *Histoire de Dannemarc* (Copenhagen: Phillibert, 1758).

Mandl, Franz, 'Das Erbe der Ahnen. Ernst Burgstaller/Herman Wirth und die österreichische Felsbildforschung,' *Mitteilungen der ANISA* 19/20 (1999): 41–67.

Marby, Friedrich Bernhard, *Runenschrift, Runenwort, Runengymnastik* (Stuttgart: Marby–Verlag, 1931).

——— *Marby-Runen-Gymnastik* (Stuttgart: Marby–Verlag, 1932).

——— *Runen raunen richtig Rat!* (Stuttgart: Marby–Verlag, 1934).

——— *Rassische Gymnastik als Aufrassungsweg* (Stuttgart: Marby–Verlag, 1935).

Marchand, Suzanne L., *Down from Olympus: Archaeology and Philhellenism in Germany, 1750–1970* (Princeton: Princeton University Press, 1996).

——— 'The Rhetoric of Artifacts and the Decline of Classical Humanism: The Case of Josef Strzygowski,' *History and Theory*, suppl. 33 (1994): 106–30.

Markey, Thomas L., 'A Tale of Two Helmets: Negau A and B,' *Journal of Indo-European Studies* 29 (2001): 69–172.

Marstrander, Carl J.S., 'Les inscriptions des casques de Negau, Styrie,' *Symbolae Osloenses* 3 (1925): 37–64.

—— 'Remarques sur les inscriptions des casques en bronze de Negau et de Watsch,' *Avh. utgitt av Det Norske Videnskaps Akademi i Oslo, Hist.-filos. Klasse* 2, 1926, no. 2.

—— 'Om runene og runenavnenes oprindelse,' *Norsk tidsskrift for sprogvidenskap* 1 (1928): 85–188.

Maser, Werner, *Hitler's Mein Kampf: An Analysis*, trans. R.H. Barry (London: Faber & Faber, 1970).

—— *Hitler*, trans. Peter and Betty Ross (London: Allen Lane, 1973).

McClelland, Charles E., *State, Society, and University in Germany 1700–1914* (Cambridge: Cambridge University Press, 1980).

Mees, Bernard, 'Linguistics and Nationalism: Henry d'Arbois de Jubainville and Cultural Hegemony,' *Melbourne Historical Journal* 25 (1997): 46–64.

—— 'Celtic Influence in the Vocabulary of Hierarchy during the Common Germanic Period,' *Zeitschrift der Savigny-Stiftung für Rechtsgeschichte, Germanistische Abteilung* 115 (1998): 361–88.

—— 'The North Etruscan Thesis of the Origin of the Runes,' *Arkiv för nordisk filologi* 115 (2000): 33–82.

—— 'Hitler and *Germanentum*,' *Journal of Contemporary History* 39 (2004): 255–70.

—— 'Germanising the East through Place-names and Pots,' in Stephan Atzert and Andrew G. Bonnell (eds.), *Europe's Pasts and Presents* (Unley SA: Australian Humanities Press, 2004), 195–211.

—— 'Runes in the First Century,' in Marie Stoklund et al. (eds.), *Runes and Their Secrets: Studies in Runology* (Copenhagen: Museum Tusculanum, 2006), 201–31

—— '*Germanische Sturmflut*: From the Old Norse twilight to the fascist new dawn,' *Studia Neophilologica* 78 (2006): 184–98.

Mehring, Reinhard, 'Tradition und Revolution in der Berliner Universitätsphilosophie,' in Rüdiger vom Bruch and Christoph Jahr (eds.), *Die Berliner Universität in der NS-Zeit*, 2 vols. (Stuttgart: Steiner, 2005), II, 199–214.

Meid, Wolfgang, 'Hermann Güntert: Leben und Werk,' in Manfred Mayrhofer, Wolfgang Meid, Bernfried Schlerath and Rüdiger Schmitt (eds.), *Antiquitates Indogermanicae; Studien zur indogermanischen Altertumskunde und zur Sprach- und Kulturgeschichte der indogermanischen Völker: Gedankenschrift für Hermann Güntert zur 25. Wiederkehr seines Todes am 23. April 1973*, Innsbrucker Beiträge zur Sprachwissenschaft 12 (Innsbruck: Institut für Sprachwissenschaft, 1974), 517–20.

Meillet, Antoine, 'Avertissement,' in Karl Brugmann, *Abrégé de grammaire comparée des langues indo-européennes*, trans. Jules Bloch, Albert Cuny and Alfred Ernout (Paris: Klincksieck, 1905), i–v.

—— *Caractères généraux des langues germanique* (Paris: Hachette, 1917).

Mentz, Arthur, 'Die notae der Germanen bei Tacitus,' *Rheinisches Museum für Philologie* 86 (1937): 193–205.

Meringer, Rudolf, 'Wörter und Sachen,' *Indogermanische Forschungen* 16 (1904): 101–96.

Meyer, Richard M., 'Runenstudien. I. Die urgermanischen Runen,' *Beiträge zur Geschichte der deutschen Sprache und Literatur* 21 (1896): 162–84.

Meyers Lexikon, 7th ed., 15 vols. (Leipzig: Bibliographisches Institut, 1924–33).

Mezynski, Andrzej, *Kommando Paulsen: Organisierter Kunstraub in Polen 1942–45*, trans. Armin Hetzer (Cologne: Dittrich, 2000).

Michelsen, Andreas Ludwig Jacob, *Die Hausmarke* (Jena: Frommann, 1853).

Mitchell, John, *A Little History of Astro-Archaeology: Stages in the Transformation of a Heresy* (London: Thames & Hudson, 1977).

Moeller van den Bruck, Arthur, *Das dritte Reich* (Berlin: Ring, 1923).

Mogk, Eugen, 'Mythologie,' in Hermann Paul (ed.), *Grundriß der germanischen Philologie*, 2 vols. (Strasbourg: Trübner, 1891–93), I, 982–1138 [= 2nd ed., 1896–1909, III, 230–406].

———— *Über Los, Zauber und Weissagen bei den Germanen (Eine Bemerkung zum 10. Kapitel der Germania des Tacitus),'* in *Kleinere Beiträge zur Geschichte von Dozenten der Leipziger Hochschule: Festschrift zum deutschen Historikertage in Leipzig, Ostern 1894* (Leipzig: Duncker & Humblot, 1894), 81–90.

———— *Über Runen und Hakenkreuz* (Leipzig: Der Ritter vom Hakenkreuz, 1921).

Mogk, Eugen, and Albrecht Haupt, 'Hakenkreuz,' in Johannes Hoops (ed.), *Reallexikon der germanischen Altertumskunde* II (Strasbourg: Trübner, 1913–15), 363–64.

Mogk, Eugen, and Konstantin Reichardt (eds.), *Sammlung altnordischer Übungstexte* 1–7 (Halle a.S.: Niemeyer, 1934–35).

Mohler, Armin, *Die konservative Revolution in Deutschland 1918–1932: Ein Handbuch*, 2nd ed. (Darmstadt: Wissenschaftliche Buchgesellschaft, 1972).

Moltke, Erik, review of Helmut Arntz, *Die Runenschrift*, *Arkiv för nordisk filologi* 53 (1937): 363–66.

Mommsen, Hans, *From Weimar to Auschwitz: Essays in German History*, trans. Phillip O'Connor (Cambridge: Polity Press, 1991).

Mommsen, Wolfgang J., *Das Ringen um den nationalen Staat: Die Gründung und der innere Ausbau des Deutschen Reiches unter Otto von Bismarck 1950 bis 1890*, Propyläen Geschichte Deutschlands 7, 1 (Berlin: Propyläen, 1993).

———— *1848: Die ungewollte Revolution. Die revolutionären Bewegung in Europa 1830–1849*, 2nd ed. (Frankfurt a.M.: Fischer, 1998).

Montelius, Oscar, 'Das Rad als religiöses Sinnbild in vorchristlicher und christlicher Zeit,' trans. A. Lorenzen, *Prometheus* 16 (1905): 241–48, 259–66 and 277–84.

———— 'Das Sonnenrad und das christliche Kreuz,' trans. Ernst Snethlagl, *Mannus* 1, 1909 (53–69): 169–86.

———— 'Das lateinische Kreuz,' *Mannus* 7 (1915): 281–314.

Montesquieu, Charles Louis de Secondat, Bon de la Brède et de, *Lettres Persanes*, 2 vols. (Amsterdam: Brunel, 1721).

———— *De l'Esprit de Loix ou du Rapport que les loix doivent avoir avec la Constitution de chaque gouvernement, les moeuers, le climat, la religion, la commerce, etc.*, 2 vols. (Geneva: Barrilot & Sons, 1748).

Morandi, Alessandro, 'Epigrafia camuna. Osservazioni su alcuni aspetti della documentazione,' *Revue belge de philologie et d'histoire* 76 (1998): 99–124.

Morpurgo Davies, Anna, *History of Linguistics. Volume IV: Nineteenth-Century Linguistics* (London: Longman, 1998).

Mosse, George L., *The Crisis of German Ideology: Intellectual Origins of the Third Reich* (New York: Grosset & Dunlap, 1964).

Much, Matthäus, *Die älteste Besiedlung der Länder des Österreichischen Kaiserstaates durch die Menschen und deren Cultur-Entwicklung* (Vienna: self-published, 1884).

—— *Die Kupferzeit in Europa und ihr Verhältnis zur Kultur der Indogermanen* (Vienna: K.-K. Hof- und Staatsdruckerei, 1886).

—— *Die Heimat der Indogermanen im Lichte der urgeschichtlichen Forschung* (Jena: Costenoble, 1902).

—— *Die Trugspiegelung orientalischer Kultur in den vorgeschichtlichen Zeitaltern Nord- und Mitteleuropas* (Jena: Costenoble, 1907).

Much, Rudolf, *Deutsche Stammessitze* (Halle a.S.: Niemeyer, 1892) [= 'Die Südmark der Germanen,' 'Die Germanen am Niederrhein,' 'Goten und Ingvaeonen,' and 'Berichtigung und Nachträge,' *Beiträge zur Geschichte der deutschen Sprache und Literatur* 17 (1893): 1–224].

—— 'Die Deutung der germanischen Völkernamen,' *Beiträge zur Geschichte der deutschen Sprache und Literatur* 20 (1895): 1–19.

—— review of Otto Bremer, *Ethnographie der germanischen Stämme*, Pauls Grundriß III, 2nd ed., *Deutsche Literaturzeitung* 23 (1902): 486.

—— 'Kelten,' in Johannes Hoops, *Reallexikon der germanischen Altertumskunde* III (Strasbourg: Trübner, 1915–16), 25–27.

—— *Der Eintritt der Germanen in die Weltgeschichte: Kaspar Zeuss zum Gedächtnis*, Sonderabdruck aus: "Germanistische Forschungen," Festschrift anläßlich des 60semestrigen Stiftungsfestes des Wiener Akademischen Germanistenvereines (Vienna: Österr. Bundesverlag für Unterricht, Wissenschaft und Kunst, 1925).

—— 'Die angebliche Keltenherrschaft in Germanien,' *Volk und Rasse* 1 (1926): 100–5.

—— 'Die Germanen bei Theodor Mommsen,' *Volk und Rasse* 3 (1928): 101–4.

—— 'Sigmund Feist und das germanische Altertum,' *Wiener Prähistorische Zeitschrift* 15 (1928): 1–19.

—— 'Bemerkung zur Feists "Entgegnung,"' *Wiener Prähistorische Zeitschrift* 15 (1928): 72–81.

Muhlack, Ulrich, 'Die Germania im deutschen Nationalbewußtsein vor dem 19. Jahrhundert,' in Herbert Jankuhn and Dieter Timpe (eds.), *Beiträge zur Verständnis der Germania des Tacitus*, 2 vols. (Göttingen: Vandenhoeck & Ruprecht, 1989), I, 128–54.

Müllenhoff, Karl, 'Ueber altdeutsche Loosung und Weissagung mit Rücksicht auf die neuesten Interpreten der Germania und die Samler deutscher Eigennamen,' *Allgemeine Monatsschrift für Wissenschaft und Literatur* (1852): 310–48 [= Rochus von Liliencron and Karl Müllenhoff, *Zur Runenlehre: Zwei Abhandlungen* (Halle a.S.: Schwetschke & Son, 1852), 26–64].

———— *Deutsche Altertumskunde*, 5 vols, Berlin: Weidmann, 1887–1900.

Müller, Jörg Jochen, 'Germanistik – eine Form bürgerlicher Opposition,' in idem (ed.), *Germanistik und deutsche Nation 1806–1848* (Stuttgart: Metzler, 2000), 5–112.

Müller, Ludvig, 'Det saakaldte Hagekor's Anvendelse og Betydning i Oldtiden,' *Det Kongelige Danske Videnskabernes Selskabs Skrifter*, 5:e Række, Hist. og Phil. Afd., Bd. 5, no. 1, 1877 (1877–92), 1–114.

Musset, Lucien, *Introduction à la runologie, en partie d'apres les notes de Fernand Mossé*, Bibliothèque du phololgie germanique 20 (Paris: Aubier-Montagne, 1965).

Nadel, Siegfried F., review of P. Hambruch, *Die Irrtümer und Phantasien des Herrn Prof. Dr. Herman Wirth* (Lübeck: German Police Press, 1931), *Mitteilungen der Anthropologischen Gesellschaft in Wien* 61 (1931): 384–85.

Nagel, Anne Christine (ed.), *Die Phillips-Universität Marburg im Nationalsozialismus. Dokumente zu ihrer Geschichte*, Pallas Athene 1 (Frankfurt a.M.: Steiner, 2000).

Nagel, Brigitte, *Die Welteislehre: Ihre Geschichte und ihre Rolle im 'Dritten Reich'* (Stuttgart: Verlag für Geschichte der Naturwissenschaften und der Technik, 1991).

Nanko, Ulrich, *Die Deutsche Glaubensbewegung: Eine historische und soziologische Untersuchung* (Marburg: Diagonal, 1993).

Naveh, Joseph, *Early History of the Alphabet: An Introduction to West Semitic Epigraphy and Palaeography* (Jerusalem: Magnes, 1982).

Neckel, Gustav, *Die germanischen Relativpartikeln* [dissertation] (Berlin: Meyer & Müller, 1900).

———— 'Zur Einführung in die Runenforschung,' *Germanisch-Romanische Monatsschrift* 1 (1909): 7–19 and 81–95.

———— *Die Überlieferungen vom Gotte Balder* (Dortmund: Ruhfus, 1920).

———— *Altgermanische Kultur*, Wissenschaft und Bildung 208, 2nd ed. (Leipzig: Quelle & Meyer, [1934]).

———— *Germanen und Kelten: Historisch-Linguistisch-Rassenkundliche Forschungen und Gedanken zur Geisteskrisis*, Kultur und Sprache 6 (Heidelberg: Winter, 1929).

———— review of Franz Rolf Schröder, *Altgermanische Kulturprobleme*, *Deutsche Literaturzeitung* 50, NF 6 (1929): 521–24.

———— review of Magnus Hammarström, 'Om runeskriftens härkomst' (*Studier i nordisk filologi* 20, 1929), *Deutsche Literaturzeitung* 50, NF 6 (1929): 1237–39.

———— review of Jan de Vries, *De germaansche oudheid* (Haarlem: Tjeenk Willink, 1930), *Deutsche Literaturzeitung* 51, NF 7 (1931): 1168–71.

———— review of Wilhelm Teudt, *Germanische Heiligtümer*, 2nd ed., *Deutsche Literaturzeitung* 51, NF 7 (1931): 1171–74.

———— review of Herman Wirth, *Was heißt deutsch?*, *Mannus* 23 (1931): 331–32.

———— 'Herman Wirth und die Wissenschaft,' in Alfred Baeumler (ed.), *Was bedeutet Herman Wirth für die Wissenschaft?* (Leipzig: Koehler & Amelang, 1932), 11–20.

——— 'Liebe und Ehe bei den vorchristlichen Germanen,' *Zeitschrift für Deutschkunde* 46 (1932): 193–207, 281–93, 386–412 [= monograph (Leipzig: Teubner, 1932)].

——— 'Die Herkunft der Runenschrift,' in Ludwig Roselius (ed.), *Erstes Nordisches Thing*, Veröffentlichung der Vaterkunde 1 (Bremen: Angelsachsen, 1933), 60–76 [= *Neue Jahrbücher für Wissenschaft und Jugendbildung* 9 (1933): 406–17].

——— 'Die Herkunft der Runen,' *Forschungen und Fortschritte* 9 (1933): 293.

——— 'Ist die Ura-Linda-Chr. echt?,' *Der Tag* 310, 29 Dec., 1933.

——— 'Germanen und Kelten,' *Zeitschrift für Deutschkunde* 47 (1933): 497–514.

——— *Kulturkunde der Germanen auf sprachwissenschaftlicher Sicht*, Wissenschaftliche Forschungsberichte zum Aufbau des neuen Reiches 2 (Berlin: Junker & Dünnhaupt 1934).

——— *Kultur der alten Germanen*, Handbuch der Kulturgeschichte 1, 1, 1 (Potsdam: Athenaion, 1934).

——— 'Zur Ura-Linda-Chronik,' *Island* 20 (1934/35): 103–7 [= (abridged) *Nationalsozialistische Monatshefte* 5 (1934): 273–75].

——— 'Die Runen,' *Acta philologica Scandinavica* 12 (1937–38): 102–15 [= *Vom Germanentum: Ausgewählte Aufsätze und Vorträge von Gustav Neckel,* ed. Wilhelm Heydenreich and Hannah M. Neckel (Leipzig: Harrassowitz, 1944), 423–35].

——— review of Hans Naumann, *Germanisches Gefolgschaftswesen* (Leipzig: Bibliographisches Institut, 1939), *Historische Zeitschrift* 163 (1941): 124–26.

Neumann, Franz, *Behemoth: The Structure and Practice of National Socialism* (London: Gollancz, 1942).

Newton, Gerold, '*Deutsche Schrift*: The Demise and Rise of German Black Letter,' *German Life and Letters* 56 (2003): 183–211.

[Nibelungenlied] *Der Nibelunge Not, mit der Klage ... in der ältesten Gestalt mit den Abweichungen*, ed. Carl Lachmann (Berlin: Reimer, 1826).

Niedner, Felix (and Gustav Neckel) (eds.), *Thule: Altnordische Dichtung und Prosa*, 24 vols. (Jena: Diederichs, 1911–30).

Nielsen, Hans F., 'Jacob Grimm and the "German" Dialects,' in Elmer H. Antonsen (ed.), *The Grimm Brothers and the Germanic Past*, Amsterdam Studies in the Science and Theory of the Linguistic Sciences, Series III: Studies in the History of the Language Sciences 54 (Amsterdam: Benjamins, 1990), 25–32.

Neim, Christina, 'Lily Weiser-Aall (1898–1987): Ein Beitrag zur Wissenschaftsgeschichte der Volkskunde,' *Zeitschrift für Volkskunde* 94 (1998): 25–52.

Nietzsche, Friedrich W., *Die Geburt der Tragödie; oder Griechenthum und Pessimismus* (Leipzig: Fritsch, 1871).

——— *Also sprach Zarathustra: Ein Buch für alle und keinen*, 4 vols. (Chemnitz: Schmeitzer and Leipzig: Naumann, 1883–91).

——— *Der Wille zur Macht: Versuch einer Umwerthung aller Werthe*, ed. Elizabeth Förster-Nietzsche (Leipzig: Naumann, 1901).

Nipperdey, Thomas, *Germany from Napoleon to Bismarck 1800–1866*, trans. Daniel Nolan (Dublin: Gill & Macmillan, 1996).

Noll, Richard, *The Jung Cult: Origins of a Charismatic Movement* (Princeton: Princeton University Press, 1994).

—— *The Aryan Christ: The Secret Life of Carl Gustav Jung* (New York: Random House, 1997).

Nordén, Arthur [G.], 'Die Frage nach den Urpsrung der Runen im Lichte der Val Camonica-Funde,' *Berichte zur Runenforschung* 1 (1939): 25–34.

—— 'Felszeichnungen und Runenschrift,' *Runenberichte* 1 (1941): 51–75.

Norden, Eduard, *Die germanische Urgeschichte in Tacitus Germania*, 2nd ed. (Leipzig: Teubner, 1922).

Nordström, Johan, 'Goter och spanjoner. Till den spanska goticismens historia,' *Lychnos* (1944–45): 257–80 and (1971–72): 171–80.

Nußbeck, Ulrich, *Karl Theodor Weigel und das Göttinger Sinnbildarchiv: Eine Karriere im Dritten Reich*, Beiträge zur Volkskunde in Niedersachsen 8 (Göttingen: Schmerse, 1993).

Oberkrome, Willy, *Volksgeschichte: Methodische Innovation und völkische Ideologisierung in der deutschen Geschichtswissenschaft 1918–1945*, Kritische Studien zur Geschichtswissenschaft 101 (Göttingen: Vandenhoeck & Ruprecht, 1993).

Ó Dochartaigh, Pól, *Julius Pokorny, 1887–1970: Germans, Celts and Nationalism* (Dublin: Four Courts, 2004).

Oesterle, Anka (Angelika), 'John Meier und das SS-Ahnenerbe,' in Helge Gerndt (ed.), *Volkskunde und Nationalsozialismus: Referate und Diskussionen einer Tagung der Deutschen Gesellschaft für Volkskunde, München, 23. bis 25. Oktober 1986*, Münchener Beiträge zur Volkskunde 7 (Munich: Münchener Vereinigung für Volkskunde, 1987), 83–93.

Oexle, Gerhard Otto, '"Zusammenarbeit mi Baal": Über die Mentalitäten deutscher Geisteswissenschaftler 1933—und nach 1945,' *Historische Anthropologie* 8 (2000): 1–27.

Olberg, Gabriele von, 'Odal,' in Adalbert Erler and Ekkehard Kaufmann (eds.), *Handwörterbuch zur deutschen Rechtsgeschichte* II (Berlin: Schmidt, 1982), 1178–84.

Olt, Reinhard, and Hans Ramge, '"Aussenseiter": Otto Behagel, ein eitel Hirngespinst und der Nationalsozialismus,' *LiLi* 14 (1984): 194–223.

Oschilewski, Walther G., *Eugen Diederichs und sein Werk* (Jena: Diederichs, 1936).

Ottaway, James Henry, 'Rudolf Virchow: An Appreciation,' *Antiquity* 47 (1973): 101–8.

Ottema, Jan Geraldus (ed.), *Thet Oera Linda Bok* (Leeuwarden: Kuipers, 1872) [= *The Oera Linda Book*, trans. William R. Sandbach (London: Trübner, 1876)].

Pape, Wolfgang, 'Zur Entwicklung des Faches Ur- und Frühgeschichte in Deutschland bis 1945,' in Achim Leube (ed.), *Prähistorie und Nationalsozialismus: Die mittel- und osteuropäische Ur- und Frühgeschichtsforschung in den Jahren 1933–1945*, Studien zur Wissenschafts- und Universitätsgeschichte 2 (Heidelberg: Synchron, 2002), 163–226.

Pascal, Roy, 'A Controversy in the German Universities,' *German Life and Letters* ns 1 (1947–48): 140–49.

Pastor, Willy, *Der Zug vom Norden: Anregungen zum Studium der nordischen Altertumskunde* (Jena: Diederichs, 1906).

———— *Aus germanischer Vorzeit: Bilder unserer Vorgeschichte* (Berlin: Haessel, 1907).

Patai, Raphael, and Jennifer, *The Myth of the Jewish Race* (Detriot: Wayne State University Press, 1989).

Pätzke, B., 'Die deutsche Wiederbesiedlung des Ostens,' *SS-Leitheft* 3/8 (1937): 55–56.

Paul, Fritz, *Fünfzig Jahre Skandinavistik an der Georg-August-Universität Göttingen: Eine vorläufige Skizze* (Göttingen: Skandinavisches Seminar der Universität, 1985).

Paul, Hermann, *Prinzipien der Sprachgeschichte* (Halle a.S.: Niemeyer, 1880).

Paul, Ina Ulrike, 'Paul Anton de Lagarde,' in Uwe Puschner, Walter Schmitz and Justus H. Ulbricht (eds.), *Handbuch zur 'Völkischen Bewegung' 1871–1918* (Munich: Saur, 1996), 45–93.

Pedersen, Holger, *Linguistic Science in the Nineteenth Century: Methods and Results*, trans. John Webster Spargo (Cambridge, Mass.: Harvard University Press, 1931) [= *The Discovery of Language* (Bloomington: Indiana University Press, 1962)].

Penka, Karl, *Origines Ariacae: Linguistisch-ethnologische Untersuchungen zur ältesten Geschichte der arischen Völker und Sprachen* (Vienna: Prochaska, 1883).

———— *Die Herkunft der Arier: Neue Beiträge zur historischen Anthropologie der europäischen Völker* (Vienna: Prochaska, 1886).

Pertz, Georg H., et al. (eds.), *Monumenta Germaniae historica inde ab anno Christi quingentesimo usque ad annum millesimum et quingentesimium* (Hanover: Hahn, and Berlin: Weidmann, 1826ff.).

Petri, Franz, *Germanisches Volkserbe in Wallonien und Nordfrankreich: Die fränkische Landnahme in Frankreich und den Niederlanden und die Bildung der westlichen Sprachgrenze* (Bonn: Röhrscheid, 1937).

Petrie, W.M. Flinders, *The Formation of the Alphabet* (London: MacMillan, 1912).

Petsch, Robert, 'Über Zeichenrunen und Verwandtes,' *Zeitschrift für den deutschen Unterricht* 31 (1917): 433–49.

Pfister, Friedrich, 'Brauch und Sinnbild,' in Ferdinand Herrmann and Wolfgang Treutlein (eds.), *Brauch und Sinnbild: Eugen Fehrle zum 60. Geburtstag* (Karlsruhe: Sudwestdeutsche Druck- und Verlags-Gesellschaft, 1940), 34–49.

Pflanze, Otto, *Bismarck and the Development of Germany, Volume 1: The Period of Unification 1815–1871*, 2nd ed. (Princeton: Princeton University Press, 1990).

Phelps, Reginald H., 'Theodor Fritsch und der Antisemitismus,' *Deutsche Rundschau* 87 (1961): 442–49.

———— '"Before Hitler Came": Thule Society and Germanen Orden,' *Journal of Modern History* 35 (1963): 245–61.

Picker, Henry, *Hitler's Tischgespräche im Führer Hauptquartier: Mit bisher un-bekanten Selbstzeugnissen Adolf Hitlers*, 3rd ed. (Stuttgart: Seewald, 1976).

Pictet, Adolphe, *Les Origines indo-européennes ou les Aryas primitifs. Essai de paléontologie linguistique*, 2 vols. (Paris: Cherbuliez, 1859–63).

Plaßmann, Joseph Otto, 'Die Prosawerke der Zuster Hadewych' (dissertation, Münster i.W., 1920) [cf. *Die Werke der Hadewych*, Schriftenreihe Kulturen der Erde. Textwerke 2 (Hanover: Lafaire, 1923)].

—— *Die Geschichte der Stadt Münster in Westfalen: Von den ältesten Zeiten bis zur Gegenwart* (Münster i.W.: Theissing, 1925).

—— *Das Leben des Kaiser Friedrich II. von Hohenstaufen*, Deutsche Volkheit (Jena: Diederichs 1927).

—— *Das Leben Kaiser Ottos des Großen*, Deutsche Volkheit (Jena: Diederichs 1928).

—— *Das Leben Kaiser Konrads des Zweiten des Saliers*, Deutsche Volkheit (Jena: Diederichs 1928).

—— *Orpheus: Altgriechische Mysteriengesänge* (Jena: Diederichs, 1928).

—— *König Heinrich der Vogler*, Deutsche Volkheit (Jena: Diederichs, 1928).

—— *Wikingerfahrten und Normannenreiche*, Deutsche Volkheit (Jena: Died-erichs, 1929).

—— 'Grundfragen zur germanischen Kultur,' *Germanien* 3 (1931/32): 76–84.

—— 'Die Ura Linda-Chronik,' *Germanien* 5 (1933): 323–29.

—— 'Sinnfälliges und Sinnbildliches: Grundsätzliches zur urgeistesgeschicht-lichen Forschungsmethodik,' *Germanien* 5 (1933): 33–41.

—— 'Runenformen in brauchtümlichen Sinnbildern,' *Germanien* 8 (1936): 105–14.

—— 'Völkisches Wollen und exaktes Forschen, *Germanien* 8 (1936): 130–33.

—— '"Ir sult sprechen willekommen,"' *Germanien* 8 (1936): 161–62.

—— 'Eröffnung der Pflegstätte für Germanenkunde in Detmold am 5. Ok-tober 1936,' *Germanien* 8 (1936): 328–31.

—— *Die Externsteine* (Berlin–Dahlem: Ahnenerbe, 1939).

—— *Ehre ist Zwang genug: Gedanken zur deutschen Ahnenerbe* (Berlin–Dahlem: Ahnenerbe, 1941).

—— 'Das Sinnbild im Märchen,' *Germanien* 13, NF 3 (1941): 201–10.

—— 'Rückblick und Ausblick,' *Germanien* 15, NF 5 (1943): 1–4.

—— 'Odal, Odalrune und Schaub: Zur Frage der Runen als Sinnbilder,' *Germanien* 15, NF 5 (1943): 237–46.

—— *Ehr is dwang gnog*, trans. A.E.C. Vuerhard-Berkhort (Amsterdam: Hamer, 1944).

—— 'Widukinds Sachsengeschichte im Spiegel altsächsischer Sprache und Dichtung,' *Niedersächsisches Jahrbuch für Landesgeschichte* 24 (1952): 1–35.

—— 'Widukind von Corvey als Quelle für die germanische Altertumskunde,' *Beiträge zur Geschichte der deutschen Sprache und Literatur* 75 (1953): 191–228.

—— *Princeps und Populus: Die Gefolgschaft im ottonischen Staatsaufbau nach der sächsischen Geschichtsschreibern des 10. Jahrhunderts*, Schriften der Forsch-ungshilfe (Göttingen: Göttinger Verlagsanstalt, 1954).

Plaßmann, Joseph Otto, and Wolfgang Krause, 'Die Hrabanische Runenreihe,' *Germanien* 15, NF 5 (1943): 171–88.

Plaßmann and Kreyenborg, 'Zum Arbeitsplan III (Plan des Archiv für germanische Vorgeschichte),' *Germanien* 1 (1929/30): 75–77.

Platz, Friedrich, 'An unsere Mitglieder!,' *Germanien* 7 (1935): 161.

Poesche, Theodor, *Die Arier: Ein Beitrag zur historischen Anthropologie* (Jena: Costenoble, 1878).

Poewe, Karla, *New Religions and the Nazis* (London: Routledge, 2006).

Polenz, Peter von, 'Sprachpurismus und Nationalsozialismus: Die "Fremdwort"-Frage gestern und heute,' in Eberhard Lämmert, Walther Killy, Karl Otto Conrady and Peter von Polenz, *Germanistik—eine deutsche Wissenschaft*, Edition Suhrkamp 204, 2nd ed. (Frankfurt a.M.: Suhrkamp, 1967), 111–65.

Poliakov, Léon, *The Aryan Myth: A History of Racist and Nationalist Ideas in Europe*, trans. Edmund Howard, Columbia Centre Series (London: Heinemann, 1974).

Poliakov, Léon, and Joseph Wulf (eds.), *Das Dritte Reich und seine Denker* (Berlin: Arani, 1959).

Pott, August Friedrich, *Etymologische Forschungen auf dem Gebiete der indo-germanischen Sprachen*, 4 vols. (Lemgo: Meyer, 1833–36).

Price, Arnold H., *The Germanic Warrior Clubs: An Inquiry into the Dynamics of the Era of Migrations and into the Antecedents of Medieval Society*, 2nd ed. (Tübingen: Niemeyer, 1996).

Pringle, Heather, *The Master Plan: Himmler's scholars and the Holocaust* (New York: Hyperion, 2006).

Puschner, Uwe, *Die völkische Bewegung im wilhelminischen Kaiserreich: Sprache – Rasse – Religion* (Darmstadt: Wissenschaftliche Buchgesellschaft, 2001).

———'"One People, One Reich, One God": The *völkische Weltanschauung* and Movement,' *Bulletin of the German Historical Institute London* 24 (2002): 5–28.

———'Germanenideologie und völkische Weltanschauung,' in Heinrich Beck et al. (eds.), *Zur Geschichte der Gleichung "germanisch-deutsch": Sprache und Namen, Geschichte und Institutionen*, Erganzungsbände zum Reallexikon der Germanischen Altertumskunde 24 (Berlin: De Gruyter, 2003), 103–29.

——— 'Anti-Semitism and German Voelkish Ideology,' in Hubert Cancik and Uwe Puschner (eds.), *Anti-Semitism, Paganism, Voelkish Religion* (Munich: Saur, 2004), 55–63.

Quinn, Malcolm, *The Swastika: Constructing the Symbol* (London: Routledge, 1994).

Raabe, Felix, *Die bündische Jugend: Ein Beitrag zur Geschichte der Weimarer Republik* (Stuttgart: Brentano, [1961]).

Rahn, Otto, *Kreuzzug gegen den Gral* (Freiburg i.Br.: Urban, 1933).

Rambach, Johan Jakob, *Versuch einer pragmatischen Literairhistorie* (Halle a.S: Gebauer, 1770).

Ranke, Friedrich, 'Das Wilde Heer und die Kultbünde der Germanen: Eine Auseinandersetzung mit Otto Höfler,' *Niederdeutsche Zeitschrift für Volks-*

kunde und Blätter für niedersächsische Heimatpflege 18 (1940): 1–33 [= idem, *Kleinere Schriften*, ed. Heinz Rupp and Eduard Studer, Bibliotheca Germania 12 (Bern: Francke, 1971), 380–408].

Raschdorff, Max, *Nordische Sinnzeichen- und Bilderschrift durch 4 Jahrtausende* (Finsterwalde: Raschdorff-Viehrig, 1939).

Rather, Lelland Joseph, *Reading Wagner: A Study in the History of Ideas* (Baton Rouge: Louisiana State University Press, 1990).

Rauschning, Hermann, *Hitler Speaks* (London: Thornton Butterworth, 1939) [= *Gespräche mit Hitler*, 2nd ed. (New York: Europa, 1940)].

Reichardt, Konstantin, *Studien zu den Skalden des 9. und 10. Jahrhunderts* [dissertation] (Leipzig: Mayer & Müller, 1928).

———— *Thule: Ausgewählte Sagas von altgermanischen Bauern und Helden* (Jena: Diederichs, 1934).

———— *Germanische Welt vor tausend Jahren* (Jena: Diederichs, 1936).

———— *Runenkunde* (Jena: Diederichs, 1936).

———— *Havard, der Mann von Ejsfjord* (Jena: Diederichs, 1940).

Reichert, Hermann, 'Much, Rudolf,' in Johannes Hoops, *Reallexikon der germanischen Altertumskunde* XX, 2nd ed. (Berlin: De Gruyter, 2002), 273–79.

Reimann, Bruno W., 'Die "Selbst-Gleichschaltung" der Universitäten 1933,' in Jörg Tröger (ed.), *Hochschule und Wissenschaft im Dritten Reich* (Frankfurt a.M.: Campus, 1984), 38–52.

Reinach, Salomon, *L'Origin des Aryens* (Paris: Leroux, 1892).

———— 'Le mirage oriental,' *L'Anthropologie* 4 (1893): 539–78 and 699–732.

———— review of Herman Wirth, *Der Aufgang der Menschheit*, *Revue archéologique*, 5ᵉ ser., 3 (1929): 136.

Reinecke, Adolf, *Die deutsche Buchstabenschrift: Ihre Entstehung und Entwickelung, ihre zweckmässigkeit und völkische Bedeutung* (Leipzig–Borsdorf: Hasert, 1910).

Reinerth, Hans, *Pfahlbauten am Bodensee* (Augsburg: Filser, 1922); 2nd ed. (Leipzig: Kabitsch, 1940); 14th ed. (Überlingen am Bodensee: Feyel, 1986).

———— 'Die deutsche Vorgeschichte im Dritten Reich,' *Nationalsozialistische Monatshefte* 3 (1932): 256–59

———— '†Gustav Kossinna,' *Nationalsozialistische Monatshefte* 3 (1932): 259–61.

———— 'Gustaf Kossinna als Vorkämpfer und Begründer der völkischen Vorgeschichtsforschung,' *Germanen-Erbe* 3 (1938): 354–62.

———— *Vorgeschichte der deutschen Stämme: Germanisch Tat und Kultur auf deutschem Boden* (Leipzig: Bibliographisches Institut, [1940]).

———— *Pfahlbauten Unteruhldingen am Bodensee um 2200 und 1100 v. d. Ztr: Führer durch das Freilichtmuseum*, 14th ed. (Überlingen am Bodensee: Feyel, 1957).

Reiss, Bernhard, *Runenkunde*, Reclams Universitäts-Bibliothek (Leipzig: Reclam, [1936]).

Renck-Reichert, Kurt, *Runenfibel* (Heilbronn: Salzer, 1935).

Repp, Kevin, *Reformers, Critics, and the Paths of German Modernity: Anti-politics and the Search for Alternatives, 1890–1914* (Cambridge, Mass.: Harvard University Press, 2000).

Resenius, Petrus J. (Peder H. Resen), *Edda Islandorum An. Chr. MCCXV. Islandice conscripta per Snorronem Sturlæ Islandiae nomophylacem nunc primum Islandice Danice et Latine ex antiquis codicibus mss. bibliothecae regis et aliorum in lucem prodit opera et studio Petri Johannis Resenii* (Copenhagen: Gödian, 1665).

Retallack, James N., *Notables of the Right: The Conservative Party and Political Mobilization in Germany, 1876–1918* (Boston: Unwin Hyman, 1988).

Reulecke, Jürgen, 'Das Jahr 1902 und die Ursprünge der Männerbund-Ideologie,' in Gisela Völger and Karin von Welck (eds.), *Männerbünde, Mannerband. Zur Rolle des Mannes im Kulturvergleich (Zweibändige Materiellensammlung zu einer Austellung des Rautenstrauch-Joest-Museums für Völkerkunde in der Josef-Haubrich-Kunsthalle, Köln von 23, März bis 17. Juni 1990)* (Cologne: Stadt Köln, 1990), I, 3–10.

Richards, Earl Jeffrey, 'Dr. Schneider gen. Dr. Schwerte: Versuch einer vorläufigen Bilanz,' in *Ungeahntes Erbe. Der Fall Schneider/Schwerte: Persilschen für eine Lebenslüge. Eine Dokumentation* (Aschaffenburg: Alibri, 1998), 212–33.

Richthofen, Bolko Freiherr von, 'Zur religionsgeschichtlichen Auswertung vorgeschichtlicher Altertümer,' *Mitteilungen der Anthropologischen Gesellschaft in Wien* 62 (1932): 110–44.

———— 'Eine Entgegnung an Prof. H. Wirth,' *Mitteilungen der Anthropologischen Gesellschaft in Wien* 62 (1932): 228–30.

———— 'Um Herman Wirth,' *Reichswart* 13/19, 7 May, 1932.

Richter, Erwin, 'Das Hakenkreuz als Führer zu altgermanischer Kultur: Ein Beitrag zur germanischen Wiederentdeckung,' *Mannus* 23 (1931): 1–23.

Ridé, Jacques, *L'Image du Germain dans le pensée et la littérature Allemande de la récouverte de Tacite à la fin du XVIème siècle (contribution à l'étude de la genese d'un mythe)*, 3 vols. (Paris: Champion, 1977).

Riehl, Wilhelm Heinrich, *Die Naturgeschichte des Volkes als Grundlage einer deutschen Sozialpolitik*, 4 vols. (Stuttgart: Cotta, 1851–69).

Ringer, Fritz K., *The Decline of the German Mandarins: The German Academic Community 1890–1933* (Cambridge, Mass.: Harvard University Press, 1969).

———— 'A Sociography of German Academics, 1863–1938,' *Central European History* 25 (1993): 251–80.

Robberstad, Knut, Magnús Már Lárusson & Gerhard Hafström, 'Odelsrett,' in Johannes Brøndsted et al. (eds.), *Kulturhistorisk leksikon for nordisk middelalder* XII (Copenhagen: Rosenkilde & Bagger, 1967), 493–503.

Robins, Robert H., *A Short History of Linguistics*, Longmann Linguistics Library, 3rd ed. (London: Longmann, 1990).

Römer, Ruth, 'Sigmund Feist: Deutscher–Germanist–Jude,' *Muttersprache* 91 (1981): 249–308.

———— *Sprachwissenschaft und Rassenideologie in Deutschland*, 2nd ed. (Munich: Fink, 1989).

———— 'Sigmund Feist und die Gesellschaft für deutsche Philologie in Berlin,' *Muttersprache* 103 (1993): 28–40.

Rose, Detlev, *Die Thule-Gesellschaft: Legende–Mythos–Wirklichkeit*, Veröffentlichungen des Instituts für deutsche Nachkriegesgeschichte 20 (Tübingen: Grabert, 1994).

Rose, Paul Lawrence, *Wagner, Race and Revolution* (London: Faber, 1992).

Roselius, Hildegard, *Ludwig Roselius und sein kulturelles Werk* (Brunswick: Westermann, 1954).

Rosenberg, Alfred, *Die Protokolle der Weisen von Zion und die jüdische Weltpolitik* (Munich: Boepple, 1923).

———— *Der Mythus des XX. Jahrhunderts* (Munich: Hoheneichen, 1930).

———— 'Germanische Lebenswerte im Weltanschauungskampf,' *Germanen-Erbe* 1 (1936).

Rotsaert, Marie-Louise, 'Etymologie et ideologie: Des reflets du nationalisme sur la lexicologie allemande 1830–1914,' *Historiographia linguistica* 6 (1979): 309–38.

Rötzer, Hans Gerd, *Geschichte der deutschen Literatur: Epochen, Autoren, Werke* (Bamberg: Buchner, 1997).

Rudbeck, Olaf (the elder), *Atland eller Manheim*, 4 vols. (Uppsala: Curio, 1679–1702).

Ruppel, Karl Konrad A., 'Das Symbol der germanischen Sippe,' *Odal* 5 (1936): 391–404.

———— *Die Hausmarke: Das Symbol der germanischen Sippe*, Schriftenreihe der Forschungsstätte für Hausmarken und Sippenzeichen im Ahnenerbe 1 (Berlin: Metzner, 1939).

Rusinek, Bernd-A., 'Ein Germanist in der SS,' in Gotthard Jasper (ed.), *Ein Germanist und seine Wissenschaft: Der Fall Schneider/Schwerte*, Erlangen Universitätsreden 53/3 (Erlangen: Friedrich-Alexander Universität Erlangen-Nürnberg, 1996), 23–46.

Salin, Bernhard, *Die altgermanische Thierornamentik: Typologische Studie über germanischen Metallgegenstände aus dem IV. bis IX. Jahrhundert, nebst einer Studie über irischer Ornamentik*, trans. Johanna Mestorf (Stockholm: Wahlström & Widstand, 1904).

Sandmann, Jürgen, *Der Bruck mit der humanitären Tradition: Die Biologisierung der Ethik bei Ernst Haeckel und anderen Darwinisten seiner Zeit*, Forschungen zur neueren Medizin- und Biologiegeschichte 2 (Stuttgart: Fischer, 1990).

Saussure, Ferdinand de, *Cours de linguistique générale*, ed. Charles Bally and Albert Sechecaye (Lausanne: Payot, 1916), 2nd ed. (Paris: Payot, 1922) [= *Grundfragen der allgemeinen Sprachwissenschaft*, trans. Hermann Lommel (Berlin: De Gruyter, 1931)].

Sax, Benjamin C., and Dieter Kuntz (eds.), *Inside Hitler's Germany: A Documentary History of the Third Reich*, Sources in Modern History Series (Lexington, Mass.: Heath, 1992).

Schama, Simon, *Landscape and Memory* (New York: Knopf, 1995).

Scharfe, Martin, 'Einschwörung auf den völkisch-germanischen Kulturbegriff,' in Jörg Tröger (ed.), *Hochschule und Wissenschaft im Dritten Reich* (Frankfurt a.M.: Campus, 1984), 105–55.

Scherer, Wilhelm, *Geschichte der Deutschen Literatur*, 13th ed. (Berlin: Weidmann, 1915).

Scheuermann, Wilhelm, *Woher kommt das Hakenkreuz?* (Berlin: Rowohlt, 1933).

Schirach, Baldur von, *Ich glaubte an Hitler* (Hamburg: Mosaik, 1967).

Schlegel, [C. W.] Friedrich von, *Ueber die Sprache und Weissheit der Indier* (Heidelberg: Mohr & Zimmer, 1808).

Schleif, Hans, 'Die SS-Ausgrabung am "Kriemhildenstuhl" bei Bad Dürkheim,' *Germanien* 10 (1938): 289–96 and 11 (1939): 340–46.

––––– 'Die SS-Ausgrabung Karnburg,' *Germanien* 12, NF 2 (1940): 63–70.

––––– 'SS-Ausgrabung Urstätt im Warthegau,' *Germanien* 14, NF 4 (1942): 431–36.

Schirmeisen, Karl, 'Buchstabenschrift, Lautwandel, Göttersage und Zeitrechnung,' *Mannus* 3 (1911): 97–120 and 225–78.

––––– 'Die Runen als Göttersymbole,' *Zeitschrift des Deutschen Vereins für die Geschichte Mährens und Schliesens* 26/4 (1926).

Schliemann, Heinrich, *Trojanische Altertümer: Bericht über die Ausgrabungen in Troja* (Leipzig: Brockhaus, 1874) [= *Troy and Its Remains: A Narrative of Researches and Discoveries made on the Site of Ilium and in the Trojan Plain*, ed. Phillip Smith (London: Murray, 1875)].

Schlottig, Kurt H. (ed.), *Beiträge zur Runenkunde und nordischen Sprachwissenschaft. Gustav Neckel zum 60. Geburtstag* (Leipzig: Harrassowitz, 1938).

Schmeja, Hans, *Der Mythos der Alpengermanen*, Arbeiten aus dem Institut für Vergleichende Sprachwissenschaft 8 (Vienna: Gerold, 1968).

Schmidt, Martin, and Uta Halle, 'On the Folklore of the Externsteine: Or a Centre for Germanomaniacs,' in Amy Gazin-Schwartz and Cornelius Holtorf (eds.), *Archaeology and Folklore* (London: Routledge, 1999), 158–74.

Schmidt-Klevenow, Kurt, 'Nordische Runen und Hausmarken in der chinesichen Schrift,' *Germanien* 8 (1936): 183–84.

Schmidt(-Rohr), Georg, *Unsere Muttersprache als Waffe und Werkzeug des deutschen Gedankens*, Tat-Flugschriften 20 (Jena: Diederichs, 1917).

––––– *Die Sprache als Bildnerin der Völker: Eine Wesens- und Lebenskunde der Volkstümer* (Jena: Diederichs, 1932).

––––– *Mutter Sprache: Vom Amt der Sprache bei der Volkwerdung*, 2nd ed. (Jena: Diederichs, 1933).

Schmitz-Berning, Cornelia, *Vokabular des Nationalsozialismus*, 2nd ed. (Berlin: De Gruyter, 1998).

Schneider, Hans Ernst, 'Das Tragische,' *Das Reich: Literatur, Kunst, Wissenschaft* 6, 7 Feb., 1943.

Schneider, Hermann (Leipzig), *Der kretische Ursprung des "phönikischen" Alphabets; Die Wanderung und Wandlung der Sündflutsage: Der herrschende Rassebegriff und die Tatsachen der Erfahrung* (Leipzig: Hinrichs, 1913).

––––– 'Ursprung und Sinn unseres Alphabets,' in *Gesammelte Aufsätze* (Leipzig: Kroner, 1924), 3–113.

Schneider, Hermann (Tübingen), *Germanische Heldensage*, 2 vols. (Berlin: De Gruyter, 1928–34).

——— 'Die germanische Altertumskunde zwischen 1933 und 1938,' *Forschungen und Fortschritte* 15 (1939): 1–3 [= 'The Study of Germanic Antiquity in the Years 1933–1938,' *Research and Progress* 5 (1939): 135–42].

Schnell, Ralf, *Literarische Innere Emigration 1933–45* (Stuttgart: Metzler, 1976).

——— 'Innere Emigration,' in Walther Killy (ed.), *Literatur Lexikon* XIII (Gütersloh: Bertelsmann, 1992), 436–38.

Schnurbein, Stefanie von, 'Geheime kultische Männerbünde bei den Germanen—Eine Theorie im Spannungsfeld zwischen Wissenschaft und Ideologie,' in Gisela Völger and Karin von Welck (eds.), *Männerbünde, Mannerband. Zur Rolle des Mannes im Kulturvergleich (Zweibändige Materiellensammlung zu einer Austellung des Rautenstrauch-Joest-Museums für Völkerkunde in der Josef-Haubrich-Kunsthalle, Köln von 23, März bis 17. Juni 1990)* (Cologne: Stadt Köln, 1990), II, 97–102.

——— *Religion als Kulturkritik: Neugermanisches Heidentum im 20. Jahrhundert*, Skandinavistische Arbeiten 13 (Heidelberg: Winter, 1992).

Schöbel, Gunter, 'Hans Reinerth. Forscher – NS-Funktionär – Museumsleiter,' in Achim Leube (ed.), *Prähistorie und Nationalsozialismus: Die mittel- und osteuropäische Ur- und Frühgeschichtsforschung in den Jahren 1933–1945*, Studien zur Wissenschafts- und Universitätsgeschichte 2 (Heidelberg: Synchron, 2002), 321–96.

Schopenhauer, Arthur, *Parerga und Paralipomena: Kleine philosophische Schriften* (Stuttgart: Cotta, 1850).

Schröder, Albert, *Ahnenerbe in der Volkskunst der Heide*, Aus Geschichte und Kultur der Heide 3 (Düben: Streubel, 1939).

Schröder, Franz Rolf, *Untersuchungen zur Halfdanar Saga Eysteinssonar* [dissertation] (Halle a.S.: Niemeyer, 1917).

——— 'Neuere Runenforschung,' *Germanisch-Romanische Monatsschrift* 10 (1922): 4–16.

——— 'Zur Runeninschrift auf dem Marmorlöwen im Piräus,' *Beiträge zur Geschichte der deutschen Sprache und Literatur* 47 (1923): 347–50.

——— *Altgermanische Kulturprobleme*, Trübners philologische Bibliothek 11 (Berlin: De Gruyter 1929).

——— 'Neuere Forschungen zur germanischen Altertumskunde und Religionsgeschichte,' *Germanisch-Romanische Monatsschrift* 17 (1929): 177–92, 241–55 and 401–20.

——— presentation of Fritz Wiegers (ed.), *Herman Wirth und die deutsche Wissenschaft*, *Germanisch-Romanische Monatsschrift* 20 (1932): 313.

——— presentation of Gustav Neckel, *Kultur der alten Germanen*, *Germanisch-Romanische Monatsschrift* 23 (1935): 230.

——— review of Bernhard Kummer, *Midgards Untergang*, 2nd ed., *Germanisch-Romanische Monatsschrift* 24 (1936): 150.

Schuchardt, Hugo, 'Sachen und Wörter,' *Zeitschrift für romanische Philologie* 29 (1905): 620–22.

Schumacher, Karl-Heinz, *Die deutschen Monatsnamen* (Griefswald: Bamberg, 1937).

Schüler, Winfried, *Der Bayreuther Kreis von seiner Entstehung bis zum Ausgang der Wilhelminischen Ära: Wagnerkult und Kulturreform im Geist völkischer*

Weltanschauung, Neue Münstersche Beiträge zur Geschichtsforschung 12 (Münster: Aschendorff, 1971).

Schumann, Wolfgang, 'Die Universität Jena in der Zeit des deutschen Fachismus (1933 bis 1945),' in Max Steinmetz (ed.), *Geschichte der Universität Jena 1548/58-1958: Festgabe zum vierhundert jährigen Universitätsjubiläum* (Jena: Fischer, 1958), 615–70.

Schultz, Wolfgang, 'Das Hakenkreuz als Grundzeichen des westsemitischen Alphabets,' *Memnon* 3 (1909): 175–200.

Schulz, Mathias, 'Der Kult der Sternenmagier,' *Der Spiegel* 48, 25 Nov. 2002, 192–206.

Schurtz, Heinrich, *Altersklassen und Männerbünde: Eine Darstellung der Grundformen der Gesellschaft* (Berlin: Reimer, 1902).

Schwerin von Krosigk, Hildegard Gräfin, *Gustaf Kossinna; Der Nachlaß: Versuch einer Analyse*, Offa-Ergänzungsreihe 6 (Neumünster: Wachholtz, 1982).

Schwerte, Hans, *Faust und das Faustische: Ein Kapitel deutscher Ideologie* (Stuttgart: Klett, 1962).

Schwierskott, Hans-Joachim, *Arthur Moeller van den Bruck und der revolutionäre Nationalismus in der Weimarer Republik*, Veröffentlichungen der Gesellschaft für Geistesgeschichte 1 (Göttingen: Musterschmidt, 1962).

Scurla, Herbert, *Wilhelm von Humboldt: Werden und Wirken* (Düsseldorf: Claasen, 1976).

See, Klaus von, *Deutsche-Germanen Ideologie: Vom Humanismus bis zur Gegenwart* (Frankfurt a.M.: Athenäum, 1970).

———— 'Das "Nordische" in der deutschen Wissenschaft des 20. Jahrhunderts,' *Jahrbuch für Internationale Germanistik* 15/2 (1983): 8–38 [= a slightly abbreviated version in *Barbar, Germane, Arier: Die Suche nach der Identität der Deutschen* (Heidelberg: Winter, 1994), 207–32].

———— 'Politische Männerbunde-Ideologie von der wilhelmischen Zeit bis zum Nationalsozialismus,' in Gisela Völger and Karin von Welck (eds.), *Männerbünde, Mannerband. Zur Rolle des Mannes im Kulturvergleich (Zweibändige Materiellensammlung zu einer Austellung des Rautenstrauch-Joest-Museums für Völkerkunde in der Josef-Haubrich-Kunsthalle, Köln von 23, März bis 17. Juni 1990)* (Cologne: Stadt Köln, 1990), I, 93–102 [= a revised version in *Barbar, Germane, Arier: Die Suche nach der Identität der Deutschen* (Heidelberg: Winter, 1994), 319–42].

———— 'Andreas Heusler in seinen Briefen,' *Zeitschrift für deutsches Altertum und deutsche Literatur* 119 (1990): 379–96 [= *Barbar, Germane, Arier: Die Suche nach der Identität der Deutschen* (Heidelberg: Winter, 1994), 261–82].

———— *Barbar, Germane, Arier: Die Suche nach der Identität der Deutschen* (Heidelberg: Winter, 1994).

See, Klaus von, and Julia Zernack, *Germanistik und Politik in der Zeit des Nationalsozialismus. Zwei Fallstudien: Hermann Schneider und Gustav Neckel*, Frankfurter Beiträge zur Germanistik 42 (Heidelberg: Winter, 2004).

Seip, Didrik Arup, *Hjemme og i fiendeland 1940–45* (Oslo: Gyldental, 1946).

Sheehan, James J., *German History 1770–1866*, Oxford History of Modern Europe (Oxford: Clarendon, 1989).

Siefert, Hermann, *Der bündische Aufbruch, 1918–1923*, Veröffentlichungen der Gesellschaft für Geistesgeschichte (Bad Godesberg: Voggenreiter, [1963]).

Siegert, Hans, 'Zur Geschichte der Begriffe "Arier" und "arisch,"' *Wörter und Sachen* 22, NF 4 (1941–42): 73–99.

Sim, Kevin (dir.), *Hitler's Search for the Holy Grail* (London: Channel 4, 1999).

Simon, Gerd, 'Wissenschaft und Wende 1933: Zum Verhältnis von Wissenschaft und Politik am Beispiel des Sprachwissenschaftlers Georg Schmidt-Rohr,' *Das Argument* 158 (1986): 527–42.

—— 'Sprachpflege im "Dritten Reich",' in Konrad Ehlich (ed.), *Sprache im Faschismus*, Suhrkamp-Taschenbuch Wissenschaft 760 (Frankfurt a.M.: Suhrkamp, 1989), 58–86.

—— *Die hochfliegenden Pläne eines "nichtamtlichen Kulturministers": Erich Gierachs ›Sachwörterbuch der Germanenkunde‹*, Wörterbücher im Dritten Reich 1 (Tübingen: Gesellschaft für Interdisziplinäre Forschung Tübingen, 1998).

—— 'Die Island-Expedition des ›Ahnenerbe‹ der SS,' <homepages.uni-tuebingen.de/gerd.simon/island.pdf>, 2002.

Simpson, John A., and Edmund S.C. Weiner et al. (eds.), *The Oxford English Dictionary*, 22 vols., 2nd ed. (Oxford: Clarendon, 1989).

Sklenář, Karel, *Archaeology in Central Europe: The First 500 Years*, trans. Iris Lewitová (Leicester: Leicester University Press, 1983).

Smith, Woodruff D., *The Ideological Origin of Nazi Imperialism* (New York: Oxford University Press, 1986).

—— *Politics and the Sciences of Culture in Germany 1840–1920* (New York: Oxford University Press, 1991).

Smolla, Günter, 'Das Kossinna-Syndrom,' *Fundberichte aus Hessen* 19/20 (1979–80): 1–9.

—— 'Gustaf Kossinna nach 50 Jahren. Kein Nachruf,' *Acta praehistorica et archaeologica* 16/17 (1984–85): 9–14.

—— review of Hildegard Gräfin Schwerin von Krosigk, *Gustaf Kossinna*, *Germania: Anzeiger der Römisch-Germanischen Kommission des Deutschen Archäologischen Instituts* 64 (1986): 682–86.

Söderberg, Sven and Erik Brate, *Ölands runinskrifter*, Sverges runinskrifter 1 (Stockholm: Norstedt & Sons, 1900–6).

Sombart, Nicolaus, 'Männerbund und Politische Kultur in Deutschland,' in Joachim H. Knoll and Julius H. Schoeps (ed.), *Typisch deutsch, die Jugendbewegung: Beiträge zu einer Phänomengeschichte* (Opladen: Leske & Budrich, 1988) [= Thomas Kühne (ed.), *Männergeschichte—Geschlechtergeschichte: Männlichkeit im Wandel der Moderne*, Reihe "Geschichte und Geschlechter" 14 (Frankfurt a.M.: Campus, 1996), 136–55].

Sonderegger, Stefan, 'Vorwort,' in Andreas Heusler, *Kleine Schriften* II, ed. Stefan Sondregger (Berlin: De Gruyter, 1969).

Sørensen, Marie L.S., 'The Fall of a Nation, the Birth of a Subject: the National Use of Archaeology in Nineteenth-Century Denmark,' in Margarita Díaz-Andreu and Timothy C. Champion (eds.), *Nationalism and Archaeology in Europe* (London: UCL Press, 1996, 24–47).

Sparnay, H., *Karl Lachmann als Germanist* (Bern: Francke, 1948).

Specht, Franz, *Der Ursprung der indogermanischen Deklination* (Göttingen: Vandenhoeck & Ruprecht, 1944 [1947]).

Spengler, Oswald, *Der Untergang des Abendlandes: Umrisse einer Morphologie der Weltgeschichte* (Munich: Beck, 1923).

Spielvogel, Jackson J., *Hitler and Nazi Germany*, 2nd ed. (Englewood Cliffs: Prentice Hall, 1992).

Stachura, Peter D., *The German Youth Movement 1900–1945: An Interpretative and Documentary History* (New York: St Martin's Press, 1981).

Stackelberg, Roderick, *Idealism Debased: From Völkisch Ideology to National Socialism* (Kent, Ohio: Kent State University Press, 1981).

Stampfuss, Rudolf, *Gustaf Kossinna: Ein Leben für die deutsche Vorgeschichte* (Leipzig: Kabitzsch, 1935).

Stark, Gary D., *Entrepreneurs of Ideology: Neoconservative Publishers in Germany, 1890–1933* (Chapel Hill: University of North Carolina Press, 1981).

Stauff, Phillip, *Runenhäuser* (Berlin–Lichterfelde: Scheffer, 1913).

Stecke, Theodor, 'Die Ura Linda-Chronik, altgermanisch oder gefälscht?,' *Völkischer Beobachter* 47/11, 11 Jan., 1934.

Steinen, Karl von den, 'Prähistorische Zeichen und Ornamente. Svastika. Triskeles. Runenalphabet?,' in *Festschrift für Adolf Bastian zu seinem 70. Geburtstag, 26. Juni 1896* (Berlin: Reimer, 1896), 249–88.

Steinmetz, Hermann, 'Versuch einer astronomischen Deutung des Hakenkreuzes,' *Archiv für Anthropologie* NF 15 (1917): 206–13.

Steinthal, Heymann, *Grammatik, Logik und Psychologie: Ihre Prinzipien und ihr Verhältnis zu einander* (Berlin: Dümmler, 1855).

—— *Einleitung in die Psychologie und Sprachwissenschaft*, Abriss der Sprachwissenschaft 1 (Berlin: Dümmler, 1871).

Stephenson, Jill, *The Nazi Organisation of Women* (London: Croom Helm, 1981).

Stern, Fritz, *The Politics of Cultural Despair: A Study in the Rise of German Ideology* (Berkeley: University of California Press, 1961).

Sterne, Carus [Ernst Krause], *Tuisko-Land: Der arischen Stämme und Götter Urheimat* (Glogau: Flemming, 1891).

Steuer, Heiko, 'Herbert Jankuhn und seine Darstellungen zur Germanen- und Wikingerzeit,' in Heiko Steuer (ed.), *Eine hervorragend nationale Wissenschaft: Deutsche Prähistoriker zwischen 1900–1995*, Ergänzungsbände zum Reallexikon der Germanischen Altertumskunde, 29 (Berlin: De Gruyter, 2001), 417–73.

Stief, Werner, *Heidnische Sinnbilder an christlichen Kirchen und auf Werken der Volkskunst: Der "Lebensbaum" und sein Gestaltwandel im Jahreslauf*, Deutsches Ahnenerbe, Reihe C: Volkstümliche Schriften 8 (Leipzig: Hase & Koehler, 1938).

Stiehl, Ruth, and Hans Erich Stier (eds.), *Beiträge zur Alten Geschichte und deren Nachleben: Festschrift für Franz Altheim zum 6.10.1968*, 2 vols. (Berlin: De Gruyter, 1969–70).

Storm, Sönje, 'Die öffentliche Aussprache über Herman Wirths "Ura-Linda-Chronik" in Berlin (1934),' in Birgitta Almgren (ed.), *Bilder des Nordens in der Germanistik 1929–1945: Wissenschaftliche Integrität oder politische Anpassung?*, Södertörn Academic Studies 11 (Huddinge: Södertörns Högskola, 2002), 79–97.

Strauss, Herbert A., 'Wissenschaftler in der Emigration,' in Jörg Tröger (ed.), *Hochschule und Wissenschaft im Dritten Reich* (Frankfurt a.M.: Campus, 1984), 53–64.

Strauss, Herbert A., and Werner Röder (eds.), *International Biographical Dictionary of Central European Emigrés 1933–1945*, 3 vols. (Munich: Saur, 1980–83).

Strobel, Hans, 'Allzu "geheim" Herr Geheimrat! Eine notwendige Erwiderung,' *Völkischer Beobachter* 47/224–225, 12–13 Aug., 1934.

Strohmeyer, Arn, *Der gebaute Mythos: Das Haus Atlantis in der Bremer Böttscherstraße; Ein deutsches Mißverstandnis* (Bremen: Donat, 1993).

Stumpfl, Robert, 'Der Ursprung des Fastnachtspiels und die kultischen Männerbünder der Germanen,' *Zeitschrift für Deutschkunde* 48 (1934): 286–97.

——— *Kultspiele der Germanen als Ursprung des mittelälterlichen Dramas* (Berlin: Junker & Dünnhaupt, 1936–37).

Suffert, Otto, review of Gustav Neckel, review of Wilhelm Teudt, *Germanische Heiligtümer* (*Deutsche Literaturzeitung* 51, 1931), *Germanien* 3 (1930/31).

——— 'Zum Streit um die Ura Linda-Chronik,' *Germanien* 6 (1934): 49–56.

Svärdström, Elisabeth, *Johannes Bureus' arbeten om svenska runinskrifter* (Stockholm: Wahlström & Widstrand, 1936).

Svennung, Josef, *Zur Geschichte des Goticismus*, Skrifter utg. av K. Human. Vetenskapssamfundet i Uppsala 44, 2 B (Stockholm: Almqvist & Wiksell, 1967).

[Tacitus, P. Cornelius] *Cai Cornelii Taciti Equitis Ro. Germania incipit* ([Nuremberg: Creusner, 1473]).

——— *Cornelii Taciti Historia Augusta additis quinque libris nouiter incientis*, ed. Andrea Alciato (Basel: [s.n.,] 1519).

——— *The Agricola and the Germania*, trans. Harold Mattingly, ed. Stanley A. Handford, The Penguin Classics, rev. ed. (London: Penguin, 1970).

Taeger, Hans, 'Germanentum und wir,' *Zeitschrift für Deutschkunde* 50 (1936): 406–13.

Tanner, Michael, 'The Total Work of Art,' in Peter Burbidge and Richard Sutton (eds.), *The Wagner Companion* (London: Faber & Faber, 1979), 140–220.

——— *Wagner* (London: HarperCollins, 1996).

Taureck, Bernhard H.F., *Nietzsche und der Faschismus: Eine Studie über Nietzsches politische Philosophie und ihre Folgen* (Hamburg: Junius, 1989).

Tenney, M.F., 'Tacitus through the Centuries to the Age of Printing,' *University of Colorado Studies* 22 (1935): 341–63.

Teudt, Wilhelm, *'Im Interesse der Wissenschaft!': Haeckels 'Fälschungen' und die 46 Zoologen etc. Die wichtigsten Dokumente zum Fall Brass-Haeckel*, Schriften des Keplerbundes 3 (Godesberg bei Bonn: Naturwissenschaftlicher Verlag des Keplerbundes, 1909).

———— *Die deutsche Sachlichkeit und der Weltkrieg: Ein Beitrag zur Völkerseelenkunde* (Godesberg bei Bonn: Naturwissenschaftlicher Verlag des Keplerbundes, 1917).

———— 'Altgermanischer Gestirndienst. I. Das Zerstörungswerk an den Externsteinen,' *Mannus* 18 (1926): 349–57.

———— *Germanische Heiligtümer: Beiträge zur Aufdeckung der Vorgeschichte, ausgehend von den Externsteinen, den Lippequellen und dem Teutoburg* (Jena: Diederichs, 1929; 4th ed., 1936).

———— 'Das Werk Gustaf Kossinnas,' *Germanien* 3 (1931/32): 73–75.

———— 'Bericht über den Stand der Detmolder germanenkundlichen Werkes und der begründenden Pflegstätte, im Brachtet (Juni) 1935,' *Germanien* 7 (1935): 257–61.

Thiele, Ernst Otto, *Sinnbild und Brauchtum: Volkskunst in einem deutschen Gau* (Potsdam: Bogenreiter, 1937).

Tiedemann, Hans, *Tacitus und das Nationalbewußtsein der deutschen Humanisten Ende des 15. und Anfang des 16. Jh.* (Berlin: Ebering, 1913).

Tilak, Bal Gangadhar, *The Arctic Home in the Vedas, Being also a New Key to the Interpretation of Many Vedic Texts and Legends* (Poona: Kesari, 1903).

Till, Rudolf, 'Die Überlieferung von Tacitus' Germania,' *Germanien* 15, NF 5 (1943): 119–29.

———— *Handschriftliche Untersuchungen zu Tacitus Agricola und Germania*, Deutsches Ahnenerbe, B. Abteilung Arbeiten zur klassischen Philologie und Altertumskunde 1 (Berlin–Dahlem: Ahnenerbe, 1943).

Timpanaro, Sebastiano, *La genesi del metodo del Lachmann*, Biblioteca di cultura; Saggi 5, 2nd ed. (Padua: Liviana, 1985).

Titzmann, Michael, 'Die Konzeption der "Germanen" in der deutsche Literatur des 19. Jahrhunderts,' in Jürgen Link and Wulf Wülfling (eds.), *Nationale Mythen und Symbole in der zweiten Hälfte des 19. Jahrhunderts: Strukturen und Funktionen von Konzepten nationaler Identität*, Sprache und Geschichte 16 (Stuttgart: Klett-Cotta, 1991), 120–45.

Trägårdh, Lars, 'Varieties of Volkisch Ideologies: Sweden and Germany 1848–1933,' in Bo Stråth (ed.), *Language and the Construction of Class Identities; The Struggle for Discursive Power in Social Organisation: Scandinavia and Germany after 1800. Report from the DISCO II Conference on Continuity and Discontinuity in the Scandinavian Democratisation Process, in Kungälv 7–9 September 1989*, ConDis Project Report no. 3 (Gothenburg: Department of History, Gothenburg Univervsity, 1990), 25–54.

Trautmann, Reinhold, *Die wendische Ortsnamen Ostholsteins, Lübecks, Lauenburgs und Mecklenburgs*, Quellen und Forschungen zur Geschichte Schleswig-Holsteins, 21 (Neumünster: Wachholtz, 1939 [1950]).

Trautmann, Thomas R., *Aryans and British India* (Berkeley: University of California Press, 1997).

Travers, Martin, *Critics of Modernity: The Literature of the Conservative Revolution in Germany, 1890–1933*, German Life and Civilization 35 (New York: Lang, 2001).

Treitel, Corinna, *A Science for the Soul: Occultism and the Genesis of the German Modern* (Balitmore: Johns Hopkins University Press, 2004).

Trevor Roper, Hugh, *The Last Days of Hitler*, 2nd ed. (London: Pan, 1962).

Trier, Jost, 'Sprächliche Felder,' *Zeitschrift für deutsche Bildung* 8 (1932): 417–27.

—— 'Das sprächliche Feld: Eine Auseinandersetzung,' *Neue Jahrbücher für Wissenschaft und Jugendbildung* 10 (1934): 428–49.

—— 'Germanische Religionsgeschichte,' *Zeitschrift für Deutschkunde* 52 (1938): 382–86.

—— 'First. Über die Stellung des Zauns im Denken der Vorzeit,' *Nachrichten von der Akademie der Wissenschaften in Göttingen, Phil.-Hist. Klasse* 1940, no. 4, 55–137.

—— 'Über das Sprechen in ringförmiger Versammlung,' *Göttingische gelehrte Anzeigen* 203 (1941): 423–64.

—— 'Zaun und Mannring,' *Beiträge zur Geschichte der deutschen Sprache und Literatur* 66 (1942): 232–64.

—— 'Zur Vorgeschichte des Wortes Reich,' *Nachrichten der Akademie der Wissenschaften in Göttingen, Phil.-Hist. Klasse* 1943, no. 14, 535–82.

Trubetskoy, Nikolay Sergeevitch [Prinz], *Grundzüge der Phonologie*, Travaux du Cercle Linguistique de Prague 7 (Prague: Cercle Linguistique de Prague, 1939).

Ulbricht, Justus H., and Meike G. Werner (eds.), *Romantik, Revolution und Reform: Der Eugen-Diederichs-Verlag im Epochenkontext 1900–1949* (Göttingen: Wallstein, 1999).

Unverzagt, Wilhelm, 'Zur Vorgeschichte des ostgermanischen Raumes,' in Albert Brackmann (ed.), *Deutschland und Polen: Beiträge zur ihren geschichtlichen Beziehungen* (Munich: Oldenbourg, 1933), 3–12 [= *Germany and Poland in their Historical Realtions*, trans. S. Miles Bouton (Munich: Oldenbourg, 1934), 3–12].

—— 'Zusammenfassung,' in Albert Brackmann and Wilhelm Unverzagt (eds.), *Zantoch: Eine Burg im deutschen Osten. 1. Zantoch in der schriftlichen Überlieferung und die Ausgrabungen 1932/33*, Deutschland und der Osten. Quellen und Forschungen zur Geschichte ihrer Beziehungen 1 (Leipzig: Hirtzel, 1936), 127–40.

Urban, Otto H., 'Much. 1) Matthäus,' *Neue deutsche Biographie* XVIII (Berlin: Dunker & Humblot, 1997), 249.

Uthmann, Jörg von, 'Ein garstig Lied? Geschichten um die deutsche National-hymne,' *Frankfürter Allgemeine Zeitung: Bilder und Zeiten* Nr. 10, 12 Jan., 1980, 2.

Vacher de Lapouge, Georges, *Les Selections sociales: Cours libre de science politique* (Paris: Fontemoing, 1896).

—— *L'Aryen: son rôle social* (Paris: Fontemoing, 1899).

Vasmer, Max, 'Beiträge zur slavischen Altertumskunde: 7. Balkangermanisches und Verwandtes,' *Zeitschrift für slavische Philologie* 18 (1942/43): 55–59.

—— 'Zur Ortsnamen in der Balkanländer,' *Zeitschrift für slavische Philologie* 18 (1942/43): 384–87.

—— 'Balkangermanisches,' *Arkiv för nordisk filologi* 44 (1944): 87–92.

Veit, Ulrich, 'Gustaf Kossinna und V.G. Childe. Ansätze zu einer theoretischen Grundlegung der Vorgeschichte,' *Saeculum* 35/3–4 (1984): 326–64.

———— 'Ethnic Concepts in German Prehistory: A Case Study on the Relationship between Cultural Identity and Archaeological Objectivity,' in Stephen Shennan (ed.), *Archaeological Approaches to Cultural Identity* (London: Unwin Hyman, 1989), 35–56.

Veld, N.K.C.A. in't (ed.), *De SS in Nederland: Documenten uit SS-archieven 1935–1945*, Rijksinstitut voor Oorlogsdocumentatie: Bronnenpublicaties; Documenten 2, 2 vols. (The Hague: Nijhoff, 1976).

Venedy, Jakob, *Römerthum, Christenthum und Germanenthum und deren wechselseitiger Einfluß bei der Umgestaltung der Sclaverei des Alterthums und die Leibeigenschaft des Mittlealters* (Frankfurt a.m.: Meidinger, 1840).

Vezina, Birgitta, *"Die Gleichschaltung" der Universität Heidelberg im Zuge der nationalsozialistischen Machtergreifung*, Heidelberger Rechtswissenschaftliche Abhandlungen NF 32 (Heidelberg: Winter, 1982).

Viehöfer, Erich, 'Der Verleger als Organisator: Eugen Diederichs und die bürgerlichen Reformbewegung der Jahrhundertwende,' *Archiv für Geschichte des Buchwesens* 30 (1988): 1–147 [= monograph (Frankfurt a.m.: Buchhändler, 1988)].

Virchow, Rudolf, comment on Ludwig Wilser, 'Die Herkunft der Germanen,' *Correspondenz-Blatt der deutschen Gesellschaft für Anthropologie, Ethnologie und Urgeschichte* 16 (1885): 124–25.

Visser, Romke, 'Fascist doctrine and the cult of *romanità*,' *Journal of Contemporary History* 27 (1992): 5–22.

Voigt, Heinrich J.F., *Eis, ein Weltenbaustoff: Gemeinfassliche Einführung in Ph. Fauths Hörbigers Glacialkosmogonie* (Berlin–Wilmersdorf: Paekel, 1920).

Vogt, Walter Heinrich, 'Altgermanische Religiosität,' *Forschungen und Fortschritte* 15 (1939): 246–48.

Vries, Jan de, *Altgermanische Religionsgeschichte*, Grundriß der germanischen Philologie 12, 2 vols. (Berlin: De Gruyter, 1935–37).

———— 'Over Germaanse wereldbeschouwing,' *Algemein Nederlands Tijdschrift voor Wijsbegeerte en Psychologie* 34 (1941): 185–204.

———— 'Germanische goden,' *Hamer* 2/5–12 (1942).

———— 'Über neuere Runenforschung,' *Geistige Arbeit* 9/8 (1942): 3–4.

———— 'Het raadsel der runen,' *Hamer* 3/5–10 (1943).

———— *Die geistige Welt der Germanen* (Halle a.S.: Niemeyer 1943), 3rd ed. (Darmstadt: Wissenschaftliche Buchgesellschaft, 1964).

———— *De Goden der Germanen* (Amsterdam: Hamer, 1944).

Wache, W., 'Die Neuordnung Europas durch die Germanen,' *SS-Leitheft* 3/3 (1937): 10–15.

Wagener, Samuel Christoph, *Handbuch der vorzüglichtes, in Deutschland entdeckten Alterthümer aus heidnischer Zeit* (Weimar: Voigt, 1842).

Wahle, Ernst, 'Zur ethnischen Deutung frühgeschichtlicher Kulturprovinzen: Grenzen der frühgeschichtlichen Erkenntnis I,' *Sitzungsberichte der Heidelberger Akadamie der Wissenschaften, Phil.-Hist. Klasse* 1940/41, no. 2.

Waite, Robert G.L., *Vanguard of Nazism: The Free Corps Movement in Postwar Germany 1918–1923*, Harvard Historical Studies 60 (Cambridge, Mass.: Harvard University Press, 1952).

Walther von der Vogelweide, *Die Gedichte Walters von der Vogelweide*, ed. Karl Lachmann (Berlin: Reimer, 1827).

Watt, D. Cameron, 'Introduction,' in Adolf Hitler, *Mein Kampf*, trans. Ralph Mannheim (Boston: Houghton Mifflin, 1943), xi–xlii.

Weber, Edmund, 'Ein Handbuch der Runenkunde,' *Germanien* 8 (1936): 257–61.

———— 'Ein alemannischer Runenbrief?,' in Kurt H. Schlottig (ed.), *Beiträge zur Runenkunde und nordischen Sprachwissenschaft: Gustav Neckel zum 60. Geburtstag* (Leipzig: Harrassowitz, 1938), 106–7.

———— *Kleine Runenkunde* (Berlin: Nordland, 1941).

———— 'Sinnbilder und Runen,' *Sigrune* 10 = 12/7–8 (1943): 10–11.

———— 'Ein wiedergefundenes Runendenkmal,' *Sigrune* 11 = 13/3–4 (1944): 8.

Wedekind, Michael, 'The Sword of Science: German Scholars and National Socialist Annexation Policy in Slovenia and Northern Italy,' in Ingo Haar and Michael Fahlbusch (eds.), *German Scholars and Ethnic Cleansing* (New York: Berghahn, 2004), 110–38.

Wedemeyer-Kolwe, Bernd, 'Runengymnastik: Zur Religiosität völkischer Körperkultur,' in Stefanie von Schnurbein and Justus H. Ulbricht (eds.), *Völkische Religion und Krisen der Moderne: Entwürfe "eigenartiger" Glaubensysteme seit der Jahrhundertwende* (Würzburg: Königshausern & Neumann, 2001), 367–85.

———— *'Der neue Mensch': Körperkultur im Kaiserreich und in der Weimarer Republik* (Würzburg: Königshausern & Neumann, 2004), 174–88.

Wegener, Alfred, *Die Entstehung der Kontinente und Ozeane* (Brunswick: Vieweg, 1915).

Wegener, Franz, *Das atlantidische Weltbild: Nationalsozialismus und Neue Rechte auf der Suche nach der versunkenen Atlantis* (Gladbeck: Kulturförderverein Ruhrgebiet, 2000).

Weigel, Karl Theodor, *Lebendige Vorzeit rechts und links der Landstraße* (Berlin: Metzner, 1934; 7th ed., 1942).

———— *Runen und Sinnbilder* (Berlin: Metzner, 1935; 4th ed. 1941).

———— 'Gibt es Runen im Fachwerk?,' *Deutsches Handwerk* 5 (1936): 361–63.

———— 'Runen am deutschen Hause,' *Nationalsozialistische Monatshefte* 7 (1936): 163–65 and 900–904.

———— 'Giebelzeichen und Sinnbilder,' *Germanen-Erbe* 1 (1936): 122–23.

———— 'Sinnbilder-Kulturerbe,' *Odal* 5 (1937): 720–26.

———— 'Sinnbilder am Hause,' *Haus und Hof im nordischen Raum* 2 (1937): 111–23.

———— 'Dachziegel als Sinnbildträger,' *Germanien* 13, NF 3 (1941): 434–38.

———— 'Ein vorrunisches Begriffzeichen aus der Mark,' *Wörter und Sachen* 22, NF 4 (1941–42): 207–10.

———— 'Gedachten over volkskunst,' Hamer 2/4 (1942): 21–24.

———— 'Lichtmis,' Hamer 2/6 (1942): 18–19.

———— 'Zinnebeelden in zand gestrooid,' Hamer 2/11 (1942).

———— *Ritzzeichnungen in Dreschtennen des Schwarzwaldes*, Wörter und Sachen Beiheft 1 (Heidelberg: Winter, 1942).

———— *Beiträge zur Sinnbildforschung* (Berlin: Metzner, 1943).

Weiner, Marc A., *Richard Wagner and the Anti-Semitic Imagination* (Lincoln: University of Nebraska Press, 1995).

Weingärtner, Wilhelm, *Die Ausprache des Gothischen zur Zeit des Ulfilas* (Leipzig: Weigel, 1858).

Weiser, Lily, *Altgermanische Jünglingsweihen und Männerbünde: Ein Beiträg zur deutschen und nordischen Altertums- und Volkskunde*, Bausteine zur Volkskunde und Religionswissenschaft 1 (Bühl: Konkordia, 1927).

Weisgerber, [J.] Leo, 'Das Problem der inneren Sprachform und seine Bedeutung für die deutsche Sprache,' *Germanisch-Romanische Monatsschrift* 14 (1926): 241–56 [= *Zur Grundlegung der ganzheitlichen Sprachauffassung; Aufsätze 1925–1933: Zur Vollendung des 65. Lebensjahres Leo Weisgerbers,* ed. Helmut Gipper (Düsseldorf: Schwann, 1964), 36–66].

———— 'Der Geruchsinn in unserem Sprachen,' *Indogermanische Forschungen* 46 (1928): 121–50 [= *Zur Grundlegung der ganzheitlichen Sprachauffassung; Aufsätze 1925–1933: Zur Vollendung des 65. Lebensjahres Leo Weisgerbers,* ed. Helmut Gipper (Düsseldorf: Schwann, 1964), 99–121].

———— '"Neuromantik" in der Sprachwissenschaft,' *Germanisch-Romanische Monatsschrift* 18 (1930): 241–59 [= *Zur Grundlegung der ganzheitlichen Sprachauffassung; Aufsätze 1925–1933: Zur Vollendung des 65. Lebensjahres Leo Weisgerbers,* ed. Helmut Gipper (Düsseldorf: Schwann, 1964), 212–30].

———— 'Die Stellung der Sprache im Aufbau der Gesamtkultur,' *Wörter und Sachen* 15 (1933): 134–224 and 16 (1934): 97–236 [= monograph (Heidelberg: Winter, 1934)].

———— 'Zweisprachigkeit,' *Schaffen und Schauen* 9 (1933): 5–10 [= *Zur Grundlegung der ganzheitlichen Sprachauffassung; Aufsätze 1925–1933: Zur Vollendung des 65. Lebensjahres Leo Weisgerbers,* ed. Helmut Gipper (Düsseldorf: Schwann, 1964), 423–30].

———— *Theudisk: Der deutsche Volksname und die westliche Sprachgrenze*, Marburger Universitäts-reden 5 (Marburg: Elwert, 1940) [= *Deutsch als Volksname: Ursprung und Bedeutung* (Stuttgart: Kohlhammer, 1953), 40–95].

———— *Deutsch als Volksname; Ursprung und Bedeutung* (Stuttgart: Kohlhammer, 1953).

Weißmann, Karlheinz, *Schwarze Fahnen, Runenzeichen: Die Entwicklung der politischen Symbolik der deutschen Rechten zwischen 1890 und 1945* (Düsseldorf: Droste, 1991).

Wells, Peter, *The Battle that Stopped Rome: Emperor Augustus, Arminius, and the slaughter of the legions in the Teutoburg Forest* (New York: Norton, 2003).

Werner, Meike G., *Moderne in der Provinz: Kulturelle Experimente im Fin de Siecle Jena* (Göttingen: Wallstein, 2003).

Wesel, Uwe, *Der Mythos vom Matriarchat: Über Bachofens Mutterrecht und die Stellung von Frauen in frühen Gesellschaften vor der Entstehung staatlicher Herrschaft*, Suhrkamp Taschenbuch Wissenschaft 333 (Frankfurt a.M.: Suhrkamp, 1985).

Westerhagen, Curt von, *Richard Wagner: Sein Werk, sein Wesen, sein Welt* (Zürich: Atlantis, 1956).

Whiteside, Andrew G., *The Socialism of Fools: Georg Ritter von Schönerer and Austrian Pan-Germanism* (Berkeley: University of California Press, 1975).

Wiegers, Fritz, (ed.), *Hermann Wirth und die deutsche Wissenschaft* (Munich: Lehmann, 1932).

Wiele, Jef van de, *Op zook naar een Vaderland* (Brussels: Steenlandt, 1942) [= *Flandern wird Leben* (Brussels: Steenlandt, 1944)].

Wieland, Hermann, *Atlantis, Edda und Bibel: Das entdeckte Geheimnis der Heiligen Schrift des deutschen Volkes Rettung aus Not und Tod* (Nuremberg: Wuzel, 1922).

Wieser, Max, *Aufbruch des Nordens: Einführung in die Forschungen Professor Herman Wirths: Vortrag* (Berlin: Boll, [1933]).

Wiggershaus-Müller, Ursula, *Nationalsozialismus und Geschichtswissenschaft: Die Geschichte der Historischen Zeitschrift und des Historischen Jahrbuchs von 1933–1945*, Studien zur Zeitgeschichte 17 (Hamburg: Kovac, 1998).

Wijk, Nicholas van, *Franck's etymologisch woordenboek der Nederlandsche taal*, 2nd ed. (The Hague: Nijhoff, 1912 [1949]).

Wikander, [O.] Stig, *Der arische Männerbund: Studien zur indo-iranischen Sprach- und Religionsgeschichte* (Lund: Gleerup, 1938).

Willoughby, Leonard Ashley, 'Coleridge und Deutschland,' *Germanisch-Romanische Monatsschrift* 24 (1936): 112–27.

Willson, A. Leslie, *A Mythical Image: The Ideal of India in German Romanticism* (Durham, N.C.: Duke University Press, 1964).

Wilser, [J. D.] Ludwig, *Ueber einen Fall von Ausgedehnter Thrombose der Sinus und Venen des Gehirns in Folge von Insolation* (Freiberg: Loggen & Son, 1875).

—— *Die Herkunft der Deutschen: Neue Forschungen* (Karlsruhe: Braun, 1885).

—— 'Die Herkunft der Germanen,' *Correspondenz-Blatt der deutschen Gesellschaft für Anthropologie, Ethnologie und Urgeschichte* 16 (1885): 122–24.

—— 'Über die Stellung der germanischen Runen,' *Der Karlsruher Altertumsverein* 1 (1892): 27ff.

—— 'Alter und Ursprung der Runenschrift,' *Korrespondenzblatt der Gesamtvereins der deutschen Geschichts- und Alterthumsvereine* 43 (1895): 137–43.

—— *Herkunft und Urgeschichte der Arier. Vortrag gehalten am 11. februar 1899 im Württembergischen Anthropologischen Verein zu Stuttgart* (Heidelberg: Hörnung, 1899).

—— 'Zur Geschichte der Buchstabenschrift,' *Beilage zur Allgemeinen Zeitung* 5 May, 1899, no. 103, 3.

—— *Zur Runenkunde: Zwei Abhandlungen* (Leipzig: Akademische Verlag für Kunst und Wissenschaft, 1905) (published as an appendix to his *Herkunft der Baiern*).

—— *Die Rassengliederung des Menschengeschlechts* (Leipzig: Thüringische Verlag-Anstalt, 1906).

—— *Rassentheorien* (Stuttgart, Strecker & Schröder, 1908).

—— 'Runen und Buchstaben,' *Hammer* 10 (1911): 228–31.

—— *Rassen und Völker* (Leipzig: Thomas, 1912).

———— 'Ursprung und Entwicklung der Buchstabenschrift,' *Mannus* 4 (1912): 123–29.

———— *Das Hakenkreuz nach Ursprung, Vorkommen und Bedeutung* (Zeitz: Sis Verlag, 1917), 7th ed., ed. D. Bernhardi (Lepizig: Fritsch, 1933).

———— *Deutsche Vorzeit: Einführung in die germanische Altertumskunde* (Berlin–Steglitz: Hobbing 1917), 4th ed. (Leipzig: Voigtländer [1934]).

Wilson, Thomas, 'The Swastika: The Earliest Known Symbol, and its Migrations; with Observations on the Migration of Certain Industries in Prehistoric Times,' *Report of the U.S. National Museum under the Direction of the Smithsonian Institution* (1894): 757–1011.

Wimmer, Ludvig F. A., 'Runeskriftens Oprindelse og Udvikling i Norden,' *Aarbøger for nordisk Oldkyndighed og Historie* (1874): 1–270 [= monograph (Copenhagen: Prior, 1874)].

———— *Die Runenschrift*, trans. Ferdinand Holthausen, rev. ed. (Berlin: Weidmann, 1887).

Windus, Astrid, and Hans-Gerd Winter, *Ernst Fuhrmann (1886–1956): Verzeichnis seines Nachlasses und des Nachlasses von Elisabeth Fuhrmann-Paulsen in der Staats- und Universitätsbibliothek Hamburg Carl von Ossietzky* (Herzberg: Traugott Bautz, 2000).

Wirth (Roeper Bosch), Herman F., *Der Untergang des niederlandischen Volksliedes* (dissertation, Basel 1910) [= monograph (The Hague: Nijhoff, 1911)].

———— *Hervorming en wedergeboorte. Een nederlandsch drama in 5 bedrijven* (Amsterdam: Van Holkema & Warendorf, 1911).

———— *National-Nederlandsche muziek politiek* (Amsterdam: Van Holkema & Warendorf, 1912).

———— (ed.), *Orkestcomposties van Nederlandsche meesters van het begin der 17de eeuw. Paduanen en galliarden van Melchior Borchgreving, Benedictus Grep en Nicolaus Gistow. Naar de uitgaven van 1607 en 1609 in partituur gebracht en met eene inleidning op nieuw uitgave*, Uitgave van de Vereeniging van Nederlandsche muziekgeschiedenis 34 (Amsterdam: Alsbach, 1913).

———— *Niederländisch-Deutsch*, Neufelds Sprachführer (Berlin: Neufeld & Henius, 1913).

———— (ed.), *Altniederländische Arméemärsche* (Berlin: Bote & Bock, 1914).

———— (ed.), *Ein Hähnlein woll'n wir rupfen: Neue Kriegslieder nach alten Texten u. Weisen*, Kriegslieder für's Deutsche Volk mit Noten 2 (Jena: Diederichs, 1914 [1915]).

———— *Das niederländische Volkslied vom Mittelalter bis zum 19. Jahrhundert im Rahmen der Geistesgeschichte. Vortrag gehalten von Lector Dr. Wirth, Mitarbeiter d. Pressedelegierten in Gent. Programm und Textbuch (1915)* (Leipzig: Breitkopf & Härtel, 1916).

———— *Programm- und Textbuch. Geistliches Konzert 1916. Die niederländischen kirchlichen Meister vom Mittelalter bis zum 19. Jahrhundert* (Ghent: [s.n.,] 1916).

———— *Flandern und sein Volk*, 2 vols. (Leipzig: Breitkopf & Härtel, [1916]).

———— *Flämisch: Eine reihe Sammlungen nützliche Gespräche mit Aussprachebezeichnungen, nebst systematicher Vokabular und kurzgefaßter Grammatik*, Neufelds Sprachlehrer (Berlin: Neufeld & Henius, 1916).

—— *Eerste uitvoering van Oud-Nederlandsche toonkunstwerken van de vroege middeleeuwen tot het einde der zestiende eeuw* (Utrecht: Bosch, 1920).

—— *Wat is en wat wil de Dietsche Trekvogel?* (Leiden: Landsbond der Dietsche Trekvogels, 1920).

—— 'Die Atlantisproblem,' in Eugen Diederichs (ed.), *Das deutsche Gesicht; Ein Weg zur Zukunft: Zum xxx. Jahr des Verlags Eugen Diederichs in Jena* (Jena: Diederichs, 1926), 69–79 [= *Germanien* 2 (1930/31): 115–22].

—— 'Zum Ursprung des Kreuzes,' in Leopold Feiler, *Die Entstehung des Christentums aus dem Geiste des magischen Denkens* (Jena: Diederichs, 1927), 150–52.

—— *Der Aufgang der Menschheit: Untersuchungen zur Geschichte der Religion, Symbolik und Schrift der atlantisch-nordischen Rasse. Textband I: Die Grundzüge* (Jena: Diederichs, 1928).

—— 'Die Rune in der Externsteingrotte,' *Germanien* 1 (1929/30): 10–19.

—— 'Deutsche Vorgeschichte und deutsche Geistesgeschichte. Eine Erklärung in einer öffentlichen deutschen Anlegenheit,' *Germanien* 1 (1929/30): 33–38.

—— 'Das Atlantisproblem,' *Germanien* 2 (1930/31): 115–22.

—— *Was heißt deutsch? Ein urgeistesgeschichtlicher Rückblick zur Selbstbesinnung und Selbstbestimmung* (Jena: Diederichs, 1931).

—— *Um die wissenschaftliche Erkenntnis und den nordischen Gedanken. Eine Antwort an Prof. F. Wiegers und Mitarbeiter* (Berlin–Steglitz: Herman-Wirth-Gesellschaft [1932]).

—— *Die heilige Urschrift der Menschheit: Symbolgeschichtliche Untersuchungen dieseits und jenseits des Nordatlantik*, Deutsches Ahnenerbe, Abt. A: Grundwerke 4, 2 vols. (Leipzig: Koehler & Amelang, 1931–36 [Frauenberg: Mutter Erde, 1979]).

—— 'Zur religionswissenschaftlichen Auswertung vorgeschichtlicher Altertümer,' *Mitteilungen der Anthropologischen Gesellschaft in Wien* 62 (1932): 227–28.

—— 'Prof. Herman Wirth für Hitler,' *Völkischer Beobachter* 11th Apr., 1932.

—— *Heilige Wende. Ein Zeitenspiel in 6 Aufz. (1909)* (Leipzig: Koehler & Amelang, 1933).

—— 'Das Felsengrab an den Externstein,' *Germanien* 5 (1933): 9–15.

—— 'Vom Ursprung und Sinn des Hakenkreuzes,' *Germanien* 5 (1933): 161–66.

—— *Führer durch die erste urreligionsgeschichtliche Ausstellung "Der Heilbringer": Von Thule bis Galiläa und von Galiläa bis Thule* (Berlin: Zentral-Institut für Erziehung und Unterricht, 1933).

—— (ed.), *Die Ura Linda Chronik* (Leipzig: Kohler & Amelang, 1933).

—— (dir.), *Nordischer Urmythus und die Fleichwerdung Christi* (Berlin: Ahnenerbe, 1935).

—— 'Die ältesten Odal-Urkunden des germanischen Bauern,' *Odal* 4 (1936): 882–90.

—— 'Die symbolhistorische Methode,' *Zeitschrift für Missionswissenschaft und Religionswissenschaft* 39 (1955): 127–39 [= monograph (Münster: Aschendorff, 1983)].

——— *Um die Ursinn des Menschseins: Die Wendung einer neuen Geisteswissenschaft*, Geistesurgeschichtliche Kleinbuchreihe 1 (Vienna: Volkstum, 1960).

——— *Allmutter: Die Entdeckung der "altitalischen" Inschriften in der Pfalz und ihre Deutung. Festschrift der Europäischen Sammlung für Urgemeinschaftskunde* (Marburg: Eccestan, 1974).

——— *Führer durch die Ur-Europa-Museum: Mit Einführung in der Ursymbolik und Urreligion* (Marburg: Eccestan, 1975).

——— *Europäische Urreligion und die Externsteine* (Vienna: Volkstum, 1980).

Herman Wirth Society, 'Aussprache zwischen Prof. Dr. Herman Wirth und seinen wissenschaftlichen Gegnern,' *Germanien* 3 (1931/32): 63–65.

Wiwjorra, Ingo, 'Herman Wirth—Ein gescheiterter Ideologe zwischen "Ahnenerbe" und Atlantis,' in Barbara Danckwott, Thorsten Querg and Claudia Schöningh (eds.), *Historische Rassismusforschung – Ideologen – Täter – Opfer*, Edition Philosophie und Sozialwissenschaften 30 (Hamburg: Argument, 1995), 91–112.

——— 'Willy Pastor (1867–1933) – Ein völkischer Vorgeschichtspublizist,' in Michael Meyer (ed.), *"... trans Albium fluvium": Forschungen zur vorrömischen, kaiserzeitlichen und mittelalterlichen Archäologie; Festschrift für Achim Leube zum 65. Geburtstag*, Internationale Archäologie – Studia Honoraria 10 (Rahden i.W.: Leidorf, 2001), 11–24.

——— '"Ex oriente lux" – "Ex septentrione lux": Über den Widerstreit zweier Identitätsmythen,' in Achim Leube (ed.), *Prähistorie und Nationalsozialismus: Die mittel- und osteuropäische Ur- und Frühgeschichtsforschung in den Jahren 1933–1945*, Studien zur Wissenschafts- und Universitätsgeschichte 2 (Heidelberg: Synchron, 2002), 73–106.

——— *Der Germanenmythos: Konstruktion einer Weltanschauung in der Altertumsforschung des 19. Jahrhunderts* (Darmstadt: Wissenschaftliche Buchgesellschaft, 2006).

Wolf, Abraham, *Higher Education in Nazi Germany; or: Education for World Conquest* (London: Methuen, 1944).

Wolff, Ludwig, 'Herman Wirth als Germanist,' in Fritz Wiegers (ed.), *Herman Wirth und die deutsche Wissenschaft* (Munich: Lehmann, 1932), 47–60.

Wolfram von Eschenbach, *Parcival*, ed. Carl Lachmann (Berlin: Reimer, 1833).

Wolfram, Richard, 'Sword Dances and Secret Societies,' *Journal of the English Folk Dance and Song Society* 1/1 (1932): 34–41

——— *Schwerttanz und Männerbund* (Kassel: Bärenreiter, 1936).

Wolgast, Eike, *Die Universität Heidelberg, 1386–1986* (Berlin: Springer, 1986).

Wormianus, Olaus (Ole Worm), *[Runer] Seu Danica Literatura antiquissima, Vulgo Gothica dicta, luci reddita* (Copenhagen: Moltke, 1638).

——— *Danicorum Monumentorum libri sex: E spissis antiquitatum tenebris et in Danica ac Norvegia extantibus ruderibus eruti ab Olao Worm* (Copenhagen: Moltke, 1643).

——— *Museum Wormiamum: Seu Historia rerum rariorum, tam naturalium, quam artificialum, tam domesticarum, quam exoticarum, que Hafniæ Danorum in ædibus authoris servantur* (Leiden: Elsevier, 1655).

Worsaae, J. Jacob A., 'Den nationale Oldkyndighed i Tyskland: Reisebe-
mærkinger,' *Annaler for nordisk Oldkyndighed og Historie* (1846): 116–40
[= idem, *Die nationale Alterthumskunde in Deutschland: Reisebemerkungen*
(Copenhagen: Eibe, 1846)].
Wühr, Hans, *Ewiger Sinn im zeitgebundenen Sinnbild: Germanisches Sagengut in
christlichem Gewand* (Stuttgart: Tuchenmüller, 1938).
Wundt, Max, *Was heißt völkisch?*, Pädagogisches Magazin 987; Schriften zur
politischen Bildung 16 (Langensalza: Beyer & Sons, 1924).
Wundt, Wilhelm M., *Völkerpsychologie: Eine Untersuchung der Entwicklungsgese-
tze von Sprache, Mythus und Sitte. I. Die Sprache*, 2 vols. (Leipzig: Engel-
mann, 1900).
——— *Sprachgeschichte und Sprachpsychologie* (Leipzig: Engelmann, 1901).
Wüst, Walther, 'Der Schaltsatz im Rgveda' (dissertation, University of Mu-
nich, 1924).
——— *Stilgeschichte und Chronologie des Rgveda*, Abhandlungen für die Kunde
des Morgenlandes 17, 4 (Leipzig: Deutsche Morgenländischen Gesell-
schaft, 1928).
——— *Indisch*, Die Erforschung der indogermanischen Sprachen IV.1 (Berlin:
De Gruyter, 1929).
——— 'Gedanken über Wirths "Aufgang der Menschheit",' *Zeitschrift für Mis-
sionskunde und Religionswissenschaft* 44 (1929): 257–74 and 289–307.
——— *Vergleichendes und etymologisches Wörterbuch des Altindoiranischen (Altind-
ischen) I*, Indogermanische Bibliothek, Reihe 2: Wörterbücher 4 (Heidel-
berg: Winter 1935).
——— 'Germanenkunde: Frage und Verpflichtung,' *Germanien* 8 (1936): 321–
27 [= 'Zur Germanenkunde,' *Odal* 5 (1936): 366–73 = *Indogermanisches
Bekenntnis: Sechs Reden*, Schriftenreihe Deutsches Ahnenerbe. Reihe B.
Fachwissenschaftliche Untersuchungen. Abteilung: Arbeiten zur indo-
germanisch-arische Sprach- und Kulturwissenschaft 1 (Berlin–Dahlem:
Ahenenerbe, 1942), 3–12].
——— *Das Reich: Gedanke und Wirklichkeit bei den alten Arier. Festrede aus An-
laß der von den Münchener Hochschulen veranstalteten Reichsgründungsfeier*
(Munich: Gässler, 1937).
——— *Deutsche Frühzeit und arische Geistesgeschichte*, 2nd ed. (Munich:
Deutsche Akademie, 1939).
——— 'Arisches zur Sinnbildforschung,' *Germanien* 12, NF 2 (1940), 212–
19.
——— 'Goten in Indien? Eine Forschungsbericht zur mittelindoarischen
Epigraphik,' in Franz Altheim, *Geschichte der Hunnen* 3 (Berlin: De Gruyter,
1961), 141–89 [= *Anzeiger für deutsches Altertum* 73 (1961), 45–74].
——— review of Annelies Kammenhuber, *Die Arier in vorderen Orient*, *Die
Sprache* 20 (1974), 136–63.
Zaborsky-Wahlstätten, Oskar von, *Urväter-Erbe in deutscher Volkskunst*,
Deutsches Ahnenerbe, Abt. C: Volkstümliche Schriftenreihe 1 (Leipzig:
Koehler & Amelang, 1936).

Zech, Mario, *Das Schwarze Korps: Geschichte und Gestalt des Organs der Reichs-führung SS*, Medien in Forschung + Unterricht, Serie A, 51 (Tübingen: Niemeyer, 2002).

Zehnpfennig, Barbara, *Hitlers Mein Kampf: Eine Interpretation*, 2nd ed. (Munich: Fink, 2002).

Zernack, Julia, *Geschichten aus Thule: Islendingasögar in Übersetzungen deutschen Germanisten*, Berliner Beiträge zur Skandinavistik 3 (Berlin: FU-Berlin, 1994).

Zeuss, [J.] Kaspar, *Die Deutschen und die Nachbarstämme* (Munich: Lentner, 1837).

Ziegler, Matthes, 'Der Lebensbaum im germanischen Brauchtum. Eine Ausstellung von Prof. Herman Wirth in Berlin,' *Völkischer Beobachter* 48/137, 17 May, 1935.

Zimmerman, Andrew, *Anthropology and Antihumanism in Imperial Germany* (Chicago: University of Chicago Press, 2001).

Zitelmann, Rainer, *Hitler: The Politics of Seduction*, trans. Helmut Bogler (London: London House, 1999).

Zmarzlik, Hans-Günter, 'Der Sozialdarwinismus in Deutschland als geschichtliches Problem,' *Vierteljahreshefte für Zeitgeschichte* 11 (1963): 246–73 [= 'Social Darwinism in Germany, Seen as a Historical Problem,' in Hajo Holborn (ed.), *Republic to Reich: The Making of the Nazi Revolution*, trans. Ralph Mannheim (New York: Pantheon, 1972), 435–471].

Zmigrodski, Michael von, 'Zur Geschichte der Suastika,' *Archiv für Anthropologie* 18 (1891): 173–84.

Zondergeld, Gjalt A., 'Hans Ernst Schneider und seine Bedeutung für das SS-Ahnenerbe,' in Helmut König, Wolfgang Kuhlmann and Klaus Schwabe (eds.), *Vertuschte Vergangenheit: Der Fall Schwerte und die NS-Vergangenheit der deutschen Hochschulen*, Beck'sche Reihe 1204 (Munich: Beck, 1997), 14–30.

Zschaetzsch, Karl Georg, *Die Herkunft und Geschichte des arischen Stammes* (Berlin: Arier, 1920), 2nd ed. = *Die Arier* (Berlin: Arier, 1934).

——— *Atlantis: Die Urheimat der Arier* (Berlin: Arier, 1922).

Index

Fidus (Hugo Höppener), 22, 62
Flemish, 136–37, 196–97, 243
folklore (*Volkskunde*), 3, 58, 64,
    86–87, 89–90, 92, 100, 123, 136,
    151, 154, 158, 167, 179–80, 182,
    199, 208–10, 216, n. 80, 228–33,
    241–42, 264, 266, 275–77
folklore atlas, German, 229–30
Fraktur, 22, 112
France, 8, 16, 18, 23, 36, 116, 127,
    148, 169, 201, 207, 247
Frank, Walter, 123
Franks, Frankish, 54, 116, 247
fraternity, warrior – see *Männerbund*
Frauenshaft – see Nazi Women's
    Group
Frauenwerk – see German Women's
    Work
Freecorps, 197
Freemasonry, 44, 141, 155, 174,
    242–43
Freiburg, Albert Ludwigs University
    of, 229
Freytag, Gustav, 40
Friends of Germanic Prehistory,
    Federation of (Vereinigung
    der Freunde germanischer
    Vorgeschichte), 192–95, 197–98,
    211, 242, 250–51
Friesen, Otto von, 63, 171
Frings, Theodor, 117
Frisia, 144, 146, 151–54, 240, 244
Fritsch, Theodor, 43–44, 205, 243
Fuhrmann, Ernst, 147, 154
fulmen, 57, 146

Gamillscheg, Ernst, 117, 258, n. 114
Gauch, Hermann, 207, 215, n. 76
General German Language
    Association (Allgemeiner
    deutscher Sprachverein), 44, 99
Genzmer, Felix, 104, n. 61
geology, 142, 148, 202–3
Germaanische Institut, 263
German Academy, Munich
    (Deutsche Akademie), 196

German Anthropological Society
    (Deutsche Anthropologische
    Gesellschaft), 62
German Archaeological Institute
    (Deutsches Archäologisches
    Institut, DAI), 120, 239
German Christianity, 20–21, 41, 71
German Faith Movement (Deutsche
    Glaubensbewegung, DGW), 227
German-Flemish Society (Deutsch-
    Flämisch Gesellschaft), 137
Germania (of Tacitus), 34, 56, 67, n.
    26, 90, 180, 202, 224
"Germanicdom and Christendom"
    Association (Arbeitsgemeinschaft
    "Germanentum und
    Christentum"), 158
Germanicness (*Germanentum*), 71,
    80–85, 91, 93, 100, 150, 152,
    167, 210, 220, 222, 244, 247,
    274–77, 279
Germanic Orders (Germanenorden),
    42, 44, 112–13, 141, 150, 189
Germanien, 156–57, 171, 192, 194–
    95, 197, 199, 206, 223, 226–27,
    231, 237, 243, 249
Germanischer Wissenschaftseinsatz
    (GWE), 241, 245–46, 248, 259
*Germanisch-Romanische Monatsschrift
    (GRM)*, 174–75, 235
German Law Institute, Bonn
    (Deutschrechtliches Institut), 129,
    239
German National (*deutschnational*),
    19, 24–25, 41–42, 70, 83, 118,
    271, 273
German National Museum,
    Nuremberg (Germanisches
    Nationalmuseum), 35
German Pharmacy Association
    (Deutscher Apothekerverein), 206
German Philological Society
    (Gesellschaft für deutsche
    Philologie), 176–77
German Research Council (Deutsche
    Forschungsgemeinschaft, DFG),

Figure 1.
The Gothic (runic) alphabet according to the Magnus brothers

Figure 2.
Iron Age spearhead from Dahmsdorf, Mark Brandenberg (reverse and obverse), featuring a runic inscription and various symbols (now lost)

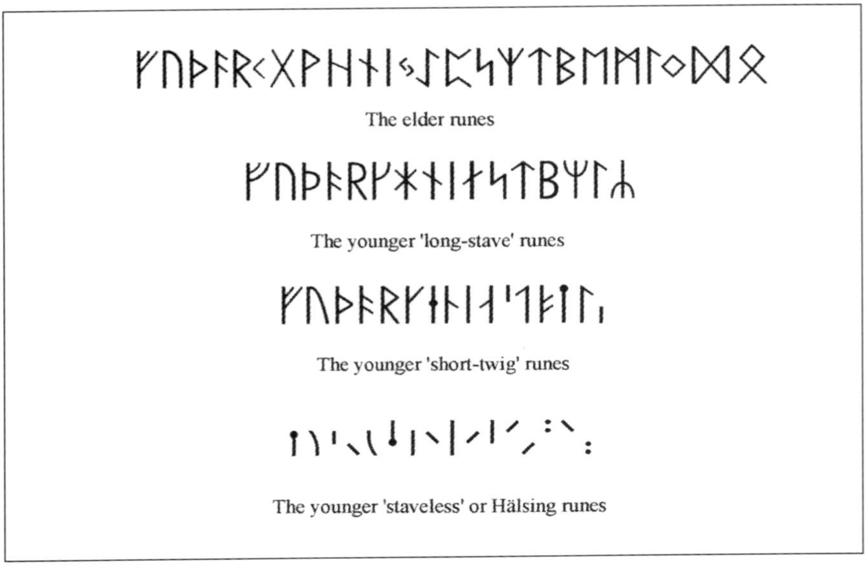

ᚠᚢᚦᚨᚱᚲᚷᚹᚺᚾᛁᛃᛇᛈᛉᛊᛏᛒᛖᛗᛚᛜᛞᛟ

The elder runes

ᚠᚢᚦᚭᚱᛋᚴᚼᚾᛁᛅᛋᛏᛒᚢᛚᛦ

The younger 'long-stave' runes

ᚠᚢᚦᚯᚱᛌᚻᚽᛁᛆᛐᛏᛓ

The younger 'short-twig' runes

The younger 'staveless' or Hälsing runes

Figure 3.
The evolution of the runic alphabets

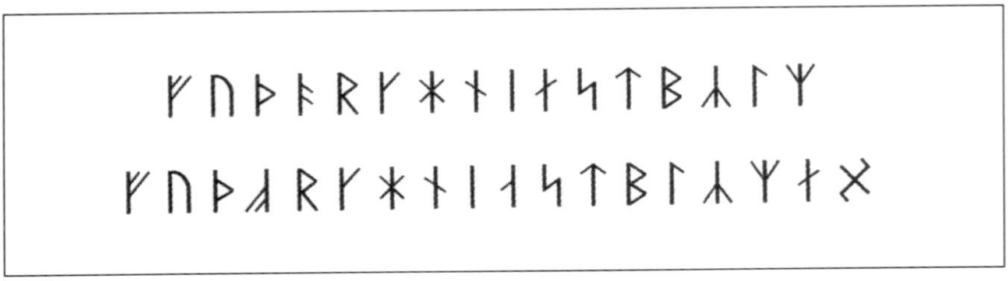

ᚠᚢᚦᚨᚱᛋᚷᚼᛁᛏᚼᛏᛒᛆᛚ�

ᚠᚢᚦᚨᚱᛋᚷᚼᛁᛏᚼᛏᛒᚱᛆᛚᚢᛏᚷ

Figure 4.
The Nordic model of the Armanen runes

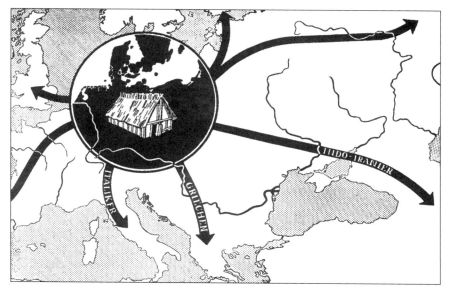

Figure 5.
The Aryan migrations out of Germany in prehistory

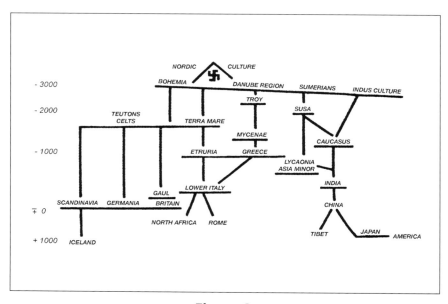

Figure 6.
The migration of the swastika according to Lechler in 1935

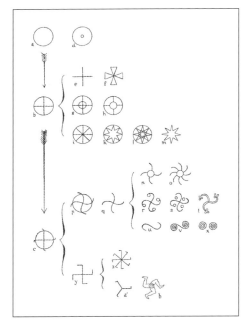

Figure 7.
The evolution of sun symbols
according to Dechelette in 1909

Figure 8.
The swastika in Scots dancing according to Richter in 1931

Figure 9.
The masthead of *Heimdall* 5 (1900), with its motto written in pseudo-runes

Figure 10.
'Anyone who claims that the Germanic peoples were cultureless heathens falsifies history and commits a crime against the German people.' Display from the 'Living Prehistory' exhibition of the Reich Institute for German Prehistory

Figure 11.
Alfred Rosenberg speaking at the Third Reich Conference for German Prehistory, Ulm, October 1936

Figure 12.
Herman Wirth (1885–1981)

Figure 13.
The cover of Wirth's *Emergence of Mankind* (1928)

Figure 14.
'Tree of life' sculpture on the Atlantis House, Bremen, by Bernhard
Hoetger (destroyed in 1944)

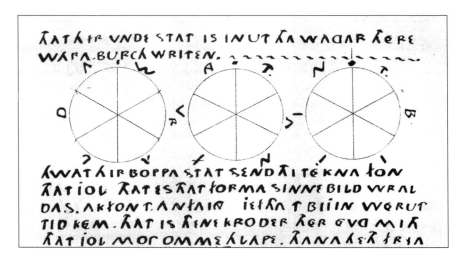

Figure 15.
'That es that forma sinnebild Wralda's' – the runic lore of the
Oera Linda Book

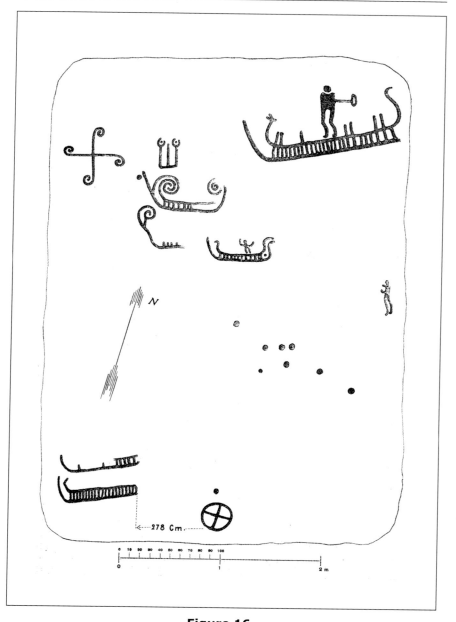

Figure 16.
A rock carving from Tose, Sweden, featuring boats, a swastika
and a circle-cross

Figure 17.
The Extern stones, Lippe, shortly before Andrée's excavation

Figure 18.
The opening of the Extern Stones Foundation by the Gauleiter
of Lippe, March 1934

Figure 19.
Wilhelm Teudt (1860–1942)

Figure 20.
Walther Wüst (1901–1993)

Figure 21.
The recreation of Irminsûl

Figure 22.
The SS yule-fire shrine featuring
the six-spoke wheel, the symbol
of Wralda in the *Oera Linda Book*

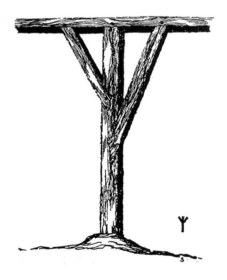

Figure 23.
The 'rune of life' in traditional
architecture

Figure 24.
Cover of the March 1935 issue of Darré's *Odal* featuring runes,
Irminsûl and a swastika

Figure 25.
An Odal rune in traditional architecture according to Weigel in 1938

Figure 26.
Children showing off festive (circle-cross) bread

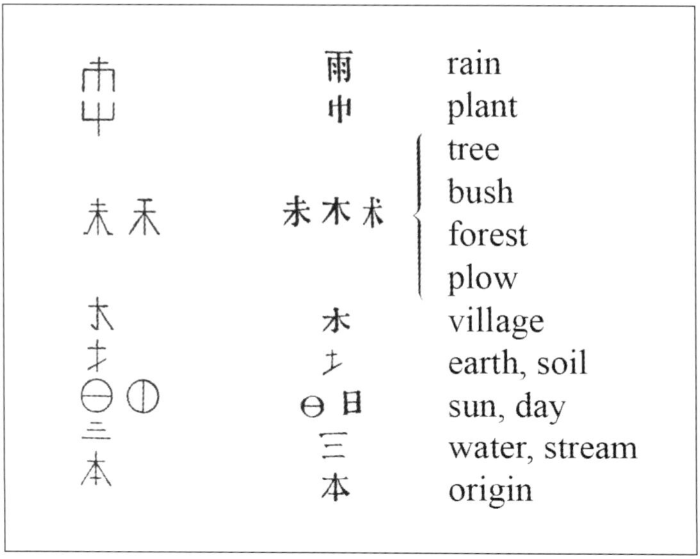

帝 屮	雨 屮	rain plant
未 禾	未 木 朮	tree bush forest plow
大 ⼟ ⊖ ① 三 本	木 ⼟ ⊖ 日 三 本	village earth, soil sun, day water, stream origin

Figure 27.
Nordic ideography and Chinese writing

Figure 28.
A steer in a folk festival apparently bearing a "rune of life" on its head.